BEST BIRDWAT

NORFOLK
(THIRD EDITION)

by

Neil Glenn

Dedicated to Pop (1924 – 2012), who used to cycle overnight
from Nottingham to East Runton to join us on our yearly family
holiday at Abb's Caravan Park!

BUCKINGHAM PRESS LTD

in
association
with

SWAROVSKI
OPTIK

First published in 2002 by:
Buckingham Press Ltd
55 Thorpe Park Road, Peterborough
Cambridgeshire PE3 6LJ
United Kingdom
This third edition published in 2013.

01733 561 739
e-mail: buck.press@btinternet.com

© Buckingham Press Ltd 2013

ISBN 978-0-9569876-4-8
ISSN 0144-364 X

Editor: David Cromack
Design and maps: Hilary Cromack
Publisher: Hilary Cromack

Cover illustration: *Geese at Holkham*, by Steve Cale.
Steve began birding at the age of 13 and started sketching birds as field notes shortly after. Over 30 years, his work has become an individually recognisable style. He has birded and painted all over the world but has made his home in Norfolk where his artwork is now well known. Contact details: Tel: 01328 862 265; (M)07866 263 673; e-mail: steveshrike@aol.com
www.steve-cale-artist.co.uk

Black and white illustrations: Cliff Robinson
Cliff Robinson is a freelance illustrator based at Gerrard's Cross, Buckinghamshire. He can be contacted on 01753 885 779.

Printed and bound in Great Britain by:
Ashford Colour Press Ltd, Gosport, Hampshire.

CONTENTS

FEATURED SITES IN NORFOLK

CONTENTS

ASK ANY GROUP of birdwatchers for their all-time favourite moment and it will be a safe bet that at least one of them will plump for 'a flock of Pinkfeet calling as they head off into a glorious Norfolk sunset'. Such evocative moments may have been happening each winter for millenia, but that knowledge will do nothing to diminish the impact of such a scene.

Of course Norfolk is capable of generating scores of other 'memorable moments' – from the massed aerobatics of waders on the Wash to the challenge of finding a freshly-arrived Yellow-browed Warbler among a throng of other autumn visitors.

Indeed, it is Norfolk's ability to constantly surprise that makes it the No1 county with birdwatchers and the biggest challenge when time is short, is deciding where to visit. That's where Neil Glenn's eagerly-anticipated 3rd edition of *Best Birdwatching Sites: Norfolk* comes in…..

The original edition, published in 2002, completely re-wrote the manual on how to create a birdwatching site guide. Readers were given the 'essential' information they needed in pages designed to be models of clarity. Maps and directions were included alongside the birdwatching advice, not buried in a separate section at the back, and each site was evaluated for wheelchair access. It quickly became the guide of choice for the county and was followed by guides to other key birding areas of the UK.

Swarovski Optik UK, as part of its commitment to supporting the wider birdwatching community, has been proud to sponsor each addition to the series, and I am convinced the release of the completely updated and enlarged new Norfolk edition (featuring nine new sites), will once again lift the quality threshold for books of this kind. Whichever of Norfolk's myriad delights you decide to explore first, I wish you a happy day's birding and, with this book to hand, I'm sure you'll have many more in the future….

Peter Antoniou
Country Manager, UK & Republic of Ireland
Swarovski Optik UK

WHY THIS SITE GUIDE?

THERE are several guides to Norfolk bird and wildlife sites available for you to buy, so why choose this one? I shall explain.

When I visit a bird site, particularly one I haven't visited before, I want to know:

i) **Exactly what I am likely to see at the time of year I am visiting.**

ii) **The likelihood of seeing the birds listed in the site guide.**

For instance, how many times have you been to a reserve in winter and seen Merlin on the sightings board? Lots. And how many Merlins have you seen? Not many, I bet! In this guide you will find Merlin listed for many reserves but you will also be given an idea of how likely you are to see one. This is expressed by a percentage score after the name of each target bird for each site. The fact that Merlins zip through Titchwell once a day in winter doesn't mean you will see one and this guide makes that obvious. In this way, the visiting birdwatcher will not let their hopes rise too high but will know which birds are most likely to be encountered.

A major feature of this guide is that **sites are listed in alphabetical order**: no more struggling to find site 3.14, or reading through reams of text to find the site you want. Sites are also cross-referenced on pages for **Wheelchair Access, Partial Wheelchair Access, Public Transport Access** and **Broadland Boat Access**. If you are visiting Norfolk for a Norfolk Broads boating holiday, for instance, this feature makes it easy to look up which sites are accessible for you. You then simply turn to the site guide page for more details.

Another bugbear of many site guides is the fact they hide the most important information in masses of text. **This guide displays the most relevant facts prominently** (when to visit, grid reference of parking area, target species, likelihood of seeing your targets). More detailed background information is given in the adjoining text but the important stuff is right there up front.

Another important feature of this book is that it is up to date. I visited every site listed in 2012 and 2013 and noted any changes to previous visits. Of course, things may have changed since I last visited. **This makes the Contacts section for each site an essential feature**, enabling visitors to check details of opening times, entrance fee, etc before their trip.

Complete beginners will find that the **Calendar section details the seasonal comings and goings of birds in Norfolk** plus a list of birdwatching sites recommended according to the season. More experienced birders may wish to visit somewhere they have heard about but not yet visited. In either case, the reader can easily locate the relevant page, as sites are arranged in alphabetical order.

The layout for each site is designed to help you make the most of your visit. As stated above, important information (e.g. parking) is easy to find but this guide comes into its own as **the background text takes you on the walk itself**. The best areas for certain target species are described, as are tips on fieldcraft, enabling birdwatchers to make the most of their visit.

In a nutshell, this book is designed to enable any birdwatcher visiting Norfolk to confidently plan a day, weekend, or holiday seeing exactly what they want to see, when they want to see it (within reason!), no matter how experienced or inexperienced they may be.

WHY THIS SITE GUIDE?

Finally, every effort has been made to check, check and check again the details for each site. If you find that this guide is incorrect in any way, please let me know so that I can amend the details in future editions. Also, I would be extremely happy to hear from you if you have enjoyed a day out at one of the sites mentioned: it would make all my hard work worthwhile!

INTRODUCTION

S O, ANOTHER edition hits the bookshelves! It still never ceases to amaze me just how many sites change in the relatively few years between editions of this Norfolk book. Yet more hides have come and gone, new trails have been opened and new bits of boardwalk have been unveiled. Incredibly, even completely new visitor centres have sprung out of nowhere since I last researched the book! It's an ever-changing world out there, even in the seemingly sleepy county of Norfolk.

When I lead bird walks and tours for local groups, some Norfolk virgins cannot believe the number of birds and bird species they see in the county. I almost envy them their first visit to this bird-filled paradise. But there is trouble in paradise...

The most worrying change since Edition 2 has been the continued decline of some of the bird species in the county. Willow Tits have all but vanished, Lesser Spotted Woodpeckers are deserting once traditional sites and Turtle Doves are hurtling towards extinction as a breeding Norfolk bird. Hopefully, if and when Edition 4 is released into the wild, I will be able to report population increases in many vulnerable species, or at the very least a flattening out of the steep declines.

On the plus side, Norfolk has seen an increase in a few bird species. Little Egrets, Marsh Harriers and Cetti's Warblers continue to flourish and spread. Several new additions to the county avifauna have been recorded in the shape of extreme rarities such as Black Lark, Western Sandpiper and Spectacled Warbler, while Spoonbill has been added to the list of birds regularly breeding in the county. It surely cannot be too long until we see Great White Egret, Purple Heron and Little Bittern taking up residence.

One thing I love about Norfolk is the fact that resident and visiting birdwatchers can almost expect the unexpected. For instance, who would have predicted that a Great Snipe would be found lekking in the county one May? There really is a sense that one can find anything at any time in Norfolk. And if this book should aid you in finding that species you have always wanted to see, whether it be common, scarce or rare, then my aim has been achieved and we can both bask in a warm glow!

Ed: We welcome readers providing updated information (eg. new hides or new species for a particular site), which we will publish in the news section of the Buckingham Press website. Please e-mail us on buck.press@btinternet.com or call on 01733 561 739.

WHY NORFOLK IS THE TOP COUNTY FOR BIRDWATCHING

FOR the bulk of the British population, Norfolk is a sleepy tucked-away county with little to make it noteworthy but, among birdwatchers, it enjoys a reputation second to none. Why is this so? Until I began to research the original edition of this book, I freely admit that I'd been content to watch the diverse bounty of birds without being particularly bothered why they were attracted to the county. However, on further reflection, this question demands some answers.

A quick glance at a map of Britain gives a simple clue to the county's importance to birds. East Anglia (of which Norfolk is the northern half) is a bulky land-mass that juts out into the North Sea, pointing towards Europe and Scandinavia. For any off-course birds migrating from these continental areas, making landfall here could be the difference between life and death.

This explains why so many rarities are discovered but many other commoner species actively choose this county as their preferred wintering or summering grounds. There must be some other attraction other than geographical positioning and that can be summed up in one word: habitat.

Many birdwatchers in Norfolk concentrate along the north coast, dominated by The Wash and large tracts of salt marsh, because this is the area with the greatest concentration of birds. The Wash is a huge estuary of mud, super-abundant in invertebrates – a crucial food supply for thousands of wintering wading birds. The 2,000 hectares of salt marsh – stretching from Holme to Salthouse – is internationally important for many breeding species and over-wintering wildfowl. For instance, up to a third of the world's population of Pink-footed Geese choose to spend the winter on these marshes. Norfolk is lucky in that most of its salt marsh has been protected from development. Similar habitat in Essex and Kent, which once supported large bird communities, has been reclaimed for housing and industrial use. As other areas of marsh disappear under housing, so the Norfolk marshes become even more important for birds.

However, it is important to remember that the interior of Norfolk contains other valuable habitats. Further south are the Norfolk Broads, a bird-rich habitat created in medieval times by people digging for peat. These waters, so beloved of boating enthusiasts, spread inland from Great Yarmouth to Wroxham and Norwich. The pure waters of The Broads attract many species of wildfowl as well as many species of insect and plant. Ironically, the activities of man are now threatening this delicate habitat through pollution, though this is being addressed by numerous conservation organisations. Most Broadland reedbeds and wet woodlands (carrs) are being restored and preserved by hard-working organisations such as Norfolk Wildlife Trust, The Broads Authority and the RSPB.

Breckland is yet another important region for birds. This is an area of some 94,000 hectares, originally of sandy heathland, located around Thetford. This nutrient-poor soil was extensively planted with Scots pines in the 1940s and these are still being harvested to this day by Forest Enterprise. This harvesting creates many clearings that are inhabited by Woodlarks and Nightjars. The other important resident of The Brecks is the humble rabbit: constant nibbling of vegetation ensures the continued presence of ground-nesting species such as Stone-curlew and Woodlark.

The Fens of East Anglia have mostly been drained and reclaimed for agricultural use, though some areas remain, most notably around The Ouse Washes. Norfolk's key site is WWT Welney and its famous wintering herds of wild swans and huge numbers of wildfowl, which find the combination of rivers, flood plains and grazing marsh to their liking. The RSPB is creating the largest wetland reserve in Britain on the Fens of Lakenheath, hoping to attract Bitterns, Bearded Tits and Marsh Harriers back to the area.

We must not forget farmland in our equation. The majority of land in Norfolk is intensively farmed and is thus inaccessible to visitors. However, it is this inaccessibility that protects some species from disturbance on farms managed sympathetically with wildlife in mind. Many of Norfolk's 100 pairs of Stone-curlews nest on farmland, free from the pressures of egg-collectors and birdwatchers. The same can be said for winter flocks of Tree Sparrows and Corn Buntings. Of course some farmers, motivated largely by EC subsidies, have much to answer for as many farms these days are completely devoid of wildlife but I feel the tide is turning.

Add gravel workings, small tracts of ancient woodland, extensive dune systems, former Victorian estates and the North Sea into the equation and the wide range of habitats in Norfolk becomes evident. There are even a couple of sea-cliffs, recently colonised by Fulmars; not bad for a "boring, flat county"!

One final thought: as Norfolk's attraction for birds became evident, more and more birdwatchers congregated in the county. Norfolk now has a large, resident population of birders, plus many more who spend their holidays there. This means that new and interesting birds are always likely to be discovered, fuelling the county's reputation as the bird capital of Britain, thus attracting more birdwatchers and so on and so forth…

THIS PART of the book is aimed at helping you plan your birding trips more effectively. For example, you may wish to observe wild geese: by reading the monthly summaries you will be able to find out which species will be present, the best time of year to visit and which sites to head for. Then simply turn to the site page in the main section to find out how to get to your chosen birding venue.

January's calendar is very comprehensive, covering species which occur throughout the period from October to March and is intended to be complementary to the calendars for each of those months.

JANUARY

MANY evocative sights and sounds can be experienced without much effort from the enthusiastic birdwatcher in this exciting month. What could be better than starting the day with thousands of Pink-footed Geese flying on the way to their feeding grounds and ending it, by watching Hen Harriers silently drifting in to roost over a reedbed? Pure magic.

Herons and Cranes: If areas of shallow water freeze over on reserves such as Titchwell, Hickling Broad, Cley, etc, keep an eye open for Bitterns in the open, as their usual feeding areas deep in the reeds become inaccessible. Little Egrets should be seen at many wetland sites, no matter what the weather conditions but if you wish to see Cranes then head for Stubb Mill.

Geese: Huge numbers of wintering wild geese can be seen at various accessible sites. Almost half of all Britain's wintering Pink-footed Geese roost on The Wash at Snettisham. Get there early in the morning for a real avian spectacular but avoid three days either side of a full moon, when the geese will remain in the fields feeding throughout the night. During the day, flocks can be encountered anywhere along the coast and surrounding fields, but it is worth noting that Holkham tends to hold birds throughout the day.

Brent Geese visit most of the salt marshes between Salthouse and Holme but try Titchwell, Holkham and Cley for close views of birds on the ground. Most of the Brents will be of the dark-bellied race (*bernicla*) but it is possible to test your identification skills by trying to pick out a pale-bellied race (*hrota*) or a Black Brant (*branta*) from their commoner cousins. The Black Brant, a vagrant from America, has become an annual visitor to Norfolk, favouring sites such as Cley and Titchwell in the last couple of years. Hybrid young (*branta x bernicla*) are identified most winters to further test the keen birder!

White-fronted Geese are best viewed from Lady Anne's Drive at Holkham or Buckenham and Cantley Marshes. Thousands of Pink-footed Geese are usually in the Holkham area and mixed in with them might be one or two Barnacle Geese, (tundra) Bean Geese or a Lesser White-fronted Goose on rare occasions. There should also be one or two Egyptian Geese at this site along with the other two 'plastic' geese, Canada and Greylag.

The other winter goose to see in the county is the (taiga) Bean, the larger of the two races. There is a wintering flock of up to 100 birds, usually to be found on Buckenham Marshes. A few individuals of the smaller (tundra) Bean Goose can sometimes be found with the geese at Holkham or the swans at Welney.

Swans: If you are looking for superb views of wild swans, then Welney is the place to head for. Most of the Bewick's and Whoopers spend the day in fields away from the reserve but return to roost in the early evening. The warden spreads grain out for the swans and ducks and the whole spectacle can be watched from the comfort of a heated hide. A small number of wild swans can sometimes be seen around Haddiscoe Marsh and occasionally in the Horsey area.

Wildfowl: Thousands of ducks make Norfolk their home in winter. These can be split into two categories: seaducks and inland ducks. Species of seaduck such as Long-tailed Duck, Common Scoter, Velvet Scoter and Red-breasted Merganser are usually best found somewhere between Hunstanton and Titchwell, though Holme seems to be the most reliable site for the former species. They can be accompanied by Red-throated, Black-throated and Great Northern Divers, or Red-necked and Slavonian Grebes. The dunes in Holkham Bay are also excellent vantage points to scan for seaduck, divers and grebes.

Species such as Wigeon, Pintail, Pochard and Mallard can be found on virtually any marsh or lake but for the most comfortable viewing try Welney. You can see all of the above species and many more from the comfort of the heated hide. Also look out for Scaup and Smew around the county: neither can be guaranteed but Snettisham occasionally attracts the former species, while Tottenhill Gravel Pits has gained a reputation for attracting the latter. Goosanders may be found at Sparham Pools, Denver Sluice and Nunnery Lakes.

Birds of prey: When I think of Norfolk in winter, I think of raptor roosts. There is nothing more evocative than ending a cold day's birding by watching Hen and Marsh Harriers drifting in to roost along with a lightning fast Merlin or two. My favourite site to head for is Stubb Mill, where Cranes can also be virtually guaranteed. Other raptor roosts include Roydon Common, Strumpshaw Fen, Warham Greens and Titchwell.

Away from the traditional roost sites, raptors during January are usually just passing through. Merlin and Peregrine scour the marshes for unwary waders, so if you see a flock of ducks or waders take to the air, always look skyward for a hunting raptor.

Waders: The north Norfolk coast is an internationally important area for wintering waders and a trip to Snettisham at high tide is a must. The sight of thousands of birds coming in to roost in front of the hide is truly awe-inspiring. Never mind trying to identify the individual species, just sit and marvel at the sight and sound of Dunlin, Knot, Oystercatcher, Bar-tailed Godwit, Redshank, Ringed Plover, Sanderling, etc as they whirl through the air, twisting and turning, seemingly at random, before landing on the beach. Magnificent!

Of course, you can see waders at many other sites in January. Breydon Water, Hunstanton, Holme, Titchwell, Cley, etc can be alive with commoner species but Purple Sandpipers are now rare winter visitors to the county. Woodcock and Jack Snipe are by far the most elusive waders. Places to try at dusk for the former species include Titchwell, Holkham Park, Blickling and Stubb Mill. Jack Snipe are very scarce in the county, the most regular site being an inaccessible area of Roydon Common, though they are occasionally seen at Surlingham Church Marshes.

Cley holds Black-tailed Godwits and maybe even an Avocet or two and Grey Plovers should grace many north coast beaches. If you feel you have to see Avocets in January, then visit Breydon Water where up to 100 can be found among the large number of commoner wader species.

Owls: One of the lasting memories of a trip to Norfolk in January – indeed any month – should be the sight of a Barn Owl silently hunting over a field or marsh. The places where I seem to have most success are Hickling, Holme, Flitcham Abbey Farm, Morston Quay and Cley, though the chances of seeing one while travelling between sites are good, especially if you are out and about at dawn and dusk. Short-eared Owls may be encountered on any marsh, but 'The Mound' at Waveney Forest seems to be the most reliable site in recent winters. By day they spend their time hunting over Haddiscoe or Berney Arms Marshes. A Little Owl or two is virtually guaranteed at Flitcham Abbey Farm or Choseley Barns.

Passerines: Small birds can seem to take a back seat at this time of year but there are plenty to see, if you have the inclination to seek them. The main target species include Twite, Snow Bunting, Lapland Bunting and Shore Lark. Numbers vary from year to year and Lapland Buntings and Twite are becoming extremely scarce. It is the best policy to monitor the bird news services for the latest site information, but make sure you don't add to any possible disturbance – these birds need to be able to feed in peace.

The best site for Shore Lark (in fact the *only* site recently) is Holkham Dunes. Titchwell, Cley and Salthouse Beach are also traditional sites for Shore Lark in a good year but never guaranteed. In addition, Titchwell is a good bet to find Snow Buntings, though Hunstanton, Holme, Salthouse Beach, Blakeney Point and Great Yarmouth Beach are all worth searching for the mobile flocks. Holkham NNR has been the most reliable site in recent years.

Buckenham Marsh is virtually guaranteed to produce a handful of Water Pipits in among the Meadow Pipits and Pied Wagtails feeding on the marsh. The fields around Cley's east Bank is also a traditional site. Large numbers of Rock Pipits spend the winter in Norfolk, the biggest flocks being on Scolt Head Island and Breydon Water. On a still day, the more colourful Bearded Tits should make an appearance at sites such as Cley, Titchwell, Welney, Gypsy Lane and Hickling.

Hawfinches should be in evidence but their numbers are declining rapidly in the county. Head for Lynford Arboretum for your best chance of seeing this elusive beauty. Resident Firecrests may be found at places, such as Sandringham Park, Felbrigg, Lynford Arboretum and Santon Downham.

Buntings and finches may form large feeding flocks during the winter months, with Flitcham Abbey Farm, Choseley Barns and East Wretham Heath being prime sites. Scan any flock carefully, as it may contain one or two Bramblings or Tree Sparrows. Catch the corvid and Starling roosts at Strumpshaw and Buckingham by the end of the month.

Rarities: Rarity-hunting can be hard work at this time of year but there are usually one or two goodies to be seen. Recent years have seen over-wintering Lesser Yellowlegs, Pine and Little Buntings, Black Brants and Arctic Redpolls, with a shorter-staying Ross's Gull. Iceland or Glaucous Gulls may be found around the county (try King's Lynn Docks or Blackborough End Tip), Mediterranean Gulls should be encountered on Breydon Water and Great Yarmouth Beach and hardy seawatchers may be rewarded with a Pomarine Skua or two.

Waxwings may be seen during irruption years, though no single site can be recommended as they head for the nearest berry bushes, stay for a couple of days to strip them bare, then move on to another area. A Rough-legged Buzzard is usually to be found wintering in the county but, as with Waxwings, no single site can be recommended. I have found single birds at Titchwell (1998) and Horsey (1999). 'The Mound' at Waveney Forest, the bridge at Haddiscoe and Holkham Marsh are the recent hotspots for Rough-legged Buzzard sightings.

Titchwell has attracted a winter Penduline Tit and any feeding finch flocks encountered on your travels should be scrutinised for Common and Arctic Redpolls (fairly regular at Titchwell by the visitor centre) and Serin. A day or weekend in Norfolk in January ensures an exciting start to the birding year for the visiting birdwatcher. For a 'sad lister' such as me, it is the ideal county to get your year-list off to a flying start!

FEBRUARY

THOUGH species largely mirror those detailed in January's calendar, spring migration gets under way during this month. This may seem unlikely as you stand birdwatching, dressed like Sir Ranulph Fiennes at the North Pole but it is true.

Geese: Many Pink-footed Geese will have moved on by mid-month but you should still be able to catch up with a few at Holkham NNR or Snettisham. Bean Geese usually leave Buckenham by the second week of February at the very latest, earlier if possible if the weather is mild. Egyptian Geese will already be nesting, though few of the first batch of chicks will survive if there is a prolonged freeze.

Wildfowl: Some wintering ducks will move out later in the month but there are still plenty at the sites mentioned for January.

Birds of prey: All the raptors previously mentioned in January will still be in evidence.

Waders: Avocets will return to their breeding grounds so try Cley, Breydon Water and Titchwell. Thousands of waders will still be viewable on the Wash at Snettisham.

Owls: Long-eared Owls begin to breed, so listen out for hooting from suitable coniferous woods in the county (e.g. Thetford Forest and Dersingham Bog). It is also a good month to search out Tawny Owls, another species that breeds early in the season. Also look out for Lesser Spotted Woodpeckers in Holham Park, Felbrigg Hall and Strumpshaw Fen.

Passerines: Early breeding species include Crossbill, which may start nesting in Lynford Arboretum, Holkham, Sandringham and Dersingham Bog. Bunting and finch flocks will still be around – check out sites such as Flitcham Abbey Farm, East Wretham Heath and Choseley Barns. Apart from the above species, you should read the calendar notes for January if visiting Norfolk in February.

MARCH

SPRING migration picks up speed in March but only just. Several early-arriving species will have been recorded by the end of the month but this is usually only a tantalising taster of the mass arrival of birds in April and May.

Herons and Cranes: It is worth pausing by any large area of reeds to listen for the evocative booming of a Bittern. This is still a rare sound but is gradually increasing at places such as Strumpshaw Fen, Cley and Lakenheath. March could be the last month for a while that you catch a glimpse of Crane around the Horsey area or at Lakenheath.

Swans: Bewick's and Whooper Swans will be leaving in their droves early in the month, so watch for flying flocks. A handful of both species remain at Welney until the last week of March but after that, only injured birds unable to fly are seen here.

Geese: Brents will still be much in evidence on the coastal marshes all month. Virtually all the Pink-feet depart, though up to 1,000 can usually be found around Holkham until the end of April. All White-fronted Geese will have departed from their favoured areas (Buckenham Marshes and Holkham NNR) by mid-month.

Wildfowl: Winter ducks remain in impressive numbers, with Smew probable at Tottenhill Gravel Pits and Red-breasted Merganser and Common Scoter on the sea between Hunstanton and Scolt Head Island. Long-tailed Duck records are few and far between in March but Goosanders are usually still present at Barnhamcross Common (the BTO lake), Denver Sluice and Sparham.

Wigeon in their thousands can still be seen at several sites (Welney, Buckenham Marshes, Holkham NNR, Halvergate Marshes), with numbers of Tufted Duck, Teal and Shoveler remaining stable at suitable sites such as Welney. Pochard and Pintail numbers start to dwindle as birds migrate north but many hang on to the end of the month.

Just one duck species moves in for the summer. By the end of the month, a few Garganeys will have returned from Africa to breed in Norfolk. The most likely sites to encounter this attractive species are Welney, Cley, Hickling Broad and the flash at Lakenheath, though any marsh or shallow pool should be carefully checked.

Waders: Another addition to the scene will be Little Ringed Plover, usually appearing during the last third of the month at any suitable wader habitat, (e.g. Titchwell and Holme) but the most likely places are Pentney Gravel Pits and Welney.

Other waders to be seen include all species mentioned in January's summary. Titchwell, Cley and Welney are the main breeding centres for Avocets but you can also check out Hickling Broad. High tides at Snettisham should still produce thousands of waders in the roost. Ringed Plovers move back to their breeding grounds in March, so check any stony beach. Black-tailed Godwits don their striking breeding plumage, thus becoming more conspicuous at sites such as Cley, Breydon Water and Welney. Stone-curlews return to Norfolk during March, though the only place to see this species without disturbing them, Weeting Heath, remains closed all month to allow the birds to settle.

Birds of prey: Raptor roosts such as Roydon Common and Stubb Mill continue to attract Hen Harrier and Merlin, though numbers dwindle as the month wears on. Wintering Marsh Harriers also continue to appear at their roost sites (mainly Stubb Mill) but their numbers are augmented by migrating birds. Any north coast watchpoint should be watched for an incoming Marsh Harrier, as well as for the odd Goshawk and Buzzard. A trip to Thetford Forest should reveal a displaying Goshawk or two on mild March mornings.

Terns: A welcome reminder that warmer weather is just around the corner comes with the appearance of the first Sandwich Terns of the year, during mid to late March. Any coastal site could be the first to record this species, though Blakeney Point or Scolt Head Island are usually ahead of the rest.

Woodland species: Lesser Spotted Woodpeckers begin to display at the end of the month. Check sites such as Holkham Park, Felbrigg Hall, Sculthorpe Moor and Strumpshaw Fen to see the fluttering display flight of this otherwise elusive species. Another species typical of a March birdwatching trip is Woodlark. Any clearing in The Brecks should be alive with their mournful song (try Santon Downham or East Wretham Heath). They should also be present at Dersingham Bog and Ken Hill Wood.

Passerines: It is a fun diversion during March to try to spot the first Swallow or House Martin of the year, though Sand Martin is more likely. Spend time at any migration watchpoint for a chance of catching these heralds of summer. Also keep an eye open for the first Wheatear, Chiffchaff and Ring Ouzel of the year: Blakeney Point or Holme are prime sites.

Any over-wintering Shore Larks and Water Pipits will be coming into their smart breeding plumage by the end of the month. Try Holkham NNR for the former species and Cley or Buckenham Marshes for the latter. A visit on a fine, mild day in March to any site where Cetti's Warblers are resident should result in a sighting of this elusive species because the bushes they favour won't yet be in leaf.

After March, Hawfinches become elusive until December, so visit Lynford Arboretum before the month is out. Other finches and buntings should still be found in feeding flocks around Flitcham Abbey Farm, Choseley Barns, etc.

APRIL

SPRING is here! By the end of the April, many of Norfolk's summer visitors will have returned, though the month may start off slowly if poor weather prevails. By poor weather, I mean low pressure over Europe or strong offshore or northerly winds.

Throughout April, any site in Norfolk could produce migrants passing through or lingering for a day or two. If the weather charts show high pressure over Europe with a low pressure system and easterly winds over the east coast of Britain, then you should head for Winterton, Holme, Blakeney Point, Weybourne, etc. If it is raining or foggy when you arrive, do not complain as you will almost certainly discover many common migrants forced to land by these 'unpleasant' conditions.

Divers and grebes: A late Red-throated moving north at sea will be the only probable diver this month. Likewise, any wintering Red-necked and Slavonian Grebes should have moved on, though there is a slight chance of Black-necked Grebes on any suitable stretch of water: try Welney, the flashes at Lakenheath, or any of the Broads. Great Crested Grebes will be nesting on any suitable pit or lake, though The Broads is their stronghold in the county.

Geese: Of the wintering geese, only Brents will be seen in any sort of number, on any coastal marsh. A few Pink-feet may remain around Holkham but cannot be guaranteed.

Wildfowl: If you wish to catch up with Red-breasted Merganser or Goldeneye, do it early in the month but those wishing to find Pintail, Long-tailed Duck and Goosander will have to wait until next winter.

Numbers of Pochard, Gadwall, Teal and Tufted Duck greatly reduce as birds move out of the county to breed, though one or two of each species remain at traditional sites all year (Welney, Snettisham, Titchwell, etc). Eider and Common Scoter may still be found around the north coast. April is probably the best month to see Garganey, with Welney, Cley and Hickling Broad the most likely sites.

Birds of prey: Raptors desert their winter roost sites in March, so concentrate on watching Marsh Harriers on their breeding grounds (e.g. Hickling Broad, Cley, Titchwell). Buzzards may also be on the move and Goshawks will still be in display flight on fine mornings in The Brecks. In late April, the first Hobbies will be arriving along with one or two Montagu's Harriers (over any watchpoint). April is a good month to scan the skies for migrating Ospreys, some dropping in on Broadland lakes for a brief fishing sortie (Ranworth Broad is the most regular stop-off site).

Gamebirds: April is a good month to locate Golden Pheasants as they are very vocal at this time of year. Visit the Wolferton Triangle or Santon Downham to hear their harsh calls.

Waders: The wader scene in Norfolk during April is a confusing mixture of returning breeding birds, lingering winter visitors and birds dropping in on migration for a quick refuelling stop. Snettisham continues to be the centre of attraction, though numbers of birds start to dwindle. Wintering Woodcock numbers begin to be augmented by migrant birds (check any coastal site for tired arrivals).

April is a good month to find species such as Green, Common and Wood Sandpipers, Whimbrel and Greenshank at any suitable marsh, scrape or gravel pit. Golden Plovers leave the county for their northern breeding grounds, while Avocets can be seen nest-building. Other waders settling down to breed include Redshank, Snipe and Lapwing on the marshes, Ringed Plover and Oystercatcher on shingle beaches and Little Ringed Plover on scrapes and gravel pits.

Weeting Heath opens its gates to visitors wishing to see Stone-curlew. This species can be particularly vocal at this time of year, especially at dawn and dusk.

Gulls and terns: Mediterranean Gulls can be virtually guaranteed on Great Yarmouth Beach while other species can be found nesting on marshes and scrapes around the county. One or two Little Gulls may be found – try Cley, Titchwell, Welney or Hickling Broad.

Activity at tern colonies increases during April and, by the end of the month, most birds will have returned to sites such as Blakeney Point. Common Terns will have also returned to nesting platforms in the Broads. One or two Black Terns may be seen at the end of the month, though they are more likely in May: check out any Broadland lake or Lakenheath.

Migrants: Latest additions to the year list will be Turtle Dove, Cuckoo and Swift, all usually reported during the last week of the month at any migration point (Holme, Blakeney Point, Winterton etc). Also look out for classic over-shooting spring scarcities such as Hoopoe, Red-backed Shrike, Wryneck and Bluethroat.

Woodpeckers: Lesser Spotted Woodpeckers may still be displaying during the first half of the month at Holkham Park, Felbrigg Hall and Ted Ellis Reserve.

Passerines: Woodlarks should still be singing throughout the month and several Shore Larks may linger at one or two sites (Holkham NNR for instance) with wintering flocks augmented by migrating birds. By now, this attractive species will have moulted into summer plumage and be sporting the elongated black feathers which give it its American name, Horned Lark.

Sand Martin numbers build up during the month (Kelling Quags, Tottenhill and Pentney Gravel Pits, etc) with Swallows and House Martins streaming in throughout. Rock and Water Pipits will desert their winter quarters by the end of April. Tree Pipits return to their breeding grounds throughout the month, with migrant birds being seen on the coast from early April. This is also an excellent month to find flocks of Yellow Wagtails in any wet field. Try Kelling Quags, Cley or Salthouse Beach. Also keep an eye open for one of the rarer races of Yellow Wagtail – usually Blue-headed – among the flocks, or possibly a White Wagtail.

A trip to Norfolk in late April would not be complete without a visit to a Nightingale site such as Pentney or Salthouse Heath. Nightingales are easier to see now than later in the season but you may still have to settle for 'just' hearing their distinctive song.

Black Redstarts can turn up anywhere along the Norfolk coast, as can Redstart. The latter species may also be encountered at inland sites such as Felbrigg Hall and East Wretham Heath. Whinchat, Wheatear and Ring Ouzel should all be looked out for in the dunes along the coast, as well as any suitable field or hedgerow. Also keep an eye open for Fieldfare and Redwing flocks leaving the county on the way to Scandinavia.

April is an excellent month to catch a glimpse of Cetti's Warbler. Try Strumpshaw Fen, Rockland Broad and Ted Ellis Reserve. Other returning warbler species in April include Chiffchaff, Willow Warbler, Blackcap, Sedge and Reed Warblers, Whitethroat, Lesser Whitethroat, Grasshopper Warbler and maybe Garden and Wood Warblers at the end of the month. The usual migration watchpoints, such as Winterton, Blakeney Point, Holkham NNR, Wells Woods and Holme, will generally be best for warblers. Also keep an eye open at these sites, as well as Felbrigg Hall and Salthouse Heath, for Pied Flycatchers. A fine April morning is the ideal time to head to Kellling Heath to listen for Dartford Warblers, but please remember this is a protected species, so be careful not to cause disturbance.

Bearded Tits can be quite showy at this time of year, especially on still days, as the males may already be collecting insects to feed to their sitting females. Any wintering Twite flocks will mostly be gone but one or two birds linger all month. Brambling may occasionally be seen, with some males sporting their fine breeding plumage.

In coniferous forest, listen out for the '*chip-chip*' calls of Crossbills. This species may already be feeding young and are particularly vocal at this time. Hawfinches become scarcer as the month wears on, though optimistic birders can still try their luck at sites recommended for March. As well as the species already mentioned, common birds such as Robin, Blackbird, Song Thrush, Goldcrest, etc can also be found in impressive numbers at migration watchpoints. If suitable weather conditions prevail, rare and scarce birds can, and do, turn up anywhere in the county.

MAY

WHAT a fantastic time to visit Norfolk – migrants will be streaming into all sites to set up breeding territories, so enjoy the show at migration watchpoints such as Blakeney Point, Winterton Dunes and Holme. High pressure over Europe encourages birds to undertake the trip across the channel, and if they hit poor weather associated with low pressure over the east coast, then look out! This inclement weather forces the migrants to take refuge at the first visible land, hopefully where you will be waiting for them. Repeat after me, "rain and fog are good……rain and fog are good…….. rain and…"

By the end of the month, the enthusiastic birdwatcher will be able to watch birds from dawn until dusk. Insomniacs may wish to start the day with a woodland dawn chorus, move on to the marshes during the day, or visit The Brecks and end the day on a heathland for Nightjar and Woodcock.

Grebes: To see any grebes, venture onto inland pits and lakes where Great Cresteds will be sitting on nests. Broadland lakes sometimes turn up a Black-necked Grebe in May, by now sporting its stunning breeding plumage.

Egrets and herons: Visit the Joe Jordan hide at Holkham to see nesting Little Egrets and Spoonbills.

Wildfowl: A few Eider and Common Scoters may linger around the coast all month, usually around Titchwell or Holme. Other than the resident 'plastic' geese, the only species to be seen with any certainty will be Brents (Titchwell, Blakeney harbour, etc).

Terns: Replacing the ducks and divers at sea will be terns. Common, Sandwich and Little Terns will all be busy settling into their colonies (Blakeney Point, Winterton etc) and can be seen fishing anywhere along the coast. Common Terns also return to their breeding platforms at inland sites such as Hoveton Great Broad, Breydon Water and Ranworth Broad. Also look out for Arctic and Roseate Terns at Blakeney and Cley.

Black Terns used to breed on Broadland lakes but sadly they can now only be encountered on passage, May being the prime month. Try Lakenheath or Hardley Flood. The first Manx Shearwaters of the year will be seen off Sheringham, Cley, Titchwell or Holme by the end of the month.

Birds of prey: Raptor enthusiasts are spoiled in May. It is an excellent time to see Honey

Buzzards in the county, as a few pass over on migration. By the 20th, the Great Wood at Swanton Novers should be occupied by this rare breeder if they are going to settle. Marsh Harriers are likely over any marsh or reedbed.

Hobbies return during the month, causing chaos among the *hirundine* flocks at Weeting Heath, RSPB Lakenheath Fen, Hickling Broad, etc. The rarest breeding raptor in the county is Montagu's Harrier, which can sometimes be seen over any coastal watchpoint on passage, so stay alert. Tune into the bird news services to learn of any raptor viewpoints being established.

Waders: Snettisham still attracts good numbers of waders to its roost and several attractive species can be seen on breeding grounds. Avocets can be seen on virtually any marsh or pit and stunning Black-tailed Godwits should be sought out at Holme and Welney etc.

If you are walking on any shingle beach, you should be careful not to disturb Ringed Plovers and Oystercatchers from their nests. Little Ringed Plover can be seen well at Welney and more distantly at Pentney Gravel Pits. Stone-curlews will be raising young at Weeting, with Woodlarks also showing well here in front of the hides or in clearings along the woodland trail.

This is a good month to find scarce and rare waders throughout the county. Regular species include Red-necked Phalarope and Temminck's Stint at Cley, with Kentish Plover and Temminck's Stint sometimes at Breydon Water.

Heathland species: From late May you can make a dusk visit to a Nightjar site (Roydon Common, Buxton Heath, Santon Downham, Salthouse Heath, Dersingham Bog). While waiting for the Nightjars to appear, you should see roding Woodcock and hear young Tawny Owls begging for food (listen out for a sound like an asthmatic smoker sprinting for a bus on a smoggy morning). Also keep an ear open for the begging squeaks of young Long-eared Owls.

Passerines: Swifts arrive from early to mid-month, as do most Turtle Doves. Listen for the latter's evocative purring calls especially at Flitcham Abbey Farm and Santon Downham. Another species that gives itself away by its song in May is Tree Pipit. Breckland is a stronghold of this species but it can also be heard at Dersingham Bog, Roydon Common and Kelling Heath as well. Woodlarks will also still be singing over any suitable clearing in the Brecks such as Santon Downham. On the subject of calling birds, listen for the evocative sounds of Cuckoos: Lakenheath is traditionally a good site.

May is a good month to scan any suitable wetland for Yellow Wagtails. Cley is a favoured haunt but also try Buckenham Marsh or Surlingham Church Marsh. This is a prime month to find scarce sub-species such as Blue-headed and White among the commoner Yellows and Pieds.

This month is a good time to see Bearded Tits in any expanse of reedbed (Hickling Broad, Cley, Titchwell, Gypsy Lane, etc). From mid-month, I strongly suggest you pay a visit to Lakenheath to try to catch a glimpse of Golden Oriole. You will almost certainly hear them from the poplars but seeing one might involve much patience!

Migrants: Migrants to watch out for include Bluethroat (Blakeney Point, Holme Dunes), Redstart and Wood Warbler (Salthouse Heath, Felbrigg Hall, East Wretham Heath) and Pied Flycatcher (Stiffkey, Wells Woods). Black Redstarts used to breed around the power station and industrial units of Great Yarmouth but have been absent for a couple of years. It is still worth listening out for them as this species is notoriously unpredictable in its breeding habits. Wryneck may be found skulking in any suitable dune system (Winterton, Holme Dunes), where you should also keep an eye open for Red-backed Shrike. Early in the month is a good time to listen for Nightingale at such sites as Pentney Gravel Pits and Salthouse Heath.

May is definitely a warbler month! As the days tick by, Sedge, Reed, Garden and Willow Warblers all arrive en masse, as well as Whitethroat, Lesser Whitethroat, Blackcap and Chiffchaff. Grasshopper Warblers may well be heard 'reeling' from suitable habitat (Wells Woods, Winterton Dunes, Horsey, etc) and rarer visitors could include Icterine and Savi's Warblers. A visit to a large wood at dawn is a must during May, so try Ken Hill Wood, Sandringham or Santon Downham.

Spotted Flycatcher is one of the latest summer arrivals but a handful will be at breeding sites late in the month (Weeting Heath, Holkham NNR).

Rarities: Rarity hunters will find themselves spoiled for choice. Regular rarities include Red-footed Falcon, Caspian Tern, Purple Heron and Broad-billed Sandpiper as well as scarcities such as Temminck's Stint, Red-necked Phalarope, Wryneck and Bluethroat. There should be at least one national rarity to see in Norfolk during the month, so good hunting.

JUNE

THOUGH June is probably the quietest month for birds in Norfolk, there is still plenty to see. As migration is at its lowest level of the year, the main interest is in watching breeding birds go about the business of raising a family. Mind you, if a rarity does turn up, it is usually a mega.

Wildfowl: Any wildfowl in the county will probably be elusive as they tend to hide while sitting on nests. Noisy Egyptian Geese will be waddling around their chosen breeding sites with large young in tow (Flitcham Abbey Farm, Holkham NNR, Pentney Gravel Pits, Norfolk Broads, etc).

Birds of prey: Many visitors to Norfolk will be enthralled by Marsh Harriers in June, as they drift over any suitable marsh or reedbed. If you are lucky, you will witness the aerobatics of a food-passing manoeuvre by these wonderful birds.

Honey Buzzard and Montagu's Harrier tend to be elusive during June but Hobbies are regularly seen at Hickling Broad, Lakenheath Fen, Weeting Heath and Upton Fen throughout the month.

Waders: Wader species will be on nests, the star attractions being Avocets at Titchwell, Cley and Welney. Common waders such as Redshank, Lapwing and Snipe nest at a few sites but can be hard to locate (try Buckenham Marshes and Welney). Little Ringed Plover, a scarce Norfolk breeder, is best viewed from the main hide at Welney. The Stone-curlews at Weeting will have large young by now but viewing them through the heat-haze can be frustrating.

Terns and seabirds: A few Manx Shearwaters may be seen off seawatching points but tern activity is usually restricted to colonies such as Blakeney Point and Winterton. Common Terns will be seen on any suitable river or pit, especially those with breeding platforms or islands. Noisy Black-headed Gulls are not hard to locate but Kelling Quags is the best site for good views of them at the nest.

Heathland species: One species that shows well throughout the month is Nightjar. Balmy June evenings are perfect to watch these moth-like creatures at such places as Dersingham Bog, Winterton Dunes and Sandringham. At Salthouse Heath, you can combine a Nightjar search with a Nightingale chorus, while at Winterton Dunes, you may also listen to the reeling of Grasshopper Warblers and the croaking of natterjack toads.

Passerines: Warblers will still be in full song throughout the month but towards the end of the month many species become more elusive after the initial explosive start to the day, so catch a dawn chorus sooner rather than later.

Bushes around any marsh, river or pit will be alive with the scratchy song of Sedge Warblers and the grumpy-sounding song of Reed Warblers will be emanating from every patch of reedbed. Cetti's Warblers should still be singing intermittently from deep cover around their Broadland strongholds but you will probably not see one!

June is the prime month for Marsh Warbler to appear, so pay attention to any strange song you may hear. The last one I saw in Norfolk was singing by a very well used footpath next to a school in King's Lynn, so be alert in any location.

Golden Orioles will still be whistling from poplars around Lakenheath during the early part of the month but then become very difficult to locate, until the young are out and about in late August.

JULY

WHILE you stand sweating on the footpath at Titchwell, watching Avocet chicks waddle after their parents, it is hard to believe that autumn migration is under way. Many non-breeding waders return to Norfolk from Scandinavia during July, so it can be an interesting diversion at the end of the month to attempt to match the number of wader species to the date (i.e. 28 species of wader on July 28 and so on).

Seabirds: Seawatching picks up slightly during July, with increased numbers of Manx Shearwaters being seen and maybe one or two Balearic Shearwaters.

Spoonbills: Once fledged, the Holkham Spoonbills go walkabout, but Cley and Titchwell tend to be their favourite hang-outs.

Wildfowl: Duck-watching becomes very dull in July, as the drakes moult into their dowdy 'eclipse' plumage.

Birds of prey: Rare breeding raptors show more often as the month wears on. Honey Buzzards should be showing well if any have bred in the locality – listen to the bird news services for reports. Listen out for any RSPB Montagu's Harrier watchpoints that may be set up to see this much sought-after species. Marsh Harriers will be much in evidence over reeds and marshes across the county, making it hard to believe this species was faced with extinction as a British breeding bird just a few years ago. Hobbies will become more obvious as they take advantage of new prey: dragonflies.

Quail: While driving around the county, it may be worth stopping at the side of any barley field to listen for the *'wet-my-lips'* call of Quail. They turn up anywhere and are almost impossible to see. Remember, it is illegal to tape-lure this species and you should never enter fields to try to flush one into view!

Waders: Young birds will be prominent and many a sigh of 'aahhh' has gone up from admiring birders at the sight of a young Lapwing/Avocet chick trotting along after its parents, only to be followed by gasps of horror as a Herring or Great Black-backed Gull swoops down and swallows the poor thing whole. Life is tough! Visit sites such as Welney, Titchwell and Cley to see nature in all its gory splendour.

By the end of July, waders such as Knot, Dunlin and Sanderling will be returning from their breeding grounds. The roost at Snettisham once again begins to attract many birds, though not as numerous as in winter. Female Red-necked Phalaropes sometimes appear at Cley or Titchwell to sun themselves after leaving the hapless males to rear their young in the bleak northern breeding grounds.

Welney is a good place to visit in July to obtain superb views of baby Little Ringed Plovers, complete with tiny yellow eye-rings. Adult and almost fully grown Stone-curlews should be showing well on Weeting Heath.

Gulls and terns: Yellow-legged Gull is a summer feature of Norfolk, prime sites being Blackborough End Tip, Cley, King's Lynn Docks and Hickling Broad. Black-headed Gull colonies become even noisier as the youngsters beg for food from harassed adults.

July is the best month to visit a tern colony. A boat trip out to Blakeney Point at this time of year is a real treat. Many a happy hour can be spent at a Little Tern colony (Winterton Dunes, etc) watching chicks run to their parents as they land close by.

Heathland species: Nightjars will be churring at dusk throughout the month at sites such as Roydon Common, Buxton Heath, Winterton Dunes, Sandringham and Dersingham Bog. Insect repellent may be advisable if waiting any length of time for the Nightjars to appear.

Passerines: The majority of warblers and woodland birds will become more elusive as the month wears on and the heat builds up. Many species will be hiding away, quietly moulting out of the reach of predators. Even more unsportingly, they stop singing, so you can't even locate them that way.

Alternatives: If things appear to be a little quiet on the birding front, don't forget that there are always plenty of plants butterflies and dragonflies to be seen.

AUGUST

IN BIRDING terms, August heralds the onset of winter with many south-bound species stopping off. Lots of young birds can still be seen, most making very unfamiliar noises that often fool even the most ardent bird-call fanatic. Because there are so many youngsters around, this is a bumper time for raptors too.

Seabirds: August is the real start of the seawatching season. Manx Shearwaters pass watchpoints in impressive numbers in some years, often joined by Balearic or Sooty Shearwaters, or maybe something rarer such as Cory's or Great Shearwaters. Many watchpoints such as Holme NOA Observatory, Cley and Sheringham will be crowded with birders hoping for the 'biggie' to come past, especially if there is a stiff north wind blowing. However, Gannets and Kittiwakes are much more likely. Tern activity will be at a peak at sea, as adults are joined by scruffy-looking juveniles learning how to fish.

All four skua species should be recorded off seawatching points (Holme Observatory, Cley, Sheringham, etc) throughout the month but concentrate your efforts if the wind is coming from the north or north-west. Auk species may also pass watchpoints in reasonable numbers.

Wildfowl: Wigeon numbers will be gradually building on the marshes, along with Teal. By the end of the month, the first returning Pintail will have been noted. Garganey begin to show again, after hiding the whole summer, with juveniles testing the identification skills of birders at Cley, Welney and Hickling Broad among others. The bad news is that male ducks will still be in their dull 'eclipse' plumage.

Birds of prey: Raptors to be seen in Norfolk during August include the first returning Merlin (maybe Blakeney Point) and any breeding of Honey Buzzards at Swanton Novers will result in the adults being accompanied by their young: catch them while you can as they usually depart late in the month. Montagu's Harriers roam far and wide during August and may be encountered anywhere. This is probably the best month to see a Hobby as the youngsters are on the wing learning how to catch Swallows, House Martins and dragonflies at sites such as Upton Fen, Lakenheath or Hickling Broad. As ever, Marsh Harriers will be seen over any marsh or reedbed, sometimes food-passing in mid-air.

Crakes and gamebirds: August is a prime month to find a Spotted Crake. Any marsh may be graced by this elusive species, though Titchwell seems to be the favourite site. Any Quail in the county should still be calling so check bird newslines to find out this year's best location

Waders: A fine selection will be on show. You may wish to visit the Snettisham roost or concentrate on finding passage birds on any suitable pool or marsh. Greenshank, Green Sandpiper, Wood Sandpiper and Common Sandpiper are guaranteed during August, the best sites being Cley, Redwell Marsh, Welney and Breydon Water. The latter site also sees a build-up in number of Avocets during the month. Cantley Beet Factory is the best site to see Green, Wood and Common Sandpipers in the autumn, though access is now tricky. If you want permission to visit this site regularly, please write to: The Site Manager, British Sugar plc, Cantley Sugar Factory, Norwich NR13 3ST or ask at the security hut by the main gate. Please obey all on-site instructions.

In general, many species of wader (Whimbrel, Ruff, Little Ringed Plover, Spotted Redshank, Little Stint, Temminck's Stint, etc) can turn up anywhere, so check any suitable-looking patch of marsh, wetland or pool to find your own. Stone-curlews will be gathering in small flocks by the end of the month.

Gulls and terns: Gull colonies will still be boisterous and Yellow-legged Gull numbers at

King's Lynn Docks or Cley can reach double figures. Terns will show well in good numbers throughout the month. Keep an eye open for migrating Black Terns at any seawatching point.

Nightjars: If you want to hear Nightjars in August, visit your chosen site (Winterton, Buxton Heath, Roydon Common, etc) sooner rather than later. On cooler evenings, Nightjars may not churr at all and, by the end of the month, most visits will be silent.

Migrants: The number of Turtle Doves, Cuckoos, Sand Martins and Swifts reported start to dwindle as the days tick by but Swallows and House Martins should still be swarming over any area of water, often pursued by a Hobby or two. Listen and look out for Tree Pipits at any migration watchpoint as they begin to move out of their breeding areas.

Heart-rates of migrant hunters begin to rise as August wears on. Common early drop-ins at watchpoints such as Winterton Dunes, Blakeney Point and Holme, include Redstart, Whinchat, Wheatear, Ring Ouzel, Spotted Flycatcher and Pied Flycatcher. By the end of the month, the first Red-backed Shrike should have been reported.

If easterly winds are forecast, it may be worth a walk to Blakeney Point for such classic species as Greenish and Barred Warblers. The trickle of migrants in August is just a taster of things to come in September and October.

SEPTEMBER

SEPTEMBER can be an amazing month in Norfolk. If strong winds blow in from the north, seawatchers come out in their droves. If easterly winds prevail, places such as Blakeney Point, Warham Greens and Holme can be full of birders looking for tasty treats such as Barred Warbler and Red-backed Shrike. If conditions are perfect (high pressure over Scandinavia and the east, with low pressure over Britain and strong easterly winds), anything can turn up.

Seabirds: Throughout the month, seawatching enthusiasts will be at such sites as Sheringham and Holme NOA Observatory searching the swell for shearwaters, skuas and petrels. Common passage birds during the month include Gannet and Kittiwake in good numbers.

The fun really starts when a prolonged period of north or north-westerly winds is experienced. If this happens, seawatching can be extremely exciting (yes, trust me, it can)! Spending a whole morning watching hundreds of terns passing your vantage point is exciting enough but add up to four species of skua occasionally pursuing them and Manx, Balearic and Sooty Shearwaters gliding just above the surface of the sea and you have the recipe for an exceptional day's birding.

Wildfowl: Duck numbers build up on marshes and pools, as winter migration gathers apace. Garganey can still be seen at Cley but still in drab eclipse or immature plumage. Make sure you catch up with this species early in the month. At the very end of September you can expect to find the first Goldeneyes and Red-breasted Mergansers of winter, though predicting where they will occur is more difficult.

A few Brent Geese will be returning to their regular haunts by mid-month (Blakeney, Brancaster, etc) as will Pink-footed Geese (Holkham).

Birds of prey: Honey Buzzard, Montagu's Harrier and Hobby all depart for warmer climes during September and can turn up at any migration watchpoint, or indeed over any other site in Norfolk. Ospreys may also pass through on the way to Africa. Peregrines arrive at their wintering grounds during early September and reports of Merlin increase as the month progresses.

Waders: September is another exciting wader month in the county. Any area, and I do mean *any* area, of marsh or water with a muddy edge should be scanned thoroughly for passage birds. Common, Wood and Green Sandpipers are classic September birds, with Cley and Redwell Marsh being favoured sites.

I feel this is the best month in which to see Curlew Sandpiper. They tend to show particularly well at Titchwell but don't expect any gaudy red birds, as most will be juveniles. Other species which should be in evidence include Ruff, Whimbrel, Spotted Redshank and Little Stint among the common species. Wader rarities in September can include such goodies as Pectoral and Buff-breasted Sandpipers and, while on the marsh, keep an eye open for a Spotted Crake creeping at the edge of the reeds (try Titchwell).

A feature of September in The Brecks is the flocking of juvenile Stone-curlews before they migrate south. In some years, more than 30 birds can be seen together at Weeting but scan any field in the area for the chance of a wonderful discovery. Up to 60 birds together have been reported on Norfolk farmland in some years.

Migrants: The majority of hirundines leave the county by the end of the month but early on, it may be worth watching reedbeds at dusk for roosting Swallows (Martham Broad, Cley, etc).

September is a superb time to find your own birds. Depending on weather conditions, numbers of migrants at coastal watchpoints can be staggering. Common species such as Robin, Chiffchaff and Goldcrest can be forced down by fog or rain. Summer warblers such as Whitethroat, Lesser Whitethroat, Garden Warbler and Blackcap should all be encountered on the coast and something special might be hiding among them.

Other common migrants at this time should include Wheatear, Whinchat and maybe a few Ring Ouzel. Redstart and Pied Flycatcher are also recorded in good numbers each September. Scarce species regularly recorded this month include Wryneck, Richard's Pipit, Red-backed Shrike, Common Rosefinch, Firecrest, Ortolan and Barred Warbler (Holme, Winterton, Blakeney Point).

Any site – and any bush! – on the coast should be checked thoroughly, though hot-spots such as Blakeney Point, NWT Holme Dunes, NOA Holme Observatory, Great Yarmouth Cemetery and Warham Greens are the most visited. Migrant-hunters will be hoping for something a bit rarer (such as Lanceolated Warbler and Pechora Pipit) for their efforts.

Passerines: In my experience, September is the best month to see Bearded Tits. Family parties are very noisy and active and usually show very well at sites such as Titchwell (around the first hide), Hickling Broad, Gypsy Lane and Brancaster Marsh. Instead of the usual fleeting flight glimpse, at this time of year the patient birdwatcher can obtain very close and prolonged views.

OCTOBER

EXCITEMENT among birders remains high this month. Not only do rarities abound, but common winter visitors arrive seemingly unnoticed. Swans, geese and ducks return in decent numbers and raptor roosts begin to attract Hen Harriers once more. Winter has arrived!

Seabirds: As in September, keep an eye on weather forecasts for northerly winds. Head for seawatching watchpoints in these conditions as skuas, shearwaters, Gannets and Kittiwakes should be seen in reasonable numbers.

October seems to be the most likely month to encounter the exquisite Sabine's Gull off the Norfolk coast but beware of confusion with immature Kittiwake (a common error). Numbers of divers, grebes and seaduck build during the month adding to the excitement of any seawatch.

Wildfowl: Wild swans gradually return to their traditional wintering grounds during the middle of the month. Pink-footed and Brent Goose numbers also build up throughout October (Holkham NNR, Snettisham) and one or two White-fronted Geese may have been recorded by the end of the month, though most return in November. The steady influx of wintering ducks which began in September continues throughout October. Welney and other wetland sites will hold thousands of Wigeon, Teal, Pintail and Pochard, by the end of the month.

Birds of prey: As mentioned before, Hen Harriers return to their traditional roosts, as do Merlins. Numbers may be small but birds should be present during the second half of the month. Peregrines slowly return to their wintering grounds and migration watchpoints may record Buzzard and Marsh Harrier, as they leave the county for the winter. Many Marsh Harriers do remain in Norfolk and can be seen over any marsh or reedbed (Cley, Horsey, etc).

Waders: Many passage waders such as Greenshank, Little Stint, Ruff, Green Sandpiper and Curlew Sandpiper will remain on muddy-edged pools and pits such as Pentney, Rush Hill scrape (Hickling) and Redwell Marsh. Thousands of common waders continue to arrive for the winter, augmenting the earlier arrivals. The roost at Snettisham attracts thousands of birds at high tide. Any beach or marsh, such as Holme Dunes, Titchwell and Cley can hold common wader species. Any Spotted Crakes that turned up in late summer may still be in residence (try Titchwell).

Terns: Numbers drop to a trickle by the end of October but Sandwich, Common, Little and Arctic Terns are all reported regularly.

Migrants: October is a fantastic month for finding your own migrant birds in Norfolk. Handfuls of Swallows, Swifts, Sand and House Martins pass over watchpoints all month and winter thrushes begin to trickle in. This trickle may become a flood if a high pressure system over Scandinavia combines with strong easterly winds and rain or fog over East Anglia. Sites such as Blakeney Point and Holme should be visited if these conditions prevail.

Experienced birdwatchers will expect something more exciting to turn up in these conditions, with such classic species as Short-toed Lark, Barred Warbler, Richard's Pipit and Red-backed Shrike all possibilities. Dune systems along the coast (Holme, Winterton, etc) may also hide exhausted Short or Long-eared Owls, Woodcock or even a Corn Crake.

Warbler numbers at migration watchpoints can be impressive in October, as birds pause on the coast to feed up or await perfect conditions before heading south. Wells Woods, Holkham NNR, Warham Greens and Stiffkey can produce many species, including Garden Warbler, Willow Warbler, Lesser Whitethroat, Whitethroat, Chiffchaff and Blackcap. Among these commoner species may be Firecrest, Red-breasted Flycatcher, Yellow-browed Warbler or Barred Warbler. Any feeding flock should be scanned thoroughly, as scarce and rare birds often latch onto such flocks: every bird should be scrutinised.

Reed Warblers can sometimes turn up in strange habitat at this time, occasionally confusing unwary birders. Many a time I have witnessed over-eager rarity hunters mistake a Reed Warbler for a rarer species, simply because it was hopping about in a tree or bush and not in reeds.

Expect to see Whinchat, Wheatear, Pied Flycatcher and Redstart, with common species such as Robin, Song Thrush and Goldcrest, sometimes appearing in their hundreds. Though Lapland Bunting is now a scarce over-wintering species in the county, one or two very occasionally drop in at Salthouse Beach (Little Eye) or Cley (Eye Field) in October.

NOVEMBER

MANY birdwatchers regard November migration as quieter than that of September and October, usually because rare species can be thin on the ground. However, common summer visitors often linger until the first half of the month and, at the same time, winter visitors stream in from Scandinavia and further north to settle until next spring. And the rarities that do show up are usually very sought-after species indeed. You cannot afford to relax just yet.

Seabirds: Divers, grebes and winter seaduck return to the seas of Norfolk during the month as winter takes a hold. Red-throated Diver is common off such places as Titchwell, Holme and Cley. Long-tailed Ducks should be seen off Holme, though numbers are small (usually only up to 30). November also seems a good month to connect with a Red-necked Grebe (try Titchwell and Wells).

The tiny Little Auks should be seen on most days if conditions are favourable, with strong northerly winds. Any flock of Starlings coming in off the sea should be scrutinised thoroughly, as Little Auks sometimes tag on to the end of such flocks and follow them inland. Sometimes, exhausted Little Auk are discovered on inland waters. Recent sites have included Snettisham and Wells boating lake.

Wildfowl: Inland duck species return in force, with Wigeon being the most obvious arrival on most coastal marshes. The only wildfowl species leaving us, Garganey, will be gone by the second week of the month.

Bewick's and Whooper Swan numbers build up at Welney along with those of common ducks, while White-fronted Geese return to Holkham and Buckenham Marshes. If visiting Buckenham, I recommend you wait until the latter half of the month by which time the (taiga) Bean Geese should have arrived, though they sometimes don't turn up until December.

Birds of prey: Hen Harrier numbers increase at their traditional roost sites (Stubb Mill, etc) as do Merlin records. Marsh Harriers become scarcer, though growing numbers remain in the county throughout winter (Stubb Mill, Horsey, etc). Short-eared Owl and Peregrine are recorded daily, though can turn up on any marsh at any time (try Haddiscoe Marsh or Waveney Forest).

Waders: Breydon Water supports up to 100 Avocets throughout the winter, the only reliable place to see them during this time. Snettisham is well worth a visit at high tide for the spectacular wader roost. Common species present include thousands of Dunlin, Golden Plover, Knot, Bar-tailed Godwit, Turnstone, Ringed Plover and Oystercatcher along with smaller numbers of Grey Plover, Snipe, Sanderling, etc.

Most of the passage waders (Green Sandpiper, Greenshank, Little Stint, etc) will have departed, though a few linger throughout the month. November seems to be a good month to see Grey Phalarope, usually from seawatching sites such as Sheringham during northerly winds.

Please read January's Calendar for a more detailed run-down of waders in the county in November.

Passerines: A tiny number of Swallows and House Martins continue to be recorded throughout November, usually at coastal sites. Any Swift seen should be studied very carefully indeed, as recent Novembers have regularly turned up Pallid Swifts.

Similarly, any November Wheatear should be scrutinised to make sure it is not of the Desert or Pied variety. November is the prime month for records of Pallas's and Dusky Warblers and Olive-backed Pipit, with Wells Woods being as good a place as any to find one.

Shore Larks, Snow Buntings and Twite may return to the marshes and saltings of Norfolk during the month and usually remain until April. Please do not harass these birds at this time (or ever) as they need time to settle down into their chosen winter home.

Woodland birds now become easier to see as the trees lose their leaves: a trip to Holkham Park, Ken Hill Wood or Sandringham may prove to be very productive. If you enjoy seeing murmurations ofr Starlings, try Strumpshaw Fen as numbers now begin to build. Similarly the famous corvid roost at Buckenham Marshes begins to grow too.

By the end of the month, winter will have arrived. Read January's Calendar section for further details of birds to be seen.

DECEMBER

THIS MONTH'S calendar is basically the same as January's, with one or two minor alterations. In my experience, December is the best month to catch up with Hawfinch.

Lynford Arboretum seems to have become the prime site for this secretive species in recent winters. Corvid and Starling roosts reach their peaks this month.

All in all, December provides the opportunity to catch up with winter species you may have missed earlier in the year. Also, there are plenty of bracing walks to help you walk-off your Christmas turkey dinner.

ACKNOWLEDGEMENTS

I WOULD LIKE to say a massive thank you to Ken and Maureen Reeves for once again allowing me the use of their bungalow in Hunstanton while updating this book. It has made visiting the sites in this book so much easier. Thank you!

A huge thank you must also go to Lynnette Dear of the Norfolk Wildlife Trust and Sophie Barker of the Norfolk Ornithologists' Association who have been paragons of patience when answering my barrage of e-mails about their organisations' sites. Brian Anderson gave an essential insight into where it is and isn't possible to get to in a wheelchair. Joint County Recorders, Dave and Jacquie Bridges, provided valuable information about the Norfolk bird list.

I would also like to thank everyone who has commented on the previous two editions of this book and to everyone who has filled in sightings boards and books at reserves. Thank you all for your stories about how Edition 2 has helped you see some sought-after species missing on your bird list. There are too many of you to thank personally but keep those comments coming in!

The following is a list of people who have been extremely helpful in compiling information for specific sites. Apologies for anyone missing off this list: please put it down to age-induced memory loss! Chris Gregory and Nick Moran (Barnhamcross Common & Nunnery Lakes); Joe Cockram (Blakeney Point); Colin Penny (Buxton Heath); Steve Harris (The Bayfield Estate & Kelling Heath); Richard Kemp, Georgie Angel and Louise Rout (Fairhaven Water Gardens); Gary Elton (Holme Bird Observatory & Hempton Marsh); Toby (Salhouse Broad & Hoveton Great Broad); Dan Hoare (How Hill); Katherine Puttick (Lakenheath); Colin Jones and Alan Wood (Norwich); Edward Bramham-Jones, Mark Noble and Tim Nevard (Pensthorpe); Leanne Thomas (Sculthorpe Moor); Chris Mills of Norfolk Birding (Sparham Pools); David Nobbs (Ted Ellis Trust Reserve & Rockland Broad); Dave Hawkins and Rob Coleman (Titchwell and Snettisham).

Finally, I would again like to acknowledge the support, encouragement and understanding of Jackie, my perfect wife, during the updating of this edition.

Key points:
Opening times, terrain, suitability for wheelchair users and other useful tips. ALWAYS check opening times with the site managers before you visit.

Title of site:
Sites are listed in alphabetical order and numbered.

Target birds and the likelihood of seeing them:
Lists the species for which the reserve is most noted. The percentage figure gives a rough idea – based on the author's experiences at the site – of how likely you are to see the target species, provided you visit the site at the correct time and stay a reasonable amount of time. Where you see 'winter raptors (25%)' this means that you have a 25% chance of seeing each species of raptor at the site.

Other possible species:
A guide to commoner species, listed in BOU order, you are likely to see, season-by-season, though space does not allow 100 per cent to be covered. Under the *Occasional birds* sub-heading you will find a list of rarer species which are not recorded enough to be included in the Target Birds section.

---

22 / FLITCHAM ABBEY FARM

Key points
• Hide is open at all times, though Wednesdays can be disturbed by management work on the farm.

• Donations box outside the hide.

• Free car park.

• Wheelchair accessible hide.

• Log book in hide.

• Fieldguide in hide.

Flitcham Abbey Farm is a hidden gem among more famous honeypot reserves. Carefully managed to ensure the maximum number of birds use the site for feeding and breeding, it is probably the best place to see Tree Sparrow, Kingfisher, Little Owl and Turtle Dove in the county.

Target birds *All year* – **Tree Sparrow (70%), Little Owl (70%), Barn Owl (70%), Marsh Tit (65%), Marsh Harrier (50%), Kingfisher (50%).** *Winter* – **Pink-footed Goose (30%), Corn Bunting (10%).**

Other possible bird species

All year		
Little Grebe	Stock Dove	Winter thrushes
Egyptian Goose	Tawny Owl	*Spring/autumn*
Teal	Kingfisher	Passage waders
Common wildfowl	Green Woodpecker	Yellow Wagtail
Common waterfowl	Great Spotted Woodpecker	
Sparrowhawk	Pied Wagtail	*Summer*
Buzzard	Corvids	Turtle Dove
Kestrel	Bullfinch	Hirundines
Red-legged Partridge	Other common finches	Summer warblers
Grey Partridge	Yellowhammer	
Water Rail	Reed Bunting	*Occasional*
Lapwing		Garganey
Snipe	*Winter*	Hobby
	Woodcock	Red Kite
	Grey Wagtail	

Background information and birding tips

THIS WORKING FARM is a hidden treasure! Money provided by the Wildfowl and Wetlands Trust, DEFRA and the Countryside Stewardship Scheme goes towards managing the site as a haven for wildlife. This is how all farms could and should be but it is a sign of the times that I feel the need to praise RS Cross & Son (the owners) for their efforts.

On a winter's day, the bushes and trees around the car park can be dripping with birds. Yellowhammer and Chaffinch numbers are impressive (75-plus of the former and more than 100 of the latter have been recorded).

Several Tree Sparrows (normally in the hedges along the road) and

a few Corn Buntings are usually present, though the former seems to be declining here. Marsh Tit is a certainty in winter, along with one or two Bullfinches. Pink-footed Geese sometimes feed in the large field opposite the car park in winter but be very careful not to flush them. In 2001, this flock was joined by a Red-breasted Goose.

From the hide, Little Owls can usually be seen in the fallen oak directly in front of you, or on the large logs in the field to the left of this tree. Kingfishers regularly sit on the posts in the middle of the pool, Barn Owls breed on site and can be quite showy, while Tawny Owls also breed but are seldom seen. Several noisy Egyptian Geese are resident.

A Buzzard is sometimes seen

Contacts
RS Cross & Son, Abbey Farm, Flitcham, Norfolk.
01485 600 227

84

Useful contacts:
Phone numbers to confirm access details etc.

Background information:
Generally, this section will take you through the walk, with details of the birds that you might see and handy tips to help you see them. It might contain more information on points which have been briefly mentioned in previous sections, e.g. more extensive bird lists, more detailed information about terrain etc.

HOW TO USE THIS BOOK

Best time of year to visit:
There may be things to see at other times of year but this season is likely to produce the best results.

Maps:
Relevant OS Landranger map number.

Grid reference(s) of parking area(s):
Giving easiest access to site.

Maps:
The larger, more detailed map shows trails, hides and other key features for the reserve. (See key to symbols below). The small thumbnail map shows the reserve's position within its county.

ALL YEAR	OS MAP 132	TF 737 266

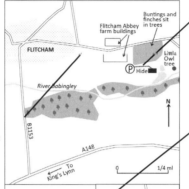

patrolling the skies throughout the year, while Hobbies occasionally fly over the farm from May to September (most in evidence between July and August). Marsh Harriers are reported daily during the spring and summer months and less frequently at other times of year, while Red Kite sightings are increasing.

Summer breeders include Whitethroats, Lesser Whitethroats, Spotted Flycatchers, Blackcaps, Willow Warblers and Chiffchaffs. This is one of the best sites in Norfolk to see Turtle Doves, which love to sit on the telephone wires running across the reserve.

In winter, pay special attention to the vegetated ditch viewable from the left side of the hide. Both Water Rail and Woodcock have been seen here and common species come to this shallow pool to drink.

All in all, this is a cracking little place with plenty to see at all times of year. It is not unusual to see most of the target birds in a single visit. I love to drop in at Flitcham for an hour or so at the end of a hard day's birding around the Norfolk coast, just to chill out and see what is around. I am rarely disappointed.

This site is a shining example of how farming and wildlife conservation can be comfortable bedfellows. It is frightening to contrast this farm with the bird-less 'agri-deserts' so often encountered these days.

How to get there
(7.5 miles E of King's Lynn).
SAT NAV: PE31 6BT. Takes you onto Abbey Road in Flitcham – then follow directions below to the farm.
GPS: 52.808972; 0.574722.

From King's Lynn take A148 (Cromer/Fakenham road) and then turn left onto B1153 at Hillington, sign-posted to Flitcham.

In Flitcham, turn right into Abbey Road and drive for half a mile until you have just passed the farm buildings on the right. Beyond the farmhouse there is a small sign

on the stone wall 'Abbey Farm Bird Hide' sending you down a short track.

Park at the end on the mud: the two hard-standing spaces are reserved for orange badge holders.

The hide is along a short concrete path and is wheelchair friendly.

Other nearby sites
Blackborough End Tip, Dersingham Bog, Hunstanton, Ken Hill Wood, King's Lynn docks, Pentney Gravel Pits, NWT Roydon Common, Sandringham, RSPB Snettisham, Tottenhill Gravel Pits, Wolferton Triangle.

85

SAT NAV:
All tested on my machine, but update your SAT NAV regularly.

GPS:
Type co-ordinates into Google Earth and pinpoint the parking area. Zoom right down to street level to see tricky road lay-outs or hidden car park entrances.

Access:
Detailed directions to the parking area(s) or reserve entrance (the harder a site is to find, the more detailed the description). For some sites, we have detailed the most straightforward route for those unfamiliar with the area, not necessarily the quickest.

Other nearby sites:
Included where space allows.

Key to map symbols:

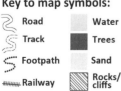

31

Key points

- Site is a designated SSSI.
- Free access at all times.
- Level terrain along muddy grass paths.
- Not suitable for wheelchairs.
- Observation blind, no seating.
- No dogs.
- Keep to colour-marked trails at all times.
- Information board in car park.
- Use insect repellent in summer.

SMALL AND SECLUDED, this Norfolk Wildlife Trust reserve on the edge of the Broads is well worth visiting at any time of year. Alderfen Broad is excellent for many common bird species, plus several scarce insects and plants – truly a site for the all-round naturalist.

Target birds *All year* – Common wildfowl (100%), Cetti's Warbler (hear 60%, see 10%). *Summer* – Common Tern (80%). *Winter* – Bittern (15%).

Other possible bird species

All year		
Cormorant	Common scrub birds	Grasshopper Warbler
Great Crested Grebe	Common woodland birds	Other warblers
Common waterbirds	Pied Wagtail	
Sparrowhawk	Siskin	*Occasional*
Regular gull species	Redpoll	Bittern (winter)
Tawny Owl	Other finches	Marsh Harrier
Green Woodpecker		Osprey (passage)
Great Spotted Woodpecker	*Summer*	Lesser Spotted Woodpecker
Kingfisher	Cuckoo	
Marsh Tit	Hirundines	Passage terns
	Sedge Warbler	
	Reed Warbler	

Background information and birding tips

SECLUSION is the chief attribute of this Norfolk Wildlife Trust reserve, which isn't to imply there are no birds or other wildlife to see, just that it lacks the drama of the top Norfolk birding sites.

The major plus-point is that I can almost guarantee you will be on your own as you wait patiently for that elusive Cetti's Warbler in the dense undergrowth to show itself, or scan the Broad to find Britain's first Cinnamon Teal!

There are two colour-marked trails from the car park. The one off to your right (as you face the info board in the car park) is along an uneven grass path and runs alongside a creek (good for dragonflies in summer) to an area of dense cover (ideal for Cetti's Warblers) and a wood (common scrub birds and warblers). This trail is 0.8km long.

Immediately you join this path

from the car park, there is a narrower grass path off to your left, leading down to a wooden screen.

The screen overlooks the 3.5ha Broad, though you may have to stand on one of the three logs provided to see anything! There is an entertaining sightings book in a sweet tin by these logs (make sure to replace its lid securely to keep the book dry).

In winter, Bittern should be your target species, most often seen in flight along the reedbed on the opposite side of the Broad from the screen. Common wildfowl and Great Crested Grebes, spend the winter on the Broad and a few remain on site to breed (e.g. Tufted Ducks).

Common Terns can be seen over the water in summer and the reeds around and opposite the screen hold good numbers of Reed and

Contacts

Norfolk Wildlife Trust
01603 625 540

How to get there

(Ten miles NE of Norwich).

SAT NAV: Neatishead > Common Road (NR12).

SatNav will get you onto Common Road to Threehammer Common. Follow detailed directions in Access Section once on Common Road.

GPS: 52.723228; 1.482069.

At Wroxham, NE of Norwich on the A1151, turn onto A1062 to Horning. In village turn left to Neatishead.

At the crossroads, turn right. In 0.3 miles, go past the Radar Museum and then after another 0.2 miles take the left turn sign-posted to Threehammer Common (Common Road).

In 0.5 miles, there is a left turn to 'the church' – ignore this and go straight on for another 0.1 miles.

Turn right down an unmarked, rough track just before the 30mph sign (the 2nd such sign in the village). Park in a grassy clearing at the end of the track.

Sedge Warblers. Cetti's Warblers may be heard and glimpsed anywhere around the reserve, Kingfishers frequent the dykes and channels, while Ospreys and Black Terns sometimes drift through on passage.

A colour-marked trail also runs from the left of the car park and then turns immediately right, down a grassy path, to run in a loop through the reserve (1.7km long). Boots are recommended for this route, which remains boggy at all times of year.

This trail takes you through a reedbed where it is worth pausing to see what you can see and hear (good for swallowtail butterflies here in summer). It opens out into a clearing where a Grasshopper Warbler or two may be heard reeling.

A short, muddy path through a small wood starts from the left of the car park. This wood can be alive with many common bird species such as Dunnock, Long-tailed and Marsh Tits, Robin, Blackbird, etc. The path leads to some fields where you may see winter thrushes and buntings.

In summer, the resident birds are joined by Willow Warblers, Chiffchaffs, Blackcaps, Whitethroats and Garden Warblers.

There is a slim chance of Lesser Spotted Woodpecker anywhere on the reserve and the whole place is packed with rare and scarce wildlife such as swallowtail butterfly, royal fern, hairy dragonfly and much more.

An all-round naturalist could spend a whole day exploring the 23ha of habitats here, while a bird specialist may perhaps spend only a couple of hours.

33

Key points

- **Free entry every day from dawn to dusk.**

- **Free parking. Car park open 9am to 5pm; at other times park on roadside and use pedestrian gate.**

- **Level terrain on grass and mud paths.**

- **Some wheelchair access when dry.**

- **No facilities (pub close by).**

- **No dogs allowed.**

- **Waymarked trail and info boards on site.**

Contacts

Norfolk Wildlife Trust,
01603 625 540

OWNED and managed by the Norfolk Wildlife Trust, Ashwellthorpe's Lower Wood comprises 37ha of ancient mixed woodland, which is home to many common woodland bird species and a range of spring flowers. A quiet stroll on a fine spring morning is medicine for the soul.

Target birds *All year* – Common woodland species (100%).
Spring/summer – Spotted Flycatcher (70%).

Other possible bird species

All year		Other common finches
Pheasant	Green Woodpecker	
Buzzard	Great Spotted Woodpecker	*Spring/summer*
Woodcock	Skylark	Cuckoo
Sparrowhawk	Jay	Hirundines
Kestrel	Other corvids	Summer warblers
Stock Dove	Common scrub birds	
Wood Pigeon	Marsh Tit	*Winter*
Little Owl	Nuthatch	Winter thrushes
Tawny Owl	Treecreeper	*Occasional*
	Bullfinch	Brambling (winter)

Background information and birding tips

ONCE YOU HAVE located the tricky-to-find car park, Ashwellthorpe Wood makes for an extremely pleasant stroll in the spring sunshine. Common woodland bird species are present all year, of course, but spring brings with it an array of wildflowers such as bluebells, wood anemones, wild garlic and primroses.

All this can be enjoyed in peace, thanks to the Trust's policy of banning dogs from its reserves: it makes a welcome change to be able to scan for birds without being slobbered on by someone's uncontrolled pooch. Absolute bliss!

The trail is obvious from the car park, though I would suggest you have a quick scan of the meadow in front of you from your car in case a Green Woodpecker or Blackbirds, Song and Mistle Thrushes are foraging. These are joined by Fieldfares and Redwings in winter. Anything in this fenced off 'paddock' will flush once you approach the reserve.

From the car park, after studying the info board and map and picking up your leaflet from the box, go through the kissing gate and follow the wide, gravel path towards the wood. You'll soon reach a T-junction where you can turn left or right along grassy/muddy paths. I usually walk clockwise around the trail.

Unlike Foxley Wood, Ashwellthorpe is open 24/7, and therefore an ideal place to experience the dawn chorus: early May is best. At all times of year, the trick is to walk slowly, listening for birds as you go. The trail is marked on posts bearing the NWT logo and is easy to follow. There are several unmarked 'rides' leading off the main path and all are worth exploring.

From the main T-junction, turn left and follow the muddy path through the wood, which will take you past an area of coppiced trees on your right, with larger trees on your left, before coming to a major crossroads. Turn right here (though you may wish to explore grassy rides straight on and to your left) and you will see a cleared area peppered with lots of majestic old trees.

Wait here for as long as possible because in my experience, this clearing produces the most birds. Nuthatches, Great Spotted Woodpeckers and Treecreepers usually show well if you are patient and you will almost certainly see a range of resident tits, finches and scrub birds as well as Blackcap, Willow Warblers and Chiffchaffs in spring and summer.

If you visit at dusk, this area could well provide you with a sighting of a Tawny or Little Owl and a Woodcock or two.

While here, don't forget to scan the sky above you: Sparrowhawks are common and Kestrels and Buzzards occasionally soar overhead.

The main path continues past a cleared area on your right. This was home to a stand of ash trees which had to be felled due to ash dieback disease in 2013. A 'ride' leads off left and then the main trail bends right and is enclosed by woodland again.

The area between here and the car park can be fairly quiet but Chiffchaffs and Blackcaps are usually seen or heard in spring and summer and the hedges bordering the reserve hold Whitethroats in the breeding season. You may even see a white admiral butterfly in summer!

Ashwellthorpe Wood can seem devoid of birds at times but patience usually pays off in the end.

How to get there

(2.5 miles SE of Wymondham).

SAT NAV: NR16 1HB (or Ashwellthorpe>The Street>No. 35).

Postcode gets you very close – follow written details when in village.

GPS: 52.534916; 1.152239.

The wood lies east of A11 between Wymondham and Attleborough. Leave A11 at signs for Mulbarton and follow signs to Mulbarton and Lotus Cars on B1135. After 3.2 miles, turn right at the T-junction onto B1113 (signposted to New Buckenham and Tacolneston).

After 1.4 miles, turn right to Ashwellthorpe (Wymondham Road, which becomes The Street). In village drive past the White Horse pub on the right and after 0.1 miles, you will see Greenwood Close on your left. Along the main road you will now see, on your right, a small white brick garage (with a round window) facing you: the entrance to the car park is immediately after this garage through a metal 5-bar gate down a grass drive (in spring there is a toad crossing warning sign immediately opposite the entrance). If you reach Woodman's Lodge and Audrey Musket Cottages you have gone too far.

35

Key points

- **Free parking and access at all times.**

- **Reserve is a designated SSSI.**

- **Terrain level along gravel footpaths and boardwalks.**

- **Toilet block (inc disabled) at main car park.**

- **Food, etc in Neatishead village.**

- **Blue Badge parking at Heron's Carr.**

- **Free 24-hour mooring available.**

- **No dogs on boardwalk.**

- **Braille signs on boardwalk.**

- **Bike rails at Heron's Carr, but no cycling on baordwalk.**

- **Boardwalk can be slippery when wet.**

Contacts

Norfolk Wildlife Trust
01603 625 540

General Broads Authority
01603 610 734

THE SECOND largest of all the broads, covering 164ha, is owned by Norfolk Wildlife Trust which continues to improve the water quality for the benefit of a wide range of wildlife, including otters. A pleasant stroll along the Heron's Carr boardwalk leads you through an extensive wet wood to a viewpoint overlooking the broad itself.

Target birds *All year* – **Common wildfowl (100%), Cetti's Warbler (hear 60%, see 10%).**

Other possible bird species

All year		Summer warblers
Egyptian Goose	Great Spotted Woodpecker	
Cormorant	Common scrub birds	*Winter*
Great Crested Grebe	Common woodland birds	Goldeneye
Common waterbirds	Pied Wagtail	Winter thrushes
Sparrowhawk	Common finches	
Kestrel		*Occasional*
Regular gull species	*Summer*	Marsh Harrier
Kingfisher	Common Tern	Osprey (passage)
Green Woodpecker	Hirundines	Lesser Spotted Woodpecker

Background information and birding tips

PREVIOUSLY, Barton Broad could only be viewed from a boat but thanks to some incredibly hard work by Norfolk Wildlife Trust and the Broads Authority, all birders should be able to enjoy the delights of this site.

There is an easy access path from the main car park to the boardwalk (just under a mile away), though blue badge holders are allowed to park at the start of the boardwalk at Heron's Carr car park.

When you enter the main car park, glance right to the treeline: this is where the path starts. The easy access route is lined with trees and bushes. Common scrub birds, including Yellowhammers and Linnets, reside here and are joined by Whitethroats, Blackcaps and other migrants in summer. Scan the fields for partridges, finches and winter thrushes.

The path emerges onto a narrow lane. Keep straight on for about 500 yards until you reach a small opening marked with three short wooden posts with red-lined tops. If you miss this opening, the Heron's Carr car park is a hundred yards further along: you cannot miss this! The boardwalk loops between these two access points so you won't miss any birds.

Take your time along the boardwalk. The wet wood is an excellent place to find resident birds such as Cetti's Warblers, Great Spotted Woodpeckers and Marsh Tits. Lesser Spotted Woodpeckers may still visit occasionally.

The path eventually leads to a viewpoint overlooking Barton Broad. The benches here allow you to sit and take in the wildlife of Barton at your leisure.

In winter, the water may be covered with common wildfowl including Goldeneye. Scarce and rarer ducks such as Smew, Ferruginous & Ring-necked Ducks have turned up, as have rarer

How to get there

(10.5 miles NE of Norwich).

SAT NAV: NR12 8XP. This postcode gets you very close, but alternatively key in: Neatishead > Long Road

GPS: 52.733931; 1.480211.

By car: In Wroxham, follow signs to Stalham/Yarmouth/Cromer/N. Walsham (along A1151). Two miles N of roundabout at junction with A1062, turn right at signs to 'Rose Centre'/Neatishead/Duck Boardwalk.

Continue into Neatishead village and turn right at Ye Olde Saddlery public house and B&B (sign-posted to Irstead and Duck Boardwalk).

After 0.7 miles, turn right at the Old Rectory, still following the brown duck signs. The car park entrance is 75 yards on the left.

Take the gravel path from the top of the car park (starts near the entrance to the car park) for just under a mile to Heron's Carr.

Wheelchair users should ignore this car park and continue past the Old Rectory to Heron's Carr (TG 358 207) where there is Blue Badge parking only.

By boat: NWT Barton Broad is situated along the River Ant, one day's sail from Wroxham. Mooring for reserve is at Lime Kiln Dyke.

Mooring with facilities is available at Neatishead, at the end of Lime Kiln Dyke, or further N at Barton Turf, though this does not give access to Heron's Carr. The whole of Barton Broad can also be seen from your boat.

grebes, so scan the flocks carefully.

In summer, broadland boats cruise the River Ant, which runs through Barton Broad, but they don't seem to disturb the Common Terns, Cormorants, Great Crested Grebes, Egyptian Geese, etc.

Now the water quality is improving, otters are being seen more frequently at Barton. Obviously, quieter times provide the best chance of a sighting and you may have to be patient but it is

well worth the effort. You never know, you may see a migrating Osprey in spring and autumn while you wait, though a Kingfisher is much more likely.

The hard work of NWT and BA ensures that NWT Barton Broad is one to watch in the future. I suggest you reward their hard work by paying Heron's Carr a visit as soon as you can and inject a little cash into the local economy. This may have the effect of damping down some local

objections to the development of the reserve.

One final thing to note is that the electric boat that used to take visitors around the Broad in summer no longer runs here. It now operates around Whitlingham Country Park.

Other nearby sites

Alderfen Broad, Hickling Broad, How Hill NNR, Hoveton Great Broad, Martham Broad.

37

Key points

- **Free admission.**
- **Car park gates locked 5pm Mon – Sat, 4pm Sundays and Bank Holidays. Out-of-hours parking at Glandford ford (TG 044 414).**
- **Permissive footpaths on the estate, so obey all signs and stay on footpaths!**
- **Toilet block in car park is wheelchair friendly.**

A THREE MILE circular walk around the Bayfield Estate takes in bird-friendly farmland, woodland and riverside, so you'll see plenty of common species. Alternatively, you may just want to browse the wonderful bird art or try out some new optical equipment available in converted barns on this rural site!

Target birds *All Year* – Declining farmland birds (95%), Barn Owl (50%), Grey Wagtail (50%).

Other possible bird species

All Year
Common wildfowl
Red-legged Partridge
Grey Partridge
Cormorant
Little Grebe
Buzzard
Sparrowhawk
Kestrel
Coot
Moorhen
Lapwing
Regular gull species
Stock Dove
Kingfisher
Green Woodpecker
Great Spotted Woodpecker

Jay
Other corvids
Common scrub birds
Nuthatch
Treecreeper
Marsh Tit
Skylark
House Sparrow
Pied Wagtail
Bullfinch
Other common finches
Yellowhammer

Summer
Hirundines
Blackcap
Lesser Whitethroat
Whitethroat

Chiffchaff
Willow Warbler

Winter
Winter wildfowl
Winter thrushes
Meadow Pipit
Reed Bunting

Occasional
Marsh Harrier
Hen Harrier
Hobby
Turtle Dove
Lesser Spotted
Woodpecker
Brambling (winter)

Background information and birding tips

THE FARMLAND Bird Project was set up in 2002 to demonstrate to farmers that crops and birds could co-exist in harmony. The small reserve was reincorporated into the Higher Level Stewardship scheme of the Bayfield Estate where bird-friendly crops are still planted annually, meaning the fields and hedgerows are usually bursting with finches, buntings and other common birds.

Parking for the estate is opposite converted farm barns which now house BIRDscapes art gallery, a cafe and the CleySpy optics and clothing store... all worth investigating.

On the Bayfield Estate there is a large tract of ancient wood,

pasture, woodland, heathy scrubland, parkland and wet grassland alongside the River Glaven. This diversity of habitat means that the Estate has a bird list of more than 130 species.

From Glandford, permissive footpaths allow visitors to explore the Estate as far as Wiveton Down LNR and along the Glaven to the Wildflower Centre and Bayfield Hall on the other side of the valley.

From the car park, walk through the yard, past the converted barns and onto a track. The 'bird field' is to your right just beyond CleySpy. Pause here to see what flies out of the field into the hedgerow, as birds can hide in the crop for long periods. You may wish to test some

Contacts

Cley Spy, Jodrell Barn, Manor Farm Barns, Glandford
01263 740 088
E-mail: enquiries@ cleyspy.co.uk
www.cleyspy.co.uk

BIRDscapes Gallery,
01263 741 742
www.birdscapes gallery.co.uk

Art Café
http://art-cafe.org/

Natural Surroundings
www.natural surroundings.org.uk/

How to get there

(Ten miles west of Sheringham).

SAT NAV: NR25 7JP.

GPS: 52.931821; 1.037391.

From the A149 by Blakeney church, follow brown tourist signs to CleySpy.

In Wiveton village, one mile from the A149 junction in Blakeney, bear right to Holt and Glandford.

After 0.8 miles you enter Glandford. Turn right into a large car park/courtyard (marked with a large pair of yellow binoculars!) where a range of small businesses includes an optics dealer, vegetarian cafe and art gallery.

The main access track can be found by walking straight on past BIRDscapes Gallery and then CleySpy on the right.

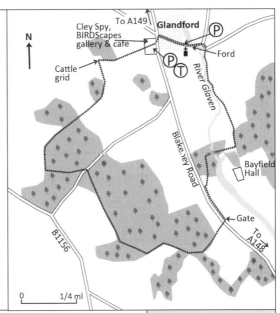

new optics from the shop while scanning!

Resident species include Yellowhammer, Greenfinch, Linnet, Chaffinch and House Sparrow and they will be joined in summer by breeding warblers such as Chiffchaff, Blackcap, etc.

Continue along the farm track, which goes slightly uphill. Bear left just before a cattle grid. The track takes you alongside fields that are excellent for partridges and also offers a panoramic view over the area to scan for Barn Owls and raptors. As well as resident Sparrowhawk and Kestrel, these have included Buzzard, harriers, Hobby, Red Kite and even Goshawk.

Check the fields for Wheatears at passage times and feeding flocks of buntings and finches in winter. Any grazing cattle on the estate will have Swallows swooping over them in summer.

The track passes through a belt of trees and then bends to the left. About 200m further on, the route turns sharply left, down hill, to meet

a public road. Turn left down this road for a short distance before turning off right along a steep(ish) track. The mature trees here are excellent for woodpeckers, Nuthatch, Treecreeper etc.

After a short climb, this path wends its way alongside a field with woodland on the left. At the end of the field (approx. 600yds) the path descends into a grassy valley with another pine plantation on the right and mature broadleaf trees on the left. The path continues along the valley bottom with ancient wood-pasture oaks on the left and lime trees. A public footpath joins from the right and a view opens up across the valley; check for circling raptors here. The path curves left, alongside the wood and downhill to another public road.

The whole of the woodland along these

Key points

- **Wildlife art gallery and cafe next to parking area.**

- **Birding equipment and optics for sale nearby.**

- **Walk leaflet available from BIRDscapes gallery and also downloadable at http://www. cleyspy.co.uk/ bayfield-birdwalk-c187. html**

- **Uneven paths, relatively undulating (for Norfolk), can be muddy.**

tracks is excellent for woodpeckers, Nuthatch, Treecreeper and other common woodland birds so take your time to maximise your chance of seeing them.

Cross the road and you will see Bayfield Hall and lake in front of you. The farm gate here is ideal to lean on while you scan the lake for common wildfowl, grebes, etc.

Go through the gate and turn left to follow the course of the park wall. There is a gate at the end leading through another small wood.

Turn right along the road and after 50 yards you reach a weir. This is the place to stand and wait for the resident Grey Wagtails to show and is also one of the best areas in which to see a Lesser Spotted Woodpecker (though you must remember they are still very scarce).

Continue up the hill and turn left through a car park. This belongs to Natural Surroundings, where you will find an extra eight acres of wildlife gardens and riverside nature reserve plus a lovely cafe where you can observe woodland birds on the feeders while partaking of refreshments yourself.

Immediately after the car park, leave the vehicle track and go through a gate into the pasture. This narrow path runs alongside the River Glaven and a marshy field.

Listen for Grasshopper Warblers in summer. The hedgerow here is excellent for scrub birds, finches, etc. Go through another gate and bear left along the road to a ford. The bridge over the ford is a good place to watch for Kingfisher, Grey Wagtail and common wildfowl. When the water level is low, the muddy edges may attract waders (a Wood Sandpiper has been recorded here!).

Follow the road past some beautiful houses and a church to a junction. Turn left and you are back at the car park/courtyard.

This is a reserve that you can drop in to while in the area visiting more famous Norfolk sites. You should see several declining bird species on this scenic, circular route, in relative solitude.

And don't forget to call in at the optics shop and bird art gallery – both adjacent to the reserve – if you have money burning a hole in your pocket (or even if you don't)!

Other nearby sites

Cley Marshes, Felbrigg Hall, Kelling Quags, Kelling Heath, Salthouse Marshes, Salthouse Heath, Stiffkey Fen, Walsey Hills, Weybourne.

BERNEY MARSHES is a huge area of marsh, farmland, pools and dykes managed by the RSPB for the benefit of thousands of wintering wildfowl and declining breeding waders. Because of its remoteness, you can feel a real sense of adventure as you step off the train in the middle of nowhere at Berney Arms Halt!

Target birds *All year* – **Marsh Harrier (90%), waders (85%), Avocet (80%), Mediterranean Gull (70%).** *Winter* – **Winter wildfowl (90%), Pink-footed Goose (75%), winter raptors inc. Short-eared Owl (25%).** *Spring/autumn* – **Passage waders (100%).** *Summer* – **Breeding waders (100%).**

Other possible bird species

All Year	*Winter*	Yellow Wagtail
Common wildfowl	Wigeon	
Red-legged Partridge	Teal	*Summer*
Grey Partridge	Pintail	Hobby
Cormorant	Golden Plover	Lapwing
Grey Heron	Winter thrushes	Little Ringed Plover
Little Egret	Stonechat	Redshank
Sparrowhawk	Rock Pipit	Hirundines
Kestrel		Whitethroat
Water Rail	*Spring/autumn passage*	Sedge Warbler
Avocet	Garganey	Reed Warbler
Lapwing	Curlew Sandpiper	Yellow Wagtail
Snipe	Little Stint	
Curlew	Ruff	*Occasional*
Regular gull species	Whimbrel	Bewick's Swan
Barn Owl	Greenshank	Whooper Swan
Kingfisher	Green Sandpiper	White-fronted Goose
Corvids	Wood Sandpiper	Rough-legged Buzzard
Skylark	Common Sandpiper	(winter)
Meadow Pipit	Other common waders	Yellow-legged Gull
Common scrub birds	Hirundines	Bearded Tit
Common finches	Wheatear	Twite
Reed Bunting	Whinchat	Snow Bunting
		Lapland Bunting

Background information and birding tips

THE RSPB RESERVE at Berney Arms covers 366 hectares of the vast Halvergate Marshes complex. The RSPB deliberately floods the reserve in winter to attract thousands of wildfowl, such as Pink-footed Geese, Wigeon and Teal, plus waders such as Lapwings and Golden Plovers.

Your first task is to actually get to the reserve. Full details can be found in the **How To Get There** panel (page 42) but you have several choices. There is a train from Great Yarmouth or you may walk from Yarmouth, Halvergate, Wickhampton and Reedham. For those birders holidaying on a Broadland boat, there is mooring (and facilities) at the Berney Arms public house.

My favourite route is to take the

Key points
• Berney Arms pub open 7 days a week, mid March to end Oct (noon to 11pm). Food 12 to 2.30pm & 6 to 8.30pm

• Berney Arms can only be reached by train (request-stop), by boat or by foot from Great Yarmouth, Reedham and Halvergate.

• Free access at all times.

• Plan your journey carefully before you set off.

• Walking boots needed at least, Wellingtons in winter.

• Dogs only allowed on public footpaths and bridleways.

Contacts
RSPB Warden
01493 700 645;
e-mail: berney.
marshes@rspb.org.uk

General Broads Authority
01603 610 734

Berney Arms public house, 01493 700 303

How to get there

(On eastern outskirts of Great Yarmouth).

SAT NAV: POI>Great Yarmouth Railway Station. Use pay-and-display car park.

GPS: 52.589788; 1.630285 (train station).

By train: Purchase ticket from Yarmouth station. Ask train driver to stop at Berney Arms Station (5 mins – TG 460 053), as this is a request stop only. Follow signs to Berney Arms Mill from Berney Arms Station.

By foot: From Yarmouth, follow the Wherryman's Way footpath (past Asda and the train station) along the north shore of Breydon Water to the RSPB reserve (4 miles). Footpaths also lead from Wickhampton and Reedham.

By car: Park in train station car park in Great Yarmouth. (See Breydon Water page for directions. Follow directions for foot or train access above.

Alternatively, park in Halvergate at TG 434 66. Turn right off the Acle to Yarmouth (A47) road, 2.2 miles from the large Acle roundabout (signed to Halvergate, opposite The Pontiac Roadhouse just after the suggested 40mph speed limit. Be aware that this is an extremely dangerous road!). After 1.4 miles, the main road

bends sharp right but you need to turn left down Stone Rd.

Park sensibly (very busy with farm vehicles so don't block access!). One small lay-by on right, room for 2 cars, or alternatively park sensibly on main road and walk back along Stone Rd. At end of Stone Rd, follow the sign posts to Weaver's Way footpath (you take the path on the right), which takes you across rough, muddy fields to Berney Arms Station (1hr walk).

By boat : Moor at the Berney Arms public house on the River Yare (free) and follow signs to RSPB reserve (down the seawall).

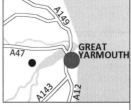

train from Yarmouth, walk to the reserve and then return to the town, via the Wherryman's Way footpath along the north shore of Breydon Water. Whichever way you choose there is usually something to see.

From Berney Arms Station, carefully cross the railway line via the obvious wooden crossing (following the exit sign). The train platform

is an ideal perch to sit and scan the marshes towards Halvergate. When you reach the Weaver's Way footpath, head left (south-east) towards the black and white mill (no sails). An RSPB information board and map is near the station. At the mill there is another RSPB information board, a donations box and some picnic tables. You may either walk left along the seawall towards the public house (there are some benches here for you to sit and scan the fields and pools to your left, though distant, and the river) or go through a gate along an obvious gravel path before you reach the mill. Either way, you can get to the RSPB viewing screen.

From the pub, go down the seawall steps, cross a track and follow the sign to 'reed screen' down a grassy path. The gravel path joins the 'reed screen' path at the back of the pub.

The screen overlooks Seago's Marsh. Wildfowl may be close in winter but birds may be distant at other times of year.

It is possible to follow the main track eastwards (scanning pools and fields on your left as you go) to where it rejoins the Weaver's Way path to Halvergate and the Wherryman's Way to Yarmouth alongside Breydon Water.

In winter, the flooded fields are home to thousands of wildfowl including Pink-footed Geese which are sometimes joined by wild swans and White-fronted Geese. The surrounding marshes are patrolled by Hen and Marsh Harriers, Peregrines, Merlins, Barn and Short-eared Owls plus the usual Kestrels and Sparrowhawks.

In spring and autumn, the shallow pools at Berney and further along towards Yarmouth on the Wherryman's Way footpath attract passage migrants such as Wood, Green and Common Sandpipers, godwits, etc.

Avocets, Oystercatchers and Lapwings breed on the islands in the pools, while Redshanks and Snipe breed on the marsh itself. Other migrant species may include Garganey, Yellow Wagtail, Wheatear and Whinchat.

If after visiting Berney Marshes, you are returning to Great Yarmouth via the main raised Wherryman's Way footpath (take the kissing gate by the Berney Arms pub and keep going for four miles keeping the river and then Breydon Water to your right), you will see many species of wader on Breydon Water itself.

Breydon is tidal and the best views of birds will be when the tide has just about covered most of the massive area of exposed mud. At this time, waders are pushed closer to the banks. If the tide is out, you will need a telescope!

When the tide is fully in, waders may well roost on the pools on the RSPB reserve itself or on the two pools closer towards Yarmouth.

Mediterranean Gulls should be present on Breydon Water all year round, while the marshes are a winter home for Rock and Meadow Pipits, occasionally joined by Snow and Lapland Buntings and Twite. Because this is such a huge area, species may be difficult to locate but the longer you stay on site, the more you will see.

The reedbed and bushes around the main pool hold resident Bearded Tits, joined by Reed and Sedge Warblers in summer. Yellow Wagtails may be seen throughout the spring and summer. Wheatears and Whinchats may drop in on passage also.

The marsh is home to many cows (in fact, if you are nervous of these inquisitive animals, I suggest you avoid the public footpath from Halvergate village to the reserve!), which in turn attract flies. These annoying insects are hunted by hundreds of hirundines, which are occasionally attacked by a Hobby!

Visitors shouldn't forget to check the River Yare when they are at Berney. Approach the seawall carefully and you may get close views of waders and a Little Egret or two on the muddy edges of Berney Arms Reach.

Because of its remoteness, Berney Arms Marsh is an under-watched site. There is a strong possibility that you'll be alone to enjoy the birds and you may even find something out of the ordinary. Previous finds include Kentish Plover, Great Reed Warbler, Terek Sandpiper, Glossy Ibis, Killdeer, Rough-legged Buzzard and American Wigeon among an impressive list of rarities.

Key points
• **Several stiles to negotiate.**

• **Well-marked footpath across very muddy, wet fields.**

• **Donations box for RSPB at Mill.**

• **Viewing screen with seat.**

• **Telescope useful.**

Key points

- **Access track is used by quarry lorries, so take extra care on site.**

- **Sundays are quiet days for gulls: no fresh rubbish to feed on!**

- **Level terrain but can be muddy with large puddles.**

- **Arrive early before gulls disperse.**

- **Free access at all times.**

- **Park sensibly. Do not block lorry access.**

B Y NO MEANS a glamorous site, Blackborough End rubbish tip continues to attract feeding gulls throughout the year and in winter, the thousands of commoner gulls may be joined by Glaucous or Iceland Gulls. At any time of year, you should also see quite a few common water and scrub birds.

Target birds *All year* – **Yellow-legged Gull (30%).** *Winter –* **Glaucous Gull (<20%), Iceland Gull (<20%).**

Other possible bird species

Resident		
Common wildfowl	Stock Dove	Turtle Dove
Egyptian Goose	Corvids	Hirundines
Cormorant	Skylark	Kingfisher
Grey Heron	Common scrub birds	Summer warblers
Common waterbirds	Goldcrest	Yellow Wagtail
Great Crested Grebe	Marsh Tit	
Little Grebe	Meadow Pipit	*Winter*
Sparrowhawk	Pied Wagtail	Redshank
Kestrel	Common finches	Grey Wagtail
Lapwing	Reed Bunting	Winter thrushes
Regular gull species	Yellowhammer	
Green Woodpecker		*Passage*
Great Spotted Woodpecker	*Summer*	Passage waders
	Hobby	
	Common Tern	*Occasional*
		Caspian Gull

Background information and birding tips

B LACKBOROUGH END Tip is a working household waste centre (a.k.a. rubbish tip!) and quarry. The foul-smelling waste is a magnet for thousands of gulls at all times of year (all common species are recorded in impressive numbers).

Some winters are good 'white-winged years', other winters they are few and far between and it is impossible to predict what sort of winter it is going to be. In general, March seems to be a good time to look for white-winged gull species in Britain.

When arriving on site, please be sure to park your vehicle away from the bend on the main road, as large lorries need space to swing in and out of the track. The site manager is a friendly chap who is pleased that his tip attracts rare birds but he asks you all for your co-operation

in leaving clear access for his trucks.

Follow the sandy track away from the road (signed 'bridleway'). After approximately 200 yards, the bridleway takes a sharp turn right but ignore this unless you want to view the fishing lake. Gulls bathe on this lake and there are usually a few common wildfowl species to be seen here. The conifers on the left are good for Goldcrest and Coal Tit.

Carry on along the wide sandy track. You will pass a sign reading 'caution gate locked ahead', then a large house on your right. The path bends, then opens out so you can see the mound of rubbish on your left (about half a mile from the car park).

Go a few yards further and there are a couple of raised grass banks by the path that are ideal platforms to view the area on the left.

Contacts

None.

In my experience, it is advisable to be on site early in the morning. The white-winged gulls tend to loaf on the banks of the tip or bathe in the two pools, visible from the path, before heading off at around 9am. If present, sightings of Glaucs and Icelands become very sporadic throughout the day from that point onwards.

The pools by the path hold bathing gulls. If the white-winged species get on here they allow very good views indeed. I have also seen Redshank and Grey and Pied Wagtails on this pool and it should also be attractive to passage waders such as Green and Common Sandpipers.

The surrounding bushes hide many species of common birds such as Bullfinch, Long-tailed Tit, Blackbird, Dunnock, Wren, Robin, Song Thrush, Yellowhammer, etc, joined by Redwing and Fieldfare in winter.

A summer visit can be unproductive, unless you like scanning through gull flocks to find a Yellow-legged Gull. Caspian Gull has also been reported from here, so you never know what is going to turn up.

The bushes and trees along the track attract several species of warbler in spring and summer. Whitethroats, Lesser Whitethroats and Willow Warblers and Chiffchaffs all visit, as do Turtle Doves.

The fishing lake usually has a swarm of hirundines hunting insects over it and one or two Common Terns can usually be seen. Egyptian Geese are ever-present on the lake.

Blackborough End Tip makes

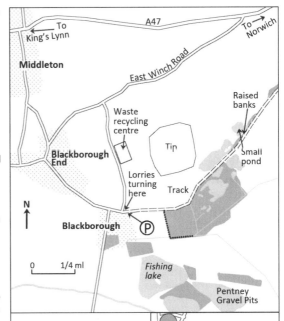

How to get there

(Five miles SE of King's Lynn).

SAT NAV: PE32 1SQ (postcode should take you to the house on the sharp bend and then follow written instructions).

GPS: Approx. 52.700284; 0.474815.

From King's Lynn, take the A47 signed to Norwich. After approx. 3 miles take East Winch Road, sign-posted to the Waste Disposal Tip.

After a mile, take the first left (sign-posted 'Waste Recycling Centre', immediately before 7.5 tonne restriction sign).

Go down the hill for 0.7 miles, (past the recycling centre) and at the sharp right bend at the bottom of the hill turn sharp left onto a wide sandy track.

Do not park on the bend (because lorries come down the hill and need room to turn onto this track). Go a little way down the track to park.

for a bracing start to a winter day's birding in Norfolk. Start here, then head for the coastal hotspots for waders, geese and ducks then end the day at a raptor roost. Does a day's entertainment come any more exciting than that?!

45

Key points

- **Keep dogs under control.**
- **No foot access to western tip (April to July), to protect terns.**
- **Phone boat companies for sailing times.**
- **Facilities at parking places (Morston and Blakeney) can be closed off-peak.**
- **Keep to boardwalks and avoid roped-off areas.**
- **Info Centre on The Point has toilet facilities (inc. disabled). Open dawn to dusk (April –Oct inclusive).**
- **Difficult wheelchair access. Phone the warden and boat companies for access info.**
- **If walking, the terrain is tough.**

BIRDWATCHERS who join the tourists on boats from Blakeney and Morston will enjoy the spectacle provided by gull and tern colonies as well as the common and grey seals. The challenge is to pick out a Mediterranean Gull or a Roseate Tern among the swirling mass of white birds. During migration, the eight mile round trip along shingle from Cley beach car park will most likely produce more species, but do not under-estimate the effort this trek takes!

Target birds
All year – **Marsh Harrier (90%).** *Summer* – **Nesting terns (100%), Mediterranean Gull (10%).** *Spring/ autumn* – **Passage seabirds, passage migrants.** *Winter* – **Waders (100%), winter raptors (20%).**

Other possible bird species

All year	*Spring/autumn (might include)*	
Shelduck	Shearwaters	Yellow Wagtail
Other common wildfowl	Gannet	Richard's Pipit
Red-legged Partridge	Whimbrel	*Winter*
Cormorant	Skuas	Brent Goose
Kestrel	Hirundines	Wigeon
Common waders	Ring Ouzel	Grey Plover
Regular gull species	Bluethroat	Winter thrushes
Corvids	Whinchat	Rock Pipit
Skylark	Wheatear	*Occasional*
Meadow Pipit	Black Redstart	Winter raptors
Pied Wagtail	Grasshopper Warbler	Short-eared Owl
Common finches	Goldcrest	Roseate Tern
Reed Bunting		

Background information and birding tips

A VISIT to Blakeney Point in ideal migrant conditions (fog, drizzle, onshore winds) can seem a very bleak experience, but visit in spring and summer sunshine for the tern and seal colonies and it can seem like a naturalist's paradise.

Summer boat trips are popular with tourists interested in seeing common and grey seals on The Point but they also provide a superb opportunity for obtaining close views of Sandwich, Common, Little and Arctic Terns busily going about the business of raising chicks. Sharp-eyed birders should manage to pick out a Mediterranean Gull or even a Roseate Tern.

Along Blakeney Channel you will see many common waders on the mud banks and see terns as they fish the large inlet. At most times, the trip takes about one hour and you do not land on The Point. However, if the tide is right, the boat does land, extending the round trip to two hours. Booking boat trips is essential, especially in school holidays.

Birdwatchers on the look-out for migrants in spring and autumn should endeavour to walk the whole length of Blakeney Point from Cley beach car park. This is an arduous walk along a shingle sea wall and, at the end of the eight mile trek (four miles each

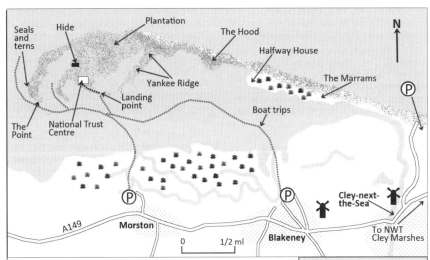

How to get there

(Eleven miles W of Cromer).

SAT NAV: NR25 7BH (postcode for Morston Quay from where boats leave for the Point).

GPS: 52.958972; 0.985848 (co-ordinates for Morston Quay car park).

You can tackle Blakeney Point the hard way or the easy way. The easy way is to travel by boat from either Morston Quay or Blakeney Harbour. Call contact numbers for sailing times, as these depend on tides.

Boats run throughout the year, though tide times dictate

whether you are able to land on The Point or not.

Morston is about two miles W of Blakeney village, both connected by A149. Obtain boat tickets where the chalk boards advertise 'Boat Trips' by The Anchor pub on A149.

Morston Quay is sign-posted on a brown tourist sign. Follow this rough track to a pay and display car park.

Blakeney Harbour is sign-posted off the A149 down Westgate Street. Follow the road to the quay car park and the moorings for the seal and bird trips are very obvious.

If you want a challenge in spring and autumn, the best way to find the birds is by walking from Cley beach car park, out of the village towards Sheringham, then turn left at the sign for 'Beach'. Walk W along the shingle bank for four miles.

way), your calf muscles will be complaining bitterly! Please keep clear of Oystercatchers and Ringed Plovers in spring, as they will be trying to nest on the shingle.

For the first mile you will have the sea on your right and a marsh on your left. Scan both at regular intervals

for passing seabirds over the former and geese, ducks and raptors over the latter. The shingle then opens out to an area of stubby vegetation, known as The Marrams. Wait here awhile as the dense plants can hold various species which tend to hide.

Wheatears are common here

on passage and look out for thrushes, warblers, Goldcrests, finches etc as they make their first landing from the continent. Such tired, small birds attract the attention of raptors, so keep one eye on the skies!

A mile further on, you reach Halfway House. Don't let

47

the name fool you: this is only Quarterway or Three-quarterway House depending if you are on your way to The Point or on your way back.

Either way, it will feel good to get your feet on solid ground for a few moments after sand and shingle. The bushes around Halfway House are excellent migrant traps. After a further half a mile, you reach a dune system, known as The Hood, which is good for migrant pipits, chats, thrushes etc. It usually pays to search the area thoroughly before continuing your journey.

Eventually, you will reach an odd-shaped blue building, which was the old lifeboat station but now houses the National Trust information centre. Just before the centre, you will see a few bushes, optimistically called The Plantation. These are an irresistible magnet for tired migrants and you should pause here for some time to see what pops into view.

The area around the lifeboat station and chalets is excellent for Wheatears, Whinchats, thrushes, etc in spring and autumn. There is also a seat here where you can look over Blakeney Channel and marsh.

When the tide permits, Grey Plovers, Curlews, Dunlins, Bar-tailed Godwits, Ringed Plovers, etc can be seen and Brent Geese are present on the marsh until May.

Terns fish the channel from April onwards but the nesting area is another half a mile from here, at the western tip of The Point. There is no access by foot to the tern colony between April and July. A boardwalk runs from behind the visitor centre to a hide overlooking a channel. This is good for fishing terns in summer when the tide is in, as well as geese and waders in winter when the mud is exposed. A telescope is useful.

The boardwalk also leads to the beach. This can be a spectacular place when the wind is blowing strongly onshore as birds seem to pass closer here than at any other seawatching site in Norfolk (with the possible exception of Sheringham), though there is no shelter. Manx Shearwater, Arctic and Great Skuas are the most likely to be seen, but Pomerine and Long-tailed Skuas and Balearic Shearwaters are also possible.

Blakeney Point also boasts a disabled toilet. The most baffling thing is exactly how the National Trust expects wheelchair users to get to it, as a steep step from the sand onto a boardwalk has to be negotiated. If you have mobility problems, I would phone the warden to clarify things first!

As mentioned before, Blakeney Point is famous for its seal colony. More than 400 animals can be seen here, a mixture of grey and common seals. The seals and terns provide a noisy spectacle on the boat trips and I thoroughly recommend it to you, even if you are prone to queasiness on boats.

Usually I feel ill at the slightest sea-swell but this trip is a breeze. I am usually more concerned with sorting out the terns ('was that a Roseate which just flew over my head?') and cooing at the baby seals!

In truth, the walk from Cley is usually only undertaken by hardened birdwatchers trying to find rare migrants in spring and autumn. Hardy, persistent searchers can turn up anything.

The list of rare and scarce birds seen on Blakeney are too numerous to mention but Alder Flycatcher, Pallas's Grasshopper Warbler, Thrush Nightingale, Desert Warbler, etc should get your mouth watering!

Contacts
National Trust warden 01263 740 241; e-mail: blakeneypoint@nationaltrust.org.uk
www.nationaltrust.org.uk/blakeney/

Boat operators
Graham Bean - 01263 740 505;

e-mail: info@beansboattrips.co.uk
www.beansboattrips.co.uk
John Bean 01263 740 038.

Bishop's Boats 01263 740 753 or Freephone 0800 740 745;
e-mail: paul@bishopsboats.com
www.norfolksealtrips.co.uk

Blakeney Point Seal Trips

01263 740 792 / 07563 332 088
www.blakeneypointsealtrips.co.uk/finding

Moreton's Boat Trips
01263 740 792 or 07563 332 088

Jim Temple 01263 740 791;
e-mail: info@sealtrips.co.uk
www.sealtrips.co.uk

BLICKLING HALL is a typical English country estate, owned and managed by the National Trust. It comprises 600 acres of ancient woodland, 800 acres of pasture and a large artificial lake. These habitats support a wide range of common resident and visiting birds throughout the year.

Target birds *All year* – **Common woodland and parkland birds (100%), Barn Owl (40%).** *Winter* – **Winter wildfowl (100%).**

Other possible bird species

All year		*Summer*
Egyptian Goose	Other corvids	Hobby
Common wildfowl	Skylark	Common Tern
Little Grebe	Common scrub birds	Cuckoo
Great Crested Grebe	Goldcrest	Turtle Dove
Buzzard	Common woodland birds	Sand Martin
Sparrowhawk	Nuthatch	Other hirundines
Kestrel	Treecreeper	Reed Warbler
Woodcock	Pied Wagtail	Sedge Warbler
Regular gull species	Meadow Pipit	Other summer warblers
Stock Dove	Common finches	
Barn Owl	Reed Bunting	Spotted Flycatcher
Little Owl	Yellowhammer	
Tawny Owl		*Occasional*
Green Woodpecker	*Winter*	Lesser Spotted Woodpecker
Great Spotted Woodpecker	Goldeneye	
Kingfisher	Goosander	Yellow Wagtail
Jay	Lapwing	Crossbill
	Winter thrushes	
	Grey Wagtail	

Background information and birding tips

THERE ARE three, circular colour-marked trails leading from the main car park. The Blue Estate Walk is five miles long, a brown-marked Mausoleum Trail is 2.25 miles in length and there is a green-signed Lakeside Trail which is also 2.25 miles long. I usually do a mixture of all three!

From the main car park, follow signs for the Lakeside Walk. Go past some beautiful cottages and through the park gates. Almost immediately, you can turn right through a small wooden gate onto a grass footpath (if you head left along the main track you reach the Great Wood). This takes you to the lake through some mature trees.

Spend time in the area as this is a good place for woodpeckers (all year round) and summer warblers. There may be Spotted Flycatchers here in summer and one or two migrants such as Pied Flycatcher, Redstart and Wood Warbler may be found at passage times.

The path reaches the lake where you will see many common waterbirds at any time of year. Expect to see Great Crested Grebe, Coot, Moorhen, Egyptian Goose, Tufted Duck and Gadwall.

In winter, these are joined by Goosander, Pochard, Shoveler, Goldeneye and maybe even one of the rarer grebes. The path encircles

Key points

- **Park open all year, dawn to dusk. Restrictions may apply when a major event is taking place.**

- **Complicated Hall opening times – check website for the day you wish to visit.**

- **Free parking.**

- **Restaurant & shop. Toilets (inc blue badge) at main entrance.**

- **Dogs on leads in park.**

- **Brown trail (2.25 miles), Lakeside trail (2.25 miles), Blue trail (5 miles). Level terrain, but muddy in parts.**

Contacts
Blickling Hall
01263 738 030 ;
e-mail: blickling@nationaltrust.org.uk
www.nationaltrust.org.uk/blickling-estate/

How to get there

(15 miles N of Norwich, 1.25 miles NW of Aylsham).

SAT NAV: NR11 6NJ (main car park).

GPS: 52.810918; 1.226504.

On the A140 Norwich to Cromer road turn off at the roundabout (signed Aylsham). Follow the road through Aylsham where you pick up brown tourist signs for Blickling Hall. Then choose your route from below:

For lake (TG 179 925 or GPS 52.819602; 1.233576): After passing through Aylsham, take the second right turn to Ingworth, (1.6 miles from the A140 roundabout). Turn left at signs for Ingworth and Blickling Lake, then after 0.7 miles turn left into the lake car park (this gives quick access to the lake and wood on the eastern side of the lake).

For Great Wood (TG 161 297) or GPS 52.821`608;1.206721): The Woodgate car park is reached by continuing along the road from the lake car park for another 1.7 miles and turning left (opposite a house where the road bends

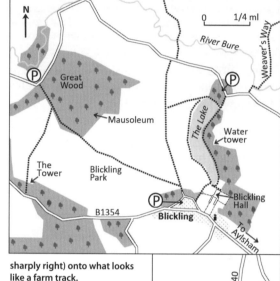

sharply right) onto what looks like a farm track.

Hall: If you want the main car park, continue on the B1149 through Aylsham and the hall is 2.2 miles from the A140 roundabout. The Common car park is on your right, 1.4 miles past the hall car park (immediately past a brown tourist sign for Mannington Hall/Tudor Tour and just before the turn off for Cawston). TG 157 289.

Blue Badge holders may park at the hall.

the whole lake, taking you back around the hall to the car park.

The reeds around the edge of the large lake hold breeding Reed Warblers in summer, but you will be lucky to see one of the resident Water Rails. There are a few muddy edges to the lake so be watchful for waders at passage time. A Hobby or two may be seen around the lake area in summer and autumn, hunting the hirundines and dragonflies.

A walk early in the morning will produce the best birding as the lake area is popular with general visitors during the day.

At the northern end of the lake, you can walk around it to another couple of stands of wood or turn left to follow the brown Mausoleum Trail to Great Wood. All these areas are good for resident woodpeckers (though not Lesser Spotted any more), Nuthatches, Treecreepers and other common woodland species.

In winter, watch for Bramblings feeding on the forest floor among Chaffinch flocks, especially if there is beech mast on the ground. Spotted Flycatchers and warblers arrive to breed in spring and summer.

The trail linking the lake with the Great Wood

is quiet as far as birds go but keep your eyes open for Little Owl, perched on fence posts and isolated trees and Barn Owls hunting over the fields at dawn and dusk (they breed in the park).

Before you get to the Great Wood, you pass a smaller wood, including some larch trees. Crossbills have been seen here but Siskin and Redpoll are more likely. This wood can be surprisingly devoid of people, making it ideal for birdwatchers to wait patiently to see what shows itself.

The footpath affords excellent overviews of several woods and it may be worth regularly scanning for birds of prey when you reach a suitable vantage point.

If you don't fancy walking all the way to the Great Wood from the main car park, there is also a car park here (see access section). This is ideal if you don't have a lot of time to spend in the park, as you can easily access different habitats from different car parks.

You eventually reach The Mausoleum, another good place from which to scan the surrounding area, especially for Barn Owls.

The trails split about 500 yards past the Mausoleum, red goes left, the blue bears right. The blue trail leads you to Great Wood and Woodgate car park. There are many smaller paths through the trees, so explore as much as you desire!

The blue Estate Trail leads south off the track by Great Wood if you wish to divert to scan a few hedgerows and fields. This trail is a bit fiddly and takes you across and along some busy roads and an incredibly muddy field, so I tend to retrace my steps to complete a circuit of the lake. This gives me a chance of seeing species I have missed earlier. The choice is yours depending on how fit you are feeling!

If I am honest, there are only three areas of great interest to birdwatchers: the lake; the wood at the back of the lake; the Great Wood. All of these have their own car parks so you can move between each site without having to bother with the less interesting bits in between.

If you have a bike, there is a marked cycle route around the park (cycles are available for hire at the hall at certain times).

You may want to spend the whole day in the park birding, visiting the hall, picnicking, etc but if you wish to tour the hall I suggest you phone to check it is open beforehand – I have lost count of the number of people who turn up to find it closed!

Key points

• **Two seated walking frames and three single-seater PMVs for hire.**

• **Two mile circular route accessible to wheelchairs (accessible map available at Hall).**

Other nearby sites

Buxton Heath, Felbrigg Hall, Hoveton Great Broad, Rockland Broad Sparham Pools, Surlingham Church Marshes.

Key points

- National Trust site – open access at all times.
- Beach car park charge cheaper after 4pm (NT members must also pay).
- Road to car park may flood at high tide.
- Toilet block near main car park.
- Footpath trail consists of railway sleepers.
- Wheelchair users restricted to Broad Lane and main car parks.
- Terrain is level but at least one stile to negotiate.
- Insect repellent advisable in summer.
- Telescope advisable.
- Tide times for Brancaster at: http://rwngc.org/

Contacts

None

PART OF THE North Norfolk Coast's Area of Outstanding Natural Beauty, Brancaster links with Gypsy Lane and Titchwell Marsh to the west and Holkham Pines to the east. Visitors may wish to view the marsh from the car park or take a stroll along the North Norfolk Coastal Path to see what birds are on offer.

Target birds *All year* – **Marsh Harrier (90%), Bearded Tit (70%), Barn Owl (50%).** *Winter* – **Brent Goose (95%), seaduck (40%), winter raptors (25%).** *Spring/autumn* – **Passage migrants.**

Other possible bird species

All year		*Winter*
Shelduck	Whimbrel	Wigeon
Little Egret	Skuas	Teal
Kestrel	Wryneck	Long-tailed Duck
Common waders	Redstart	Common Scoter
Regular gull species	Whinchat	Goldeneye
Green Woodpecker	Wheatear	Red-breasted Merganser
Skylark	Ring Ouzel	Red-throated Diver
Meadow Pipit	Winter thrushes	Hen Harrier
Pied Wagtail	Barred Warbler	Merlin
Bullfinch	Yellow-browed Warbler	Peregrine
Reed Bunting	Firecrest	Grey Plover
Spring/autumn	Pied Flycatcher	Short-eared Owl
(might include)	Yellow Wagtail	Stonechat
Garganey	*Summer*	Winter thrushes
Shearwaters	Terns	Twite
Gannet	Hirundines	Snow Bunting
Hobby	Common warblers	

Background information and birding tips

BRANCASTER MARSH is another coastal site neglected by birders, making it ideal for those wishing to birdwatch on their own. It is an extension of the Gypsy Lane walk to the west.

Close to the small lay-by along the road, listen out for the '*ping-ping*' calls of Bearded Tits in the surrounding reedbed: they can show well here. The start of the track is marked by a National Trust ("Norfolk Coastal Path – Brancaster Manor") sign about 75 yards back towards the village from the small lay-by.

The path starts off along a rough track through a small reedbed. This is frequented by Reed Warblers in summer. The trees and bushes around the start of the track are alive with species such as Goldfinch, Greenfinch, Reed Bunting and other common birds.

The path narrows and continues east until it reaches a stile from where you start to get a great overview of the marsh. This is also a good place to watch for Sedge Warblers. Until this point, the vertically-challenged among us will have seen very little of the marsh over the reeds!

All along this section there are

bushes to scan for common birds and migrants in spring and autumn. There is a distinct possibility of the occasional Redstart, Pied Flycatcher, Barred Warbler or Firecrest turning up here in May or, more likely, in September/October.

After the stile, the path consists of two railway sleepers side by side (quite narrow when passing other walkers, especially those clad in winter woollies). The whole path gives excellent views over the marsh.

In winter, expect Hen Harriers and maybe a Merlin with a distinct possibility of a Barn or Short-eared Owl. Flying in and out of the marsh will be small flocks of Brent Geese and Wigeon. Little Egrets are resident but can be hidden in the channels.

The marsh is quieter in summer but you should obtain reasonable views of a Marsh Harrier or two. Hirundines should be seen overhead, sometimes being pursued by a Hobby.

The path reaches a beautiful cottage with views over the marsh and, if I win the lottery, I shall be knocking on the owner's door to make them an offer they can't refuse! Just after this cottage, you come across a creek, which is a good place to scan for waders and Little Egrets when the tide is out.

From here the path continues with good views over the marsh to your left and bushes to your right. The longer you walk along towards Holkham, the more birds you are likely to see, especially in winter.

If you fancy a bit of seawatching, park in the main car park at the end of Broad Lane but be aware

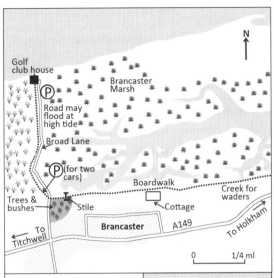

How to get there

(6.5 miles E of Hunstanton).

SAT NAV: PE31 8AX.

GPS: 52.973397; 0.637009.

Enter Brancaster village on A149 Norfolk coast road and take Broad Lane, sign-posted 'The Beach'.

There is a small pull-in on the left with room for two cars at the point where the road splits the reedbed. If this is full, follow the road to the car park (you may have to pay the attendant, depending on time of year).

The car park is also an ideal place to sit and scan the marsh, particularly in

The footpath is 75 yards back towards the village from the small lay-by. Turn left along a track in the reeds and follow for as far as you like (this path is part of The Peddar's Way long distance footpath).

that this may be cut off at particularly high tides. Brancaster is adjacent to Titchwell Marsh, so see that site (page 208) for details of likely species at sea.

winter when raptors may pass through on their way to roost.

If you fancy walking along the beach to Titchwell, only attempt it at low tide – there is a deep channel between the two reserves!

53

Key points

- **Free access at all times.**
- **Terrain level on narrow, muddy path, not suitable for wheelchairs.**
- **Hide overlooks Breydon Water (accessed up steep steps).**
- **Great views from 'sea-wall'. Telescope essential.**
- **Best viewed an hour before high tide when birds are pushed into NE corner.**
- **Morning 2hr boat trips run through the winter from Burgh Castle. Booking essential on 01603 715 191.**
- **Car parking restrictions (see access details).**
- **Nearest facilities at Asda store.**

Contacts

General Broads Authority
01603 610 734

THE EXTENSIVE mud flats of Breydon Water (when exposed) are usually covered with waders and gulls, and the north shore is easily accessible from Great Yarmouth. Birdwatchers can walk as far as they like to get the best out of their visit – the marshes beyond the hide are home to winter wildfowl and raptors.

Target birds
All year – **Marsh Harrier (95%), Mediterranean Gull (90%), Avocet (80%).** *Winter* – **Short-eared Owl (10%).** *Spring/summer* – **Little Gull (50%), Roseate Tern (<10%).** *Spring/autumn* – **Passage waders, Little Gull (60%).**

Other possible bird species

All year	Curlew Sandpiper	Tufted Duck
Shelduck	Black-tailed Godwit	Pintail
Common wildfowl	Whimbrel	Goldeneye
Grey Partridge	Greenshank	Golden Plover
Red-legged Partridge	Spotted Redshank	Grey Plover
Cormorant	Green Sandpiper	Knot
Little Egret	Wood Sandpiper	Bar-tailed Godwit
Marsh Harrier	Common Sandpiper	Rock Pipit
Sparrowhawk	Black Tern	
Peregrine	Arctic Tern	*Spring/summer*
Kestrel	Hirundines	Garganey
Common waders		Sandwich Tern
Regular gull species	*Winter*	Common Tern
Barn Owl	Bewick's Swan	Little Tern
Pied Wagtail	Whooper Swan	
	Pink-footed Goose	*Occasional*
Passage	Wigeon	White-fronted Goose
Ruff	Teal	Hen Harrier (winter)
Little Stint	Pochard	Merlin

Background information and birding tips

BREYDON WATER is at the confluence of the Rivers Bure, Waveney and Yare. It forms the only tidal flats on the east coast of Norfolk and is internationally important for wintering waterbirds.

Such a huge area can seem a very daunting place to watch birds but getting there at the right time makes it more accessible, as the tide will do all your hard work for you. The north-east area is the last to be covered by the tide, so if you reach here about 60 or 90 minutes before high tide, all the waders and roosting terns will be pushed towards you.

Breydon is one of the most reliable places to see wintering Avocets in Norfolk. There may be one or two at other sites in the county but more than 50 stay here from October to March. These are joined by others in summer, with numbers reaching up to 300 in July and August. Dotted among the Avocets you should see one or two Grey Plovers and Bar-tailed Godwits, along with other species of commoner waders and a Little Egret or two.

If you follow the path from the Asda car park along the north shore, passing the hide, you are

How to get there

(On outskirts of Great Yarmouth).

SAT NAV: NR30 1SF.

GPS: 52.612903; 1.717813.

By car: Take A47 into Great Yarmouth, heading straight over the first roundabout (junction with A12) towards the town centre.

Move immediately into the right hand lane and turn right at the traffic lights (50 yards after the A12 island) signed to the train station.

Either park in the station's pay-and-display car park or follow the road round to park in the Asda car park (maximum 3 hours' stay – free). Keeping Asda on your right and the water on your left, follow the path to the info board.

The Weavers Way footpath starts here, going under the road bridge and following the north shore of Breydon Water to the hide and beyond to Berney Marshes.

By boat: There is free 24hr mooring on the River Bure at Great Yarmouth, near the tourist information centre at TG 521 083.

Walk south and cross A47 road bridge to the train station and Asda supermarket. Follow directions above.

Alternatively, be 'green' and catch a train to Great Yarmouth or Berney Arms.

able to look out over Acle Marshes on your right. In winter, Hen Harriers and Merlins occasionally pass through and in some winters a Short-eared Owl or two may roost on the marsh. A Barn Owl is far more likely, though.

The marshes around Breydon also hold varying numbers of wintering wildfowl. White-fronted Geese numbers seem to be declining here but Wigeon are numerous and you might pick out a few Bewick's or Whooper Swans in the fields. You should also find one or two Rock Pipits as 100 or so over-winter.

Common waders will be joined by more exciting species at passage times in spring and autumn. These can include Whimbrel, Spotted Redshank, Little Stint, Ruff and Green, Common, Wood and Curlew Sandpipers. Numbers are usually better in autumn. Also look out for Black and Arctic Terns.

In summer, Breydon is frequented by several species of roosting tern. Sandwich and Common Terns are the most numerous but watch out for Little and Roseate Terns among them. The hide overlooks the tern platforms.

If you wish, you can continue along the north shore path across the Halvergate Marshes to Halvergate village, or on to Berney Arms RSPB. An infrequent bus service runs back to Yarmouth from the former and an even more infrequent train service runs from the latter. Or just retrace your steps back to Yarmouth to scan the fields and water again.

If you are visiting The Broads area by boat, you can get excellent views of Breydon Water's birds from your vessel. Alternatively, the RSPB organise two-hour boat trips across Breydon in winter. The boat runs from Goodchild Marina, Burgh Castle. It is essential to book in advance as the boat only holds 12 people (see Key Points).

55

Key points

- **Free parking.**

- **Access via a rough track that may be wet at all times of year. Boots or wellies recommended.**

- **Wheelchair access possible to new hide, but not to riverside path.**

- **Telescope essential as target species are invariably distant.**

- **Please leave sightings information in hide.**

- **Bike racks on reserve side of Buckenham railway line.**

Contacts

RSPB Mid Yare Office
01603 715 191

RSPB East Anglia Office
01603 661 662;
e-mail: strumpshaw@ rspb.org.uk

IN WINTER, RSPB Buckenham and Cantley Marshes continue to host the only wintering flock of (Taiga) Bean Geese in England, along with other species of wildfowl. In the breeding season the marshes are home to several sought-after species. Perhaps the most underrated wildlife experience in Britain can be witnessed here: tens of thousands of corvids gathering in the surrounding fields to feed before noisily flying to roost like a scene from a Hitchcock movie!

Target birds *All year* – **Marsh Harrier (80%), Cetti's Warbler (hear 60%, see 20%).** *Winter* – **(Taiga) Bean Goose (85%), White-fronted Goose (85%), Water Pipit (60%).** *Summer* – **Breeding waders (100%), Hobby (40%).**

Other possible bird species

Winter	Short-eared Owl	Reed Warbler
Mute Swan	Corvids	Sedge Warbler
Pink-footed Goose	Winter thrushes	Whitethroat
Wigeon		Blackcap
Teal	*Summer*	Chiffchaff
Pintail	Egyptian Goose	Yellow Wagtail
Other wildfowl	Gadwall	
Common waterbirds	Shoveler	*Spring/autumn*
Winter raptors	Oystercatcher	Garganey
Golden Plover	Avocet	Passage waders
Ruff	Lapwing	Little Gull
Redshank	Snipe	
Regular gull species	Curlew	*Occasional*
Barn Owl	Redshank	Bittern
	Black-headed Gull	

Background information and birding tips

ENGLAND'S only regular wintering flock of Bean Geese has made the RSPB's Buckenham Marshes famous. These birds are usually present from November through to the end of January. They sometimes linger until mid-February but I recommend you visit earlier in the year to be sure of connecting with this scarce species.

A small flock of White-fronted Geese also over-winters on the marsh. A Lesser White-fronted Goose occasionally joins the flock, so study the distant geese very carefully!

The goose flock can sometimes be hard to locate. If you choose

to park at Buckenham station, carefully cross the railway line to follow the wide, rough track straight ahead to the riverbank. Then turn left to follow the riverside footpath all the way to Cantley, scanning the marshes as you go.

Alternatively, you can park very carefully on Burnthouse Road, Cantley, and follow the well-marked footpath signs across the marsh to the riverbank. Turn right and follow the raised 'seawall' for 2.5 miles towards Buckenham, scanning all the way.

These walks can seem an awfully long way on cold winter days but the River Yare can hold many a wild duck, especially when the marsh pools are frozen. I disturbed a Bittern in riverside reeds at the Cantley end one snowy February morning!

In winter, as well as Bean and White-fronted Geese, you will also see thousands of Wigeon and Teal and maybe a few Pink-footed geese too. These birds allow you superb views from the access track, as they are too busy feeding to be disturbed. The Teal flock is occasionally joined by a Green-winged Teal. Scan the marshes either side of the access track for waders such as Redshank, Curlew and Ruff.

Raptors and owls regularly patrol the fields in winter, Peregrine being the most regularly noted. Barn Owls can be encountered at most times of year but I have never been very lucky at this site. Up to half a dozen Water Pipits can usually be found on the marshes, though they are elusive at times.

At dusk in winter – best witnessed in December through to late January – an enormous corvid roost of tens of thousands of birds provides one of the best bird spectacles in Britain. The Crows, Jackdaws and Rooks gather in fields north of Buckenham Station (please watch from your car to avoid disturbance) before heading to roost in the carrs to the north of the reserve.

You may have to search for the field they are in, as the corvids can change location each night. The noise as they pass over you is deafening.

In summer, Buckenham is an important breeding area for several species that are declining

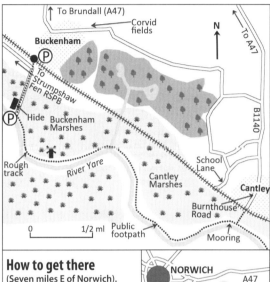

How to get there

(Seven miles E of Norwich).

SAT NAV: NR13 4HW.

GPS: 52.597721; 1.470267.

From Norwich take A47 east to roundabout sign-posted to Brundall. Continue on minor road for 0.4 miles and bear left at the sharp bend onto The Street (sign-posted Brundall Station). Follow the road around mini-roundabouts and across the traffic-calmed area.

After 1.1 miles you go under a railway bridge, then reach a sign for RSPB Strumpshaw Fen. Turn right (Stone Road) and follow signs for the Household Waste Disposal Centre.

Go past this centre, then turn right after 0.7 miles, sign-posted to Buckenham Station (Station Road).

After half a mile, park in the RSPB car park behind the railway station. Carefully cross the railway line and follow the obvious wide track ahead to the hide. From here turn left towards the derelict windmill where you can pick up the riverside path.

rapidly on the national stage. These include Skylark, Yellow Wagtail, Redshank, Snipe, Shoveler and Lapwing. Egyptian and Greylag Geese also breed, as does Meadow Pipit.

Marsh Harriers and Hobbies frequently cause panic as they hunt. Avocets now breed on site and Cetti's Warblers can be heard from riverside bushes and reeds throughout the year.

57

In spring and autumn, the site attracts passage waders. Ruff, Black-tailed Godwit, Green and Wood Sandpipers and Little Stint are the most regular but recent rarities include Pacific Golden Plover and Pectoral Sandpiper. Little Gulls and Garganey are recorded regularly on passage.

Many of the birds mentioned above may be viewable from the new hide at the bottom of the rocky track from Buckenham Station. Wheelchair users (and lazy birders such as myself) can park by the hide (TG 348 050) by crossing the manned level crossing at Strumpshaw and then following the road/track to the pull-in by the hide. The hide is fully wheelchair accessible.

From the hide, the riverside footpath to Cantley is accessed by following the main track towards the derelict windmill and then climbing a few steps onto the raised path (not wheelchair accessible).

This is an important reserve for birds, both for wintering wildfowl and breeding waders. The birds can be distant and elusive but patience will be rewarded. There is no boat mooring facility at Buckenham, though you may moor at Cantley, a distance of about 2.5 miles.

Avocet numbers in the county have increased steadily and the Buckenham Marshes reserve is just one of their many breeding sites.

Other nearby sites

Breydon Water, Burgh Castle, Great Yarmouth Beach, Hardley Flood, Rockland Broad, Sparham Pools, Strumpshaw Fen, Surlingham Church Marshes, Ted Ellis Reserve.

THERE ARE two options at Burgh Castle: take a long walk along the southern shore of Breydon water for waders, wildfowl and raptors or simply sit in the grounds of a Roman fort and wait to see what comes to you. The grassland surrounding the ruin is superb for insects in summer.

Target birds *All year* – **Marsh Harrier (85%), Avocet (80%), Cetti's Warbler (hear 80%, see 20%).** *Winter* – **Winter raptors (25%), Short-eared Owl (15%).**

Other possible bird species

All year
Common wildfowl
Cormorant
Little Egret
Little Grebe
Great Crested Grebe
Common waterbirds
Marsh Harrier
Sparrowhawk
Kestrel
Red-legged Partridge
Grey Partridge
Common waders
Regular gull species
Barn Owl
Great Spotted Woodpecker
Corvids
Skylark
Common scrub birds

Common woodland birds
Meadow Pipit
Pied Wagtail
Common finches
Reed Bunting

Winter
Bewick's Swan
Whooper Swan
White-fronted Goose
Wigeon
Goldeneye
Hen Harrier
Merlin
Peregrine
Winter thrushes
Stonechat

Summer
Hobby
Common Tern

Cuckoo
Hirundines
Sedge Warbler
Reed Warbler
Whitethroat
Lesser Whitethroat
Blackcap
Willow Warbler
Chiffchaff

Spring/autumn
Passage waders

Occasional
Rough-legged Buzzard (winter)
Lesser Spotted Woodpecker
Bearded Tit

Background information and birding tips

THE ROMAN fort at Burgh Castle affords superb views over the marshes of Langley, Beighton, Reedham, Halvergate, Chedgrave, Acle, South Walsham and Burgh Castle. In winter, this is a great place to sit and scan for raptors and wildfowl. There is a bench and an ID information panel at the edge of the cliff within the fort's grounds.

A telescope is essential to get the best out of your visit and it can get very cold up there on the hill but your reward should include views of Marsh and Hen Harriers, along with Peregrine, Merlin, Short-eared Owl

and wild swans and geese.

The bushes and trees around the fort are magnets for common woodland birds, including occasional Lesser Spotted Woodpeckers. Search these trees in spring and autumn for migrants such as Redstarts, Pied Flycatchers and Firecrests. Below the fort is a reedbed that sometimes attracts Bearded Tits but more likely will hold a Reed Bunting or two.

The path below the fort can be reached down steep steps in the grounds of the ruin. Alternatively, if you need a much shallower path,

Key points
- Terrain is mainly level along tracks and grass paths. Some steep steps, though most can be avoided.

- Path alongside Breydon Water is level and well maintained – good for wheelchair users.

- Telescope essential for good views of raptors.

- Free access at all times.

- Free 24-hour mooring close by.

- Boat trips available from Goodchild's Marina (NR31 9PZ), just to the south of the Roman ruin.

Contacts
General Broads Authority
01603 610 734
Boat trips
01603 715 191

How to get there

(Three miles W of Great Yarmouth).

SAT NAV: NR31 9QG. Postcode for Church Lane, Belton. Follow directions below to parking area.

GPS: 52.586796; 1.654138.

By car: From Great Yarmouth, head S on A12. Follow tourist signs for Burgh Castle and Belton (also holiday parks, caravan and camping site and marina) along A143.

In Belton, take first right turn, following sign for Burgh Castle. At T-junction, turn left into Chuch Road and then either park carefully around the turning circle by the church sign, or continue past the church, past the Old Rectory and down a slight incline to park on the next open area on the left (NOTE: It's strictly private access after the gravel area).

From the gravel parking area, walk back towards the church for a few yards to a metal kissing gate on the right. Take the hard path downhill through some trees to the Angles Way at the bottom: turn left to walk below the Roman remains or right along a raised path overlooking Breydon Water.

Alternatively, at the church's turning circle, go through the gate, past the church and follow signs to the Roman Villa. There is a watchpoint by the ruins.

By boat: Nearest mooring is at Burgh Castle Marina, along the River Waveney at the western end of Breydon Water. A (sometimes muddy) public footpath runs north to the Roman fort.

Map labels:
To Herbert Barnes Riverside Park
BREYDON WATER
Church Farm Country Club
Church Road
Burgh Castle
Metal kissing-gate
To Belton
Steps
Gate
Angles Way
Fields
Fields
Roman ruins
Burgh Castle Reach
Track
N
Viewpoint
Mooring at marina
Steps
0   220 yds
A149
A47
GREAT YARMOUTH
A143
A12

look for a large metal kissing gate just up the hill from the gravel parking area. This path brings you much closer to the reedbed and bushes (you should hear a Cetti's Warbler even if you don't see one!).

Turn right and the path leads you along the southern shore of Breydon Water.

Time your visit correctly and you should get close views of many species of wader from this footpath. The best time to arrive is about an hour before high tide when the waders are pushed up to this western end of Breydon Water.

Avocets can be found here all year round and are joined by species such as Dunlin, Ringed Plover, Bar-tailed Godwit, Greenshank, Green Sandpiper and Little Stint at various times of the year. Spoonbills, Glossy Ibises and Rough-legged Buzzards turn up very occasionally.

Much more likely are Mediterranean Gulls: the

further you walk towards Yarmouth and the Herbert Barnes Riverside Park, the more likely you are to see one.

The Angles Way, a wide, well-maintained footpath, runs for about three and a half miles to Great Yarmouth (part of a 78 mile walk!). This is ideal if you are travelling by public transport, as you can catch a bus to Burgh Castle and walk back to Yarmouth or vice versa.

There is always something to see, though

views of most birds may be distant. Whether you choose to stay around the ruins (the surrounding meadows are superb for insects and wild flowers in summer) or go on a longer trek, you should see a good range of species at Burgh Castle.

Finally, you may wish to take an organised boat trip from Goodchild's Marina, which lies to the south of the Roman fort, to get close views of the thousands of waders on Breydon Water. Phone 01603 715 191 for further details.

Key points

- **No facilities other than a car park.**

- **Take a torch (to find your way back to the car park NOT to point at the Nightjars!!)**

- **Insect repellent advised.**

- **Level terrain but paths can be muddy so wear boots, especially early in the season (May).**

- **Stay on tracks at all times to protect delicate plants on site.**

- **Managed by Norfolk WT/ Natural England / Buxton Heath Wildlife Group on behalf of Hevingham Relief in Need charity.**

- **Dogs on leads.**

- **2.17 metre height barrier at car park.**

Contacts

Norfolk Wildlife Trust
01603 625 540
Buxton Heath Wildlife Group: http://www.freewebs.com/bhwg/
Also a Facebook page

BUXTON is a large area of heath and mire which is home to the closest Nightjar colony to Norwich. The maze of footpaths around the site gives access to several scarce species of plants and birds, so please keep to the path at all times to avoid disturbance!

Target birds *Summer* – **Woodcock (99%), Nightjar (90%), Woodlark (60%).**

Other possible bird species

Summer		
Sparrowhawk	Great Spotted Woodpecker	Grasshopper Warbler
Kestrel		Reed Warbler
Hobby	Jay	Sedge Warbler
Turtle Dove	Skylark	Goldcrest
Cuckoo	Hirundines	Common finches
Tawny Owl	Common scrub birds	Yellowhammer
Green Woodpecker	Lesser Whitethroat	Reed Bunting
	Whitethroat	

Background information and birding tips

BUXTON HEATH is a handy site for Nightjars if you are staying in Norwich or Wroxham. The Norfolk Wildlife Trust has cleared bracken from large areas, thus Nightjar numbers are increasing.

Nightjars and Woodlarks may be found in any cleared area at Buxton but I have found the best views are to be had in the north-west part of the reserve.

As you drive/walk down the access track from the minor road opposite Meadow View House, look straight ahead as the track opens into the car park. You will see a metal kissing gate and this is the path you need to follow.

Walk through the trees along the muddy path (common woodland birds). This soon opens onto a sandy track heading slightly uphill (an excellent area for Green Woodpeckers).

This path joins a wide main track: turn right and again follow this until it leads you slightly uphill. At the top of the rise is a large cleared area where you can wait for the

Nightjars to appear. Woodlarks can be elusive but Woodcocks show very well in flight here.

If you arrive early, it is worth exploring the track that runs from the right of the car park. Go over the cattle grid and follow the muddy path until it overlooks a reedbed. This is still establishing itself but you should see Reed Warblers and Reed Buntings and hear Grasshopper Warblers in the surrounding scrub (very difficult to see).

You may also wish to explore the Great Wood to the north of the reserve, accessed through a metal gate along the wide, sandy track.

Once in place, wait for dusk when the Nightjars become active. You should get excellent flight views of one or two roding Woodcock, which seem to come out much earlier here than at other sites.

You should also hear Tawny Owls hooting and may see Green Woodpecker, Jay, Yellowhammer, Turtle Dove, Stock Dove, Sparrowhawk or Kestrel along with common woodland and scrub birds.

Overhead, Swallows, Swifts and House Martins help keep the midges away from you but they may fall prey to a dashing Hobby.

The Nightjars here seem to like a lie-in, as they always start 'churring' later than at other sites. In fact, they sometimes fail to 'churr' at all and the first you will know of their presence is when something silently flaps, ghost-like, past your ear.

You will have just become accustomed to the owl hooting, the pipistrelle bats fluttering overhead and the Woodcocks squeaking and honking, when a suggestion of a dark shape startles you. Eerie but strangely tranquil!

I can personally guarantee that the midges will love you for your effort, especially if you forget your insect repellent but, with luck, you may also find one or two glow worms on your way back.

In winter, Buxton holds a few resident common scrub birds, woodland species and visiting winter thrushes. Jack Snipe occasionally visit the wetter areas but are hardly ever seen.

Woodlarks may be singing on fine days from late February, but it is from late spring through to the end of August when Buxton Heath really comes into its own. This is also the best place in Norfolk to see silver-studded blue butterflies and adders, which like to bask by the main track on warm days.

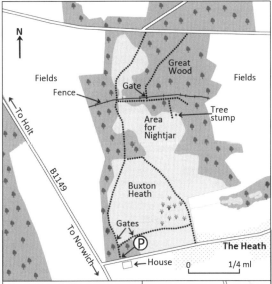

How to get there

(7.5 miles N of Norwich).

SAT NAV: NR10 4DA or Hevingham>The Heath (Minor road leading to car park).

GPS: 52.746229; 1.215584.

From Norwich, head N on A140 (towards Cromer), then left along B1149 (sign-posted to Horsford). After about five miles, turn right into The Heath sign-posted 'Buxton Heath' on a white wooden road sign (third minor road right after Horsford village).

After about 200 yards look for a narrow track on left, sign-posted 'Buxton Heath' opposite first house (Meadow View) on right. Park in small car park at the bottom of the track (75 yards from the road).

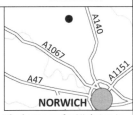

The best area for Nightjars is straight ahead from the car park (as if continuing along the access track).

Follow narrow path for 50 yards to a metal gate. Go through the gate and follow the wide path through the trees until it opens out into a cleared area and finally onto a sandy track.

The whole of this cleared area is excellent for Nightjars. Explore the tracks but do not stray off them.

63

Key points

- **Open access at all times.**

- **Best views in early mornings and evenings when birds not disturbed by farm traffic.**

- **Level terrain along an uneven, grass path.**

- **The farmyard can be viewed from the road.**

- **Birds are easily disturbed in the farmyard, so please be quiet and keep a respectable distance.**

- **Birds need to feed as much as possible in winter, so any disturbance could literally mean the difference between life and death at this critical time.**

Contacts
None

WHILE NO LONGER attracting the number of birds that it used to in its pomp in the 1990s and noughties, Choseley Barns remains an easy site to drop into when visiting RSPB Titchwell Marsh and other North Norfolk coastal sites. It is still the best site in Norfolk at which to see Corn Bunting.

Target birds *All year* – **Corn Bunting (70%), Yellowhammer (70%), Marsh Harrier (30%).** *Spring/autumn* – **Passage migrants.**

Other possible bird species

All year	Whitethroat	*Winter*
Red-legged Partridge	Blackcap	Pink-footed Goose
Grey Partridge	Yellow Wagtail	Hen Harrier
Sparrowhawk	Turtle Dove	Peregrine
Kestrel		Merlin
Stock Dove	*Spring/autumn*	Meadow Pipit
Skylark	Redstart	Reed Bunting
Common scrub birds	Whinchat	
Corvids	Wheatear	*Occasional*
Common finches	Winter thrushes	Dotterel (passage)
Summer	Ring Ouzel	Barn Owl
Quail	Goldcrest	Brambling (winter)
Hirundines	Pied Flycatcher	Snow Bunting (winter)
		Lapland Bunting (winter)

Background information and birding tips

CHOSELEY BARNS is an unlikely looking site to go birdwatching but it is the best place in Norfolk to see Corn Buntings. They usually feed around the large drying barn just off the minor road near the RSPB Titchwell Marsh reserve.

They are usually joined by many Yellowhammers and a variety of finches and other common birds. Tree Sparrows are rare here now but it is still worthwhile waiting to see what joins the common species feeding on the spilt grain. A Pine Bunting was found in 2004!

Birds also like to perch on the telephone wires in the fields – including occasional Turtle Doves in spring – before dropping into the fields to feed, so you will have to stay alert. I suggest you sit quietly in your car by the barn and it won't

be long before several of the above species hop into view.

Birds can be present throughout the day, though early mornings and evenings are best because farm traffic is less frequent at these times.

If you fancy a walk, a public footpath runs east and west from the barns. The footpath is bordered by trees and bushes which are full of common scrub birds and summer warblers. Little Owls seem to have deserted the site but it is still worth checking any mature trees.

There are regular gaps in the hedge from which to scan the fields. Past winters have produced Lapland and Snow Buntings (though Meadow Pipits and Skylarks are much more likely) and recent springs and autumns have produced regular sightings of Ring Ouzels and Dotterels.

Buntings and finches love to hide in the hedges of the eastern section of the path, so approach very carefully.

The bounty of small birds inevitably attracts raptors such as Marsh Harriers, Sparrowhawks, Kestrels and Peregrines all year round, joined by occasional Hen Harriers and Merlins in winter.

If you stand on the footpath at the RSPB Titchwell Marsh reserve and look inland, you will see the communications mast and hedge on the hill, demonstrating what an irresistible magnet the area makes for tired migrants. Everything from the humble Goldcrest to the mega-rare Pied Wheatear has been recorded!

In summer, look out for Blackcap, Whitethroat and Yellow Wagtail, which return to breed in May. One or two Quails have been heard in recent summers ('*wet-my-lips*') but you won't see one: PLEASE NOTE THAT IT IS ILLEGAL TO TAPE LURE THIS SPECIES!

Summing up, Choseley Barns makes an ideal quick call-in spot as you travel between more well known sites along the Norfolk coast at any time of year.

NB: If using the public footpath past the barn, approach carefully or you may scare off any birds hiding in the hedgerow.

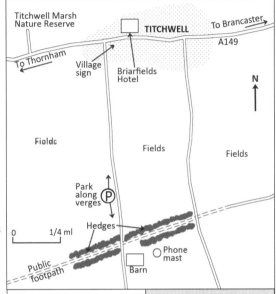

How to get there

(Six miles E of Hunstanton).

SAT NAV: PE31 8ED (Postcode for Titchwell village – from here follow directions below).

GPS: 52.947619; 0.613736.

From the entrance to RSPB Titchwell Marsh on A149, head E to Titchwell village. After 0.4 miles, take the first right turn (where the Titchwell village post is situated on a small green, by the farm. If you reach the Briarfields Hotel you have gone too far).

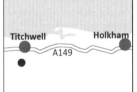

Keep on this minor road up the hill for one mile. Park sensibly on the verges: DO NOT BLOCK FARM ACCESS.

Scan the farmyard for birds, plus walk west (away from the barn) down the footpath to view the fields and hedgerows.

Other nearby sites

Brancaster Marsh, Gypsy Lane, Holme Bird Observatory, Holme Dunes, Hunstanton, Redwell Marsh, Sandringham, Titchwell Marsh, Wolferton Triangle.

Key points

- **Open daily except Dec 25, but free access at all times to East Bank, shingle ridge and Beach Road.**

- **Visitor centre open 10am-4pm (Nov 1 to March 1); 10am- 5pm (March to Oct). Cafe closes 30 mins earlier.**

- **Permits issued at visitor centre (NWT members, carers accompanying disabled visitors and children free; charge to non-members).**

- **NWT members may visit hides before centre is open – collect permit at 10am.**

- **Early access for non-NWT members only when a rare bird is sighted. Non-members may collect permits at centre in advance if they want early access – no telephone bookings.**

CLEY MARSHES was the first reserve set up by a county Wildlife Trust (in 1926) and it continues to be one of the premier birdwatching sites in the country. Visitors can watch Marsh Harriers, wildfowl and waders when enjoying a cup of tea in the centre, while the hides allow close-up views of many more species – the reserve has now attracted 50 species of wader! If Cley Marshes were a musical instrument, it would undoubtedly be a Stradivarius.

Target birds *All year* – Marsh Harrier (90%), Bearded Tit (75%), Barn Owl (50%), Cetti's Warbler (hear 60%, see 15%), Bittern (10%). *Winter* – Winter raptors (25%), Water Pipit (20%). *Spring* – Avocet (99%), Garganey (75%). *Summer* – Avocet (99%), Marsh Harrier (95%), Garganey (60%), Spoonbill (60%). *Autumn* – Passage seabirds, passage waders.

Other possible bird species

All year
Egyptian Goose
Shelduck
Other common wildfowl
Cormorant
Little Grebe
Sparrowhawk
Kestrel
Water Rail
Black-tailed Godwit
Other common waders
Regular gull species
Guillemot (at sea)
Razorbill (at sea)
Kingfisher
Skylark
Common scrub birds
Corvids
Meadow Pipit
Pied Wagtail
Common finches
Reed Bunting

Spring
Little Ringed Plover
Whimbrel
Greenshank
Arctic Tern
Yellow Wagtail
Whinchat

Wheatear
Ring Ouzel

Summer
Yellow-legged Gull
Sandwich Tern
Common Tern
Little Tern
Hirundines
Sedge Warbler
Reed Warbler

Autumn
(might include)
Fulmar
Manx Shearwater
Balearic Shearwater
Gannet
Whimbrel
Little Stint
Curlew Sandpiper
Ruff
Spotted Redshank
Greenshank
Green Sandpiper
Wood Sandpiper
Common Sandpiper
Temminck's Stint
Red-necked Phalarope
Skuas
Kittiwake

Whinchat
Wheatear

Winter
Brent Goose
Wigeon
Pintail
Goldeneye
Red-breasted Merganser
Red-throated Diver
Great Crested Grebe
Hen Harrier
Merlin
Peregrine
Golden Plover
Bar-tailed Godwit
Rock Pipit
Stonechat
Winter thrushes

Occasional
Rarer divers and grebes
Temminck's Stint
Jack Snipe (winter)
Roseate Tern (summer)
Short-eared Owl (winter)
Shore Lark (winter)
Twite (winter)
Snow Bunting (winter)
Lapland Bunting (winter)

How to get there

(10.5 miles W of Cromer)

SAT NAV: NR25 7SA.

GPS: 52.954505; 1.056462.

Main car park (TG 053 441): The main (free) car park is sign-posted off A149 half a mile E of Cley-next-the-Sea village (car park is landward side of the road).

From here, an easy access path and boardwalks allows access to four hides.

Beach Road car park (TG 0484 52): This is sign-posted 'Beach' off A149 just E of Cley village. Small fee payable for car parking at peak times.

East Bank car park (TG 059 442): This small car park is on the seaward side of A149. Heading E from Cley village, go past the visitor centre car park for about 300 yards. If you reach the Walsey Hills 'NOA Watchpoint' sign-post you have gone too far.

This car park gives easiest access to the East Bank area of the reserve.

Map labels:
To Blakeney Point
The Eye
Brick shelter
Rough track
North Scrape
Arnold's Marsh
Big Pool
Beach Road
Simmond's Scrape
Whitewell Scrape
West Bank
River Glaven
Pat's Pool
Bittern Pool
Carter's Scrape
South Pool
Boardwalk
East Bank
To Salthouse
A149
Warden's House
Easy access track
Easy access track
Walsey Hills
Cley-next-the-Sea
NWT Visitor centre

Hides
1. Avocet
2. Dawke's
3. Teal
4. Bishop's
5. Swarovski Optik

0   1/4 ml

Holkham
A149
Cley-next-the-Sea
A148

Background information and birding tips

THIS NORFOLK Wildlife Trust reserve is a large area to cover but there are three access points to ease the way. The main entrance is at the visitor centre.

Before entering the reserve you must obtain a permit from the visitor centre. Norfolk Wildlife Trust members should obtain a permit from the centre when open, or carry their membership cards at all times if the centre is closed.

Non-members are not allowed on the reserve until they have obtained a permit, though access along the East Bank or Beach Road to the shingle beach is free from dawn to dusk.

After obtaining your permit, cross the busy coast road and follow the easy access path and boardwalks to the hides. This is the site's only wheelchair-friendly trail but it can be very productive.

The wide channel running adjacent to the road should be scanned for Kingfishers and Little Grebes and the fields behind usually hold Wigeon and Teal all year (with larger numbers present in winter). The flooded fields around here are a favoured haunt of Rock Pipits in winter.

Along the boardwalk, Bearded Tits and Reed

67

Key points

- **Permit half price for public transport users (bus stop by visitor centre).**

- **Visitor centre has extensive range of books, bird food, etc.**

- **Toilets (including disabled) at visitor centre.**

- **Wheelchair access OK to all hides except Swarovski Optik.**

- **Wheelchair users can access centre by lift at main entrance. Easy access path leads from centre to four hides, Beach Road and main village footpath.**

- **East Bank is a public footpath: narrow & muddy (no wheelchair access). Shingle ridge has been levelled to allow easier walking.**

- **No dogs allowed on reserve.**

Buntings can be seen all year, joined by Reed Warblers in the breeding season.

The three hides (Avocet, Dauke's and Teal) look out over Simmonds's Scrape and Pat's Pool, which can be covered in waders at all times of year. Avocets, Redshanks, Dunlins, Black-tailed Godwits, etc are present in varying numbers, and are joined by passage waders such as Little Stints, Greenshanks, Green, Wood and Curlew Sandpipers in spring and autumn.

Garganeys breed on site but can be elusive. Keep a careful eye on the large gulls for a lurking Yellow-legged in summer. Also look out for Red-necked Phalarope and Temminck's Stint, which have become something of a Cley speciality on passage, though certainly not guaranteed.

These hides are a good place to sit and watch the resident Marsh Harriers drift over or witness a Bittern lazily flapping above the reeds. Keep your eyes peeled!

You now have to retrace your steps to the road, as there is no circular route from here. Instead of crossing the road to the visitor centre, keep on the path towards the East Bank. This easy access path brings you to Bishop's Hide, which allows you to view Pat's Pool from a different angle.

After Bishop's Hide, follow the easy-access path, adjacent to the road, to the East Bank. Listen out for the resident Cetti's Warblers that sing from the bushes along this path. When you reach the East Bank car park, turn left along the raised bank and walk towards the sea wall, scanning for Bearded Tits, which should be seen all year round in the reeds.

Water Pipits often feed in the field to the right of the bank from December to March, though Wigeon and Brent Geese are much more frequent, with an occasional Black Brant accompanying the latter.

In spring, this marshy field is a favourite haunt of Yellow Wagtails. Occasionally, the wagtail flock contains one or two of the scarcer races, such as Blue-headed and White. Also look out for the resident Barn Owl over the fields.

At all times of year, the fields and marsh to your right along East Bank will hold waders. Avocets show well here in summer and it is a favoured spot for Whimbrels and Curlews in spring and autumn. Egyptian Geese breed here also.

Closer to the sea wall, you will see Arnold's Marsh to your right. This is usually home to several species of wader, with Avocets guaranteed in spring and summer. This is also a favoured roost site of a Roseate Tern or two among the mixed tern flock, but their appearance is unpredictable.

Once on the shingle sea wall, you can turn back the way you came, left to the beach car park, or right to Salthouse. If you choose left or right, scan the sea carefully at all times of year.

Cley is renowned as a prime seawatching site and if you turn up

Contacts

Visitor centre - 01263 740 008
Norfolk Wildlife Trust
01603 625 540
www.norfolkwildlifetrust.org.uk/cley.aspx

Cley Bird Club:
Peter Gooden, 45 Charles Road, Holt, Norfolk, NR25 6DA.

Further reading: *The Birds of Cley* by SJM Gantlett, available from 'Books for Birders' 01263 741 139.

in favourable conditions – strong onshore winds – during September and October, you will find many telescopes set up on the shingle or in the brick shelter by the beach car park, with eager birdwatchers all hoping for something special to pass.

In winter scan for grebes, divers and ducks; in summer watch out for terns. In autumn, anything can go past!

From the shingle sea wall, you have the option of diverting to the Swarovski Optik I lide (formerly known as North I lide). Several species of wader can be seen here all year round and it is another good viewpoint to scan for Marsh Harriers, Bitterns, wildfowl, etc.

From July, the Spoonbills that have bred at Holkham have a habit of bringing their young to feed at Cley, usually on North Scrape: double figures are possible!

The field by the beach car park is known as The Eye. This is another favourite spot of

Wigeon and Brent Geese in winter (occasionally joined by a Black Brant), passage waders in spring and autumn and very occasionally a Lapland Bunting puts in an appearance (usually in autumn).

It is perfectly possible to spend the whole day at Cley, gently strolling around, stopping off at the hides, seawatching and generally feeling all is well with the world.

Whichever of the car parks you start from, it is possible to take a two-mile circular route encompassing the whole of the reserve. And don't forget to pause awhile on the shingle sea wall to take in the famous vista of Cley windmill.

As I write, there is a public appeal by the Norfolk Wildlife Trust to help raise funds to purchase 143 acres adjoining Cley Marshes to the east. It seems that this reserve will continue to improve for wildlife and visitors, if such a thing is possible.

Key points

- Site is a designated SSSI.
- Free access at all times.
- Narrow access road prone to flooding.
- Boardwalk trail on level terrain.
- Free 24-hour mooring at the reserve entrance.
- Wheelchair-accessible hide.
- Free parking but can get full in summer.
- Use insect repellent in summer.

Contacts

Norfolk Wildlife Trust
01603 625 540

Natural England
0845 600 3078; e-mail:
enquiries@natural
england.org.uk

Broadland Conservation
Centre 01603 270 479

General Broads
Authority
01603 610 734

COCKSHOOT BROAD is a secluded reserve managed by Norfolk Wildlife Trust. Even though the River Bure and the nearby public house become very crowded, one can be sure of a tranquil stroll along the boardwalks of a reserve that is home to rare plants, butterflies and dragonflies.

Target birds *All year* – **Common wildfowl (99%), Marsh Harrier (75%), Cetti's Warbler (hear 75%, see 20%).**

Other possible bird species

Resident	Common scrub birds	Cuckoo
Egyptian Goose	Marsh Tit	Hirundines
Common wildfowl	Common woodland birds	Sedge Warbler
Great Crested Grebe	Siskin	Reed Warbler
Common waterbirds	Redpoll	*Occasional*
Sparrowhawk	Common finches	Osprey (passage)
Regular gull species	Reed Bunting	Marsh Harrier
Kingfisher		Lesser Spotted
Great Spotted Woodpecker	*Summer*	Woodpecker
	Common Tern	

Background information and birding tips

PREVIOUSLY a privately owned shooting site, Cockshoot Broad is now part of the Bure Marshes National Nature Reserve (along with Ranworth Broad and Hoveton Great Broad), managed by Norfolk Wildlife Trust. This five hectare reserve consists of open water, carr and fen. Ongoing management continues to improve water quality to benefit wildlife.

The fun starts along the approach road to the car park where you can play the little known game of 'Dodge the Dragonfly', as black-tailed skimmers love to rest on the road, only zipping away at the last minute.

The site includes a short but pleasant circular walk along a boardwalk (and is thus fully wheelchair accessible) through reeds and alder carr (wet woodland).

In summer, the river can be quite noisy with boat traffic and boaters enjoying themselves. Even so, the riverside path has a couple of viewpoints from which to scan the extensive sedge bed for swallowtail butterflies in summer and Marsh Harriers all year round.

Once on the reserve itself (reached by crossing the second wooden bridge at the end of the mooring channel), the path runs adjacent to a channel where you may hear the explosive song of a Cetti's Warbler from thick cover, or catch a glimpse of a Blackcap or Garden Warbler. Marsh Tits are relatively common in the woodland.

Stay on the main path to the hide at the end, or fork left through some reeds (excellent for swallowtail butterflies in summer). Both ways can be productive and if you choose one way up to the hide, you can always return via the other route.

The hide overlooks Cockshoot Broad itself and birds seen here regularly include Kingfisher, (perched in the trees on the island) Common Tern, Shelduck, Egyptian Goose, Grey Heron and other common waterfowl. There is a wipe-clean sightings board in the hide.

In winter, the broad holds Pochards, Teal, Shovelers, Cormorants etc. Reed Buntings are resident, as are the commoner woodland species and they are easier to see because of the lack of leaves on the trees. This is a walk for hardy souls at this time of year though. The riverside boardwalk may flood in poor weather years, so I would stick to spring and summer.

This reserve is also renowned for its dragonflies and butterflies in summer. The channel is an excellent place to see red-eyed damselflies and Norfolk hawkers while black-tailed skimmers are common along the whole length of the boardwalk. I suggest an early morning walk for the best of the bird activity followed by a search for the dragonflies as the heat of the sun brings them out.

As the water quality of Cockshoot Broad improves, the wildlife variety and quality can only improve with it. A Bittern is occasionally reported and Ferruginous Duck has turned up, showing the potential of this quiet, picturesque place.

Other nearby sites

Breydon Water, Buxton Heath, Great Yarmouth Beach, Hickling Broad, Horsey, Hoveton Great Broad, How Hill, Ranworth Broad, Strumpshaw Fen, Ted Ellis Reserve, Upton Fen, Winterton Dunes.

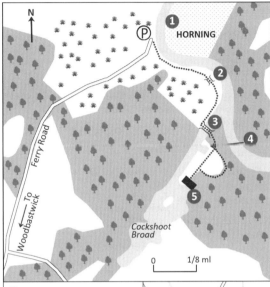

Key

1. Ferry Inn
2. Bridge - good for Reed Warbler
3. 24hr mooring
4. Dragonfly viewing platform
5. Hide

How to get there

(Eight miles NE of Norwich).

SAT NAV: Horning > Ferry Road. IMPORTANT. This only works if you are SOUTH of the River Bure. If you are north, it will take you to the Ferry Inn on the opposite side of the river to the reserve!

GPS: 52.69498; 1.46701.

By car: From B1140 (Acle to Wroxham road), turn off at the signs for Woodbastwick. In the village, head E past the church, following signs for Ranworth.

Out of the village, the road bends sharply right but you go straight on down a narrow road sign-posted 'River Only'. It ends in a small car park at the River Bure, opposite the Ferry Inn at Horning. The boardwalk to the reserve is on the right of this car park.

By boat: Head E from Wroxham along River Bure to Horning. In Horning, about 100 yards after the Ferry Inn on the left, there is a mooring channel on the right, maximum 24 hours stay. The path into the reserve starts at the end of this channel (TG 346 160).

71

Key points

- **Mill open every day (10am to 5pm) apart from December 25.**

- **Free parking, but height restriction applies at entrance.**

- **Can be very bleak and birdless!**

- **Not suitable for wheelchair users.**

- **Wrap up warm!**

- **Terrain is level but uneven grass paths can be muddy.**

- **Walking boots recommended.**

- **Height barrier on car park gate.**

Contacts

The Borough Council of King's Lynn & West Norfolk, 01553 692 722 www.west-norfolk. gov.uk

Denver Windmill, Denver, Downham Market PE38 0EG 01366 384 009; e-mail: enquiries@ denvermill.plus.com www.denvermill.co.uk

HERE IS a site best visited in harsh weather when wintering wildfowl are forced onto the unfrozen waters of the Hundred Foot Drain – and that's bad news for fair-weather birders, because on this walk there is nowhere to shelter from the wind, rain or snow. Non-birding partners can now take refuge in the restored mill's tea-room while you brave the elements.

Target birds *Winter* – Goosander (65%), Winter raptors (30%), Smew (10%).

Other possible bird species

Winter	Barn Owl	Common finches
Winter wildfowl	Skylark	Yellowhammer
Common waterfowl	Winter thrushes	Reed Bunting
Lapwing	Corvids	Corn Bunting
Redshank	Starling	*Occasional*
Curlew	Meadow Pipit	Winter raptors
Regular gull species	Pied Wagtail	

Background information and birding tips

DENVER SLUICE is at its best when all other lakes and pools are frozen, because it keeps the Hundred Foot Drain free of ice even in the most hostile of conditions. In turn, this makes it *the* place to see Goosanders in west Norfolk.

Once you have climbed the bank near the pub, turned left and negotiated the stile, you will see the Hundred Foot Drain stretching in front of you. There is a sluice gate in the distance. The best birds are usually between Denver Sluice and the distant sluice. Walk as far as you like along this raised bank watching the water and fields for anything that moves.

On a particularly good 'Denver Day' the first thing you might see is a limping brass monkey. If you are the sort of birdwatcher who moans when your feet and hands go numb in the cold then this is not the walk for you.

Scan towards the distant sluice gate to check if there are many birds on the Drain, as this is not always the case. As you walk along the raised path keep scanning the fields for raptors such as Peregrine and Hen Harrier.

Barn Owls are seen regularly and Short-eared Owls may also be encountered. Also keep an eye on the telephone wires as they make good perches for Corn Buntings, Yellowhammers, Starlings, Linnets, Goldfinches, etc.

If the fancy takes you, you can keep going past the distant sluice gate (1.5 miles from the main sluice) to WWT Welney, where a warm soup and a spell in the heated main hide goes down a treat!

A round walk from the Denver car park to Welney is about 9.5 miles and comes with this warning: there is no respite from the cold wind/snow/rain as there isn't a scrap of cover the whole way. On the other hand, on a frosty, bright morning, this can be a superbly bracing day out!

Non-birding members of the

family may choose to visit the mill while you are freezing to death on the footpath! The mill was built in 1835 and has now been restored to working order. There is also a bakery and tearoom here.

The area is of little interest at other times of the year, though Turtle Doves and hirundines can usually be seen around the car park and sluice. At this time of year, you may as well go straight to Welney in your car and save yourself a long, birdless walk.

If you enjoy walking, there are one or two footpaths leading the opposite way (NE) from Denver Sluice. You can walk all the way to King's Lynn alongside The River Great Ouse on the Fen Rivers Way footpath or alongside The Black Bank Dyke. All areas can be good for common wildfowl and winter raptors.

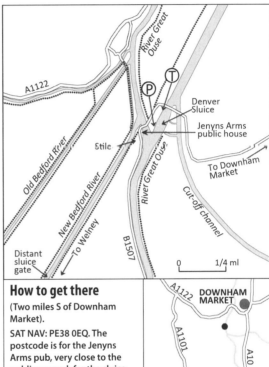

How to get there

(Two miles S of Downham Market).

SAT NAV: PE38 0EQ. The postcode is for the Jenyns Arms pub, very close to the public car park for the sluice.

GPS: 52.584503; 0.343646.

On the A10 bypass, about one mile S of Downham Market. turn on to B1507 (sign-posted Denver/Denver Complex/Denver Mill).

Pass the recently renovated mill, following signs for Denver Sluice. Cross first bridge then park in the obvious large gravel car park on the left (height barrier). There is a toilet block here but it is sometimes locked in winter.

From the car park, follow

Other nearby sites

Blackborough End Tip, King's Lynn Docks, Ken Hill Wood, Pentney Gravel Pits, Roydon Common, Sandringham, RSPB Snettisham, Tottenhill, WWT Welney.

the road to a second bridge (this is Denver Sluice) and a few yards further on you will see the Jenyns Arms public house with a telephone box opposite.

The footpath starts on the top of the bank (above the phone box) and over a stile. Turn left and walk as far as you desire, checking the channel for birds as you go.

The sluice gate you can see in the distance is 1.5 miles from the pub, WWT Welney is 5 miles away.

Key points

- **Reserve open at all times.**
- **Keep to paths at all times and obey all no-entry signs.**
- **Wide tracks, though some steepish steps and short, steep banks.**
- **Difficult for wheelchair users, though Nightjars are occasionally viewable by the roadside gate (TF 663 284).**
- **Boardwalk trail through the bog. Paths can be muddy after rain.**
- **Insect repellent essential in summer.**
- **Dogs should be kept on leads.**
- **Leaflet available by gate.**

Contacts

Natural England,
0845 600 3078;
e-mail: enquiries@
naturalengland.org.uk

IN MY OPINION, Dersingham Bog is the best place in Norfolk to see Nightjars in summer, but the site also contains some of the rarest habitats in Britain: acid mire and lowland heath. There are also areas of mixed woodland. The reserve is home to many rare birds, insects and plants, making it a must-visit site for the all-round naturalist.

Target birds *All year* – Crossbill (45%), Golden Pheasant (20%), Long-eared Owl (5%). *Summer* – Nightjar (95%), Tree Pipit (65%), Grasshopper Warbler (hear 60%, see 5%), Woodlark (55%), Marsh Harrier (40%).

Other possible bird species

All year	Common woodland birds	Summer warblers
Shelduck	Goldcrest	Spotted Flycatcher
Buzzard	Corvids	
Sparrowhawk	Meadow Pipit	*Occasional*
Kestrel	Siskin	Rough-legged Buzzard (winter)
Woodcock	Redpoll	
Tawny Owl		Hen Harrier (winter)
Green Woodpecker	*Summer*	Goshawk
Great Spotted Woodpecker	Hobby	Lesser Spotted Woodpecker
Skylark	Cuckoo	
Common scrub birds	Sand Martin	Short-eared Owl
	Other hirundines	

Background information and birding tips

DERSINGHAM BOG is a 159 hectare area of intensively-managed heath and bog that is part of the Sandringham Estate, managed by Natural England. The reserve is not visited by a huge number of people and in winter you will find you have the whole place to yourself.

There are three well-marked trails and several offshoots at Dersingham that lead you through the main areas of interest. Along all of them, listening for birds is as important as watching for them.

The main reason most birders come to the site is for Nightjars in summer. Braving the midges is well worthwhile, as up to 26 Nightjars should be entertaining you and taking your mind off the annoying insects. The boardwalk area is the best place to see the birds, as

they usually sit on telephone wires here, or display above your head. Magical!

From the Scissors Crossroad car park, follow the path on the right onto the reserve (do not go up the steps) and the habitat soon opens out to Nightjar country. Keep on the wide path to reach the boardwalk area. From the village end car park, follow the path down some steps to the boardwalk.

Woodcocks should be roding over the woods, Tawny Owls may be hooting and Long-eared Owl chicks might be begging for food from the pines. The perfect dusk chorus!

A visit on a winter morning will produce skeins of Pink-footed Geese overhead. The woodland trail offers the best chance to see the resident, but shy, Golden Pheasants – walk very quietly

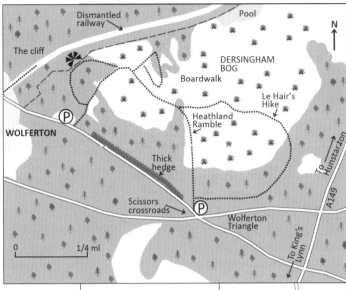

along the path to see one, or sit patiently by a tree for one to come out from the rhododendron hedge. Do not leave the path!

Winter also brings Fieldfares, Redwings and Reed Buntings onto the reserve. From mid-February, listen for the mournful song of Woodlarks anywhere on the reserve. Also listen out for the moaning call of a Long-eared Owl as it establishes its territory.

All three woodpecker species have been recorded but Great and Green Woodpecker are the two most likely.

Common warblers, including Blackcaps, Chiffchaffs, Willow and Garden Warblers arrive to breed in summer. Listen out for the display song of Tree Pipits, which breed on the reserve.

Marsh Harriers sometimes quarter the heath for prey, including the chicks of Shelduck which breed on the reserve in good numbers (you can see them displaying on the heath at the back of the pool in spring).

The Cliff viewpoint affords superb views over The Wash. This is a peaceful place to linger at any time of year. In winter, Pink-footed Geese fly from their roost at dawn, returning at dusk,

How to get there

(5.5 miles N of King's Lynn). SAT NAV: PE31 6HF.

GPS: 52.827456; 0.466510 or 52.824027; 0.474436.

Take A149 N towards Hunstanton. After three miles, turn left to Wolferton. After about 300 yards this road reaches a crossroads. Park on the grass near the wooden 'No overnight parking' sign and enter reserve through a kissing gate down a narrow path from this pull-off. This is known as the Scissors Crossroads entrance.

Alternatively, at the crossroads bear right and continue for half a mile until

hopefully silhouetted against an orange sky. In summer, just enjoy the view and you should be joined by

you see a large lay-by on right. The reserve gate is visible from here and there are usually some leaflets at the gate for visitors. If you reach Wolferton village you have gone too far.

When on the reserve, follow the footpaths as sign-posted. The bog and heath habitats here are extremely fragile so stay on the paths at all times.

Woodcock and Nightjar at dusk (and, unfortunately a few midges too!). In spring and autumn, keep an eye

Dersingham Bog offers visiting birdwatchers their best chance of seeing Nightjars on summer evenings.

the most evocative songs in Britain. Tree Pipits also breed here and Grasshopper Warblers are present most summers.

Scan the open areas for Marsh Harriers quartering the bog and you may be lucky enough to find a rarer species such as a Rough-legged Buzzard or a Great Grey Shrike which have both overwintered in the past.

Both the Heathland Ramble and the Le Hair's Hike will lead you to the boardwalk where you can see some very specialised plants and insects. As mentioned before, it is also an excellent place from which to witness the antics of Nightjars and Woodcocks at dusk and to listen for owls.

There are several other unmarked tracks leading to some interesting habitats. One such path leads from the north-western edge of the Le Hair's Hike through heathland. After a while, you reach a pool: Shelducks breed in this area. Crossbills may come down to drink and don't forget to keep looking skywards for raptors passing overhead.

Birdwatching at Dersingham Bog can be hard work at times. The whole reserve can seem devoid of birds but the longer you linger the more species materialise. And you cannot beat a still summer evening on the bog watching Woodcocks and Nightjars flitting above you silhouetted against a blazing orange Norfolk sunset.

open for birds arriving or leaving our shores (visible migration).

Both the Heathland Ramble and the Le Hair's Hike start from the Scissors Crossroad car park. Go down the muddy, zig-zag slope and through the large kissing gate. The colour-coded, circular trails are well-marked and join up with each other on the heath and also link with the Clifftop Stroll path and Wolferton village car park.

Once through the kissing gate, you can either turn left into the rhododendron hedge (towards the village car park), right into the woodland (both routes accessed up a set of steps) or straight on directly to the heath.

Any tract of woodland on the reserve should produce birds such as Goldcrest, Treecreeper, Siskin, Redpoll, tit species, woodpeckers, etc. Crossbills are extremely mobile and may be encountered anywhere. Listen for their sharp 'chip, chip, chip' calls.

Whichever way you go, you will eventually emerge onto open heath and bog. From February, Woodlarks take up residence and on a still day you should at least hear one displaying, its mournful refrain being one of

Best Birdwatching Sites

The trusted name for accurate, accessible site information

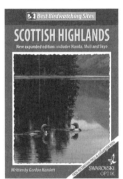

Best Birdwatching Sites in the Scottish Highlands *(2nd edition)* by Gordon Hamlett. Features 26 birding routes from John O'Groats to Pitlochry, including Mull, Skye and Handa.
Price: £17.95

Best Birdwatching Sites: North-East England by Brian Unwin.
Features 17 birding sites in Cleveland; 37 sites in Co Durham and 42 sites in Northumberland. 308 pp. **Price £17.95**

Best Birdwatching Sites: The Solway by John Miles. Features 76 birding sites in Cumbria and 84 in Dumfries & Galloway. 260 pp.
Price £17.50

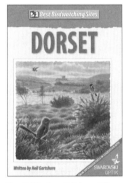

Best Birdwatching Sites: Dorset by Neil Gartshore. Features 65 reserves and birding areas, including a full range of habitats from heathland to coastal sites.
248 pp. **Price £17.95**

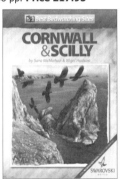

Best Birdwatching Sites in Cornwall & Scilly by Sara McMahon and Nigel Hudson. Features 52 mainland sites, plus seven routes around the key islands of Scilly. 208pp.
Price: £17.50 15.00

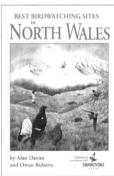

Best Birdwatching Sites in North Wales by Alan Davies and Owen Roberts. Features 58 major sites in Gwynedd and Clwyd, plus 11 smaller birding spots around Wrexham. 192pp.
Price: £15.95

Key points

- **Wildlife Trust SSSI reserve open daily (8am to dusk).**

- **Free access and parking when reserve open.**

- **No dogs in some areas.**

- **Keep dogs on a short lead March-July to avoid disturbing ground-nesting birds.**

- **All species can be seen from a public footpath when reserve is closed.**

- **Public footpath terrain is flat along a wide sandy track.**

- **Can be boggy after rain.**

- **Use insect repellent in summer.**

- **Torch needed for walking after seeing the Nightjars.**

Contacts

Norfolk Wildlife Trust
01603 625 540

A FINE SPRING morning visit to East Wretham Heath and its surrounds can produce several sought-after species such as Woodlark and Redstart, while mid-morning sun could tempt a Goshawk out of hiding. Summer evenings may be enlivened by Nightjars and a Long-eared Owl. Birdwatching on the reserve can be hard work but persistence should pay dividends!

Target birds *Spring/summer* – **Nightjar (90%), Woodlark (90%), Tree Pipit (80%), Redstart (30%), Crossbill (15%), Long-eared Owl (5%).**

Other possible bird species

All year		*Summer*
Common wildfowl	Great Spotted Woodpecker	Hobby
Ruddy Duck	Green Woodpecker	Cuckoo
Little Grebe	Jay	Warblers
Sparrowhawk	Nuthatch	Spotted Flycatcher
Kestrel	Treecreeper	
Woodcock	Siskin	*Occasional*
Stock Dove	Redpoll	Goshawk
Barn Owl	Yellowhammer	Stone-curlew
Tawny Owl	*Spring/autumn*	
Kingfisher	Passage waders	

Background information and birding tips

E AST WRETHAM HEATH is a superb 143ha reserve that holds many sought-after Breckland species. The best time to visit is an early spring morning for Woodlark and a late spring evening (May/June) for Nightjar. If the reserve is closed, all species can be seen from a public footpath running south of the NWT reserve.

The reserve itself opens at 8am but in spring and summer I usually arrive earlier and walk along the footpath (part of the Hereward's Way) towards Brandon. On a warm morning, you may see (or hear) Woodlark, Crossbill, Redstart and Tree Pipit. Keep your eyes to the skies for an occasional Goshawk over the distant pine woods.

There are two gates along this footpath leading to the meres. The left gate leads you to Fenmere and Ringmere and the right gate to Langmere (both gates are locked when the reserve is closed). Take either on the return leg of your walk to see what is about.

The meres can dry out at any time of year, but when full of water, Little Grebes and common wildfowl may be present and may even linger to breed. When muddy edges are exposed, scan for passage waders such as Green and Common Sandpipers in spring and autumn.

Continue along Hereward's Way, listening for Crossbills, Siskins and Redpolls in the trees along the path and on the reserve. After about a quarter of a mile, there is a clearing on your right, which is an excellent place to listen for Woodlark on the reserve. You should have seen Green and Great Spotted Woodpeckers by now, as well as Coal Tit, Long-tailed Tit and Mistle Thrush.

April is a good time for displaying Sparrowhawks and Goshawks. Crossbills will have young by now and will be very vocal.

From mid May, this footpath is a great place from which to see and hear Nightjars at dusk. Follow the path until you reach a wide, sandy track on your left. The land opens out to a bracken-covered area with mature pine trees dotted around. Between mid-May and the end of August, this is a superb place to see Nightjars at dusk, especially the old beech stump by the path.

Long-eared Owl is another Wretham breeding speciality, so listen for the begging squeaks of the young at dusk in May. In summer, look out for Redstarts and Spotted Flycatchers in the trees and bushes along the whole length of this track, though the former is easier to see on East Wretham reserve itself.

A little further on, the path is enclosed by mixed woodland, a good place to see Redpolls.

You can follow this track to where it joins a T-junction of two minor roads. Straight ahead leads to Fowl Mere, which is good for common waterfowl and wildfowl.

On the NWT reserve itself, there is a marked trail past Langmere and through mixed woodland (pick up trail leaflet in the reserve car park). Redstarts and Crossbills breed here in the ancient pines, along with many common birds in the mixed woodland areas.

The open areas hold Woodlarks, Tree Pipits (check the tops of isolated hawthorn bushes) and occasional Wheatears. In winter, the heath is home to large mixed

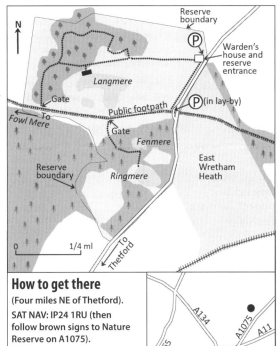

How to get there

(Four miles NE of Thetford).

SAT NAV: IP24 1RU (then follow brown signs to Nature Reserve on A1075).

GPS: 52.462002; 0.814621.

From Thetford head E on A11 to roundabout and take A1075 (sign-posted to Watton and East Dereham). After level crossing, reserve car park is sign-posted on a brown tourist sign, just over two miles from the roundabout.

The reserve can be viewed from public footpath, which starts from lay-by 200 yards

S of the car park. Follow directions above to the level crossing. Cross that, then there is a left-hand bend with a deer warning sign. The lay-by is on the left immediately after the sign (1.2 miles after the level crossing). Public footpath is signed to Brandon 16km and Peddar's Way 2km.

feeding flocks of finches and buntings.

I have to say that the track from the lay-by to Fowl Mere is possibly the best public footpath for birds in Norfolk, with the exception of the one that cuts through the RSPB

Titchwell Marsh reserve.

Starting from the late February Woodlark/Goshawk/Crossbill extravaganza through to the summer Nightjar spectacular, this is the perfect place to be.

Key points

• **Open every day except Dec 25. March – Nov 10am -5pm, Dec – Feb 10am – 4pm (9pm on Weds from May – Aug).**

• **Free parking, charge for entry to gardens.**

• **Paths OK for wheelchairs, though some are bumpy.**

• **Boat trip on private Inner Broad (April – Oct, extra charge + weather permitting). Hearing loop installed.**

• **2 wheelchairs, 3 mobility scooters (book in advance).**

• **Dogs on leads (not in tearoom).**

• **Boat mooring on South Walsham Outer Broad. 15 min walk along footpath signed to 'village' for the gardens.**

Contacts

Fairhaven Garden Trust 01603 270 449; www.norfolkbroads.com/fairhaven

O CCUPYING 131 ACRES of private ancient woodland and water gardens open to the public, Fairhaven is home to many species of common woodland birds. There is the added attraction that non-birders have plenty to see too. A boat trip on South Walsham Broad completes an ideal day out in spring and summer.

Target birds *All year* – Kingfisher (50%), Cetti's Warbler (see, 45%, hear 75%), Lesser Spotted Woodpecker (<15%). *Spring/ summer* – Common Tern (85%). *Winter* – Water Rail (70%).

Other possible bird species

All year	Great Spotted Woodpecker	Sedge Warbler
Common wildfowl	Pied Wagtail	Reed Warbler
Pheasant	Common scrub birds	Blackcap
Little Grebe	Goldcrest	Garden Warbler
Great Crested Grebe	Blue Tit	Whitethroat
Cormorant	Great Tit	Chiffchaff
Grey Heron	Coal Tit	Willow Warbler
Buzzard	Marsh Tit	*Winter*
Sparrowhawk	Nuthatch	Winter wildfowl
Kestrel	Treecreeper	Winter thrushes
Coot	Jay	
Moorhen	Other corvids	*Occasional*
Regular gull species	Starling	Bittern (winter)
Tawny Owl	Common finches	Osprey (passage)
Barn Owl	Yellowhammer	Marsh Harrier
Little Owl	Reed Bunting	Hobby (summer)
Wood Pigeon		Black & Arctic Terns
Stock Dove	*Spring/summer*	(passage)
Green Woodpecker	Hirundines	Grasshopper Warbler
	Cuckoo	Brambling (winter)

Background information and birding tips

F AIRHAVEN GARDENS provides a very pleasant stroll through woodland at all times of year. Birding starts around the car park, where the hedgerows bordering the fields may hold Yellowhammers and common scrub birds such as Wren, Blackbird, Dunnock, etc. There are nest boxes around the reception area, usually occupied in spring and summer by Blue and Great Tits.

After paying (and collecting your map if you haven't yet downloaded one), don't forget to book on the boat trip should you wish to do so. I can recommend this leisurely cruise of Inner South Walsham Broad, as you will get up close and personal views of Great Crested Grebes, ducks and geese, etc. and Common Terns from early May to September. This is your best chance of seeing a Marsh Harrier too. Wheelchairs are not allowed on the boat but if you can get to the staithe (the boat landing) and negotiate three steps, the boat will be accessible.

Follow any of the paths through the woodland and you should see a wide variety of woodland birds. Kingfishers love the quiet water channels in the garden, so go

How to get there

(Approx. 10 miles NE of Norwich)

SAT NAV: NR13 6DZ.
GPS: 52.665667;
1.501866.

Sign-posted on brown tourist signs off the A47 Norwich to Great Yarmouth Road. Turn off the A47 onto the B1140 just west of Acle (signed Wroxham, S. Walsham & Fairhaven Gardens). After about 2 miles, turn right down Newport Road and then bear right onto Burlingham Road (signed to the Gardens and South Walsham). At the next T-junction (at The Kings Arms), turn right towards Upton and Acle and the Gardens. Go through the village and in 0.4 miles, turn right onto School Lane signed to Fairhaven on brown signs. The entrance is 0.1 miles on the left.

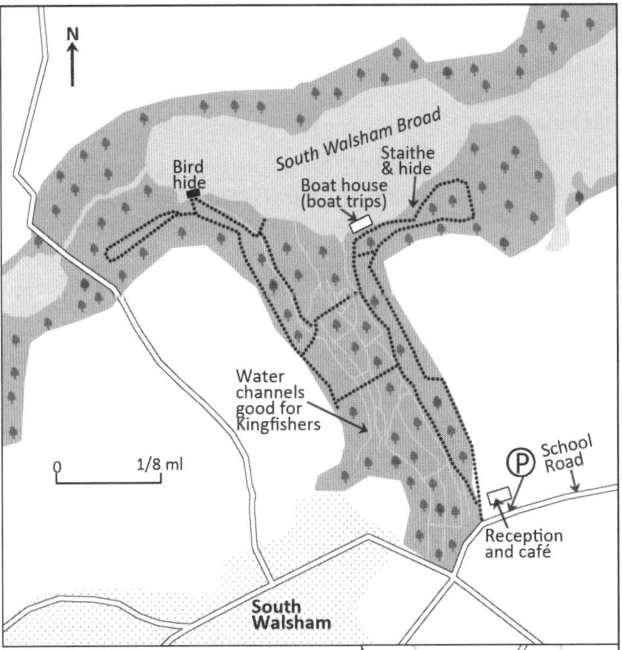

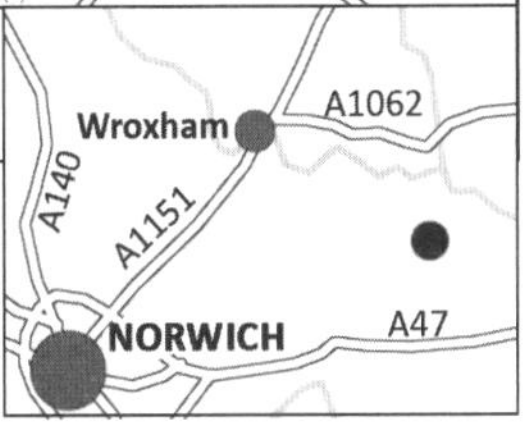

quietly and you should be lucky with a sighting. Lesser Spotted Woodpeckers still inhabit the woods here but are being seen less frequently these days. Great Spotteds are very showy, though.

Follow the paths to the western edge of the gardens. There is a wheelchair-friendly bird hide nestled in the trees on the edge of the broad. This is an excellent place from which to actually see a Cetti's Warbler! Listen for the explosive song and watch for movement in the thick undergrowth around the hide. Woodpeckers, finches and tits visit the feeders here too. In spring, Cuckoos can be seen in the trees across the broad.

Leave the hide and follow the paths across the creeks, through woodland to the boat staithe. In winter, this is an ideal viewpoint from which to scan the water for species such as Pochard,

Goldeneye and Tufted Duck, as well as the resident geese, Coots, Cormorants and Mallards.

From the staithe, take the muddy path to your right (as you face the water) and walk for about 400 yards to another bird hide. In winter, look for Water Rails under the feeders to your right and otters are regularly seen here too, so be very quiet!

Fairhaven will produce best results if you take your time on the paths and walk quietly. The gardens can get busy, so try and pick a few of the more secluded areas. Nevertheless, many of the birds are used to human visitors and can show well.

81

Key points

- **Car park charge for non-members.**

- **Free access to woodland and lake trails from dawn to dusk (except Christmas Day).**

- **Lake trail unsuitable for wheelchairs.**

- **Part of woodland trail is gravel, quite steeply uphill.**

- **Shop, gardens, and other attractions not open until 11am. Mostly closed during winter (toilets usually open year round)**

- **Terrain is along rough tracks or across fields.**

- **Some paths muddy at all times of year.**

- **Close all gates. Dogs on leads in parkland.**

Contacts

Felbrigg Hall
01263 837 444

The National Trust, East Anglia Regional Office 01263 733 471; www.nationaltrust.org

FELBRIGG HALL is a National Trust property set in 520 acres of rolling countryside. Habitats include a tract of ancient woodland, extensive farmland and a small lake so you can expect a reasonable array of birds. Non-birding members of the family can look around the house, visit the restaurant or café, or spend all your money in the Trust shop.

Target birds *All year* – **Common woodland birds (100%), Mandarin Duck (75%), Firecrest (40%), Lesser Spotted Woodpecker (10%).** *Spring/autumn* – **Passage migrants (15%).**

Other possible bird species

All year		Reed Warbler
Egyptian Goose	Jay	Blackcap
Common wildfowl	Skylark	Chiffchaff
Little Grebe	Goldcrest	Willow Warbler
Cormorant	Common scrub birds	Grasshopper Warbler
Sparrowhawk	Nuthatch	Spotted Flycatcher
Kestrel	Treecreeper	
Woodcock	Pied Wagtail	*Winter*
Regular gull species	Siskin	Wigeon
Stock Dove	Common finches	Goosander
Barn Owl	Reed Bunting	Winter thrushes
Little Owl		Meadow Pipit
Tawny Owl	*Summer*	Brambling
Green Woodpecker	Hobby	
Great Spotted Woodpecker	Cuckoo	
	Sand Martin	
	Other hirundines	

Background information and birding tips

FELBRIGG HALL itself is of little interest to birdwatchers but the grounds of the 520 acre estate are fantastic for a leisurely stroll. There is a small lake, which holds several species of common wildfowl and waterbirds and an expanse of ancient woodland that is home to many common breeding birds. Redstarts and Wood Warblers have bred here in the past.

For the lake trail, follow the signs from the car park along purple way-marked paths. Basically, you head for the small church, then aim diagonally right up the hill. Head for the two tall trees on the hilltop to reach a gate. Go through the gate and turn right, down the hill to the lake.

The footpath circles the lake and leads back to the hall. Scan the water for common ducks (Pochard, Mallard, Gadwall and Tufted Duck) which are sometimes joined by one or two Goosanders in winter. Mandarins are now resident on the lake but may be tucked away under overhanging branches.

There is a small reedbed at the northern end of the lake, home to Reed Buntings all year round and Reed Warblers in summer.

The marshy field adjacent to the lake is a good place for Grasshopper Warbler (and I have heard several young Tawny Owls calling from the trees in the marsh). Sand Martins nest in the muddy bank at the southern end of the lake and can be seen from late March to August. Scan the lake and adjoining fields for Egyptian Geese, joined by Wigeon in winter.

The woodland trail starts from the entrance to the walled garden. Take the gravel path up a steepish hill, through a stand of mature trees. Fifty yards up this path, a paddock-type area, where the trees are less densely spaced, is the best place to look for passage Redstarts, Wood Warblers and Pied Flycatchers in spring and autumn. In summer, look out for Spotted Flycatchers in the woods. Firecrests are present all year round. Listen for their 'more-insistent-Goldcrest' song on sunny days. Tape-luring this species is ILLEGAL!

Further on, the gravel track splits into several muddy grass tracks, all of which criss-cross the woodland. At the top of the hill is a bench around a large tree (the Victory V, planted to commemorate VE Day), an excellent place to sit and wait for the birds to come to you. From here, there is a hard surface path leading down the hill to the estate road and back to the hall (part of the white-marked Tree Trail).

In the wood, Great Spotted Woodpeckers are usually much in evidence but Lesser Spots can be very elusive. I have found the large trees closest to the car park to be best for the latter species, especially in late March when they give themselves away with their harsh calls, drumming and butterfly-like display flight. Occasionally, they even get in the large, lone trees in the fields towards the lake, where they show really well.

All in all, Felbrigg Hall grounds are a superb place for a stroll at any time of year. Visiting birdwatchers wandering around

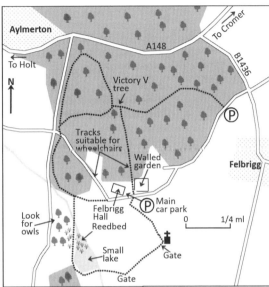

How to get there

(2.5 miles SW of Cromer).

SAT NAV: Felbrigg (The postcode allocated to the hall (NR11 8PR), results in SAT NAVS taking you a very strange route, so use Felbrigg and then follow brown signs).

GPS: 52.906954; 1.262142.

Site is well sign-posted off A148 (Cromer to Holt/ Fakenham road). Follow these

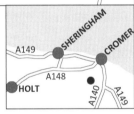

signs to the car park by the hall. From the car park, the two trails (woodland and lake) are well sign-posted.

the woods or lake (or both) are likely to encounter many common species of bird along the way. Even without a map you cannot get lost on the estate, as the hall is usually in sight.

For people who like a more secluded walk, there is a small car park on the right just before the first metal gate on the estate after you

have turned off the B1436. The footpath from here joins the main trail at the Victory V tree.

Other nearby sites

Blakeney Point, Blickling Hall, Cley Marshes, Kelling Heath, Kelling Quags, Salthouse Beach, Salthouse Heath, Sheringham, Swanton Novers, Walsey Hills, Weybourne.

Key points

- **Hide is open at all times, though Wednesdays can be disturbed by management work on the farm.**

- **Donations box outside the hide.**

- **Free car park.**

- **Wheelchair accessible hide.**

- **Log book in hide.**

- **Fieldguide in hide.**

FLITCHAM ABBEY FARM is a hidden gem among more famous honeypot reserves. Carefully managed to ensure the maximum number of birds use the site for feeding and breeding, it is probably the best place to see Tree Sparrow, Kingfisher, Little Owl and Turtle Dove in the county.

Target birds *All year* – **Tree Sparrow (70%), Little Owl (70%), Barn Owl (70%), Marsh Tit (65%), Marsh Harrier (50%), Kingfisher (50%).** *Winter* – **Pink-footed Goose (30%), Corn Bunting (10%).**

Other possible bird species

All year		
Little Grebe	Stock Dove	Winter thrushes
Egyptian Goose	Tawny Owl	*Spring/autumn*
Teal	Kingfisher	Passage waders
Common wildfowl	Green Woodpecker	Yellow Wagtail
Common waterfowl	Great Spotted Woodpecker	*Summer*
Sparrowhawk	Corvids	Turtle Dove
Buzzard	Pied Wagtail	Hirundines
Kestrel	Bullfinch	Summer warblers
Red-legged Partridge	Other common finches	*Occasional*
Grey Partridge	Yellowhammer	Garganey
Water Rail	Reed Bunting	Hobby
Lapwing	*Winter*	Red Kite
Snipe	Woodcock	
	Grey Wagtail	

Background information and birding tips

THIS WORKING FARM is a hidden treasure! Money provided by the Wildfowl and Wetlands Trust, DEFRA and the Countryside Stewardship Scheme goes towards managing the site as a haven for wildlife. This is how all farms could and should be but it is a sign of the times that I feel the need to praise RS Cross & Son (the owners) for their efforts.

On a winter's day, the bushes and trees around the car park can be dripping with birds. Yellowhammer and Chaffinch numbers are impressive (75-plus of the former and more than 100 of the latter have been recorded).

Several Tree Sparrows (normally in the hedges along the road) and a few Corn Buntings are usually present, though the former seems to be declining here. Marsh Tit is a certainty in winter, along with one or two Bullfinches. Pink-footed Geese sometimes feed in the large field opposite the car park in winter, but be very careful not to flush them. A Red-breasted Goose has also been recorded with this flock on one occasion.

From the hide, Little Owls can usually be seen in the fallen oak directly in front of you, or on the large logs in the field to the left of this tree. Kingfishers regularly sit on the posts in the middle of the pool, Barn Owls breed on site and can be quite showy, while Tawny Owls also breed but are seldom seen. Several noisy Egyptian Geese are resident.

Contacts

RS Cross & Son, Abbey Farm, Flitcham, Norfolk.
01485 600 227

A Buzzard is sometimes seen patrolling the skies throughout the year, while Hobbies occasionally fly over the farm from May to September (most in evidence between July and August). Marsh Harriers are reported daily during the spring and summer months and less frequently at other times of year, while Red Kite sightings are increasing.

Summer breeders include Whitethroats, Lesser Whitethroats, Spotted Flycatchers, Blackcaps, Willow Warblers and Chiffchaffs. This is one of the best sites in Norfolk to see Turtle Doves, which love to sit on the telephone wires running across the reserve.

In winter, pay special attention to the vegetated ditch viewable from the left side of the hide. Both Water Rail and Woodcock have been seen here and common species come to this shallow pool to drink.

All in all, this is a cracking little place with plenty to see at all times of year. It is not unusual to see most of the target birds in a single visit. I love to drop in at Flitcham for an hour or so at the end of a hard day's birding around the Norfolk coast, just to chill out and see what is around. I am rarely disappointed.

This site is a shining example of how farming and wildlife conservation can be comfortable bedfellows. It is frightening to contrast this farm with the bird-less 'agri-deserts' so often encountered these days.

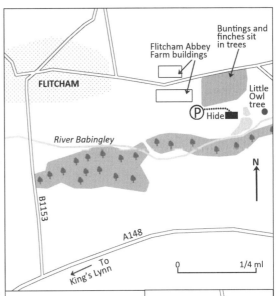

How to get there

(7.5 miles E of King's Lynn).

SAT NAV: PE31 6BT. Takes you onto Abbey Road in Flitcham – then follow directions below to the farm.

GPS: 52.808972; 0.574722.

From King's Lynn take A148 (Cromer/Fakenham road) and then turn left onto B1153 at Hillington, sign-posted to Flitcham.

In Flitcham, turn right into Abbey Road and drive for half a mile until you have just passed the farm buildings on the right. Beyond the farmhouse there is a small sign 'Abbey Farm Bird Hide' on the stone wall, sending you down a short track.

Park at the end on the mud: the two hard-standing spaces are reserved for Blue Badge holders.

The hide is along a short concrete path and is wheelchair friendly.

Other nearby sites

Blackborough End Tip, Dersingham Bog, Hunstanton, Ken Hill Wood, King's Lynn Docks, Pentney Gravel Pits, Roydon Common, Sandringham, Snettisham, Tottenhill Gravel Pits, Wolferton Triangle.

Key points

- **Free admission.**

- **Open all year round from 10am – 5pm. Closed on Thursdays.**

- **Please keep to signed trails.**

- **No wheelchair access.**

- **Can be very, very muddy all year round.**

- **Level terrain on grass paths.**

- **No dogs.**

- **Wood chips for sale (in bulk only) at certain times of year. Contact NWT for details.**

- **Check with Trust about dawn chorus walks in spring.**

Contacts

Norfolk Wildlife Trust, 01603 625 540

Download reserve leaflet at: www. norfolkwildlifetrust. org.uk/ Documents/ Reserves/Foxley-Woods. pdf

FOXLEY WOOD is the largest remaining tract of ancient woodland in Norfolk and as such it is a great place in which to encounter many common woodland bird species, plus the increasingly hard-to-find Turtle Dove and Grasshopper Warbler in spring and summer. It is also home to more than 250 species of plant, making this a fascinating place for all-round naturalists to visit.

Target species *All year* – **Common woodland birds (100%).**
Spring/summer – **Turtle Dove (40%), Grasshopper Warbler (hear 60%, see 15%).**

Other possible bird species

All year		
Sparrowhawk	Other corvids	Hirundines
Kestrel	Skylark	Common warblers
Woodcock	Common scrub birds	Spotted Flycatcher
Stock Dove	Marsh Tit	*Winter*
Barn Owl	Nuthatch	Winter thrushes
Little Owl	Treecreeper	Brambling
Tawny Owl	Bullfinch	
Green Woodpecker	Other common finches	*Occasional*
Great Spotted Woodpecker	*Spring/summer*	Buzzard
Jay	Hobby	Red Kite
	Cuckoo	Goshawk

Background information and birding tips

THIS quintessential English forest, the largest remaining stand of ancient woodland in the county, is bursting with wildlife.

The NWT is managing the 300 acre wood by traditional methods (coppicing) and removing conifers planted in the 1960s, along with other non-native species. This coppicing (cutting trees close to the ground) means there are plenty of woodland products for the visitor to purchase to help fund future management.

When visiting Foxley, it is advisable to take one's time. This is a large wood and the birds may be scattered over the whole area. The more time one spends in the wood, the more species of bird will be seen.

The circular walk is well marked on posts with green arrows, accessed at the rear of the grassy parking areas, with smaller paths leading into the wood for more intrepid birders.

There are information boards at regular intervals to tell the visitor what they may encounter at various times of year.

All of these paths can produce birds. In winter, birds gather together in feeding flocks and roam widely in the wood. You can either stroll through the wood to find them or wait patiently for them to come to you (but always stay on the paths).

Bramblings can sometimes be seen feeding on beech mast on the floor, Siskin and Lesser Redpolls move in to feed on alders, or a flock of agitated birds may lead you to a roosting Tawny Owl. Huge numbers of Woodpigeons can be seen in the quieter areas of the wood in winter.

Foxley really comes into its own in spring. The wood is bursting with bird song as the resident species are joined by a host of summer visitors.

Blackcaps, Whitethroats, Lesser Whitethroats, Garden Warblers, Grasshopper Warblers, Chiffchaffs and Willow Warblers can all be heard along with Cuckoos and Spotted Flycatchers. At dusk, you may also hear and see roding Woodcock.

One cautionary word: Foxley can be very busy in spring, as it is a famous bluebell wood. Visitors flock from miles around to experience the spectacular rivers of blue running through the trees.

Great Spotted Woodpeckers will be hard to miss and Green Woodpeckers are common. Lesser Spotted Woodpeckers haven't been seen here for at least five years now. However, Foxley is one of the best places in Norfolk to see Nuthatch and Treecreeper.

Spring and autumn may also produce a few passage migrants such as Redstart, Pied Flycatcher and Wood Warbler. At all times of year, you should occasionally glance upwards as Sparrowhawk, Kestrel, regular gull species and Buzzard may all be seen. Goshawk has also been recorded over the wood.

In short, there is always something of interest to see in Foxley Wood. As well as the bird species, the all-round naturalist will be able to enjoy butterflies, flowers and fungi.

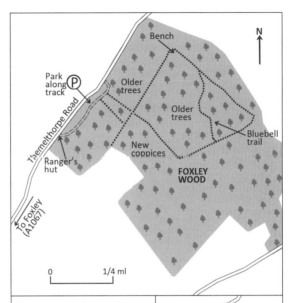

How to get there

(Approx 10 miles SE of Fakenham).

SAT NAV: NR20 4QR. Postcode gets you to within 200 yards of the entrance to car park. Or try Foxley>Themelthorpe Road, which takes you past the sign-posted reserve entrance.

GPS: 52.764918; 1.036192.

The reserve is sign-posted on brown tourist signs from the A1067 Norwich to Fakenham road, approximately one mile north of Bawdeswell, 10 miles south east of Fakenham.

Turn off A1067 (The Street) and follow the minor, narrow road through Foxley village (20mph limit) to the NWT-signed turn-in to the car park on the right (1.3 miles from main road).

Other nearby sites

Hempton Marsh, Pensthorpe Wildlife Park, Sculthorpe Moor, Sparham Pools, Swanton Novers, north coast sites.

Key points

- **Parking fee at beach. Free on-road parking for cemetery.**

- **Promenade is level concrete; cemetery paths (some hard and some grassy) are all level.**

- **Dunes not accessible to wheelchair users.**

- **Mediterranean Gulls viewable from piers and promenade.**

- **Many facilities in town. Public toilets at Marine Parade car park.**

- **Cemetery gates open 7.30am - 4.30pm (October 1 to March 31) and 7.30am - 7pm for rest of year.**

- **No dogs in cemetery.**

- **Show due consideration for graves.**

D ESPITE BEING the county's most garish, bustling seaside town, Yarmouth can boast two sites of interest to birdwatchers. Its beach is the best place in Norfolk to see Mediterranean Gulls, while the cemetery remains a magnet for migrants in spring and autumn. Sadly the Little Tern colony has moved away but the Denes still attract passage migrants and winter visitors.

Target birds *All year* – **Mediterranean Gull (95%).** *Winter* – **Snow Bunting (15%).** *Spring/summer* – **Passage migrants.**

Other possible bird species

All year	*Spring/autumn (might include)*	
Cormorant	Wryneck	Other warblers
Kestrel	Hirundines	Pied Flycatcher
Oystercatcher	Bluethroat	Red-backed Shrike
Ringed Plover	Black Redstart	
Turnstone	Redstart	*Autumn (might include)*
Regular gull species	Whinchat	Sooty Shearwater
Skylark	Wheatear	Manx Shearwater
Meadow Pipit	Ring Ouzel	Balearic Shearwater
Common finches	Winter thrushes	Gannet
	Barred Warbler	Arctic Skua
Summer	Firecrest	Great Skua
Little Gull	Yellow-browed Warbler	Little Gull
Common Tern		Kittiwake
Sandwich Tern		

Background information and birding tips

G REAT YARMOUTH beach can hold double figures of Mediterranean Gulls all year round. Take some bread and a camera with you and I am sure you will obtain mouth-watering views and/or shots of this attractive gull. In between the two piers seems to be the best place to find them.

The ends of the piers provide excellent places from which to seawatch when the tide is in. During the breeding season, you will see terns passing offshore, even though the town's hard-pressed Little Tern beach colony finally conceded defeat. They have dispersed to other sites such as Winterton and Caister.

At passage times, especially autumn, a seawatch may produce a few Gannets, Arctic and Great

Skuas, shearwaters and terns, depending on whether there is an onshore wind or not. Seaducks and divers (Red-throated most likely) should be passing by in winter.

Further north, there is a large expanse of rough grass and low dunes bordering the beach, known as The Denes. This habitat is home to Skylarks and Meadow Pipits throughout the year, joined by a few migrants in spring and autumn.

There may be a small flock of Snow Buntings overwintering from November to March but it can be extremely difficult to locate thanks to major disturbance by dog walkers. The Denes is designated as a SSSI site, so this constant uncontrolled disturbance is disgraceful.

Park near the junction of North

How to get there

SAT NAV: NR30 2DJ (postcode for hotel opposite car park). Travel to the end of the road and the car park is opposite. Walk onto promenade for gulls.

NR30 4HU (postcode for 24 Kitchener Road which is the closest house to the cemetery entrances).

GPS: 52.609859 1.737900.

Beach: From A47 follow signs to Town Centre/ Seafront onto St. Nicholas Drive. Go over the traffic lights (the road is now called Euston Road) to the pay and display car park at the end, adjacent to the toilet block. Walk on to the beach to search for the Med Gulls, usually between the two piers.

For Snow Buntings, park in the area described in the Denes section below and search the dunes.

Denes: Follow directions as above but instead of parking, turn left (N) and follow this road for about a mile. Park on road near turn-off sign-posted to Caistor (Jellicoe Road) by The Iron Duke pub (just at the start of the caravan park).

Cemetery: From A47, follow signs to 'Town Centre/ Sea Front' to St. Nicholas Drive. Turn left at traffic lights into North Dene Road (sign-posted to coach/ lorry car park). Turn left on to Kitchener Road (which is just after the coach park) and follow down to the cemetery gates, about 150 yards along. The cemetery is split into two sections, North and South and both can be accessed on foot from the road.

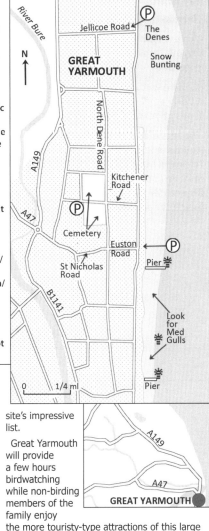

Drive and Jellicoe Road and explore the dunes carefully. On the beach you should see Oystercatchers, Ringed Plovers, Turnstones, and loafing gulls on any visit, and terns from spring to autumn.

Further inland, Great Yarmouth Cemetery is a superb place in which to find migrants in spring and autumn, especially after a spell of easterly winds.

Common species such as Goldcrest, Chiffchaff and Blackcap may be joined by migrants such as Redstart, Pied Flycatcher, Spotted Flycatcher, Whinchat, Wheatear and even rarer goodies such as Yellow-browed Warbler, Wryneck, Firecrest and Barred Warbler.

Many rarities have been discovered in the trees and bushes of the cemetery, so you may be lucky and find another 'mega' to add to the site's impressive list.

Great Yarmouth will provide a few hours birdwatching while non-birding members of the family enjoy the more touristy-type attractions of this large seaside town.

Further birdwatching opportunities near the town include Breydon Water, accessed via a footpath from Yarmouth railway station and Asda supermarket (see separate site page).

Key points

- **Terrain is level.**

- **Access along a narrow, uneven grass path.**

- **Can be wet and muddy at all times of year.**

- **No facilities (toilets at RSPB Titchwell Marsh reserve and Brancaster beach car park).**

SANDWICHED between Brancaster Marsh and Titchwell, this is a quiet area for birdwatchers to enjoy a variety of habitats, including marsh, reedbed, beach and sea. This site doesn't have the extensive wader scrapes of its more illustrious RSPB neighbour but close views of several sought-after species can be enjoyed in solitude.

Target birds *All year* – **Marsh Harrier (95%), Bearded Tit (60%).** *Winter* – **Sea duck (80%), raptors (35%), Snow Bunting (30% on beach).** *Spring* – **Garganey (30%).**

Other possible bird species

All year
Little Grebe
Cormorant
Shelduck
Sparrowhawk
Kestrel
Barn Owl
Red-legged Partridge
Grey Partridge
Common waders
Little Egret
Skylark
Stonechat
Cetti's Warbler
Linnet
Bullfinch

Reed Bunting

Spring/autumn
Shearwaters
Gannet
Passage waders
Skuas
Passage migrants
Yellow Wagtail

Summer
Terns
Cuckoo
Hirundines
Sedge Warbler
Reed Warbler
Lesser Whitethroat

Whitethroat
Blackcap
Chiffchaff
Willow Warbler

Winter
Brent Goose
Winter raptors
Grey Plover

Occasional
Hobby
Short-eared Owl
Avocet
Water Pipit
Twite

Background information and birding tips

THIS WALK will suit people who prefer to do their birdwatching away from the crowds. The range of birds is similar to that encountered on RSPB Titchwell Marsh reserve, though numbers are lower because there are no wader scrapes.

It is worth remembering to use this more easterly footpath when the sun is shining in your eyes at Titchwell (in the mornings), as you can look across to the same reedbed from Gypsy Lane.

From the car park, the footpath is bordered by trees and bushes which are home to Cetti's Warblers and common scrub birds all year, joined by warblers in spring and summer. Check carefully for migrants in spring and autumn.

After about 400 yards, the path opens out onto an extensive reedbed where you should see Marsh Harriers and Bearded Tits. Because this walk is quiet, you may get harriers flying overhead. They are present all year, though can be elusive in winter. Bitterns are present in the extensive reedbeds but are much easier to see from Fen Hide on the RSPB reserve.

Once past the reeds, the raised path crosses a marsh. One or two Little Egrets should be patrolling the channels alongside common wading species (such as Redshank) throughout the year and this is also an excellent spot for raptors, geese and ducks in winter. Garganey are regular visitors in spring and the summer months bring Sedge and

Contacts
None

How to get there

(5.5 miles E of Hunstanton).

SAT NAV: PE31 8BA (postcode for east side of Titchwell. Follow further directions in main access section.)

GPS: 052.961864; 0.625898.

On entering Titchwell village on A149 from Thornham (travelling E), park in small lay-by on left, opposite the national speed limit sign. If travelling W, the lay-by will be on the right just before the 40mph signs. There is room for about four cars. Follow the public footpath N.

Alternatively, park in Brancaster Beach car park (TF 772 451) and walk W along the beach to where it meets this footpath on the shore.

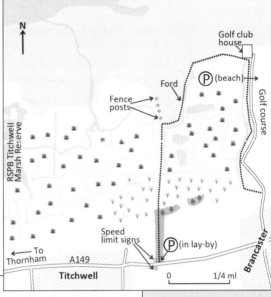

Reed Warblers to the area.

As the path bears right, look for raptors perched on old fence posts. Merlin, Peregrine, Hen Harrier, Short-eared and Barn Owls all hunt the area in winter, with the latter species present all year.

Follow the path east across a ford to the beach. In winter, all the species encountered at Titchwell on the beach and on the sea can be seen here, though there will be fewer pairs of eyes to spot things.

Waders on the beach should include Ringed Plover, Knot, Oystercatcher, Turnstone, Sanderling, Bar-tailed Godwit, Grey Plover, etc and the sea should produce Red-breasted Merganser, Goldeneye, Slavonian Grebe, Eider, Common Scoter, Long-tailed Duck and Red-throated Diver.

Summer will see a similar range of waders with Little, Sandwich and Common Terns passing constantly. Be aware that the beach may be relatively crowded with summer tourists, accessing the beach from the Brancaster car park.

Autumn seawatching should produce Manx Shearwater. Keep an eye open for any of the four species of skua harassing the terns, though Arctic Skua will be the most numerous.

This walk will almost certainly not produce as many birds as the adjoining RSPB reserve but with patience, you should be rewarded with an impressive array of species. For instance, on a 30 minute power-walk one August (just to see what was around), I saw five Little Egrets, several family parties

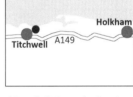

of Bearded Tits and a female and juvenile Marsh Harrier being mobbed by a pair of Sparrowhawks over my head. All this without another person in sight. Bliss!

Other nearby sites

Brancaster Marsh, Choseley Barns, Dersingham Bog, Holme Dunes, Holkham Hall, Holkham NNR, Ken Hill Wood, King's Lynn Docks, Sandringham, Snettisham, Swanton Novers, Redwell Marsh, Roydon Common, Titchwell Marsh, Wolferton Triangle.

91

Key points

- Telescope essential.

- Terrain is uphill on a surfaced pavement.

- Very exposed, with no shelter. Bring warm clothes and footwear.

- Excellent vantage point for wheelchair users to scan for raptors, though the bridge slope is relatively steep.

VIEWING Haddiscoe and Thorpe Marshes from the side of a busy road isn't necessarily the most pleasant of experiences, but this site does afford wheelchair users a safe and completely accessible watchpoint for wintering birds of prey, geese and swans.

Target birds Winter – Marsh Harrier (85%), Peregrine (40%), Hen Harrier (20%), Merlin (15%), Short-eared Owl (15%).

Other possible bird species

Winter	Buzzard	Winter thrushes
Whooper Swan	Sparrowhawk	Corvids
White-fronted Goose	Kestrel	Meadow Pipit
Shelduck	Lapwing	Pied Wagtail
Wigeon	Curlew	Common finches
Teal	Regular gull species	Reed Bunting
Cormorant	Barn Owl	*Occasional*
Grey Heron	Corvids	Bewick's Swan
Little Egret	Skylark	Rough-legged Buzzard
Common waterbirds	Common scrub birds	

Background information and birding tips

THE VANTAGE point overlooking Haddiscoe, Fritton, Thorpe, Thurlton and Norton Marshes offers no shelter from the elements, so I suggest you only visit in fine weather with good visibility. In these conditions, views of the marshes from the bridge are superb.

A wide range of raptors grace the marsh, though none can be guaranteed on any given visit. Overall, there is always something to see, though you may have to wait two or three hours to produce a decent list of desired species. By this time, your toes will no longer feel a part of your body.

Marsh Harriers, Kestrels and Sparrowhawks are the most likely raptors, though Short-eared Owls are recorded regularly.

Barn Owls and Peregrines are frequent visitors to the marsh but Merlins and Hen Harriers are seen less regularly. Scan the pylons and fence posts very carefully as raptors love to use them as look-out perches. The area is a favoured wintering ground of a Rough-legged Buzzard or two.

While scanning for raptors and owls, you may find Bewick's and Whooper Swans as well as Pink-footed Geese. White-fronts used to be regular visitors, so scan any goose flocks thoroughly.

The marsh also holds many common species ranging from Goldfinch, Greenfinch and Meadow Pipit, to grazing Wigeon, Teal and Mute Swan and nervous Lapwing and Curlew.

If you are a hardy sort of birdwatcher you may wish to walk across the marsh and you can choose to use one of several public footpaths all accessed from close to the bridge viewpoint. One is sign-posted across from the parking area, another leads from underneath the bridge and a couple start over the bridge towards St. Olaves.

Contacts
None

How to get there

(6.5 miles SW of Yarmouth).

SAT NAV: NR31 9JA (postcode for the access road to Haddiscoe Station: park in the large lay-by at the junction with the A143). If not try POI>Railway Station>Haddiscoe.

GPS: 52.532633 1.614281.

From Great Yarmouth: Head S on A12 to junction with A143 (sign-posted Belton, Burgh Castle and Beccles). Continue for 5.5 miles to St. Olaves. Pass through the village and after half a mile cross the steep bridge (over the canal and railway).

At the bottom of the bridge, turn immediately left and park on the wide, Tarmac verge (sign-posted Haddiscoe Station – if you reach Haddiscoe village, you have gone too far). Walk back to the road bridge to view the marsh on your left.

From Norwich: Leave A47 Norwich bypass on A146. Head SE for approximately 13.5 miles.

Take first exit at roundabout with the junction of A143 (sign-posted

Great Yarmouth). After approximately five miles, pass through the village of Haddiscoe and continue for another 1.5 miles.

Park on the right, just before the steep bridge over the canal and railway (park by signs for Haddiscoe station).

One option is a long, bracing circuit of 'Haddiscoe Island' (walking out as far as The Berney Arms – but on the other side of the river – and Breydon Water and returning via Seven Mile House and Toft Monks Mill).

These footpaths may result in close encounters with birds but be careful not to flush them: it is vital they are allowed to feed during limited daylight hours at this harsh time of year.

Whether you choose to observe from the bridge or the footpaths, a winter visit to these marshes may well provide you with a range of much sought-after species, especially raptors. As ever, the longer you stay on site, the more

chance you have of compiling a decent bird list!

If you ask me, it is much more sensible (if standing on a high bridge in a wind-chill of -10°C can be called sensible) to scan the area from Haddiscoe bridge, from where you can dash occasionally to the car for a respite from the elements.

Other nearby sites

Berney Arms Marshes, Breydon Water, Burgh Castle Marshes, Great Yarmouth Beach, Hardley Flood, Herbert Barnes Riverside Park, Waveney Forest.

93

Key points

- **Free access at all times along public footpaths.**

- **Terrain is level, mainly along an uneven, narrow, grass path, though there is a stretch of easy-access path to the moorings.**

- **Not suitable for wheelchair users.**

- **Free 24-hour mooring at Chedgrave.**

- **Telescope useful.**

- **Hide accessed up a ramp.**

- **ID chart inside hide. Info board and map in church car park.**

- **Toilets and shops available in Chedgrave (1 mile).**

- **Part of the Wherryman's Way Footpath.**

Contacts

General Broads
Authority
01603 610 734

A PLEASANT stroll along the banks of the River Chet brings you to a bird hide overlooking a large, reed-fringed lake. Common wildfowl should be present all year round (except when hunting is taking place!) and you may even be lucky enough to glimpse an overwintering Bittern.

Target birds *All year* – Cetti's Warbler (hear 60%, see 10%), Kingfisher (40%).

Other possible bird species

All year	Common scrub birds	Reed Warbler
Egyptian Goose	Cetti's Warbler	Whitethroat
Common wildfowl	Common woodland birds	Other warblers
Cormorant	Meadow Pipit	
Little Grebe	Pied Wagtail	*Spring/autumn*
Great Crested Grebe	Common finches	Passage waders
Common waterbirds	Reed Bunting	Yellow Wagtail
Sparrowhawk		
Kestrel	*Summer*	*Winter*
Water Rail	Marsh Harrier	Goldeneye
Regular gull species	Hobby	Goosander
Green Woodpecker	Common Tern	Winter thrushes
Great Spotted Woodpecker	Cuckoo	*Occasional*
Corvids	Hirundines	Bittern (winter)
Skylark	Sedge Warbler	Marsh Harrier
		Osprey (passage)

Background information and birding tips

HARDLEY FLOOD is a privately-owned stretch of water that holds many species of common waterfowl. In winter, the large lake can be covered in Tufted Duck, Goldeneye, Wigeon, Pochard, Teal, Mallard, Gadwall, Shoveler, Shelduck, feral geese, Coot and Great Crested Grebe.

This stretch of water is regularly used by the shooting fraternity in winter, so listen out for gun shots when you get out of your car/boat to avoid a disappointing visit.

Park by the information board next to the church. Go into the dip of the play area, past the swings etc, to find a narrow gravel path (past a cottage).

Turn right along the hard-surfaced lane (Pitt Lane) past the houses to where the boatyard access peels

off to the right. Keep straight on here through a kissing gate onto an easy access path. Follow this along the banks of the River Chet. DO NOT PARK ON PITS LANE!

To your left, a grazed marsh can hold Snipe in winter, plus summer warblers in the breeding season. The path passes the free mooring site and continues alongside the river. Kingfishers love this quiet stretch and you should get very close views of Reed and Sedge Warblers in season.

There is an open area of sedge on your left along with some dead trees which may hold an Osprey on passage (spring and autumn) though a drumming or calling Great Spotted Woodpecker is more likely. Look for swallowtail butterflies in summer.

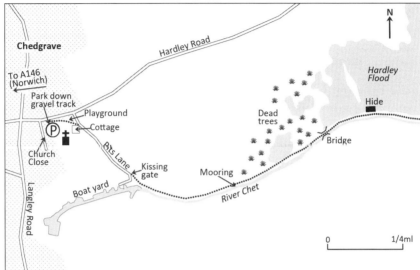

Plan to spend as long as you can in the hide. Winter will produce the highest number of wildfowl, possibly including one of the scarcer species such as Smew or Scaup (and Blue-winged Teal has been recorded, demonstrating that anything can show up). It is also an excellent place to see an otter!

If water levels drop in spring or autumn, scan the muddy edges for passage waders such as Common, Green and Wood Sandpipers.

The number of birds will dwindle in summer but Common Terns grace the Flood, sometimes joined by Black and Arctics in spring and autumn.

Many Swallows, Swifts and House Martins feed over the water, which may attract a Hobby or two (they also love the dragonflies from July onwards).

The path continues along the River Chet and then loops back through Hardley Hall to Chedgrave, though I usually go to the hide and then retrace my steps to the church.

How to get there

(Ten miles SE of Norwich).
SAT NAV: NR14 6NF (postcode for houses opposite church).
GPS: 52.541163; 1.482897.

By car: Leave A47 Norwich bypass at A146 (sign-posted to Lowestoft & Norwich). Head SE for seven miles, turning left to Chedgrave and Langley. In Chedgrave village, take the first left, sign-posted Langley.

At crossroads, go straight across (Hardley Road). After 100 yards, go past Church Close on your right and almost immediately afterwards, turn right up a narrow, gravel track signed 'church'. Park by the church overlooking the play area. If there is no room here, park in the village.

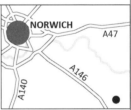

At the rear of the play area, go past a cottage and turn right along the road to its end and go through a kissing gate. Follow public footpath signs alongside the channel, then alongside the River Chet for about half a mile to view Hardley Flood.

By boat: Mooring on River Chet, approximately a 30 minute sail from the junction with the River Yare. Moor at Chedgrave Common, not at the boatyards.

Key points

- **Permit needed by non-NOA members. Hides open when wardens on site.**
- **Hide keys for NOA members (01485 525 406 or info@noa. org.uk)**
- **Boardwalk trail throughout site.**
- **Access difficult for wheelchair users due to lack of safe parking near entrance.**
- **Two bird hides, but no other facilities. Nearest toilets/ shops etc in Fakenham town centre.**

Contacts

Norfolk Ornithologists'
Association,
01485 525 406;
e-mail: info@noa.org.uk
www.noa.org.uk

DISCOVERING a new inland nature reserve is always welcome and this 28-acre SSSI in the Upper Wensum Valley is an ideal place to observe many common woodland birds and in the future may provide a home for declining breeding waders such as Snipe, Lapwing and Curlew.

Target birds *All year* – Marsh Tit (95%), Kingfisher (35%).

Other possible bird species

All year	Other corvids	Winter thrushes
Mallard	Skylark	Siskin
Red-legged Partridge	Goldcrest	Lesser Redpoll
Pheasant	Treecreeper	
Grey Heron	Bullfinch	*Occasional*
Little Grebe	Other common finches	Goosander (winter)
Common Buzzard	Reed Bunting	Little Egret (marsh)
Sparrowhawk		Marsh Harrier
Kestrel	*Spring/summer*	Winter raptors
Lapwing	Hirundines	Hobby (summer)
Regular gull species	Blackcap	Oystercatcher
Tawny Owl	Willow Warbler	Curlew
Barn Owl	Chiffchaff	Snipe
Stock Dove		Little Owl
Collared Dove	*Spring /autumn*	Lesser Spotted
Green Woodpecker	Yellow Wagtail	Woodpecker
Great Spotted Woodpecker	*Winter*	Willow Tit
Jay	Winter wildfowl	Brambling (winter)
	Woodcock	

Background information and birding tips

COMPRISING wet marsh and carr woodland, Hempton Marsh is the Norfolk Ornithologists' Association's seventh reserve, having been bought in 2000. This relatively small site is perfectly placed to be included in a visit to the cluster of reserves nestled around Fakenham or on your way to the north Norfolk coast.

After parking in the lay-by on the minor road adjacent to the A1065, cross the busy main road and head for the reserve entrance gate. If a warden is on site, you may be asked to pay for an entry permit if you are not an NOA member.

Wheelchair users and people with mobility problems could possibly park on the grass verge near to the reserve entrance, but I wouldn't recommend it as the ground is soft and fast-moving traffic passes very close.

It is always worth pausing at the gate to scan for any waders making use of the marsh, especially in winter. It is hoped that management of this declining habitat will encourage breeding waders to return to the reserve.

Walk along the boardwalk, scanning either side as you go. There is a bridge over a stream on your right, a favourite perching place for the Kingfisher. Winter thrushes should be present in the fields from November to March,

How to get there

Fakenham town centre is one mile.

SAT NAV: NR21 7LH (postcode for Fakenham Garden Centre). Then follow directions to parking below. Or try Fakenham>Gogg's Mill Road.

GPS: 52.831212; 0.838308.

Hempton village lies on the A1065 SW of Fakenham. Where it meets the A148 at the Shell garage roundabout on the Fakenham bypass, take the A1065 signed to Swaffham, Racecourse, Dereham and Hempton. Follow this for 0.8 miles and turn left towards the Fakenham Garden Centre. Turn immediately left again onto Gogg's Mill Road.

The road winds for 0.25 miles and then you reach a wide lay-by on the left side of the road (adjacent to the main road). Park here, walk up the shallow muddy bank to the main road. Cross the very busy A road to the reserve entrance gate. Follow the boardwalk around the reserve to the hides.

Alternatively, from the Shell roundabout, take the exit for Fakenham Town Centre (past the Shell garage) and take the next right turn (Sandy Lane). Follow this straight through the housing estate for 0.5 miles (this road eventually becomes Gogg's Mill Road) and park in the large lay-by on the right adjacent to the main A road (on a sharp left bend).

while Barn Owls and Marsh Harriers may drift across the fields at any time of year.

The boardwalk leads you to the wood, which is jam-packed full of woodland species, including Marsh Tit. Unfortunately, Willow Tits are in steep decline in this area of Norfolk, though one or two are occasionally reported.

The best place to observe the birds is from the two hides (obtain a key from the NOA before visiting – keys fit all of the NOA hides on all of their reserves). If that is not possible ahead of a visit, non-members will be allowed to use hides on payment of an entrance fee, but only if a warden is on duty.

The first hide, on the right of the boardwalk, looks out over the marsh and fields to the north of the reserve (see previous paragraphs for possible species). Continue along the boardwalk, which then splits, keeping your eyes open for a wintering Woodcock in the leaf litter along the way.

Straight on leads to a platform overlooking an oxbow diversion of the River Wensum. Approach very quietly and carefully and you may be lucky enough to encounter a Kingfisher or even an otter! Stand quietly here and the birds should come to you.

Retrace your steps to the junction. The

offshoot of the boardwalk leads to a second hide, which overlooks a clearing stacked with well-stocked feeders. Marsh Tits are the star species and views are good enough to note the diagnostic tiny white mark on the bill which distinguishes this species from Willow Tit.

Other species include Jay, Great Spotted Woodpecker, Bullfinch, other tits and finches and a variety of thrushes, etc. No doubt a rarity will turn up at these feeders one day!

Just off the boardwalk near this second hide is a narrow grass path which leads to the River Wensum. Approach very quietly and you may be rewarded with a sighting of an otter or water vole. Goosanders occasionally fly up the river in winter.

NOA Hempton Marsh is a lovely little reserve which is well worth visiting regularly should you have the opportunity.

Though the reserve is small in size, Hempton Marsh is already proving attactive to a wide variety of species. Look for Little Egret in the marshy areas.

I HAVE INCLUDED this small riverside park because it is an ideal place for wheelchair users and people with mobility difficulties to obtain superb views over Breydon Water. If you catch the tide right, waders can be very close to this park.

Target species *All Year* – **Avocet (90%), Mediterranean Gull (40%).** *Spring/autumn* – **Little Gull (60%), passage waders.** *Winter* – **Winter raptors (30%).** *Summer* – **Terns.**

Other possible bird species

All year
Shelduck
Common wildfowl
Cormorant
Little Egret
Marsh Harrier
Sparrowhawk
Kestrel
Common waders
Regular gull species
Barn Owl
Pied Wagtail

Winter
Pink-footed Goose
Wigeon
Pintail

Goldeneye
Golden Plover
Grey Plover
Knot
Bar-tailed Godwit

Spring/summer
Garganey
Sandwich Tern
Common Tern
Little Tern

Passage
Ruff
Little Stint
Curlew Sandpiper
Black-tailed Godwit
Whimbrel

Greenshank
Spotted Redshank
Green Sandpiper
Wood Sandpiper
Common Sandpiper
Arctic Tern
Black Tern
Hirundines
Yellow Wagtail

Occasional
Bewick's Swan (winter)
Whooper Swan (winter)
Marsh Harrier
Hen Harrier (winter)
Merlin
Peregrine

Key points

- **Free access at all times.**

- **6ft 6in height barriers on car park entrances.**

- **Site is fully wheelchair accessible.**

- **Info boards (inc map) in car parks.**

- **No facilities but Great Yarmouth is only a mile away.**

- **Telescope useful.**

Background information and birding tips

THE HERBERT BARNES Riverside Park is named after the late councillor for Cobholm, a district of Great Yarmouth. It was previously a 'hidden gem', frequented by local birdwatchers only but came to national prominence in 2005, when a Killdeer was found in the area.

From the rugby club car park, or the car park further along the lane, there is a network of hard surface paths across the park. All are easy access.

The grassy areas are magnets for Meadow Pipit and Skylarks, with Pied Wagtails dropping in regularly.

The Park really comes into its own when you reach the seawall because wheelchair users can view Breydon Water from here. At

certain times of the day the light can be more favourable here than from the hide near Asda, in Great Yarmouth.

The tide may also push birds closer to the park as it fills Breydon and, if you sit quietly on the benches on the seawall, you may get very close views of waders indeed!

If the tide is out you are still able to 'scope Breydon Water from this position, though birds may be distant. At all times of year you should expect to see Avocets, Redshanks, Lapwing, Oystercatchers, Ringed Plovers, Dunlin, Turnstones, Curlews, Shelduck and Little Egrets.

In winter, you should encounter

Contacts

Great Yarmouth
Borough Council,
Town Hall, Hall Quay,
Great Yarmouth
NR30 2QF
(01493 856 100)
www.great-yarmouth.
gov.uk

Grey and Golden Plovers, Bar-tailed Godwits and Ruff, and in summer Black-tailed Godwits and Little Ringed Plovers.

Passage waders may include Green, Wood and Common Sandpipers, Little Stints, Curlew Sandpipers and Whimbrels among others.

When the tide is in during the summer, terns fish Breydon Water, sometimes coming close to shore at the park (the channel here is narrower than at Great Yarmouth). Common and Sandwich Terns are the commonest species but they are joined by Little and Arctic.

You may be lucky and find a Roseate Tern here and on passage you might see Black Terns patrolling the area. Scan the gull flocks carefully, as they are often joined by Mediterranean Gulls (though Great Yarmouth beach is a more reliable site).

A scan of the distant fields across Breydon Water may reveal a resident Marsh Harrier, Barn Owl or Peregrine, or a wintering Hen Harrier, Merlin or Short-eared Owl. Look for flocks of Pink-footed Geese or wild swans.

From the park you may wish to walk further. The footpath along the seawall forms part of Angles Way. Head left and you reach Burgh Castle. Keep going (for 70 miles) and you reach Knettishall Heath in Suffolk but that's probably too far for one day!

Head right along the footpath and you find yourself in Great Yarmouth.

The whole walk along the southern shore is an excellent one for people who like to stretch their legs and work a bit for

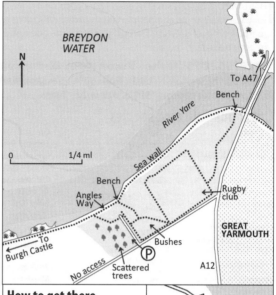

How to get there

(On the edge of Great Yarmouth).

SAT NAV: NR31 0AY.

GPS: 52.607706; 1.710561.

Take the A47 into Great Yarmouth. At the first roundabout, turn right onto the A12 (sign-posted Lowestoft).

Go to the next roundabout and turn 180 degrees (going back towards Yarmouth). In 0.7 miles, turn left and drive down this un-named lane for 0.2 miles to the car park.

their birds. If you are like me however and you like the birds to come to you, this is a quiet little place to sit and see what turns up. I think Herbert Barnes would be proud such a place bears his name.

Other nearby sites

Berney Arms Marshes, Breydon Water, Burgh Castle, Great Yarmouth beach and cemeteries, Haddiscoe Marsh, Hardley Flood, Waveney Forest.

THIS NATIONAL NATURE RESERVE, a huge site comprising extensive reedbeds, wader scrapes, marshes and a few trees, is home to a wide range of bird and other wildlife species. It will take you the whole day if you wish to explore the area fully! In summer, a trip on the electric boat to usually inaccessible parts of Hickling is a must.

Target birds *All year* – **Marsh Harrier (95%), Bearded Tit (65%), Bittern (30%), Cetti's Warbler (hear 70%, see 20%), Crane (5% on reserve, 50% in general area).** *Winter* – **Smew (35%), winter raptors (25%).** *Summer* – **Hobby (80%), Avocet (75%), Garganey (25%), Yellow-legged Gull (20%).** *Spring/ autumn* – **Passage waders, passage terns.**

Other possible bird species

All year
Common wildfowl
Cormorant
Little Egret
Great Crested Grebe
Little Grebe
Sparrowhawk
Kestrel
Water Rail
Woodcock
Regular gull species
Barn Owl
Tawny Owl
Kingfisher
Green Woodpecker
Great Spotted
Woodpecker
Skylark
Jay
Other corvids
Marsh Tit
Meadow Pipit
Pied Wagtail

Redpoll
Common finches
Reed Bunting

Summer
Little Gull
Yellow-legged Gull
Common Tern
Turtle Dove
Cuckoo
Hirundines
Sedge Warbler
Reed Warbler
Grasshopper Warbler
Lesser Whitethroat
Whitethroat
Garden Warbler
Blackcap
Chiffchaff
Willow Warbler

Spring/autumn
Slavonian Grebe
Black-necked Grebe

Little Ringed Plover
Ringed Plover
Little Stint
Curlew Sandpiper
Dunlin
Ruff
Greenshank
Green Sandpiper
Wood Sandpiper
Common Sandpiper
Little Gull
Black Tern
Yellow Wagtail

Winter
Goldeneye
Winter thrushes

Occasional
Smew (winter)
Red-footed Falcon (spring)
Savi's Warbler (spring)

Background information and birding tips

HICKLING is my favourite Broadlands reserve because it never fails to deliver a great day of nature watching.

All trails start at the visitor centre. From there you have a choice of several paths and all can produce the goods. Any patch of thick cover on the reserve may hold a Cetti's Warbler or two; listen out for their explosive song. In summer, it is worth booking a boat trip in a traditional 'reed lighter' from the Norfolk Wildlife Trust's visitor centre upon your arrival. This warden-guided trip explores areas not normally open to visitors and is well worth the cost.

Key points

- **Reserve open every day, dawn to dusk.**

- **Reserve is a designated SSSI.**

- **Access by permit - pay at visitor centre.**

- **Visitor centre open daily between Easter and Sept (10am-5pm). From Oct open weekends and half-term only.**

- **Refreshments available from shop (plus books etc).**

- **Toilets, including wheelchair access.**

- **Extensive boardwalks. Other paths can get muddy after rain.**

- **Telescope useful.**

- **Most hides are wheelchair-friendly, but a circular route not available yet for wheelchair users.**

How to get there

(13 miles NE of Norwich).

SAT NAV: NR12 0BW (then follow 'brown duck' signs - from here follow signs to reserve car park).

For Rush Hill scrape public hide parking enter: Potter Heigham > Church Road.

GPS: 52.742189; 1.595232.

From Great Yarmouth head N towards North Walsham on A149. About one mile N of Potter Heigham turn right at the signpost to Hickling.

Follow to Hickling Green, then turn right at Greyhound pub (following brown tourist signs with a duck logo). Turn left about 300 yards past the pub, still following the brown duck signs. This leads down to the Norfolk Wildlife Trust's car park, about 1.5 miles from the pub.

To view Rush Hill scrape from The Weavers' Way footpath, park at Potter Heigham Church (TG 419 199, GPS 52.722352; 1.581126, NR29 5LL). This is reached by turning right (if approaching from Yarmouth) off the A149 down Station Road (sign-posted Village Hall & Church).

After 0.2 miles, turn right at the T-junction (School Road and Church Road). The church is 0.4 miles on the left. Park on the grass in front of the church.

Walk up Church Lane, keeping the church on your right side. After 100 yards, turn right along a farm track, marked by a wooden footpath sign. After 75 yards, bear left down a wide, uneven, grassy path.

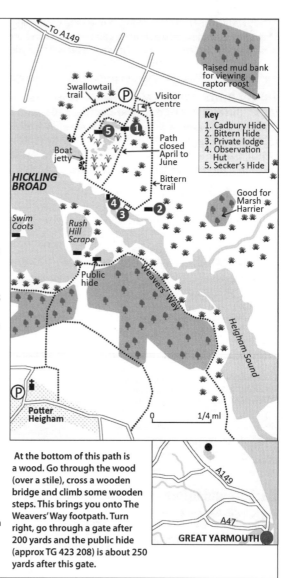

At the bottom of this path is a wood. Go through the wood (over a stile), cross a wooden bridge and climb some wooden steps. This brings you onto The Weavers' Way footpath. Turn right, go through a gate after 200 yards and the public hide (approx TG 423 208) is about 250 yards after this gate.

Key
1. Cadbury Hide
2. Bittern Hide
3. Private lodge
4. Observation Hut
5. Secker's Hide

There is nothing more pleasant on a hot day than cruising along the channels with the wind rustling the reeds and your hair (if, unlike me, you have any to rustle).

My normal summer route starts along the Bittern trail, accessed from the road immediately behind the visitor centre. It wends its way along a wide, sandy track to the Bittern hide (don't mistake the small boathouse for the hide as you will get your feet wet and see nothing)!

Along the way you should already have ticked off Reed, Sedge and Willow Warblers as well as Chiffchaff, Whitethroat and Reed Bunting and most probably Bearded Tit in the trackside reeds.

The Bittern hide (fully wheelchair-accessible) overlooks reeds that are good for Marsh Harriers, as well as Bitterns. The harriers are usually near the trees at the back of the marsh.

Be patient if you definitely want to see a Bittern: they usually show every couple of hours or so! While you are waiting, look out for dragonflies on the pond and there should be several Hobbies patrolling the sky above the dead trees in the distance (in recent years more than ten birds have been recorded, occasionally accompanied by a vagrant Red-footed Falcon).

The track continues to Whiteslea Lodge which is strictly private and is the summer home of the Cadbury family.

Bear right onto a rough grass path, which runs through bushes to the Observation Tower. This path is not yet wheelchair accessible – surely it can only be a matter of time before NWT join it with the boardwalk to make a circular route for wheelchair users.

From the tower you will get a good overview of the reeds and marsh but it is impossible to sit at the windows unless your legs are less than six inches long! You should see Marsh Harrier and Bearded Tit.

Where the rough grass path joins the boardwalk of the Swallowtail Trail, there is a short boardwalk leading to a viewing platform complete with screen, which offers a chance to scan Hickling Broad for waterfowl such as Tufted Duck, Great Crested Grebe, Mute Swan, Grey Heron, etc.

This is also a superb place to linger awhile to see what pops up. In one particular July I had a pair of Marsh Harriers food-passing, an adult Bearded Tit feeding a juvenile and a swallowtail butterfly all in the same field of view.

If you wish to go on a boat trip, they leave from a jetty near this boardwalk. On your trip, you will visit the Tree Tower, which is a metal structure giving superb views of the whole reserve. You should see Marsh Harrier from here but sufferers of vertigo should stay on solid ground.

On the boat trip, you will next visit either Swim Coots or Rush Hill Scrape. These parts of Hickling are similar in that you reach them via narrow, reed-fringed channels, good for Reed Warblers, swallowtail butterflies, Norfolk hawker dragonflies, etc.

Each has a single, thatched hide overlooking a scrape and both are good places to see Marsh Harrier, Garganey, Teal, Avocet, Yellow-legged Gull, Little Gull, breeding Black-headed Gull, Reed Warbler, Sedge Warbler and Reed Bunting.

Key points

• **Summer boat trips available May 18 to September 15 but booking essential (only way of reaching Swim Coots and Rush Hill Scrape).**

• **Free use of binoculars on board the boat.**

• **Close all gates.**

• **No dogs on reserve.**

Contacts

The Warden, Hickling Broad National Nature Reserve, Stubb Road, Hickling, Norfolk NR12 0BW.
01692 598 276.

The scrapes are also excellent places to encounter passage waders such as Little Stint and Green, Wood, Common and Curlew Sandpipers in both spring and autumn. The boat runs from mid-May to mid-September. Check with the visitor centre for details but prior booking is strongly advised, if not essential.

Rush Hill Scrape can be viewed from the Weavers' Way public footpath, accessed from Potter Heigham Church (see Access Section) and a basic hide affords satisfactory views. Sightings (among other things!) are sometimes chalked on the hide walls. A telescope is useful here.

Back on the main reserve, the boardwalk continues to the visitor centre, thus completing a circular route. Along the way, you may wish to visit one or both of the hides overlooking the pools (both of which are fully wheelchair-accessible) for the chance of more waders, usually the same range of species encountered on the boat trip.

Alternatively, from the jetty, you could retrace your steps towards the tower, then cut across a narrow grass path off to your left (closed April-June). This cuts through the marsh back to the hides and visitor centre.

In winter, the Hickling area is renowned for its raptors. These are best seen from the Stubb Mill roost (see Stubb Mill page196) but may be encountered anywhere on the reserve during the day.

By day, Hen Harriers, Merlins, Marsh Harriers and Peregrines patrol the extensive marshes and dunes in the area, spreading from Sea Palling in the north to Haddiscoe Marshes to the south. This means that they can be very elusive during the day but come in to roost about an hour before dark every evening.

The summer walk described above can seem quiet in winter but Bearded Tits should still show well during windless days. Cetti's Warblers sing occasionally when it is sunny and Bitterns sometimes fly over the reeds to new feeding areas.

If the pools are frozen, Bitterns may be seen feeding out in open areas and the Bittern hide is a very good place to watch from in these conditions.

Cranes are resident in the Hickling area but they are best seen at dusk from Stubb Mill or in fields around the Horsey Mere area. You may see one or two flying over Hickling reserve, usually betraying their presence by their evocative 'cronk, cronk' calls.

In recent winters, Hickling Broad has hosted one or two Smew among the common wildfowl. The Broad should be scanned for Tufted Duck, Goldeneye, Teal, Gadwall, Mallard, Pochard and Shoveler.

If you are unlucky, this place can seem deserted, especially in winter, but patience is usually rewarded with some very good birds at all times of year.

For me this is a fantastic reserve, not only for birds but also for people and other wildlife. The whole place abounds with animals, plants and insects, making it a 'must visit' destination for the all-round naturalist.

A visit to Hickling will not produce all the target species (unless you are very lucky) but there is always something to see.

Other nearby sites

Barton Broad, Breydon Water, Buckenham Marshes, Buxton Heath, Cockshoot Broad, Horsey area, How Hill NNR, Rockland Broad, Stubb Mill, Upton Fen, Winterton Dunes.

THIS QUINTESSENTIAL country estate holds many species of common woodland birds and is the best place to see Lesser Spotted Woodpecker in Norfolk. The park's lake is home to several species of waterfowl. The best birding habitat can be found along the waymarked Nature Trail but the more you explore the estate, the more you will find.

Target birds *All year* – **Lesser Spotted Woodpecker (spring 40%, rest of year 20%).** *Winter* – **Brambling (25%).**

Other possible bird species

All year	Barn Owl	Goldeneye
Egyptian Goose	Green Woodpecker	Winter thrushes
Other common wildfowl	Great Spotted	Grey Wagtail
Red-legged Partridge	Woodpecker	
Grey Partridge	Jay	*Summer*
Cormorant	Other corvids	Hobby
Common waterbirds	Skylark	Cuckoo
Great Crested Grebe	Common scrub birds	Hirundines
Little Grebe	Goldcrest	Warblers
Sparrowhawk	Marsh Tit	Spotted Flycatcher
Kestrel	Nuthatch	*Occasional*
Woodcock	Treecreeper	Honey Buzzard (passage)
Lapwing	Common woodland birds	Goshawk (passage)
Regular gull species	Meadow Pipit	Redstart (passage)
Stock Dove		Wood Warbler (passage)
Tawny Owl	*Winter*	Pied Flycatcher (passage)
	Pink-footed Goose	Hawfinch (winter)

Background information and birding tips

THE GROUNDS of Holkham Hall provide the visiting birdwatcher with some of the best woodland birding in Norfolk. It is worth spending a bit of time in the car park, as common birds visit the trees in the area. Walk right out of the car park along the access road and head for the imposing estate gates ahead.

Once through the gates, I like to head west (right) along the muddy path but not before scanning the ground beneath the trees along the main drive for finches (including Bramblings in winter).

Almost immediately, look into the garden on your right and scan the feeders. Nuthatches, Marsh Tits,

Great Spotted Woodpeckers and other common woodland birds should be much in evidence.

Continue along the muddy 'path', which leads to the 'Coke of Norfolk' Monument, checking the understory for feeding finches, tits, Green Woodpecker and winter thrushes, as you go. Don't forget to look up for woodland species such as Nuthatches, Treecreepers and Great Spotted Woodpeckers should all be present.

The monument is the best place to encounter Lesserpeckers; the ideal time is early spring (Feb – March) is the ideal time, as they will be displaying on fine days. Tawny Owls may be roosting in any

Key points

• Private estate with open access. Check website for specific park closure days.

• Mostly level terrain, mainly on muddy tracks or surfaced roads.

• Wheelchair access not possible on woodland paths.

• Deer Park is open daily 7am - 7pm in summer, (6pm in winter), closed Dec 25.

• Limited access to other parts of grounds – remain on designated routes.

• Facilities on site include toilets, a pottery, a café (open from Easter) and a public house.

• Map and info board just inside main pedestrian access gate.

• Nature trail starts near hall: leaflets in container by lake.

of these old trees, so keep your eyes peeled or listen for agitated small birds mobbing the owl: ones covered in ivy are the most likely sites.

At the monument, keep straight on along the grass path or turn left (slightly uphill) and you will find yourself at the lake. You can walk all around the lake and there are 28 information points along the route (leaflets can be obtained from the wooden holder by the lake near the hall, or download before you go from http://www.holkham.co.uk/downloads/NatureTrail.pdf).

The lake hosts Egyptian, Greylag and Canada Geese (occasionally joined by Pink-feet in winter), as well as Great Crested and Little Grebes (sometimes joined by one of the rarer grebes in winter).

Tufted Ducks, Pochards, Goldeneyes, Gadwall and Teal join the resident Mallards in winter (though some may linger throughout the year), and gulls come in to bathe at regular intervals.

Woodcock are present in the park grounds in excellent numbers but seeing one involves looking over the woods at dusk. You may come across one skulking in the leaf litter but this is unlikely.

In spring and summer, the woods are alive with bird activity. Summer warblers join the resident species and, if you are lucky, you might find a Pied Flycatcher, Redstart or Wood Warbler during spring migration times.

Blackcap, Willow Warbler, Chiffchaff and Whitethroat all breed on site. Another delightful summer visitor to the estate is Spotted Flycatcher; listen out

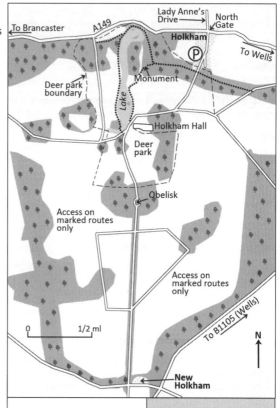

How to get there

(12 miles E of Hunstanton). SAT NAV: NR23 1RQ. GPS: 52.957011; 0.814663.

Holkham Hall's northern entrance is sign-posted to 'Holkham Hall, Bygones and Pottery' off A149 between Burnham Overy Staithe and Wells-Next-The-Sea.

Turn off the main road and follow the access road past the estate cottages to the car park about 300 yards on the right. This is free but can be muddy in winter.

Walk S (right) along access road through the estate's main gates.

My most productive walk is on the muddy track W to the lake through an area of mature woodland.

for their call which sounds like a squeaky wheelbarrow.

The south side of the park is usually the least disturbed by people. Hawfinches are occasionally seen in the trees along the long, straight access road to the south entrance. Most of the species mentioned above should also be in evidence. Be aware though that public access is strictly limited to connected roads in this area of the park.

Several trails zigzag around the estate, (marked by different colours), including Park Trail, Lake Trail and Farm Trail.

Each trail has a downloadable leaflet on the website or there is a large map at the north entrance gates (take a photo when you arrive in case there are no leaflets in the containers or at the hall!). If you still haven't had enough, you can extend your walk down to Holkham Pines NNR!

Key points
• **Free parking.**

• **Can get busy with tourists in summer.**

• **Early morning is best.**

• **Also visit the house and garden centre.**

• **Dogs on leads at all times.**

An early spring visit to the grounds of Holkham Hall will provide one of your best opportunities to see elusive Lesser Spotted Woodpeckers.

Contacts
The Site Manager
Hill Farm Office
Main Road,
Holkham,
Wells-next-the-Sea,
Norfolk NR23 1AB
01328 710 227;
e-mail: enquiries@holkham.co.uk
www.holkham.co.uk/html/park_01.html

107

Key points

- Reserve open at all times (gates close at 9pm on Fridays and Saturdays in summer).

- Pay-and-display car parking on Lady Anne's Drive.

- Two hides (wheelchair access to one), plus two viewing platforms on sea side of dunes.

- Several bench seats along track to Washington Hide.

- Tracks and boardwalks are flat. Saltings reached across a beach, wet mud and vegetation.

- Woodland paths can be narrow and steepish.

- Leaflet available from dispenser in car park.

Contacts

Site Manager
01328 711 183
www.holkham.co.uk/
naturereserve/

PROBABLY my favourite birding spot in winter, with the possibility of geese close to the access track, Shore Larks on the saltings and general panic spread by a passing winter raptor. In summer, Spoonbills and waders breed and who knows what might turn up at passage times. In short, this National Nature Reserve is alive with birds and other rare and scarce wildlife.

Target birds

All year – **Marsh Harrier (90%).** *Winter* – **Pink-footed Goose (99%), Snow Bunting (90%), seaduck (80%), White-fronted Goose (60%), Shore Lark (60%), winter raptors (50%), divers (50%).** *Spring/autumn* – **Passage migrants.** *Breeding season* – **Spoonbill (90%).**

Other possible bird species

All year	Jay	Terns
Egyptian Goose	Skylark	Avocet
Shelduck	Siskin	Common waders
Little Egret	Redpoll	Cuckoo
Grey Partridge	Reed Bunting	Hirundines
Red-legged Partridge		Spotted Flycatcher
Little Grebe	*Spring/autumn (might include)*	
Sparrowhawk	Wryneck)	*Winter*
Kestrel	Bluethroat	Brent Goose
Lapwing	Black Redstart	Wigeon
Snipe	Redstart	Teal
Woodcock	Whinchat	Common waders
Redshank	Wheatear	Rock Pipit
Water Rail	Grasshopper Warbler (passage)	Stonechat
Barn Owl		Winter thrushes
Tawny Owl	Barred Warbler	
Green Woodpecker	Firecrest	*Occasional*
Great Spotted Woodpecker	Red-breasted Flycatcher	Bean Goose (winter)
Treecreeper	Pied Flycatcher	Barnacle Goose (winter)
Common woodland birds		Rough-legged Buzzard (winter)
Common scrub birds	*Summer*	Bearded Tit
	Hobby	Crossbill
		Twite (winter)

Background information and birding tips

THOUGH Holkham National Nature Reserve (owned by the Earl of Leicester and the Crown Estates and managed by Natural England and Holkham Estate) is an excellent site for all kinds of nature, it is also popular with humans.

However, once on the reserve in summer it is easy to get away from the crowds as they are more interested in the beach than the marsh, which is overlooked by a hide.

In winter, Holkham is a superb place to encounter wild geese at close range. Slowly cruise down Lady Anne's Drive, scanning the fields either side for geese. Pinkfeet seem to prefer the first few fields, while the White-fronts seem to favour the fields at the far end. Either way, watch the birds from your car as they can easily be spooked.

Scan the goose flocks carefully, as regular interminglers include Barnacle, Bean, Greylag and Egyptian Geese, while Lesser White-fronted, small race Canada and Red-breasted are also possibilities for the alert birder. Among the geese will be large numbers of Wigeon.

For those birdwatchers who like hides, wander left at the gate at the bottom of Lady Anne's Drive. The sandy track will take you to the George Washington hide, where you can 'scope the geese and Wigeon flocks on the marsh.

The pools here will also hold common ducks such as Mallard, Gadwall, Pochard, Shoveler, Teal and Tufted Duck. Also look out for Curlew, Golden Plover, Lapwing, Snipe and Redshank.

At the rear of Washington Hide is a boardwalk that leads to a viewing platform overlooking the west end of the saltings. It provides the best place for wheelchair users to scan for Snow Buntings, pipits and larks, etc. Though these species tend to favour the eastern end, they occasionally wander west.

There is always the possibility of a raptor flying over the marsh too. Regular species include Peregrine, Merlin, Hen Harrier, Kestrel and Sparrowhawk, with Barn Owl and Short-eared Owl also possible.

From the Washington hide, walk either along a boardwalk to the beach, then turn right back to Holkham Gap for the winter finches, larks and buntings (see

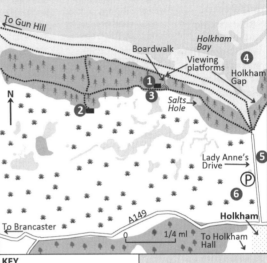

KEY
1 - George Washington Hide
2 - Joe Jordan Hide
3 - Meols House
4 - Snow Bunting area at low tide.
5 & 6 - Fields for geese.

How to get there
(13.5 miles E of Hunstanton).

SAT NAV: NR23 1RJ (postcode for A149 near Holkham Hall's main gate).

GPS: 52.966552; 0.814241.

From A149 between Burnham Overy Staithe and Wells-next-the-Sea, turn down Lady Anne's Drive towards the sea (opposite the brown tourist sign to the Pottery

below) or continue on past Meols House to the Joe Jordan hide.

At the point where the main track turns into a grass path, turn left down a very narrow path through the bracken, to the Jordan hide. Access is

and Holkham Hall). Parking is permitted all along this road, on the verges.

Follow the boardwalk to the Gap or turn left along a sandy track to the hides. For this guide, I have classed the sandy track to the right as Wells Woods.

up steep steps, so it is not suitable for wheelchair users.

This hide also looks out over Holkham Marsh but at a slightly different angle. Look straight out from here and you will see a raised, grassy ridge. This is the remains of an Iron

109

Key points

- **Bike parking rails behind Washington Hide and at Holkham Gap viewing platform.**

- **Telescope very useful.**

- **Use insect repellent in summer.**

- **Do not touch any strange objects on the beach – unexploded missiles turn up occasionally.**

- **Keep dogs under close control at all times.**

Age Fort. Beyond the ridge is a small pool with a dead tree at one end. This tree should hold several Little Egrets and Cormorants.

In recent winters Holkham Gap has become a reliable site to see Shorelarks and Snow Bunting but Twite have been very scarce. Their feeding area is reached from the car park by walking along the boardwalk straight ahead to the beach (about 300 yards). There is a viewing platform here but the birds tend to be further out in the short vegetation that is uncovered when the tide retreats.

Head right from the boardwalk along the beach/mud (you can walk as far as Wells Harbour if you wish) and scan the area. Wheelchair users may scan the saltings from this viewing platform, though the birds will almost certainly be too far away to identify!

Also note that when sand has been blown over the boardwalk it will make wheelchair access to the platform difficult.

Walking boots or Wellingtons are recommended as you may need to walk across the saltings to find the birds. I am not advocating flushing these flocks but if you wander a few yards then scan, wander and scan, then you should get good views without disturbing the birds.

The Snow Buntings and Shorelarks will be so busy feeding that if you stay still they will probably edge closer to you.

Other common birds here can include Greenfinch, Goldfinch, Meadow Pipit, Skylark

and Pied Wagtail and you should also see a Rock Pipit or two. Raptors such as Peregrine and Merlin regularly sweep across the saltings in pursuit of the feeding birds.

If you walk to the raised grassy dune at the back of the saltings you can obtain reasonable views of winter seabirds such as Red-breasted Merganser, Eider, scoters, Goldeneye, Great Crested Grebe, Slavonian Grebe and Red-throated Diver.

In some years, seaducks congregate here in impressive numbers, but can be scarce in others. When many birds are on the sea, scan the flocks carefully, as King Eider and Surf Scoters have been found along the coast!

Dunlin, Sanderling, Turnstone and other waders should also be encountered in the saltings and on the beach.

In summer, Holkham Gap is of very little interest to birdwatchers as the area is badly disturbed by beach-loving holiday makers. I suggest you walk left along the sandy track from the car park to the hides. Along the track, you will get good views of species such as Wren, Long-tailed Tit, Blackbird, Blackcap, Whitethroat, Willow Warbler and Chiffchaff.

Always check the first pond on your left as a pair of Little Grebes is usually present. In the reeds and scrub by the hide you should see Reed and Sedge Warblers and maybe even a Bearded Tit. The pools hold breeding ducks such as Gadwall, Tufted Duck, Shoveler and Pochard as well as Coot and Moorhen.

Marsh Harriers regularly hunt over the marsh and may give closer views from the Jordan hide. Avocets, Lapwings, Redshanks, Snipe, Shelduck, Oystercatchers, Skylarks, Yellow Wagtails etc can all be seen on the marsh but can be distant.

Large numbers of Swifts, Swallows and House Martins hunt over the pools, sometimes swooping over you along the path. Hobbies sometimes hunt here too.

In recent years, Spoonbills have bred at Holkham and these are best seen from the Joe Jordan hide. After fledging (July), the family parties soon begin to wander, usually to Cley Marshes and back.

While non-birders are building sand castles on the pristine beach, you can watch Sandwich, Common and Little Terns fishing in the sea. The latter species sometimes nest on the beach, so watch out for any fenced-off areas. However, most seem to have moved to Gun Hill to the west, a long walk along the beach for humans but a mere minute's flight for a tern!

In spring and autumn, the woods and dunes hold the greatest attraction. These areas attract migrants freshly arrived from the continent. Regular spring arrivals include Whinchats, Wheatears, Ring Ouzels, Goldcrests and various warblers.

Autumn seems to be the best time to find Pied Flycatchers, Wood Warblers and Redstarts in the woods, along with some scarcer visitors such as Firecrests, Red-breasted Flycatchers and Yellow-browed Warblers.

This is a (if not *the*) prime site for Pallas's Warbler. These Siberian jewels usually join up with roving tit flocks which follow circuits through the woods. So, rather than trying to follow the birds, stay in one place and wait for them to come to you. Meols House is a good spot.

Wrynecks are relatively frequent visitors to the dunes. Rarities include Dusky and Radde's Warblers and Britain's one and only Red-breasted Nuthatch! There is often an influx of continental Jays in autumn as well as Woodcock.

There are many paths criss-crossing the woods and dunes, which offer the visiting birdwatcher ample opportunity to find their own special birds at migration time. Please stick to these paths though, as the dunes and woods are home to other rare and scarce wildlife such as the natterjack toad. A walk eastwards will bring you to Wells Woods (page 224).

Birding interest at this National Nature Reserve is high throughout the year and in autumn you may see a Redstart, just one of the many passerines that pass through on passage.

Key points

- **SSSI owned by the Norfolk Ornithologists' Association.**
- **Get permit from NOA Office. Fee for non-members. NOA permit doesn't cover neighbouring NWT reserve.**
- **Dawn to dusk access for NOA members (track access gate is unlocked at all times). Non-members 9am to 5pm.**
- **Five hides and a viewing platform; two of the former and the latter are wheelchair friendly.**
- **Blue Badge parking. Boardwalk and flat path to hides /office.**

Contacts

Norfolk Ornithologists' Association
01485 525 406; e-mail: infonoa@btinternet.com
www.noa.org.uk/

HOME OF NORFOLK'S only accredited observatory, Holme is a delight to visit at any time of year. There is a seawatching hide, an extensive marsh, a stretch of freshwater and during passage times the bushes on the reserve can be crawling with migrants. As well as common species, rarities are always a possibility.

Target birds *All year* – **Marsh Harrier (90%), Barn Owl (85%).** *Summer* – **Black-tailed Godwit (90%), Avocet (80%).** *Spring/ autumn* – **Passage migrants (80%).** *Winter* – **Winter raptors (35%).**

Other possible bird species

All year	Sedge Warbler	Wheatear
Fulmar	Reed Warbler	Yellow Wagtail
Cormorant	Whitethroat	
Little Grebe	Blackcap	*Winter*
Great Crested Grebe	Other warblers	Pink-footed Goose
Peregrine	Spotted Flycatcher	Brent Goose
Sparrowhawk		Wigeon
Kestrel	*Spring/autumn*	Teal
Red-legged Partridge	*(might include)*	Goldeneye
Grey Partridge	Shearwaters	Red-breasted Merganser
Oystercatcher	Gannet	Hen Harrier
Lapwing	Skuas	Divers
Tawny Owl	Kittiwake	Grebes
Great Spotted	Terns	Golden Plover
Woodpecker	Auks	Grey Plover
Goldcrest	Wryneck	Winter thrushes
Treecreeper	Red-backed Shrike	Siskin
Reed Bunting	Redstart	
	Barred Warbler	*Occasional*
Summer	Yellow-browed Warbler	Hobby (spring/autumn)
Terns	Firecrest	Grasshopper Warbler (spring/summer)
Cuckoo	Red-breasted Flycatcher	Merlin (winter)
Hirundines	Pied Flycatcher	Short-eared Owl (winter)
	Whinchat	

Background information and birding tips

THIS SMALL reserve attracts migrants by the mist net full in spring and autumn. Ringing takes place all year round and you may be lucky to witness birds being ringed at the observatory when you visit.

You should be observant all the way along the access track to the grass car park, as the fields to your right are one of the best places in Norfolk to see Barn Owl at all times of year.

Park in the roped-off grass car park **to the right of the track and not by the white house on the left.** Follow the Shrike signs to the entrance of the NOA reserve, to the right of the white house. Before doing any more birding, obtain your permit from the Observatory office situated along the only path on the reserve.

In spring and autumn, a spell in the seawatching hide could prove a profitable starting point, provided you are able to negotiate the steep flight of steps. Obtain a key for this hide from the Observatory office. The best time for seawatching is at high tide when the birds will be much closer. And don't ignore this hide in winter, as this stretch of coast is excellent for divers and seaduck.

There are also two hides along the footpath to the Observatory office, both overlooking a sheltered 'valley'

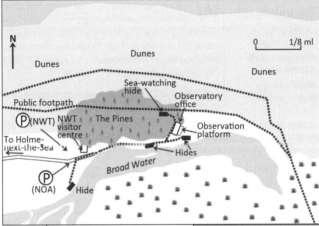

populated by thick bushes. In spring and autumn, sit quietly in one of these hides and you will be amazed at what pops out of the thick cover. The sun seems to catch this spot in the afternoons and due to the shelter of the surrounding pines, the area is highly attractive to tired migrants. Spend as long here as you can.

The only other hide on the NOA reserve overlooks Broadwater and the marsh beyond. This is a good place to watch breeding waders in spring and summer. Avocets and Black-tailed Godwits are virtually guaranteed at these times. In winter, watch out for raptors and wildfowl.

Broadwater itself holds common wildfowl species and Reed and Sedge Warblers can be seen in the surrounding vegetation in summer. Marsh Harriers quarter the marsh at most times of year.

A wheelchair-accessible viewing platform adjacent to the Obs Office affords excellent views across the marshes to the ridge. Keep an eye open for visible migration (vis-mig) over

How to get there

(Two miles NE of Hunstanton).

SAT NAV: PE36 6LQ (postcode for entrance track) or Holme-next-the-Sea> Broadwater Road

GPS: 52.973718; 0.551067.

From Hunstanton head E for two miles on A149 to left turn (sign-posted NOA Watchpoint/NNT Reserve). Continue on this road for about half a mile, then turn right onto a rough track just before you reach the toilet block (use these as there are no facilities on site). Drive slowly as track is very bumpy.

Pass through the entrance gate to the NWT and NOA reserve, telling the person in the hut

you are only visiting the NOA part of Holme. If you intend visiting the NWT part of the reserve, you MUST purchase a separate permit.

Follow the gravel track down to the end and park on the right in the roped-off grass car park. Do not park by the white house unless you have purchased a permit for the NWT reserve.

this ridge. The longer you stay here, the more you are likely to see!

Other nearby sites

Blakeney Point, Cley Marshes, Holkham NNR, Kelling Quags, Kelling Heath, Salthouse Beach, Salthouse Heath, Swanton Novers, Walsey Hills, Wells Woods.

Key points

- **Access by permit: NWT members and children free, adult non-members pay fee. Permits from access track hut or NWT visitor centre.**

- **Open 10am – 5pm every day except Christmas Day.**

- **Visitor centre open 10am – 5pm from Easter to October & weekends from Nov – March**

- **Footpath to beach along dunes and open at all times.**

- **Toilets at the start of rough access track.**

- **The visitor centre sells books, snacks and drinks (no toilet here).**

- **Three hides on Holme Marsh.**

Contacts

NWT Holme Dunes
01485 525 240

WHILE Holme Dunes has a proven track record of attracting rare, scarce and common migrants in spring and autumn, there is something to see at all times of year. It is probably the best site in the county to see resident Barn Owls, wintering Long-tailed Ducks and breeding Lesser Whitethroats. It could take you a whole day to cover this site properly, especially at migration times.

Target birds *All year* – **Marsh Harrier (85%), Barn Owl (85%).** *Summer* – **Black-tailed Godwit (90%), Avocet (80%), Little Tern (75%).** *Spring/autumn* – **Passage migrants, passage waders.** *Winter* – **Long-tailed Duck (75%), Snow Bunting (70%).**

Other possible bird species

All year
Fulmar
Cormorant
Little Egret
Little Grebe
Great Crested Grebe
Sparrowhawk
Kestrel
Oystercatcher
Lapwing
Ringed Plover
Turnstone
Tawny Owl
Great Spotted
Woodpecker
Corvids
Skylark
Goldcrest
Nuthatch
Treecreeper
Meadow Pipit
Pied Wagtail
Bullfinch
Reed Bunting

Summer
Hobby
Common Tern
Little Tern
Sandwich Tern
Cuckoo
Hirundines
Sedge Warbler

Reed Warbler
Whitethroat
Lesser Whitethroat
Blackcap
Grasshopper Warbler
Other warblers
Spotted Flycatcher

Spring/autumn
(might include)
Garganey
Shearwaters
Gannet
Little Ringed Plover
Little Stint
Ruff
Whimbrel
Greenshank
Green Sandpiper
Wood Sandpiper
Common Sandpiper
Skuas
Kittiwake
Terns
Auks
Long-eared Owl
Wryneck
Red-backed Shrike
Barred Warbler
Yellow-browed
Warbler
Firecrest
Ring Ouzel

Winter thrushes
Redstart
Whinchat
Wheatear
Red-breasted
Flycatcher
Pied Flycatcher
Richard's Pipit
Tawny Pipit
Yellow Wagtail

Winter
Brent Goose
Wigeon
Teal
Common Scoter
Velvet Scoter
Goldeneye
Red-breasted Merganser
Divers
Grebes
Merlin
Peregrine
Hen Harrier
Short-eared Owl
Golden Plover
Grey Plover
Knot
Stonechat
Winter thrushes
Siskin

How to get there

(Two miles NE of Hunstanton).

SAT NAV: PE36 6LQ.

GPS: 52.974320; 0.551907.

Holme Dunes: From Hunstanton head E. Take next left turn off A149, (sign-posted NOA Watchpoint/NNT Reserve). After about half a mile turn right onto a rough track just before you reach the toilet block (if you need the facilities, go now as there are none on site). Travel slowly down this very rough track to avoid car damage and park on left by the visitor centre (the white house). The hides are accessed by walking back past the NOA grass car park, the beach is along the footpath through the pines.

Holme Marsh: Heading E into

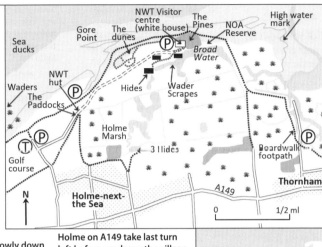

Holme on A149 take last turn left before you leave the village (Eastgate Road). Along this road bear right (signed to 'Sunnymead Holiday Park'). Park carefully by the concrete bollards after about 100 yards. Take the kissing gate to your right and follow the obvious path to the three hides overlooking a pool and bushes.

Background information and birding tips

WHERE do you start with a site as good as this designated SSSI managed by Norfolk Wildlife Trust? There are numerous access points to view the reserve, all of which produce good birds at most times of year. Here I will describe the key areas worth exploring:

Gore Point: This is an excellent place to see seaduck in winter, particularly at high tide. Park by the toilet block (pay and display) near the golf course and then walk across the golf course (watch out for stray golf balls and obey all course officials' instructions), through the dunes and onto the beach.

Gore Point is to your right. Long-tailed Duck is a speciality here but there may be thousands of Common Scoter on the sea as well.

Directly to the left of the junction of the

beach and golf course, a receding tide reveals a small marsh, which is a haven for waders. If you approach quietly and slowly, you will obtain stunningly close views of Knot, Dunlin, Sanderling, Bar-tailed Godwit, etc. Good fieldcraft is needed to avoid disturbing these waders as they busily feed on the saltings.

If you are lucky, you may find the small flock of Snow Buntings on the beach in winter, though these birds roam far and wide. In summer, several species of wader nest on the raised shingle bank by the beach, so take care not to disturb them.

Little Terns occasionally nest here too. If they don't, you will still see them out to sea, along with Common and Sandwich Terns. Please be aware that the tides and currents along this

115

Key points

- **Four hides at eastern end of main reserve.**

- **Boots recommended for Holme Marsh.**

- **Keep dogs under control or on a short lead to avoid disturbance to livestock and wildlife.**

- **Terrain is mainly level along rough tracks, grass paths and boardwalks.**

- **Limited wheelchair access.**

- **Stick to paths to avoid dune erosion.**

- **Report unusual sightings at Holme Marsh to gary.aitch@ norfolkwildlife trust.org.uk (+ sightings books in each hide).**

coast have claimed many a life.

The Paddocks: In spring and autumn, head for The Paddocks. Drive along the rough access track and park just past the warden's hut. Walk up the bank onto the dune footpath boardwalk and turn left. After about 100 yards there is a field on your left with many thick bushes scattered around.

Do not enter the Paddocks but view from the perimeter fence. Wait patiently for birds to appear out of the thick cover: possibilities include Ring Ouzel, Barred Warbler, Red-backed Shrike, Redstart, Pied Flycatcher, Turtle Dove, etc. The Paddocks also attract Wheatear in spring and autumn.

If you keep walking left, you reach the golf course and dunes, which may hold pipits and larks. Do not trespass onto the golf course, as the budding Tiger Woods become very grumpy.

The dunes: You may follow the boardwalk east from the beach car park all the way to the NWT visitor centre and the area of pines. If you choose to walk, scan the dunes and bushes regularly for anything that moves! Do not stray from the paths as you might trample a natterjack toad or a scarce plant or two.

Alternatively, once you have scanned The Paddocks, drive down the track and park by the white house at the end which is the NWT visitor centre. The roped-off grass car park on the right is for visitors to the adjoining NOA Holme Observatory site only.

The pines: These are at the back of the NWT visitor centre and attract migrants during spring and autumn. Regular drop-ins include Pied and Spotted Flycatchers, Redstarts, Firecrests and Crossbills

while Red-breasted Flycatchers and Yellow-browed Warblers are autumn specialities. Again, check the surrounding dunes for pipits, larks and Wrynecks.

The wader scrapes: These are reached by walking from the NWT visitor centre, past the NOA car park then bearing immediately left down a wheelchair-accessible track. The bushes along here hold Sedge Warblers in summer, along with common scrub birds.

The first hide is wheelchair-friendly but the path beyond becomes rough grass. The hides overlook a couple of scrapes made famous as the site of the first Norfolk breeding record of Black-winged Stilt.

Spring and autumn should produce a number of species including Greenshank, Whimbrel, Green Sandpiper and Ruff. In summer, you may get very close views of Avocet and Black-tailed Godwit.

Holme Marsh: This is an excellent place to see Barn Owl and Lesser Whitethroat. The three hides (with cushions!) overlook a pool surrounded by bushes, home to Whitethroat, Blackcap, Sedge Warbler and Lesser Whitethroat. The latter species tend to show well from these hides. The large tree to the left of the first hide is a favoured perch of the local Barn Owl.

If you don't see an owl here walk back to the road and follow the public footpath (a rough, wide track) to the right. The path ends at a gate (do not go over the gate) and overlooks several fields, which, with patience, are almost certain to produce a Barn Owl sighting.

AS WELL AS BEING one of the best places in Norfolk for raptors, Horsey is also one of the few places in Britain where you might see Cranes during the year. Incorporating Horsey Mill, Horsey Mere and Horsey Gap, this is a large area to cover, but there is usually much to see.

Target birds
All year – **Marsh Harrier (90%), Crane (60%), Bearded Tit (30%), Bittern (15%).** *Winter* – **Hen Harrier (50%), Merlin (25%).** *Summer* – **Hobby (30%).** *Spring/autumn* – **Passage migrants.**

Other possible bird species

All year
Common wildfowl
Cormorant
Common waterbirds
Grey Heron
Little Egret
Little Grebe
Great Crested Grebe
Sparrowhawk
Kestrel
Lapwing
Common waders
Regular gull species
Barn Owl
Green Woodpecker
Jay
Skylark
Stonechat
Meadow Pipit
Pied Wagtail
Common finches
Reed Bunting

Winter
Bewick's Swan
Whooper Swan
Pink-footed Goose
Long-tailed Duck
Red-breasted Merganser
Common Scoter
Velvet Scoter
Red-throated Diver
Slavonian Grebe
Red-necked Grebe
Winter thrushes

Summer
Hobby
Sandwich Tern
Common Tern
Little Tern
Hirundines
Sedge Warbler
Reed Warbler
Grasshopper Warbler
Other warblers

Spring/autumn might include
Manx Shearwater
Balearic Shearwater
Gannet
Arctic Skua
Little Gull
Ring Ouzel
Redstart
Whinchat
Wheatear
Firecrest
Pied Flycatcher
Yellow Wagtail

Scarce passage migrants
Wryneck
Red-backed Shrike
Woodchat Shrike
Red-breasted Flycatcher
Firecrest
Bluethroat
Yellow-browed Warbler

Occasional
Short-eared Owl

Background information and birding tips

THOUGH a large area to cover, Horsey can be well worth the effort at any time of year but, as winter is the most exciting from a birdwatching point of view, that's where I will start.

The main targets in winter are raptors and Cranes. The small, resident Crane population roams widely during the day but the birds have several favourite areas. These include the fields around Brograve Farm (TG 444 242), Walnut Farm (TG 452 246) and Horsey Mill itself.

I have found the best place for Cranes (and raptors) is the pull-in on the right 0.6 miles to the south of Horsey Mill on the B1159.

If you wait in your car for a while (the longer the better) you should

Key

1. Pillbox good for Stonechat
2. Mooring
3. Boat trips leave from here
4. Viewpoint for wheelchair users
5. Lay-by for raptor watching

How to get there

(Ten miles N of Yarmouth).

SAT NAV: NR29 4EF (postcode close to Horsey Mill on B1159 – then follow brown tourist signs to Horsey Mill (or Windpump).

Horsey Mill: The car park is between Stalham and Martham on B1159, a loop road to the coast off A149 between Great Yarmouth and North Walsham/Stalham. The main Horsey Mill car park is well sign-posted on brown tourist signs about two miles N of West Somerton.

Horsey Gap: Exactly one mile N of Horsey Mill car park. Heading N on B1159, there is a sharp left bend with a very rough track to the right. This track leads to a large beach car park with access to coast and dunes.

see Crane, Hen Harrier, Barn Owl and Marsh Harrier, and possibly Short-eared Owl and Merlin.

Keep a watch on the surrounding fields as raptors and Cranes appear as if out of thin air and usually vanish just as quickly! If you miss any of the above species during the day, visit Stubb Mill in the evening for almost guaranteed views of them.

Also along this road from Horsey Mill to West Somerton, you may find small numbers of Bewick's or Whooper Swans but I haven't seen any during numerous visits in recent winters.

The wintering Pink-footed Goose flock seems to be becoming more elusive too but again, scan the fields thoroughly along the B1159. They are usually seen in flight, either side of the road in the morning and at dusk.

Fancy stretching your legs? Well, you have

118

a couple of choices. Park in Horsey Mill car park, and then cross the main road along the permissive footpath directly to the dunes.

Scan the fields on the way for Cranes and raptors plus winter thrushes, Meadow Pipits, Skylarks and waders. Once you have reached the dunes, you can walk left or right along the footpath, or down to the sea. Left is to Horsey Gap, right is to Winterton Dunes.

Horsey Gap is good for seaduck such as Long-tailed Ducks, Red-breasted Mergansers, Common and Velvet Scoters, or scarcer grebes such as Slavonian and Red-necked. You should also get reasonable views here of Red-throated Divers.

Along the dune footpath, you will almost certainly encounter one or two handsome Stonechats: the derelict pillbox seems to be a favoured perch. A few Snow Buntings may be present on the beach during some winters.

Of course, you can also gain access to the coast by parking in the Horsey Gap car park (see Access section) and this may be a wise alternative in bitterly cold weather!

Alternatively, from the mill car park, you can walk past the mill to a viewpoint over the mere and reeds. This is an excellent place for wheelchair users to scan for raptors, Cranes, Bitterns, wildfowl and Bearded Tits.

The viewpoint is part of the new 'Easy Access' network of trails. The longer you sit here, the more you will see, with Marsh Harrier being virtually guaranteed.

Across the dyke from the viewpoint is a narrow, muddy footpath running along the northern edge of Horsey Mere, accessed from the mill car park. Along this path, you cross a rough field, before going up a couple of steps to a raised bank. This does not give views over the mere but is a suitable place to wait for raptors and Cranes coming in to roost, though not as productive as Stubb Mill.

This footpath continues to Horsey Corner, from where you can get back to the car park by taking either the road, or the dune footpath via Horsey Gap. The choice is yours.

The centre of attention at times of spring and autumn passage will be the dunes (as far south as Winterton and as far north as Sea Palling). I suggest you park in the Horsey Gap car park and explore the dunes and bushes as far as your energy levels allow.

Wheatears are seen regularly, as early as mid to late March, with Ring Ouzels not far behind. Bushes should be scanned for Redstarts, Wrynecks, Pied Flycatchers, Goldcrests, warblers, Whinchats, Tree Pipits, Red-backed Shrikes, etc. Anything is possible, so keep your eyes peeled.

Whimbrels may be passing overhead or stopping off in the fields around the dunes. Marsh Harriers will almost certainly be seen but Hen Harrier sightings drop off during these periods. Barn Owl is another resident species that can still be seen in the fields and dunes at these times.

Key points

- **Boats for hire in summer from shop at mill.**

- **One-hour boat trips from Horsey Staithe (near Mill). Book in advance or write name on chalkboard at end of mooring channel. Signposted from Mill car park. Wheelchair-users can be accommodated if booked in advance.**

- **Telescope recommended.**

- **Obtain footpath map from shop.**

At sea, the wintering ducks will be departing, being replaced by Little, Sandwich and Common Terns. In autumn, the ducks return and the terns may well be harassed by passing skuas. All four species are recorded annually, though Arctic Skua is the most common.

Other possible passage birds at sea include Razorbill, Guillemot, Manx and Balearic Shearwaters, Kittiwake and Little Gull.

Summer is probably the quietest time to pay a visit. Marsh Harriers usually show well in the fields across the road from Horsey Mill but the Cranes will be very elusive.

On Horsey Mere itself, Common Terns are very active and noisy, while common wildfowl and Great Crested Grebes can be seen at close range. You can do this from your Broadland boat (if it is small enough to negotiate Potter Heigham bridge!), a hired boat (from Horsey Mill) or from the dedicated wildlife boat trips which leave at regular intervals from near Horsey Mill.

I heartily recommend the latter boat, which is captained by a knowledgeable and entertaining local wildlife guide. The last time I went on this trip it was raining so hard it almost wrecked the canvas roof of the boat! However, I was treated to incredibly close views of several Marsh Harriers, Hobbies, Common Terns, Reed Buntings and Reed Warblers, etc and a couple of swallowtail butterfly caterpillars.

A Bittern also flew over the boat and remained in view for five minutes as it flew up the river. Every trip will be different but there is always something to see.

Reed and Sedge Warblers are common around the Mere and hirundines sweep across the car park, dodging the visitors as they go. Swallows even nest in the thatched toilet block in the car park. At this time of year they are sometimes pursued by a Hobby or two.

In the dunes, Stonechats are raising their families. Grasshopper Warblers can be heard reeling from nearby bushes but are hard to locate. Whitethroats and Reed Buntings are busily feeding their young and usually show well in the bushes along the dune footpath and around the Horsey Gap car park.

At sea, terns are constantly coming and going, while Ringed Plovers trot along the beach. Also look out for grey seals offshore.

The dunes in summer attract a wide range of scarce species including grass snake, natterjack toad, emperor dragonfly, Essex skipper and dark green fritillary and also many different varieties of plants. The all-round naturalist could spend the whole day in the dunes area of Horsey alone!

The sheer variety of species to be seen is worth the effort of covering this extensive area. In winter, I tend to drive around, scanning for birds, or pull over and wait for an hour or two at a good vantage point.

In times of passage, it can be an exciting place to explore to find your own birds – concentrate on hedgerows and bushes and you may strike lucky.

Though most famous as a winter site, Horsey is well placed to attract a wide variety of small birds, such as Firecrest, on passage in spring and autumn.

HOVETON GREAT BROAD National Nature Reserve is a scenic site reached by Broadland boat or by a small ferry from Salhouse Broad car park. From April to September, the reserve is packed with birds, flowers and insects, making it an excellent site for the all-round naturalist.

Target birds *May to July* – **Common Tern (95%).** *All year* – **Marsh Tit (60%), Marsh Harrier (20%), Cetti's Warbler (hear 70%, see 15%).**

Other possible bird species

All year	*Great Spotted Woodpecker*	Hirundines
Gadwall	Jay	Sedge Warbler
Teal	Goldcrest	Reed Warbler
Other common wildfowl	Long-tailed Tit	Blackcap
Great Crested Grebe	Other common	Chiffchaff
Cormorant	woodland birds	Willow Warbler
Common waterfowl	Treecreeper	*Occasional*
Buzzard	Pied Wagtail	Osprey
Kingfisher	*Summer*	Red Kite
Green Woodpecker	Cuckoo	Hobby

Background information and birding tips

THE FIRST THING to note is that the Salhouse Broad walk is open all year round, but Hoveton Great Broad is only open from Easter to September.

From the Salhouse car park, follow the marked path (near the toilet block) downhill through woodland. Though hard-standing all the way to the privately-owned Salhouse Broad quay, there are muddy bits which wheelchairs may struggle to cross.

This stretch of wood is full of resident birds such as Marsh Tits, Cetti's Warblers, Great Spotted Woodpeckers and Treecreepers, joined by Spotted Flycatchers, Chiffchaffs, Willow Warblers, Garden Warblers and Blackcaps in spring and summer. There is a boardwalk that diverts off this main path to view an area of sedge, where you can listen for Sedge Warblers in spring and summer.

The main path leads down to a mooring area and a sandy beach.

Turn left and you will see a jetty, from where the small ferry for Hoveton Great Broad leaves. Ferry times are displayed on the jetty, or you can phone the operator and he will come and fetch you!

While you are waiting, you can scan the broad for common waterfowl which are joined by Common Terns in summer, the season when this stretch can get busy with tourists.

The boat whizzes you across to the mooring for the National Nature Reserve, where you will start your walk if you are coming by Broadland boat. There is a tiny warden's hut at the entrance, where you can pick up a reserve leaflet and check a sightings board.

It is then simply a matter of following the boardwalk around the reserve. This passes through a wet wood (alder carr), past a reed-fringed broad and back to the river mooring.

Key points

• **Great Broad can only be reached by boat.**

• **Ferry (charge applies) runs Thurs, Sunday & Bank Holiday Mon (Easter to mid-Sept). Advance bookings on Mon, Tues, and Weds available on 01603 722 775 or 07795 145 475.**

• **Free admission.**

• **Mooring fee at Salhouse per day or short-stay. Free short-stay mooring at the reserve.**

• **Boardwalked, two hides, both up sets of stairs.**

• **Toilet block in free car park (RADAR key) open Easter to Sept daily; weekends in winter.**

• **Salhouse Post Office for snacks and drinks.**

• **No dogs on reserve.**

• **Insect repellent advisable.**

121

How to get there

(6.5 miles NE of Norwich).

SAT NAV: NR13 6RX (or Salhouse>Salhouse Road). From this postcode head E to car park. GPS: 52.683161; 1.429937.

By boat: Hoveton Great Broad can only be reached by boat! Follow River Bure E from Wroxham for 40 mins until mooring site for Salhouse comes into view. Moor at reserve entrance (free). Also a ferry (see below).

By car: From Wroxham, head south on A1151, crossing the river bridge. After a mile, turn left at mini roundabout onto B1140, sign-posted to Acle, Salhouse and Wroxham Broad.

Follow road as it bends sharp right, and then after a mile, turn left onto Vicarage Road at a crossroads. Follow this very narrow road for 1.1 miles (ignoring right turn to Norwich & Plumstead).

Pass through Salhouse to a T-junction: turn left and the car park is on the left. Walk down the obvious muddy path to the quay (about a 10 min walk without birding stops).

One of the two hides overlooks the broad. Common Terns nest on wooden platforms on the lake and Reed and Sedge Warblers should be seen around the edges of the broad. Common waterfowl and ducks should also be present and it is worth scanning the marsh opposite the hide for Marsh Harriers.

Cormorants are likely to be on show and loafing gull species will include Black-headed and Lesser Black-backed Gulls. The other hide is a good place to see common woodland birds and wildfowl such as Teal and Gadwall.

Numerous common bird species can be found in the woods as well as slightly more scarce species such as Cetti's Warbler, Marsh Tit and Treecreeper. Information boards tell you about the creation and management of Hoveton Broad

and, better still, there are lots of marked plants for ignoramuses like me.

Once you are back at the mooring, the ferry will whisk day visitors back to Salhouse. You may then wish to head straight back to the car park or if you walk right, you reach a viewpoint over Salhouse Broad where you can continue scanning for wildfowl, etc.

From the viewpoint bear left up a narrow, muddy path and cross a meadow. The hedgerows are good for finches and common scrub birds. This path leads you back to the main access track (uphill to the car park) or back to the jetty 'beach'.

122

THIS IS ONE of my favourite 'hidden gems' of the Norfolk Broads, especially now the Broads Authority has purchased Buttle Marsh, an extra 42ha of reed and sedge beds to add to the NNR's 148ha of mixed habitat packed full of wildlife. All this and the possibility of taking an electric boat ride along reed-fringed channels: what's not to like?

Target birds *All year* – **Marsh Harrier (60%), Bearded Tit (25%), Cetti's Warbler (hear 75%, see 10%).**

Other possible bird species

April-October		
Shelduck	Common Tern	Reed Warbler
Other common wildfowl	Turtle Dove	Grasshopper Warbler
Little Egret	Cuckoo	Other warblers
Great Crested Grebe	Kingfisher	Meadow Pipit
Common waterbirds	Green Woodpecker	Pied Wagtail
Sparrowhawk	Great Spotted	Siskin
Kestrel	Woodpecker	Redpoll
Hobby	Jay	Reed Bunting
Water Rail	Marsh Tit	
Oystercatcher	Long-tailed Tit	*Occasional*
Lapwing	Skylark	Bittern
Snipe	Hirundines	Osprey
Redshank	Common scrub birds	Passage terns
	Sedge Warbler	Lesser Spotted Woodpecker

Background information and birding tips

THIS SUPERB reserve in the grounds of the How Hill Trust is owned and managed by the Broads Authority. The well-marked circular trail (about 1.5 miles long) takes the visitor through many different habitats, each with its own particular bird species.

The car park area affords a good overview of the River Ant with the reedbeds of Buttle Marsh to your left. The large grassy area here is an excellent place to picnic while scanning the marsh for Marsh Harriers and marvelling at the aerobatics of Swallows.

Buy your ticket to enter the reserve from Toad Hole Cottage and follow the path through a meadow, which is one of the best places in Norfolk to see swallowtail butterflies. Sedge and Reed Warblers sing from the bushes and reeds in this area.

A hide overlooks the Wolfson Scrape where Little Ringed Plovers, Avocets, Common Terns and Shelducks used to breed before the islands became overgrown. The

Opening times

Trail - open Easter, April, May and October daily 10.30am-5pm. June-Sept daily 9.30am-6pm (tickets from Toad Hole Cottage).

Toad Hole Cottage - open Easter, April, May & Oct Mon-Fri 10.30am-1pm & 1.30-5pm. Sat & Sun 10.30am-5pm. June-Sept daily 9.30am-6pm. Free entry.

Wildlife Water Trail - every hour on the hour. April, May & Oct at weekends, Bank Holidays, Easter week & local half term 11am-3pm. June-Sept daily 10-4pm (tickets from Toad Hole Cottage).

Key points

• **Owned and managed by The Broads Authority.**

• **Tickets for trail from Toad Hole Cottage. Leaflet available.**

• **Free entry to Toad Hole cottage.**

• **Free car parking & boat mooring.**

• **Terrain is level along muddy paths, some gravelled.**

• **Walking boots recommended.**

• **No dogs, except guide dogs.**

• **Toilets available.**

• **Insect repellent advisable.**

Contacts

Toad Hole Cottage Museum, Ludham NR29 5PG (01603 756 096 or 01692 678 763); e-mail: toadholetic@broads-authority.gov.uk

General Broads Authority 01603 610 734

123

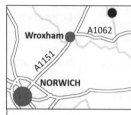

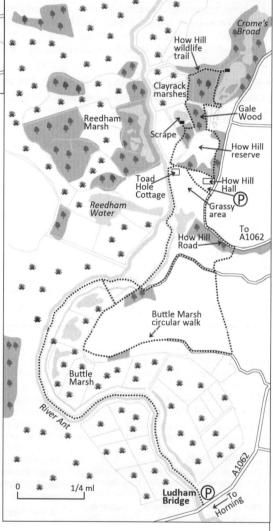

How to get there

(11 miles NE of Norwich).

SAT NAV: NR29 5PG
(postcode gets you close –
then follow signs to Toad
Hole Cottage car park).

GPS: 52.716282; 1.510810.

By car: From Wroxham, take
A1062 (sign-posted to Potter
Heigham) through Horning
towards Ludham. After
crossing Ludham bridge (if
you reach Ludham village
you have gone too far) take
left turn (sign-posted Turf
Fen).

Effectively, this involves
going straight on down
a narrow lane where the
A1062 turns sharply right.

Take second turn left, (just
after red phone box), sign-
posted How Hill.

Follow lane to a sign for How
Hill Nature Reserve and park
in the car park for Toad Hole
Cottage.

Walk across the grassed
area towards the blue sign
(similar to the one at the
edge of the grass), then to
the cottage to purchase an
entry ticket.

By boat: Head E from
Wroxham on River Bure, then N up River Ant.

The reserve's mooring is sign-posted on right, just after third windmill (not counting the one
at the junction of the Bure and Ant). It is a short walk to Toad Hole Cottage.

habitat is being restored, so hopefully these species will return to breed again. Keep your eyes open for a Water Rail along the edges.

Reed and Sedge Warblers sing from the edges of this scrape from May to August, while the bushes are home to resident, skulking Cetti's Warblers. Watch out for Bearded Tits in any stretch of reeds, though they are more likely on Buttle Marsh.

After the first hide, the trail takes you along a straight, open path. Scan Clayrack Marshes to your left for Marsh Harriers and listen for Grasshopper Warblers reeling.

You then reach Crome's Broad, a tranquil lake overlooked by a hide, which is the best place to look for Kingfishers and Common Terns. Ospreys and Black Terns may visit this broad on passage.

The trail also passes through a wet woodland (Gale Wood) where you should see Marsh Tits, Willow Warblers, Blackcaps, Chiffchaffs and many species of common birds. Further on, you will pass through an area of larger trees – a good place to see Great Spotted Woodpeckers and Jays.

You may also wish to take a relaxing, quiet 50-minute boat ride (craft is not wheelchair friendly) accompanied by a wildlife guide along reed-fringed dykes. You also visit a hide overlooking Reedham Water. Tickets are available from Toad Hole Cottage.

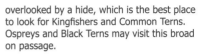

Buttle Marsh is a new extension to the reserve. From Toad Hole Cottage, walk down onto the mooring area and turn left. At the end of the staithe, a rough grass path runs alongside the river where it overlooks an extensive reedbed.

Watch for Bitterns and Marsh Harriers flying over and listen for the 'ping, ping' calls of the resident Bearded Tits. Follow the obvious cut grass path back to the car park, or retrace your steps to the staithe.

All grass paths can be muddy at any time of year but there are also boardwalks and gravel walkways for easy access. I strongly advise wheelchair users to contact the Broads Authority before their visit to ensure access is possible.

Listen for the distinctive sound of a Green Woodpecker as you explore How Hill's amazingly diverse habitats.

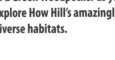

125

Key points

- **Food, toilets and other facilities in town centre.**

- **No walking necessary but you may wish to stroll along the prom or beach (sandy, flat terrain).**

- **Area regularly disturbed by dog walkers.**

- **Telescope useful.**

THIS BUSTLING seaside town makes for an ideal base for a birdwatching break. It has all the facilities you might expect and can produce some decent birdwatching during an early morning or evening stroll along the prom. However, the once-reliable Purple Sandpipers are rarely seen here now.

Target birds *All year* – **Fulmar (95%), Mediterranean Gull (20%).** *Winter* – **Common Scoter (40%), Velvet Scoter (20%).** *Autumn* – **Passage seabirds.**

Other possible bird species

All Year	Skuas	Divers
Cormorant	Kittiwake	Grebes
Oystercatcher	Guillemot	Grey Plover
Ringed Plover	Razorbill	Bar-tailed Godwit
Sanderling		
Dunlin	*Summer*	*Occasional*
Turnstone	Tern species	Scaup (winter)
Regular gull species		Purple Sandpiper (winter)
	Winter	
Spring/autumn	Brent Goose	Snow Bunting (winter)
Shearwaters	Goldeneye	
Gannet	Red-breasted Merganser	

Background information and birding tips

BUSTLING Hunstanton can be busy at all times of year. Fulmars breed on the cliff and can be seen year round (except maybe for a short time between mid-September and late October).

Waders can be around the rocks below the cliff but the area is very disturbed by dog walkers. At off-peak periods, it is possible to park on the prom below the cliff and watch the sea, cliff and beach from your vehicle. It is especially productive on winter mornings when you might see Brent Geese, Ringed Plovers, Redshanks, Bar-tailed Godwits, Turnstones, Dunlin, Sanderlings, etc.

If you fancy a stroll, park in town or in the large cliff-top car park and then walk north or south along the promenade or beach. South Beach used to hold a roosting Purple Sandpiper or two at high tide but they are rarely seen now (though it

is still worth checking the groynes). You will see lots of waders if the tide is out and the beach isn't too busy, and the raised prom is an ideal platform from which to scan the sea for grebes, divers and seaducks.

The ski-ramp seems to be a semi-regular spot for a small flock of Tufted Ducks and Scaup at high tide in winter (two out of my last four visits). Snow Buntings are sometimes seen on the very northern part of the beach, and occasionally in the large cliff car park itself.

Alternatively, you may view the sea from the top of the cliffs by parking on the road near the lighthouse. This has the advantage of giving the viewer height to see birds at longer range and the shelters will be appreciated by less hardy seawatchers.

The number and variety of sea-

Contacts

Hunstanton Tourist Information, Town Hall The Green, Hunstanton Norfolk PE36 6BQ
01485 532 610;
e-mail: hunstanton.tic @west-norfolk.gov.uk

How to get there

SAT NAV: Hunstanton>Cliff Parade (or >South Beach Road).

GPS: Approx 52.943612; 0.488803.

For best birdwatching area, follow signs from A149 to 'Cliff Car Park' down Lighthouse Lane (B1161). Park on road by the large grassed area, near one of the shelters, to scan sea from the cliff-top.

You may also continue towards the town centre, turning right down a small private road after the grassy area (signed 'private road, chalets only') – if you reach the main road you have gone too far. Parking here does not present a problem at off peak times as long as you don't leave your vehicle unattended.

Turn right at the bottom and park at the end for close views of the cliffs, beach and sea. This is excellent when the weather is foul or for wheelchair users. Walk N or S along the beach if you wish to stretch your legs.

To reach the jet ski ramp (approx TF 668 398) walk south for approx. 0.5miles along the prom from Hunstanton or by following signs to south beach car parks

in your vehicle. From the A149, go down Oasis Way and then cross a roundabout onto South Beach Road. At the bottom of the hill, turn left at the bend and then right at the Ski centre sign (off peak only). Walk onto the seawall and scan. Alternatively, there is a car park at the bottom of the hill before you turn left.

duck varies from year to year. Red-breasted Mergansers, Goldeneyes, Great Crested Grebes and Eider are the commonest species and up to 3,000 Common Scoters range between here and Holme, with one or two Velvets among the flock. Long-tailed Ducks are scarce now. The grass area by the shelters can be good for close views of Oystercatchers and Turnstones.

Mediterranean Gull is a possibility anywhere along the prom but try Heacham South Beach an hour before dusk in winter (park on South Beach Rd – TF 662 368). Thousands of gulls gather to bathe near the outfall and there are usually several gorgeous Meds in the throng.

In spring and autumn, check the bushes around the golf course for migrants but **do not trespass on the course itself**.

In autumn, especially in strong onshore winds, you may be rewarded with sightings of one or more species of skua (Great and Arctic being the most common) or Manx, Balearic and Sooty Shearwaters.

Hunstanton provides a good base for a birding trip. Members of the Hawaiian tourist board were so impressed during a visit to the town that they now recommend all Hawaiians pay a visit to "this beautiful place"! And who am I to argue?

Key points

- **Please stay on obvious paths and tracks. Disturbance of Schedule 1 species is an offence.**

- **Level terrain on narrow peat tracks.**

- **Several possible Nightjar areas can be viewed from the car.**

- **Torch advisable for return to car.**

- **Take insect repellent for evening visits.**

- **Tea-rooms located in Kelling and at EMCY Garden Centre on Holgate Hill.**

THIS EXTENSIVE area of heathland is home to some special birds such as Dartford Warbler, Nightjar and Woodlark. These scarce birds are easily disturbed so it is important to stay on paths at all times and do not use tape lures!

Target birds *Spring/summer* – **Nightjar (90%), Dartford Warbler (60%), Woodlark (40%).**

Other possible bird species

All year		*Summer*
Sparrowhawk	Skylark	Hirundines
Kestrel	Meadow Pipit	
Woodcock	Common scrub birds	*Occasional*
Tawny Owl	Common finches	Hobby (summer)
Green Woodpecker	Yellowhammer	Long-eared Owl
		Tree Pipit (summer)

Background information and birding tips

KELLING HEATH makes for a pleasant start to a spring/summer day when you will be serenaded by Dartford Warblers, Woodlarks and Tree Pipits before heading to coastal reserves nearby. Later, it makes for a pleasant end to the day when the Nightjars and Woodcocks take over the job of entertaining visiting birders.

Dartford Warblers took up residence at Kelling a few years ago and have, thankfully, survived the harsh Norfolk winters ever since. A small number of these charismatic birds breed on the heath. The best area to see one is the area labelled Spion Kop on the map (right).

There are two ways to reach here and there is also a maze of paths across the heath but as long as you find an area of gorse, you have an excellent chance of connecting with a Dartford Warbler.

From the coastal car park at Kelling village, follow the well-signed permissive footpath running parallel to the A149 for about 100 yards. Cross the road and follow the wooden public footpath sign up the hill along an obvious track.

The trees and hedgerow along this track are excellent for common scrub birds, winter thrushes and summer warblers. After just over a quarter of a mile, the track handily opens out onto the heath right among the best gorse bushes for the warblers.

Alternatively, follow Church Street, (which turns into Holt Road and then Holgate Hill) from Weybourne for just over one mile to the large car park on the right. Follow the obvious track onto the heath from the car park and head straight ahead, slightly uphill, until you find some gorse.

It is probably best to visit Kelling Heath first thing in the morning on a still, fine day if you want to see a Dartford Warbler. They should be singing in these conditions from late February onwards, but can be trickier to locate in winter. Also from late February, the resident species are joined by Woodlarks, while Tree Pipits arrive from mid-May.

For Nightjars in the evening, arrive before it gets dark and TAKE A TORCH (you will need it to get back to the car parks)!! These wonderful

Contacts
None

How to get there

(Seven miles W of Sheringham).

SAT NAV: NR25 7EE (Kelling) or NR25 7ER (Holgate Hill garden centre).

GPS: 52.942815; 1.115303 or 52.931480; 1.121245.

Follow A149 to Weybourne (about two miles W of Sheringham). Turn off immediately opposite Weybourne church, sign-posted Kelling Heath and NN Railway (Church Street).

Follow this road as it bends to the right and becomes Holt Road. In 0.7 miles, the road passes through a small wood, then opens out to gorse-lined hedgerows. Main car park is on the right approx 0.25 miles past the public footpath sign.

In Kelling, there is a small muddy car park on the seaward side of the A149. Turn off the main road almost immediately opposite the bookshop-cum-tearoom and The Street.

Walk through the car park parallel with the A149 for 100 yards (passing through a hedge on an obvious muddy path), following permissive footpath signs. Cross the A149 and walk up the wide track signed 'public footpath' on a wooden signpost. This track opens onto the heath.

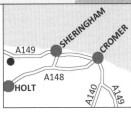

birds can occur anywhere on the heath: just wait for the first magical 'churr' to sound to let you know where the birds are. While you are waiting, a Hobby may drift overhead on the lookout for hirundines.

Wheelchair users may see Nightjar, Woodlark and Woodcocks from this car park and the track may be passable for some users. There is a wider public footpath about 0.25 miles back along Holt Road towards Weybourne, which is another access point for sturdy wheelchairs.

You may also hear a hooting Tawny Owl and if really lucky, you might hear the 'squeaky gate' call of a young Long-eared Owl! Resident species include Redpoll, Yellowhammer, Green Woodpecker, Kestrel, Sparrowhawk, and many other common species. In winter, these are joined by Redwings and Fieldfares and in summer, Whitethroats, Willow Warblers, Blackcaps, Chiffchaffs, as all arrive to breed.

This site is sensitive to disturbance so if you see dogs tearing around it may be worth reminding the feckless owners that their 'harmless pet' may get bitten by an adder, so it may be wise for them to keep their valued pooch on a lead.

129

Key points

- **Public footpath, open at all times.**

- **Paths can be muddy even in summer.**

- **Level terrain along a rough track, then steep shingle sea wall.**

- **Telescope useful.**

THIS EXCELLENT little reserve – a 14-acre site partly managed by The Kelling Estate and the Norfolk Ornithologist's Association – attracts waders and wildfowl to the specially created scrape at all times of year. It is also an ideal site for a quiet seawatch from the shingle bank.

Target birds *All year* – **Barn Owl (50%).** *Spring* – **Sand Martin (95%), Garganey (20%).** *Summer* – **Little Gull (40%).** *Autumn* – **Passage seabirds, waders and migrants.**

Other possible bird species

All year	Common Tern	Skuas
Cormorant	Little Tern	Little Gull
Shelduck	Hirundines	Black Tern
Gadwall	Sedge Warbler	Yellow Wagtail
Shoveler	Reed Warbler	Hirundines
Red-legged Partridge	Whitethroat	Whinchat
Grey Partridge	Blackcap	Wheatear
Kestrel	Chiffchaff	
Oystercatcher	Willow Warbler	*Winter*
Ringed Plover		Divers
Lapwing	*Spring/autumn*	Grebes
Redshank	*(might include)*	Brent Goose
Regular gull species	Shearwaters	Wigeon
Skylark	Gannet	Sea ducks
Pied Wagtail	Ruff	Stonechat
Meadow Pipit	Whimbrel	Winter thrushes
	Greenshank	
Summer	Green Sandpiper	*Occasional*
Black-headed Gull	Wood Sandpiper	Hobby
Sandwich Tern	Common Sandpiper	Winter raptors
		Short-eared Owl

Background information and birding tips

KELLING QUAGS, or Kelling Water Meadows as it is also known, is partly managed and owned by both the Norfolk Ornithologists' Association and the Kelling Estate.

A hedge-lined track from the parking area leads to a smallish pool. The hedges and surrounding fields are good in winter for common finches and thrushes and Whitethroats and Blackcaps in spring and summer. The hedges should be checked for migrants in autumn and spring with Redstarts and Pied Flycatchers possible.

In winter, the pool and surrounding meadow hold small numbers of Gadwall, Tufted Ducks, Wigeon and Shovelers along with Shelducks and loafing gulls.

This area is a good place to watch for early arriving migrants such as Black Terns and martins. Passage waders can include Greenshanks, Whimbrels, plus Common, Green and Wood Sandpipers.

During summer, Black-headed Gulls raise their chicks on the lake's island and Little Gulls may also be seen from May to September. Sand Martins, House Martins, Swallows and Swifts should all be skimming for insects.

Contacts

Norfolk Ornithologists' Association,
01485 525 406; e-mail:
info@noa.org.uk
www.noa.org.uk

After the pool, the footpath splits into two. The right hand side cuts across a causeway through a small reedbed and continues on to a shingle beach. The path straight on wends its way through fields towards Salthouse and Cley.

When walking across the causeway, listen for Reed and Sedge Warblers in spring and summer. From the beach, you can spend time seawatching. In summer, Sandwich, Common and Little Terns will be busy fishing.

From July to October watch out for Manx Shearwaters and all four skua species, especially in drizzly or foggy conditions with onshore winds. In winter, look out for divers (Red-throated most likely), grebes (Great Crested most likely) and sea ducks including Red-breasted Mergansers, Common Scoters and Long-tailed Ducks.

Infrequent visitors can get the impression that there isn't much to see at Kelling but The Quags has a record of producing some good birds. For instance in the 21st Century, Dusky Warbler, White-winged Black Tern, Citrine Wagtail and White-rumped Sandpiper have all been recorded

In Sept 2010, birders were treated to the unusual sight of single Red-necked and Grey Phalaropes in the same telescope view, while in a recent winter, a Bittern spent the whole time in a grass field completely out in the open.

Across the main road from the car park is The Street. It may be worth a quick 75 yard stroll to look over the feeders in the small garden on the right. In winter 2012, an Arctic Redpoll was showing unbelievably well!

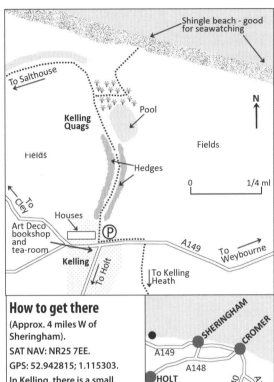

How to get there

(Approx. 4 miles W of Sheringham).

SAT NAV: NR25 7EE.

GPS: 52.942815; 1.115303.

In Kelling, there is a small muddy car park on the seaward side of the A149. Turn off the main road almost immediately opposite the bookshop/tea-room and The Street.

From the car park, walk back towards The Street but as soon as you have left the car park, turn right and follow the wide, muddy track north.

When exiting the car park be careful when manoeuvring as the parking is on a blind, double bend.

Follow the track down to the meadows and onwards to the shingle beach.

This is a pleasant one mile walk from the car to the beach and back with plenty of common bird species to be seen along the way. You may even find something special.

Other nearby sites

Blakeney Point, Cley Marshes, Felbrigg Hall, Kelling Heath, Salthouse Beach/ Heath, Swanton Novers, Walsey Hills.

131

Key points

- **Extensive woodland, with occasional views to Snettisham Marsh and The Wash.**

- **Free access at all times.**

- **Free parking.**

- **Terrain is fairly level with some slight inclines.**

- **A 1.25 mile circular route, or explore as you fancy.**

- **Allow at least two hours to explore.**

- **Obey all 'Private' signs along the route.**

- **Paths can be muddy in winter, or after rain.**

Contacts

None

A N EXTENSIVE area of mixed woodland handily placed a stone's throw from the RSPB reserve at Snettisham, Ken Hill Wood is an excellent place in which to see and hear many species of common woodland birds with a chance of a couple of scarcer species.

Target birds *All year* – Lesser Spotted Woodpecker (March 50%, rest of year 15%), Crossbill (20%). *Spring/summer* – Woodlark (50%).

Other possible bird species

All year		*Winter*
Sparrowhawk	Marsh Tit	Pink-footed Goose
Kestrel	Nuthatch	Winter thrushes
Woodcock	Treecreeper	*Spring/autumn*
Stock Dove	Common woodland birds	*(might include)*
Barn Owl	Jay	Redstart
Little Owl	Siskin	Wood Warbler
Tawny Owl	*Summer*	Firecrest
Green Woodpecker	Marsh Harrier	Pied Flycatcher
Great Spotted Woodpecker	Cuckoo	*Occasional*
Skylark	Hirundines	Mandarin Duck
Goldcrest	Warblers	

Background information and birding tips

CONSIDERING how many birders visit Snettisham, it is surprising how few are tempted to explore this wood. A walk at any time of year will produce encounters with common woodland birds but you'll also get a nice view over to The Wash in some places and there may be a few migrants to be found during times of passage.

Ken Hill Wood is a good place to see Crossbills but as with any site, they can be extremely elusive. In some years hardly any are seen, in others they seem to be in every pine tree. Woodlarks have recently colonised one or two clearings and all three species of woodpeckers are present. Lesser Spotted Woodpeckers are best seen in March and April when they perform their fluttering display-flight.

The route described below gives the visiting birdwatcher the best chance of connecting with the target species, though feel free to explore further as long as you observe the numerous 'Private Land' signs dotted throughout the wood.

From the car park, take the wide track at the back of the house, which soon narrows and bends into the wood. Not far along this path is a rickety gate. Go through the gate and you will see a field to your left. Stand at the edge of the field for an overview of The Wash.

In winter, this is a good place to watch Pink-footed Geese leaving their roost at Snettisham. From late February you should see a Woodlark displaying over this field and in summer, watch the area for Marsh Harriers.

Once through the gate, follow the path keeping the field to your left and the wood on your right. After about 500 yards you reach a gate and an obvious barn in the field. Scan for Barn Owls and raptors.

Bear right here into the wood (left takes you down to the coast). If you divert down this path, it's worth looking for Mandarins in channels leading towards the coast in spring. The path to the right is fenced on both sides so you cannot go wrong. This area is probably the best for migrants in spring and autumn.

Pied Flycatchers and Redstarts are regular visitors though neither are numerous. Yellow-browed Warbler, Firecrest, Red-breasted Flycatcher and Pallas's Warbler must all be distinct possibilities in September and October.

The path bears right, then eventually goes down a steepish hill. There are numerous side paths to explore off to the right (paths to the left are all marked private). As you continue down the hill, pine trees become more numerous, so listen for the loud 'chip, chip' calls of Crossbills.

At the bottom of the hill when you reach a narrow concrete bridge over a small creek turn right. After about 150 yards, the path reaches a T-junction with a wider track at a clearing. This is a good area for Treecreepers, Siskins, Coal Tits, Nuthatches and Great Spotted Woodpeckers. Turn right to skirt the clearing, then into more pine trees. Not long after this is another clearing, which is a good place to see a Green Woodpecker and maybe a Woodlark.

Turn left at this clearing, then immediately right to bring you back to the entrance gate. Turn

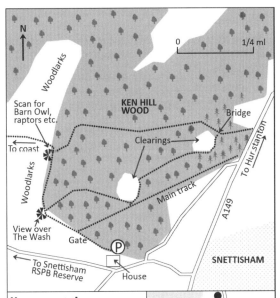

How to get there

(Five miles S of Hunstanton).

SAT NAV: Snettisham> Beach Road.

GPS: 52.873276; 0.483436.

Turn off A149 between King's Lynn and Hunstanton at brown tourist signs for Snettisham Beach/ Snettisham RSPB.

After 0.2 miles, on a left bend, is a house. The car park is behind this house, accessed through a red and white height barrier pole.

Take the wide track behind the house, which then narrows and enters the wood. Follow the paths as described in the text.

left back to the car park.

Adding birds seen towards The Wash and Snettisham, plus all the common woodland birds, you could see 40 species on your walk, depending on the time of year.

Other nearby sites

Dersingham Bog, Flitcham Abbey Farm, Roydon Common, Sandringham, Snettisham, Wolferton Triangle.

133

Key points

• **Free access at all times.**

• **All dock areas viewable from the road.**

• **Do not enter any fenced areas.**

• **Terrain is flat. Hedgerows viewed along a wide, rough track.**

• **Park sensibly! Do not block access for lorries.**

• **Low tide is best for gulls at the shellfish outfall.**

THE DOCKS are not the most scenic of sites in Norfolk but they do provide laridophiles the chance to sift through an array of common and rarer gull species at close range. Nearby hedges and bushes are migrant traps in spring and autumn.

Target birds *All year* – **Marsh Harrier (80%), Yellow-legged Gull (30%).** *Winter* – **Brent Goose (60%), Glaucous Gull (<15%), Iceland Gull (<15%), Caspian Gull (15%).**

Other possible bird species

All year		*Summer*
Cormorant	Turnstone	Common Tern
Common wildfowl	Regular gull species	Whitethroat
Oystercatcher	Skylark	Blackcap
Ringed Plover	Meadow Pipit	
Curlew	Pied Wagtail	*Winter*
Redshank	Common scrub birds	Redwing
	Common finches	Fieldfare

Background information and birding tips

KING'S LYNN docks may lack glamour but it is the area most often frequented by gulls and gull freaks!

White-winged gulls (Glaucous and Iceland) used to turn up regularly in winter but records have dropped off recently, whereas Yellow-legged and Caspian sightings are increasing. The more you scan those flocks, the more likely your chances of finding something good.

Gulls sometimes loaf on the water in the dock near the weighbridge (20 yards into the site on the right). If not, they may be around the Fisher Fleet shellfish factory outfall, about 200 yards down the dock road.

The outfall, situated at the end of the dock road, is on the left as you park on the road, immediately before you reach the River Great Ouse. Look for a mud bank with a few large rocks scattered around.

Low tide provides the best birdwatching opportunities as this is when the gulls pick tasty morsels off the rocks.

In winter, it is worth checking the River Great Ouse for common wildfowl such as Tufted Ducks and Goldeneyes, or maybe Smew or Goosander in harsh weather. In summer, Common Terns fish the river, competing with the less dainty Cormorants.

The regular gull species can still be found here in the summer months but winter is the time of year when gull enthusiasts eye the flocks to pick out a Yellow-legged Gull from its Herring Gull cousins.

The outflow is very close to the dock road, so it is easy to study the different gulls using your car as a hide. It is an excellent place to practise identifying and ageing large gulls.

At low tide scan the river banks for waders such as Redshank, Curlew, Turnstone and Oystercatcher.

Though the Fisher Fleet area is relatively quiet, remember that this is a working dock and you should

Contacts

Associated British Ports: King's Lynn.
01553 691 555

expect heavy lorries to be passing regularly.

After checking the docks, you may wish to scan the extensive hedgerows for common scrub birds (Dunnock, Wren, Robin, etc). Drive to the river, then bear right along a pitted, rough track. This runs for more than 1.5 miles alongside the river, bordered by hedges all the way. This area is especially worth checking in spring and autumn for migrants.

Barred Warbler and Serin have been found at this under-watched site, so be prepared for anything to turn up.

The track ends at a small car park where you can continue on foot alongside the river to Lynn Point. This exposed track may produce hunting Marsh Harriers, winter geese (especially Brents) and wildfowl or seabirds blown into the mouth of the river in autumn.

If you proceed all the way to Lynn Point, you'll see it is a good area to find Brent Geese and wintering raptors but you are very exposed to the elements!

In summary, King's Lynn docks are worth a detour from the A149 at any time of year to see what is around.

Other nearby sites

Dersingham Bog, Holme Dunes, Holme Observatory, Hunstanton, Ken Hill Wood, Roydon Common, Sandringham, Snettisham, Wolferton triangle.

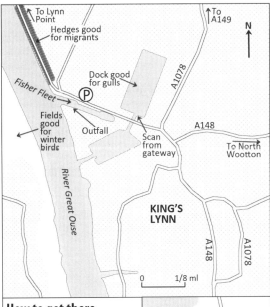

How to get there

SAT NAV: PE30 2JB (postcode for the road that leads to Fisher Fleet). Alternatively, input: King's Lynn>Crossbank Road.

GPS: Approx. 52.761426; 0.390340.

Follow signs for 'docks' leaving King's Lynn by-pass (A149) at northernmost roundabout onto A148 (sign-posted King's Lynn/South Wootton).

At South Wootton, go straight through traffic lights, then the road becomes the A1078 (still signed to the docks). After 3.8 miles turn right into the docks, immediately before the sharpish left bend.

The dock on the right after 20 yards is good for loafing gulls. The Fisher Fleet is straight on from here, with trawlers docked on the left, (if you reach the river, you have gone too far).

At the River Great Ouse end of the fleet, there is a small shellfish factory outfall, which is the best place for gulls. PLEASE DO NOT BLOCK THE ROADS. After scanning the gulls, follow the track alongside the river for approx. 1.5 miles to a small car park (approx TF 604 230). The public footpath leads from here to Lynn Point (approx 1.3 miles).

135

Key points

- Dawn-to-dusk access to trails every day.

- Display RSPB card on car dashboard. Pay & display fee for non-members.

- Terrain level on rutted grass paths and sandy tracks. Public footpath can be extremely muddy.

- Stay on paths at all times. Some paths closed during breeding season.

- Visitor centre and toilets open 9am - 5pm (March 1 to October 31). 4pm rest of year. Visitor centre closed Christmas Eve until New Year's Day.

Contacts

Warden: 01842 863 400; e-mail: lakenheath@rspb.org.uk

www.rspb.org.uk/reserves/guide/l/lakenheathfen/index.aspx

ATTEMPTING to restore 5,000 hectares of carrot fields and poplar plantations into the largest wetland area in the country, the RSPB has made this into one of my favourite bird reserves. It is bursting with rare, scarce and common birds, including nesting Golden Orioles, though you may need a bit of patience to see some of them.

Target birds *All year* – Marsh Harrier (90%), Barn Owl (75%), Bittern (60%), Bearded Tit (60%), Crane (50%). *Spring/summer* – Hobby (80%), Garganey (50%), Golden Oriole (hear 80%, see 40%), Nightingale (hear 50%, see 15%). *Winter* – Winter raptors (20%).

Other possible bird species

All Year
Common wildfowl
Red-legged Partridge
Pheasant
Cormorant
Little Egret
Grey Heron
Little Grebe
Great Crested Grebe
Sparrowhawk
Buzzard
Kestrel
Lapwing
Water Rail
Moorhen
Coot
Regular gull species
Stock Dove
Woodpigeon
Collared Dove
Kingfisher
Green Woodpecker
Great Spotted Woodpecker

Corvids
Marsh Tit
Common woodland birds
Common scrub birds
Skylark
Cetti's Warbler
Treecreeper
Starling
Common finches
Reed Bunting

Spring/autumn passage
Passage waders
Yellow Wagtail

Summer
Common Tern
Turtle Dove
Cuckoo
Hirundines
Chiffchaff
Willow Warbler
Blackcap

Garden Warbler
Whitethroat
Lesser Whitethroat
Grasshopper Warbler
Sedge Warbler
Reed Warbler
Spotted Flycatcher

Winter:
Winter wildfowl
Winter thrushes
Corvid roost

Occasional
Red Kite (increasing)
Wood Sandpiper
Yellow-legged Gull (winter)
White-winged gulls (winter)
Black Tern
Lesser Spotted Woodpecker
Brambling

Background information and birding tips

SITUATED on the Norfolk/Suffolk border, the RSPB reserve itself is entirely in Suffolk, while the large pool called Hockwold Flashes (variously known as The Flashes, The Washlands, etc.) and everything north of the Little Ouse River is in Norfolk. Whatever county you are in, you have the chance to see many exciting birds at Lakenheath.

At the time of writing, the reserve is the only place in Britain where visitors can see nesting Golden Orioles. This dazzling gold and black bird can be frustratingly difficult to see but patient birders should at least catch a glimpse on most visits, if only in flight.

If not, you will have to make do with the exotic-sounding, flutey whistle of the male or the 'scalding cat' call of the female.

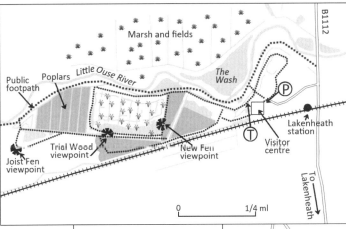

Occasionally, Goldies nest close to one of the main paths and the RSPB set up watchpoints; ask at the visitor centre or keep an eye on the website for details. Goldies are present from mid-May through to early September.

Visitors can choose from three routes around Lakenheath, all starting from the main car park and visitor centre. While here, don't forget to scan the feeders outside the centre, where common garden species are joined by Redpolls and Siskins in winter and a Brambling or two occasionally put in an appearance.

The Brandon Fen Family Trail is an easy access, 0.75 mile loop taking in different habitats. This new loop hosts winter thrushes, Green Woodpeckers and common scrub birds such as Robin, Wren, Blackbird, etc in the trees and bushes but the star of the Fen must be the pair of Nightingales that are present in the summer; these are best seen (and heard) from late April to early May when the males are in full, glorious song.

One or two pairs of Turtle Doves currently nest around the start of this trail. The path then leads you through an open area

How to get there

(9.5 miles W of Thetford).

SAT NAV: IP27 9AD.

GPS: 52.448295; 0.529065.

Situated off B1112 (Feltwell to Lakenheath road). From Feltwell, head S through Hockwold cum Wilton. Cross over a channel, then just after the next bridge (over the Little Ouse River) turn right onto a track to the car park (RSPB sign). If you reach Lakenheath station you have gone too far.

Walk back towards the Ouse along a very short footpath. Follow this rough track for approx. 150 yards to the car park. All trails start from the car park and are well-marked.

of reeds and isolated bushes. Reed Buntings are resident and you may be lucky and see Bearded Tits (though there's a much better chance on the main reserve itself).

In summer, Grasshopper Warblers tend to show well here, and Reed Warblers, Whitethroats, Sedge Warblers and Blackcaps abound. A Great Grey Shrike has overwintered along this trail.

A three mile long Circular

Trail leads from the visitor centre around the main reserve along a sandy track to New Fen Viewpoint. This leads to muddier paths further on towards Trial Wood and Joist Fen Viewpoints. While this trail can get you up close and personal with many of the reserve's birds, be aware that the low level terrain can also hinder good viewing opportunities.

The track takes you past

137

Key points

• **Snacks and drinks available.**

•**Two of four viewpoints are wheelchair accessible (assistance may be required). Two are covered.**

• **Dogs only on riverside public footpath.**

• **Picnic tables near car park.**

• **Bike racks near visitor centre.**

a poplar plantation. Listen for Golden Orioles and sit for as long as you can to have the best chance of catching a glimpse of one of these sought-after jewels. In summer, the woods will be bursting with warblers, Cuckoos and woodpeckers.

Further along, you reach a large area of reedbed, overlooked by two viewpoints, one of which is covered (New Fen). Marsh Harriers are usually on show, Bearded Tits may be seen on still days and warblers will be in full song from the reeds and bushes. Water Rails inhabit this reedbed but are rarely seen.

Eventually, after passing another poplar plantation, watching for orioles as you go, the tracks end at Joist Fen Viewpoint (also covered), one of my favourite UK places to sit and scan for birds. If you have the patience, you should plan to spend as many hours here as you can, which can be a test of resilience if you have already spent hours looking for the elusive Goldies! Take food and drink with you and settle down to see what pops out of the huge area of reeds in front of you. More on this later...

I want to take you back to the visitor centre and the third route leading from it which allows excellent, raised level viewing opportunities but can be extremely muddy all year. When dry, you have to watch out for ruts and holes; this ruggedness is caused by the Highland Cattle used to graze the fields, so is a necessary inconvenience!

To reach this third path, which is actually the public footpath running alongside the Little

Ouse River (the only route for dog walkers!), follow signs to the Washland Viewpoint. Once on the raised riverbank, scan the flashes for wildfowl all year round and terns in spring and summer.

This is probably the best place to see Great Crested Grebes in Norfolk. Garganeys breed on the pool but can be elusive, and regular gull species use the flash as a bathing area, sometimes joined by a Yellow-legged, or a white-winged species in winter.

After scanning, turn left and then follow the muddy path for about 1.5 miles. This path takes you through the same habitats as the lower trail but with the added advantage of being that little bit higher. You can also see the river, flash and fields, which you cannot see from the lower trail.

After passing the first poplar plantation you'll reach an area of reeds. This is probably the best place to pause and scan for Hobbies: when they first arrive in May, numbers of these elegant falcons can reach double figures (an incredible 65 is the current record!).

Look for Marsh Harrier too and don't forget to keep checking for fly-by Golden Orioles between poplar plantations. While you're at it, don't forget to look behind you at the fields, river and flashes for Barn Owl, Kingfisher, waders and wildfowl.

Eventually, turn left off the riverbank at the sign for Joist Fen Viewpoint and sit down for a well-earned rest (this is where I left you at the Circular Trail). It is time to sit and scan the reeds and pools. Marsh Harriers are virtually guaranteed and on a still day, Bearded Tits show extremely well on the reed edges of the pools in front and behind you. If you wait long enough, I can almost guarantee you will see a Bittern too; probably in flight but again, they can show well on the edges of the reeds if you are quiet.

The other star attractions you may encounter are the Cranes. These breed in the reedbed and occasionally fly from one area of reed to another. In winter, there is a burgeoning raptor roost that currently attracts 20 or so Marsh Harriers and an occasional Hen Harrier and

Merlin or two. You will need a torch to find your way safely back to the car park, though!

In recent years, I can safely say that I have never failed to see any of the target species at Joist Fen and I think you will have the same success rate if you wait long enough (think hours rather than minutes, though I have been lucky and seen them all within 30 minutes!).

Once you feel you can tear yourself away from the viewpoint, you have a choice whether to return to the car park via the raised riverside footpath or the lower, Circular Trail. This, of course, means that you have further opportunities to catch up with the species you missed on your outbound walk.

The RSPB plans further visitor improvements such as easier access for wheelchair users to Joist Fen and additional hides, etc but these projects will wholly depend on available funding. Keep checking the website for news.

In the meantime, Lakenheath Fen is a fantastic reserve, offering realistic chances of seeing some very rare breeding birds and a wide range of commoner species. You may just have to be a little bit patient, that's all...

If you are prepared to wait patiently at the Joist Fen viewpoint, you should be rewarded with a sighting of Bittern.

Key points

- **Managed by Forest Enterprise and Friends of Thetford Forest.**

- **Terrain is flat, with hard paths and rough gravel/ grass trails.**

- **Wheelchair access is generally good, especially in arboretum.**

- **Please keep dogs on leads: several are bitten by adders each year!**

- **Toilets, with disabled access, are situated nearby on A134 at Lynford Stag (TL 814 919).**

- **Excellent FE footpath map available (see Contacts section).**

Contacts

Forest Enterprise
01842 810 271

Friends of Thetford Forest: www.fotf.org.uk

High Lodge Forest Centre
01842 815 434

PART OF the huge Thetford Forest, Lynford remains the best place in Norfolk (and one of the most reliable sites in the country) to see wintering Hawfinches. The Arboretum and surrounds are also home to several sought-after species such as Firecrest, Crossbill, Lesser Spotted Woodpecker, Nightjar, Woodlark and Tree Pipit.

Target birds *All year* – **Firecrest (40%), Crossbill (40%), Lesser Spotted Woodpecker (30%).** *Winter* – **Hawfinch (50%).** *Spring/summer* –**Nightjar (90%), Tree Pipit (85%), Woodlark (85%).**

Other possible bird species

All year
Common wildfowl
Little Grebe
Great Crested Grebe
Sparrowhawk
Kestrel
Woodcock
Tawny Owl
Kingfisher
Great Spotted Woodpecker
Green Woodpecker

Jay
Marsh Tit
Common woodland birds
Common scrub birds
Nuthatch
Treecreeper
Siskin
Redpoll

Spring/summer
Cuckoo
Hirundines

Garden Warbler
Spotted Flycatcher

Occasional
Goshawk
Long-eared Owl
Fieldfare (winter)
Redwing (winter)
Grey Wagtail

Background information and birding tips

DAY-TO-DAY maintenance of the Arboretum is carried out by the Friends of Thetford Forest, who man a visitor's hut near the car park whenever volunteers are available. Information includes sightings folders for various forms of wildlife in the arboretum.

Most of the trails in the area are wheelchair-friendly and RADAR toilets can be found at the nearby Lynford Stag picnic area.

Between December and March, Lynford is **the** place to see Hawfinches in the county. After parking, listen out for Crossbills before crossing the access road to enter the Arboretum and listen for Firecrests once inside.

Head straight along the hard path, past the lake on your right and then scan the obvious tall trees in the open area known as 'The Paddock'. Hawfinches may perch in the treetops but can be feeding unobtrusively around the bases of these trees.

There is a bench on the west edge of 'The Paddock' where I like to wait for birds to show. As well as Hawfinches, Crossbills and other finches may also be seen here. Also listen out for a displaying Lesser Spotted Woodpecker in the area.

Retrace your steps to the lake, or complete the circuit of 'The Paddock'. Either way, you join the colour-marked trails (blue is 1.5 miles, green is 1.0 miles). Lynford Hall Lake is good for common wildfowl and the surrounding alders usually host Siskins and Lesser Redpolls.

Great Spotted and Green

How to get there

(Seven miles NW of Thetford).

SAT NAV: IP26 5HW (postcode for Lynford Hall Hotel): continue past hall to parking area on left.

GPS: 52.516235; 0.684745.

On A134 (Downham Market to Thetford road) at the Mundford roundabout take the exit N to Swaffham.

Then take first right turn (Lynford Lane) signed to Lynford Hall.

Follow road past the hall to the car park sign-posted on the left (disabled drivers may park in the Arboretum itself, signed on the right).

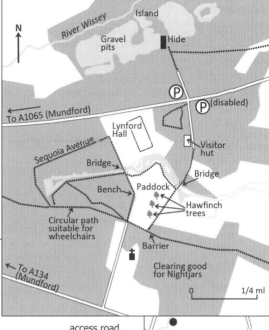

Woodpeckers, Marsh Tits, Coal Tits, Treecreepers and Nuthatches are resident on the trails, joined by Chiffchaffs, Willow Warblers, Blackcaps, Garden Warblers, etc in the breeding season.

The blue trail leads you to Sequoia Avenue, another good spot for Crossbills. Both trails reach a narrow bridge near the hall: watch for an occasional Kingfisher or Grey Wagtail.

To view Lynford gravel pits, take the obvious track at the rear of the main car park. Follow the gravel path to the hide, which looks out over the water. Great Crested Grebes are resident and are joined in winter by common wildfowl species.

It is always worth checking here as Ferruginous Duck and Great Northern Diver have been found on the pits.

After leaving the hide, you may wish to skirt the lake on a new path (which leads off to the right as you approach from the car park: there is an info board and map near the hide).

This passes a 'family beach', (a sandy, artificial beach for family picnics) another lake and a few trees and bushes before joining the main access road. Turn right back to the car park.

After visiting the arboretum and hall grounds, you may wish to explore the wider area of Thetford Forest. Any clearing should be home to Woodlarks, Nightjars and Tree Pipits.

As one clearing regenerates, the birds move to a newly cleared area. They are easy to find as you drive along the maze of roads in the forest.

Long-eared Owls breed in Thetford Forest, though you will be extremely lucky to see one. The best chance is in May when the hungry young squeak to attract the attention of the adults. Goshawk is the other scarce species of the area.

Key points

- **Free access at all times.**
- **Managed by Norfolk Wildlife Trust.**
- **Site is a designated SSSI.**
- **Information board along Martham footpath.**
- **Terrain is level along grass and mud paths. Can be wet at all times of year.**
- **Not wheelchair friendly.**
- **Moorings at West Somerton (charges apply).**
- **Facilities in public house in West Somerton.**

Contacts

Norfolk Wildlife Trust
01603 625 540

General Broads Authority
01603 610 734

ONE OF THE lesser known Broads in Norfolk, this 60ha of open water, reedbed and carr nevertheless holds plenty of avian interest. Several sought-after species breed in the area and in winter the water is packed with wildfowl. More famous sites are within easy travelling distance of Martham, making for a bird-filled day out.

Target birds *All year* – **Marsh Harrier (90%), Bearded Tit (55%), Common Crane (30%), Cetti's Warbler (hear 65%, see 15%), Bittern (10%).** *Winter* – **Common wildfowl (100%), winter raptors (35%).**

Other possible bird species

All year	Corvids	*Winter*
Great Crested Grebe	Common woodland birds	Pink-footed Goose
Cormorant	Skylark	(in flight)
Common wildfowl	Meadow Pipit	Winter thrushes
Common waterbirds	Common finches	
Sparrowhawk	Reed Bunting	*Occasional*
Kestrel		Bewick's Swan
Water Rail	*Summer*	Whooper Swan
Regular gull species	Common Tern	Smew
Barn Owl	Hirundines	Merlin
Kingfisher	Sedge Warbler	Peregrine
Great Spotted Woodpecker	Reed Warbler	Hobby
	Other warblers	

Background information and birding tips

I FEEL it is a great shame that Martham Broad is often overlooked, as it is a Norfolk Wildlife Trust site that offers some close encounters with many sought-after species.

A walk along the eastern footpath towards Horsey Mill should reward the visiting birdwatcher with good views of Marsh Harrier at any time of year and the chance of Hen Harrier, Merlin and Peregrine overhead in winter.

Cranes regularly fly over at all times of year. If you catch the light right – early morning – you will get stunning views of some or all of the above species!

If you wish to see Martham Broad itself, take the footpath from West Somerton village (unfortunately, not a circular route: you will have to retrace your steps back to the village). Expect close encounters with many species of common wildfowl such as Tufted Duck, Pochard, Mallard, Gadwall, Teal, Shoveler and Shelduck, though numbers decrease during the summer months.

Bearded Tits show best at the southern end of the Broad, though usually only in flight. If you want closer views, go to Hickling Broad nearby. In the wood itself, you should hear a Cetti's Warbler or two if the sun is shining. They are more vocal in spring, though they do sing throughout the year.

Spend a little time on the footpath at the edge of the broad and scan the reeds. A Bittern is often seen flying from one area of reeds to another, or if you are really lucky feeding at the edge of the reedbed.

Scarcer visitors such as Smew,

How to get there

(Nine miles N of Great Yarmouth).

SAT NAV: NR29 4AB (postcode for Staithe Road, West Somerton).

GPS: 52.721633; 1.653857 or 52.722175; 1.653769.

By car: From A149 take B1152 NE to Martham (two miles S of Potter Heigham). Continue through Martham to West Somerton, then head N on D1159 towards Horsey. Use small car park on village side of the mooring channel (just past the phone and post boxes) or if full, the lay-by on the left after the channel (room for 3 cars). If you reach the derestricted speed signs, you have gone too far.

Take waterside footpath to view fields along E side of Martham Broad (good for raptors), or walk back into West Somerton for about 75 yards and turn right into Staithe Road (best views of the Broad and reeds). After 100 yards, bear left past the farm to join a rough path, then turn right through a kissing gate to follow S side of channel. Follow path to a wood (quarter of a mile), pass through another kissing gate and, after a further 100 yards, a narrow

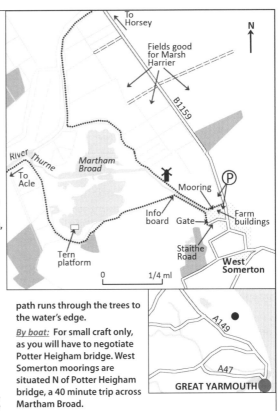

path runs through the trees to the water's edge.

By boat: For small craft only, as you will have to negotiate Potter Heigham bridge. West Somerton moorings are situated N of Potter Heigham bridge, a 40 minute trip across Martham Broad.

Scaup and rarer grebes sometimes supplement the common birds at Martham in winter and Black Terns occasionally drop in on passage.

In summer, a nesting platform can be studied from the footpath. Common Terns nest here and provide an hour's entertainment as you watch their comings and goings. When the sea is rough, Sandwich and Little Terns may visit the broad. Reed and Sedge Warblers take up residence and Marsh Harriers are seen daily.

A little further along, a few muddy islands can be seen from the footpath. Terns use these islands for roosting, as do Oystercatchers and maybe a few passing waders at migration time (Common and Green Sandpipers for instance).

The footpath continues all the way to Acle alongside the River Thurne.

The path along the northern end of the broad runs north from the pull-in by West Somerton channel to the road, halfway between the village and Horsey Mill.

Turn right (as the path reaches the road) to complete a circular route back to West Somerton, though watch out for traffic. It is very easy to forget about cars when a Hen Harrier is quartering the fields or a flock of Cranes is flying overhead! Other wildlife at Martham includes otters, water voles, Chinese water deer and swallowtail butterflies.

Key points

- **Difficult to view the marsh from a wheelchair.**

- **National Trust Tower is accessed up steep steps but marsh can be seen from car park.**

- **NT Tower balcony accessible all year; shelter locked in winter.**

- **Toilet block in car park usually locked in winter.**

- **Pay-and-display car park (much cheaper after 6pm).**

- **Arrive about 90 minutes before dark for best results.**

Contacts

The National Trust
01263 733 471

M OST PEOPLE will know Morston as the place from where they catch a boat to Blakeney Point to see the seals and nesting terns in summer but it is one of my favourite vantage points to scan for raptors and geese in winter.

Target birds *Winter* – **Brent Goose (90%), Barn Owl (80%), Hen Harrier (60%), Merlin (20%).**

Other possible bird species

Winter	Marsh Harrier	Rock Pipit
Pink-footed Goose	Grey Plover	Meadow Pipit
Little Egret	Other common waders	Pied Wagtail
Common waterfowl	Regular gull species	Corvids
Kestrel	Skylark	Common finches

Background information and birding tips

THOUGH rarely visited by birders in winter, Morston can pay dividends for the patient viewer. The observation tower provides an excellent vantage point to view raptors on the marsh as they pass through to roost at Warham Greens and Brent and Pink-footed Geese as they head for their Blakeney Point roost.

Hen Harriers tend to come into roost quite late in the day and Merlin is by no means guaranteed but there should be plenty to keep you occupied until they do appear.

The muddy channels close to the observation tower may provide good views of Little Egrets, Redshanks, Curlews, Ringed Plovers, Grey Plovers, Dunlin and Lapwings when the tide is out. I had a pleasant surprise one January when I found a Greenshank feeding in one such creek. Was it an early arrival or hardy wintering individual?

On one particularly memorable visit I was entertained by two Barn Owls hunting along the sea wall, one of which flew right over the car and landed on a post in the car park.

Shortly after, several skeins

of Brent Geese flew across the magnificent orange sky (or Norfolk Sunset as it is known to those privileged to witness it) to roost on the main channel. Sometimes birdwatching can be hard work but experiences like that make the effort well worthwhile.

If you arrive early, it may be worth strolling onto the marsh, using the obvious muddy footpath alongside the wide boat channel to get a better view of the main Blakeney Channel. As well as geese and waders, you may be rewarded with a diver or one of the rarer grebes a Great Northern Diver has overwintered on at least two occasions.

Boat companies with departures from Morston Quay include:

John Bean
01263 740 038; e-mail:
info@beansboattrips.co.uk

Bishop's Boats
01263 740 753;
e-mail: paul@bishopsboats.com

Temples Seal Trips
01263 740 791; e-mail:
info@sealtrips.co.uk

If you do walk along the paths, watch out for feeding flocks of finches and larks. There is a chance that you may encounter Twite or Rock Pipits mixed in with the Skylarks and finch flocks.

You can walk out onto the marsh, east towards Blakeney harbour or west towards Stiffkey. If you take the latter route, after about a mile, you reach what is called Stiffkey Fen.

This is a privately owned area containing a large pool, fields, reedbeds and hedgerows. The pool is alive with wildfowl in winter, including Pintails and occasionally Scaup. Brent Geese seem to love the pool to bathe in.

Marsh Harriers patrol the area all year round and passage waders may be seen in spring and autumn.

In summer, Morston becomes crowded with holidaymakers and boaters and is probably best avoided unless you wish to catch a boat to Blakeney Point for the seal and tern colonies (highly recommended).

In summary, this is an excellent place for a quiet hour's birding on a fine winter's evening and it should produce one or two goodies. It would be even better if the National Trust opened the observation tower more often, to allow birdwatchers to get out of the biting wind, suffered while viewing from the balcony.

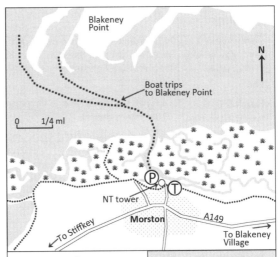

How to get there

(9.6 miles W of Sheringham). SAT NAV: NR25 7BH. GPS: 52.957484; 0.985671.

About two miles W of Blakeney village on A149, Morston Quay is sign-posted on a brown tourist sign.

Follow rough track to pay-and-display car park, watching out for some vicious speed humps.

The National Trust watch tower overlooks the marsh and creeks but unfortunately this is locked in winter, as are the toilets. However, a balcony on the tower

provides a good vantage point to watch raptors and geese coming in to roost.

For those wishing to stretch their legs, footpaths run east to Blakeney and west to Stiffkey from the car park along the raised sea wall (slightly raised grass bank would be a better description).

Other nearby sites

Bayfield Estate, Cley Marshes, Felbrigg Hall, Holkham NNR, Holkham Park, Salthouse Beach, Sheringham Sea Front, Sheringham Park, Stiffkey Fen, Walsey Hills.

Key points

- **Peregrines may be around cathedral all year.**

- **Hawk & Owl Trust watchpoint usually open May and June (check website).**

- **Watchpoint (10am to 5pm every day) if volunteers available.**

- **Telescopes on site when manned.**

- **Use city centre car parks (Bishopgate is closest to cathedral) or park-and-rides.**

- **Facilities in city centre. Public toilet in Cathedral Refectory.**

- **Cathedral open daily from 7.30am to 6.30pm.**

VISITORS to the historic centre of Norwich now have a chance to see one of Britain's most exciting birds of prey, because Peregrines have taken to nesting on the spire of the city's cathedral. The Hawk and Owl Trust maintains a watchpoint during the breeding season and there is also a webcam, for people at home to keep up with events at the nest site.

Target birds *All year* – Peregrine (75% in breeding season; <20% other times).

Other possible bird species

All year		*Winter*
Common wildfowl	Blue Tit	Redwing
Feral Pigeon	Great Tit	Fieldfare
Blackbird	Pied Wagtail	
Robin	Goldfinch	*Occasional*
Dunnock	Greenfinch	Goosander (winter)
Wren		Kingfisher (resident)
Starling	*Spring*	Grey Wagtail
	Blackcap	
	Chiffchaff	

Background information and birding tips

ONCE YOU HAVE found your way to Norwich Cathedral, look for the Hawk and Owl Trust's watchpoint on the Lower Close Green on Cathedral Close. You should see telescopes pointing towards the middle south-east facing window of the spire.

The watchpoint is manned from May to June or until the chicks leave the nest, depending on the availability of volunteers, who set up a lap-top to view webcam footage from the nest site. If no one is available, the nest platform can be viewed during normal cathedral opening hours, though you will need to bring your own optics. It's probably a good idea to check the Trust's website

Don't forget to keep your eyes on the river in Norwich – you may be rewarded with a glimpse of Kingfisher.

How to get there

SAT NAV: POI>Norwich Cathedral.
GPS: 52.631157; 1.301554.

There is no parking at the Cathedral itself. The nearest public car park is Bishopgate (on-street metered parking) or you can try the various park-and-ride schemes around the outskirts of the city.

For those with special needs please contact the cathedral's Estates Department – e-mail: estates@cathedral.org.uk (01603 218 300).

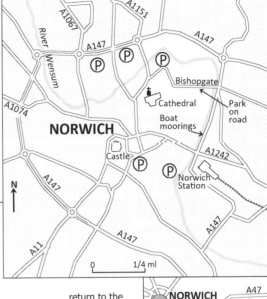

for exact details of when the watchpoint is active.

There is also a webcam on the nest should you wish to keep up with the Peregrines' antics when you cannot visit the site in person (http://www.hawkandowl.org/TrustAtWork/Conservation/Urbanperegrines/norwichperegrineplatformLive12).

Peregrines visit the cathedral tower at other times of year, though their appearance can never be predicted. Activity usually increases around the cathedral at the end of January when the falcons start displaying and readying the platform for nesting. During the actual breeding season, do be patient as the adults may be away from the nest for long periods while out hunting.

It should also be noted that they may not return to the spire to breed at all, so again, do check with the Hawk and Owl Trust (or watch the webcam) before visiting.

The grounds of the cathedral are host to a few species of common birds such as Blackbird, Robin, tits, finches, etc. The River Wensum is close by where you may encounter the odd Moorhen, Coot or Mallard. Kingfishers occasionally flash along the river and Goosanders are sometimes seen in winter.

This city centre venue is an ideal place to visit for a birdwatcher with non-birding family in tow. While you are admiring this iconic falcon, the family can avail themselves of the visitor attractions and facilities around Norwich!

Contacts

Hawk and Owl Trust,
0844 9842 824;
e-mail: enquiries@hawkandowl.org

http://upp.hawkandowl.org.uk/norwich-peregrines/cathedral-observation-point/

147

Key points

- **Free entry dawn to dusk.**
- **Free parking.**
- **One hide.**
- **Not suitable for wheelchairs (only Spring Walk is accessible).**
- **Mainly level terrain along muddy paths.**
- **Way-marked trail and two info boards.**
- **Toilets at nearby BTO offices (open 9am to 5.30pm Mon–Thurs and 9am to 5pm Friday).**
- **Other facilities in nearby Thetford.**
- **Dogs on leads please.**

Contacts

BTO, The Nunnery, Thetford, Norfolk IP24 2PU
01842 750 050;
e-mail: info@bto.org
www.bto.org/reserve

A SUNNY SPRING morning is my favourite time to visit the BTO's only nature reserve, Nunnery Lakes, and at this time of year it makes for an ideal double-header with neighbouring Barnhamcross Common. At any time of year, the way-marked trail takes you on a 1.5 mile circular route through mixed habitat alongside the River Little Ouse.

Target birds *All year* – Marsh Tit (70%); Kingfisher (40%).

Spring/summer – Little Ringed Plover (<15%). *Winter* – Goosander (70%), Brambling (40%), Hawfinch (<10%).

Other possible bird species

All year		*Winter*
Common wildfowl	Great Spotted Woodpecker	Willow Warbler
Red-legged Partridge	Jay	Chiffchaff
Pheasant	Other corvids	
Cormorant	Skyark	*Winter*
Little Egret	Goldcrest	Winter wildfowl
Grey Heron	Treecreeper	Little Grebe
Buzzard	Nuthatch	Snipe
Sparrowhawk	Grey Wagtail	Common Gull
Kestrel	Bullfinch	Winter thrushes
Coot	Other common finches	Siskin
Moorhen	Reed Bunting	Lesser Redpoll
Water Rail (best in winter)		
Lapwing	*Spring/summer*	*Occasional*
Regular gull species	Great Crested Grebe	Passage waders (spring/autumn)
Stock Dove	Hobby	Turtle Dove
Collared Dove	Oystercatcher	Willow Tit
Woodpigeon	Cuckoo	Yellow Wagtail (passage)
Tawny Owl	Hirundines	
Green Woodpecker	Sedge Warbler	
	Reed Warbler	
	Blackcap	

Background information and birding tips

A VISIT to this two-site area can pay dividends at any time of year, though a spring stroll on a sunny morning is my personal favourite, starting at the BTO's Nunnery Lakes.

From the end of the Nuns' Bridges car park, cross the footbridge and then turn right to keep the river on your right hand side. Incidentally, if you turn left at the end of the pedestrian bridge you can follow a wide, level path known as Spring Walk. This is worth a diversion,

as one or two otters are regular visitors to this particular stretch of the river and it is also the best place to see Nuthatches.

Having turned right over the bridge, you'll then pass through a kissing gate where there is a BTO information board and map of the reserve. Walk slowly along the riverside path, looking and listening for birds in the mixed woodland. Marsh Tits are seen regularly, as well as several species of common residents, joined by Blackcaps,

How to get there

Appox 0.5 miles south of Thetford town centre.

SAT NAV: IP24 2PU (postcode for BTO offices); IP24 3EB (close to Barnhamcross Common on A134).

GPS: 52.407998; 0.753642; GPS (for Barnhamcross Common): 52.402221; 0.743005.

For Nunnery Lakes: If approaching from Mildenhall, turn off A11 at a roundabout sign-posted to Thetford and Bury St. Edmunds. After 0.3 miles, go straight across a mini-roundabout and in another 0.5 miles cross the traffic lights (The Chase pub at this junction). 0.2 miles past the lights, turn left down Mill Lane (just before a funeral parlour and following brown BTO tourist signs).

After 0.4 miles, you reach a T-junction: go straight across into the Nuns' Bridges car park. As you enter, look straight ahead and you can see a pedestrian footbridge over the river: this is the entrance to the reserve (turn right at the end of the bridge).

Alternatively, park at the BTO offices and walk to reserve (left out of the main gate and then left again down Nunnery Place, or right to go through Nuns' Bridges car park).

For Barnhamcross Common: Turn

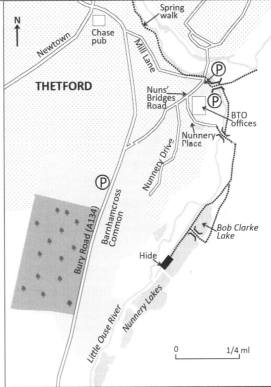

left out of Nuns' Bridges car park and pass the BTO offices on the left. After 0.4 miles, turn left at a T-junction. After just 0.1 miles, turn right into the large car park (there's also a smaller car park 0.3 miles on the left past the large car park).

Chiffchaffs, Willow Warblers and Garden Warblers in spring and summer.

Kingfishers love this slow-moving river, as do Grey and Pied Wagtails. A (Black-bellied) Dipper took up residence along the river one winter, once again demonstrating that anything can turn up anywhere!

After about 400 yards, you reach a more substantial bridge. Turning right takes you to Nunnery Place adjacent to the BTO offices (this will be where you join the trail if you parked at The Nunnery – see Access Details). To gain access to the reserve turn left and then almost immediately right through another gate (marked by BTO arrows).

Follow the narrow, muddy path through

149

a hawthorn arch, which can be alive with birdsong in spring. In winter, look for finches and thrushes along this arch. You then reach a junction with a bench, where you can sit and wait for a Kingfisher to show.

The left fork leads you through a wood while the right fork drops to follow the river bank. You can take either, as they join at a bridge further along the trail. I usually walk alongside the river, always alert for the blue bullet-like shape of a Kingfisher whizzing past. When you spot the 'Kingfisher Viewpoint' sign on the left, look across the lake to the mud bank where these popular birds like to dig a nest hole.

In spring, you should now encounter a Sedge Warbler – or five – singing from riverside bushes as well as the resident Reed Buntings. Patience will be rewarded with close views of this scratchy songster. Hirundines may be hunting over the fields across the river.

Further along, you'll reach another junction at another bridge. Take the right path to reach the hide but scan the lake to your left before progressing, as birds on here are easily flushed. These may include wintering Goosanders and Little Grebes, as well as Great Crested Grebes in summer among the common wildfowl species such as Egyptian and Greylag Geese, Mallard, etc.

The hide overlooks a newly-refurbished scrape across the Little Ouse River. Viewing can be difficult through the poolside vegetation, so sit here for as long as you can to give birds chance to walk or float into view.

There is every chance that a Kingfisher will zip past, though you may have to stand up in the hide to see it as it will be so close! Breeding waders on the scrape have included Little Ringed Plovers, Redshanks, Oystercatchers and Lapwings. Currently, only Lapwings breed regularly but LRPs still visit in spring.

Other wader species may drop in on passage in spring and autumn, so scan the muddy edges of this scrape carefully. Snipe and Water Rails are present in winter. A Hobby may hunt, especially in autumn when their young are about and dragonflies are on the wing.

Return to the bridge junction and you can choose to go back via the riverside path, or cross the bridge and turn left (again pausing to scan for wildfowl on the lakes either side of you). The path leads you through a wood and back to the 'bench junction' and then the car park.

Just a short walk/drive away is Barnhamcross Common. From the large car park on the common, head away from the town and explore the large area of common land either side of the road. Woodlarks and Turtle Doves used to breed here but have deserted the site in recent years.

It may still be worth listening for the larks' mournful song (as well as the more buoyant song of Skylarks) on fine spring mornings and Turtle Doves may well pass through occasionally (they like to perch on exposed telephone wires). Willow Tits are clinging to existence on the common but who knows for how much longer?

At any time of year, the trees on the common are home to woodland species such as Nuthatch, Treecreeper, Great Spotted Woodpecker, etc. and the bushes are magnets to breeding warblers in spring and summer. The grassy areas attract Green Woodpeckers and resident thrushes, joined by Fieldfares and Redwings in winter.

Also on the common are a couple of vantage points overlooking Nunnery Lakes: walk out of the main car park, cross the busy main road and head diagonally away from the town (south east) for several hundred yards. You eventually reach a fenceline where you can search for suitable viewpoints of the BTO reserve (see above for possible birds).

In winter, Hawfinches occasionally visit the blackthorn hedge and the one remaining large tree around the Pumping Station. To reach here from the large car park, carefully cross the busy A134 and walk back towards Thetford. When you reach the 30mph sign, turn right down a wide sandy track and walk 300 yards to the pumping station (this track is gated but you can walk around the gate. When the gate is open, wheelchairs can gain access).

CONSISTING of 243ha of former gravel workings, Pensthorpe sprang to fame when it became host to the BBC's *Springwatch* for a couple of years. Around 100 species of wild birds breed among the reserve's varied habitats and there are also many captive species for visitors to admire.

Target birds *All Year* – **Common wildfowl (100%), Lesser Spotted Woodpecker (<5%).** *Spring/summer* – **Little Ringed Plover (90%), Avocet (75%), Marsh Harrier (60%), Cetti's Warbler (hear 60%, see 5%), Grey Wagtail (40%), Honey Buzzard (<10%).** *Autumn* – **Passage waders.** *Winter* – **Bittern (15%).**

Other possible bird species

All year
Great Crested Grebe
Little Grebe
Cormorant
Grey Heron
Little Egret
Egyptian Goose
Shelduck
Common waterbirds
Sparrowhawk
Buzzard
Kestrel
Red-legged Partridge
Grey Partridge
Water Rail
Oystercatcher
Lapwing
Woodcock
Snipe
Regular gull species
Stock Dove
Barn Owl
Little Owl
Kingfisher
Green Woodpecker
Great Spotted Woodpecker
Skylark
Pied Wagtail
Starling
Common scrub birds
Goldcrest
Marsh Tit
Nuthatch
Treecreeper
Bullfinch
Common finches
Jay
Other corvids
Tree Sparrow
Reed Bunting

Winter
Goosander
Meadow Pipit
Winter thrushes
Siskin
Lesser Redpoll

Spring/summer
Hobby
Common Tern
Turtle Dove
Cuckoo
Sand Martin
Other hirundines
Sedge Warbler
Reed Warbler
Lesser Whitethroat
Whitethroat
Garden Warbler
Blackcap
Grasshopper Warbler
Chiffchaff
Willow Warbler
Spotted Flycatcher

Spring/autumn
Ringed Plover
Dunlin
Redshank
Greenshank
Green Sandpiper
Wood Sandpiper
Common Sandpiper
Curlew
Black-tailed Godwit
Ruff
Yellow Wagtail

Occasional
Bewick's Swan (fly-over)
Whooper Swan (fly-over)
Scaup (winter)
Smew (winter)
Bittern (winter)
Winter raptors
Osprey (passage)
Red Kite
Jack Snipe (winter)
Long-eared Owl (winter)
Nightingale (summer)
Bearded Tit

Background information and birding tips
YOU MAY BE wondering why I have included a wildfowl collection in a wild bird site guide and I must admit to thinking long and hard about whether to incorporate Pensthorpe into this

Key points
• **Free parking.**

• **Open every day except Dec 25 and 26: 10am to 4pm (Jan and Feb), 10am to 5pm rest of year.**

• **Check website for up-to-date admission prices. Wensum Discovery tours are extra.**

• **Only guide dogs allowed.**

• **Level terrain; most paths good for wheelchairs, but some muddy at times.**

• **Book group visits at least 10 days in advance.**

• **Wheelchairs available (first come, first served).**

• **Disabled toilets.**

• **Restaurant and shop.**

Contacts
Visitor Centre
01328 851 465;
e-mail: info@ pensthorpe.com
www.pensthorpe.com

book. However, once you visit, you will realise that Pensthorpe is much more than a 'bird zoo', being set in 243ha of land including several SSSIs. The estate is owned and managed by Bill Jordan, of Jordan's cereals fame and serves as a benchmark for wildlife-friendly farming practices in the UK. Some of the estate is run as a Conservation Grade farm bursting with wildlife. It is hoped to provide improved viewing facilities of this Conservation Grade farmland in the future.

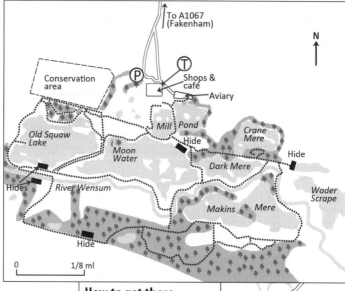

The Pensthorpe Conservation Trust is also instrumental in the Corn Crake release scheme in the Cambridgeshire Fens and the nationwide attempt to reintroduce Common Cranes.

When you have turned off the main A1067, keep one eye on the fields either side of the access road for corvids and Green Woodpeckers all year round and thrushes in winter. There are bird feeders in the car park, which attract the usual common species. Look for the play area: the surrounding grassland is an excellent spot for Barn Owls, especially at dusk.

You will then pass through reception to pay the entrance fee and pick up a reserve map (if you haven't already downloaded one from the website). All facilities are situated in this main area, including a cafe, a shop and the toilets.

How to get there

(One mile E of Fakenham).

SAT NAV: NR21 0LN.

GPS: 52.824331; 0.887932.

From the Fakenham bypass roundabout (adjacent to the football ground), take the A1067 signed to Norwich. Go straight on at the next roundabout, then left onto Pensthorpe Road at the next roundabout (still signed to Norwich).

The park entrance is 1 mile

along this road on your right (signed Waterfowl Park & Nature Reserve).

Download a reserve map at: www.pensthorpe.com/user_files/downloads/pensthorpe-park-guide-rso.pdf

Once outside again, you will pass through the captive bird pens, but I usually make straight for the revamped wader scrape, where a large hide overlooks the recently restored pools and islands. In winter, there should be a wide range of wild ducks, including Tufted Ducks, Teal, Wigeon and Goosanders, along with occasional wild swans, Smew and Scaup. Bittern sightings are increasing in winter.

Spring and summer brings the breeding

stars such as Little Ringed Plovers (remember cooing at their antics on *Springwatch*?), which nest on the scrapes. Lapwings, Shelduck and Oystercatchers add to the entertainment and Avocets are regular visitors. A nesting wall has been constructed to encourage Kingfishers to breed, and this jewel of a bird can be seen from the hide all year round. Sand Martins also nest in the wall and these arrive from early March.

Autumn and spring brings passage waders such as Ringed Plovers and Common and Green Sandpipers. Don't forget to scan the fields at the rear of the lake: the captive cranes sometimes attract wild Common Cranes down to feed and there are usually plenty of corvids and thrushes, especially in winter.

From here, retrace your steps for a short distance and then head towards the ancient wildflower meadow. A boardwalk leads you through this fascinating habitat, which is good for botanists and entomologists in summer and can attract warblers to the surrounding trees and bushes. Listen out for Grasshopper Warblers, Lesser Whitethroats, etc in spring and summer and Cetti's Warblers all year round.

Continue your walk through a wet woodland, the most likely place to encounter a Lesser Spotted Woodpecker. Sightings of this species are now few and far between but Pensthorpe hopes to manage the woodland to increase the number of this dramatically declining species.

It is worth spending a bit of time here to see what turns up: Spotted Flycatcher is a target bird in the breeding season and Treecreepers are present year round.

It is then a short walk to the woodland hide. This overlooks a set of well-stocked feeders which attract the usual suspects as well as the nationally declining Marsh Tit. You may be lucky enough to hear a Nightingale in April and May.

Continue along the footpath, which leads to a marshy area on one side and a grassy area on the other (around J3 on the reserve leaflet). If it is quiet, you may be lucky enough to stumble upon a wintering Jack Snipe in the former

habitat (though far more likely is a Common Snipe or two) and a Barn Owl in the latter.

Visitors can now take a short cut back to the main reception area (straight on) or turn left. Both paths skirt Old Squaw Lake and you will find a small hide overlooking the lake on the latter route. Here, you may find Little and Great Crested Grebes among the common wildfowl and Reed and Sedge Warblers in the breeding season.

Whenever you reach a spot where you can scan your surroundings, look out for Honey Buzzards passing over in summer. Pensthorpe is very close to the Sennowe Estate, hence HBs are seen occasionally between mid May and early September.

Also keep an eye open for Marsh Harriers, Goshawks and Buzzards all year round and Peregrines, Merlins and Hen Harriers in winter, though sightings are few and far between.

Dotted around the estate are several feeding stations allowing visitors to get close up views of many common passerine species.

An entry fee of nearly a tenner seems a bit steep to get onto a reserve but one has to bear in mind the other attractions available. This is a great place to bring your kids to learn about wildlife and conservation and you may even go on a 'safari tour' to learn more about Conservation Grade farming methods.

At the moment, there is good access for wheelchair users but the management team hopes to improve this even further in the future.

I would like to see a separate fee for birders and casual visitors, though I realise this is impractical. In the meantime, if a rare bird turns up, a reduced fee is usually negotiated for 'twitchers' (such as when a Squacco Heron turned up a few years ago).

Other nearby sites
Flitcham Abbey Farm, Hempton Marsh, King's Lynn Docks, Pentney Gravel Pits, Roydon Common, Sculthorpe Moor, Swanton Novers.

Key points

- **Access at all times.**
- **Park sensibly – all roads heavily used by gravel lorries.**
- **Be careful of heavy trucks in the bridge area.**
- **Telescope very useful.**
- **Best to arrive early in summer, as the Leisure Park area is busy with holidaymakers.**
- **Viewing the Leisure Lake is from the road, so wheelchair access is good.**

Contacts
None

THERE ARE two main areas of interest at Pentney: the gravel pits accessed along a public footpath alongside the River Nar and the easily-disturbed lakes near the caravan park. In spring, the bushes at either site can be full of the song of warblers and in winter the pits can be crowded with wildfowl and gulls.

Target birds *All year* – **Common wildfowl (100%), Yellow-legged Gull (30%).** *Summer* – **Little Ringed Plover (75%), Nightingale (hear 60%, see 5%).** *Spring/autumn* – **Passage waders.**

Other possible bird species

All year
Great Crested Grebe
Cormorant
Egyptian Goose
Water Rail
Common wildfowl
Common waterbirds
Sparrowhawk
Kestrel
Regular gull species
Kingfisher
Green Woodpecker
Great Spotted Woodpecker
Skylark
Pied Wagtail

Jay
Other corvids
Bullfinch
Other common finches
Yellowhammer
Reed Bunting

Spring/autumn
Ringed Plover
Little Stint
Curlew Sandpiper
Ruff
Whimbrel
Greenshank
Green Sandpiper
Wood Sandpiper

Common Sandpiper
Black Tern
Yellow Wagtail

Summer
Common Tern
Hobby
Hirundines
Grasshopper Warbler
Sedge Warbler
Reed Warbler
Lesser Whitethroat
Other common warblers

Winter
Goldeneye
Winter thrushes

Background information and birding tips

A CASUAL glance might suggest Pentney Pits has little to offer birdwatchers but it is worth a diversion off the A47 at all times of year.

The main area of interest consists of working pits, accessed from the track running east from High Bridge. Follow the rough, grass path (checking the ditch for Sedge Warblers in summer and Kingfishers all year round) until it joins a wide gravel track. There are many viewpoints along the way and several paths down to the pits.

The first pit holds many loafing gulls throughout the year, which may include Yellow-legged and Caspian, possibly joined by Iceland and Glaucous in winter. These birds

visit from the Blackborough End Tip, visible in the background.

The second pit along has a couple of sandy islands and muddy edges. This is the best area for Little Ringed Plover in summer and any passage waders in spring and autumn. Check the reeds for Reed Warbler and Reed Bunting. Also scan the fields to your right for thrushes, gamebirds, Lapwings and grazing wildfowl.

Further along, you come to a large pit which attracts Common Terns in summer (and maybe Black and Arctic Terns on passage) and winter ducks. Eventually, you reach the main working pit with a poplar plantation to your right.

If you fancy a really long walk,

How to get there

(5.5 miles SE of King's Lynn).

SAT NAV: Blackborough>New Road. (Probably best to follow written directions instead of SAT NAV).

GPS: 52.693996; 0.169323

Map labels: To A47; Blackborough End; To East Winch (A47); N; Blackborough; West Bilney Wood; Viewpoint for Pentney Lakes (OK for wheelchairs); Viewpoint for working pits; P; P; Pentney Lakes Leisure Park; P; River Nar; Working pits; Cover for Nightingales; Ashwood Lodge; To Wormegay; No vehicular access; 0   1/2ml; KING'S LYNN; A47; A10; A1122

Working pits: From King's Lynn, take the A47 signed to Norwich (ignoring brown signs for "Pentney Lakes"). After approx. 3 miles take East Winch Road, signed to Waste Disposal Tip. After 1 mile, take first left (sign-posted "Waste Recycling Centre", immediately before 7.5 tonne restriction sign). Go past recycling centre, down hill, right at sharp bend to a T-junction. Turn left and drive 0.4 miles to bridge. Park carefully in small lay-by on right before you cross the bridge (room for two cars). The public footpath is signed both ways along the River Nar (take the left track as you face the bridge, crossing the ditch and then over a stile). DO NOT BLOCK ANY FARM GATES.

Caravan site lakes: From King's Lynn take the minor road off to the right following the brown tourist signs for 'Pentney Lakes'. Follow to the entrance of Pentney Lakes Leisure Park. The area of bushes just before this entrance used to be good for Nightingales, as did the area around the sandy pull-in for West Bilney Wood (TF 699 133).

To view the pits, go past the Leisure Park entrance and turn left at the sharp bend by the house (straight on is access for lorries only). After one mile, park on the left-hand verge opposite track to Ashwood Lodge (if you reach the ancient cross on the right you have gone too far).

continue along the footpath until it meets a road. Turn left and follow the road to the Leisure Park entrance (beware of fast-moving heavy lorries!). Just after the entrance, there is an obvious track on the left leading into West Bilney Woods. Go through the wood and turn left at the top of the track to return to the public footpath by the River Nar, via the gravel pits. Turn right on the path to return to your car at High Bridge.

The pit by the Leisure Park lakes can be viewed from the verge opposite the track to Ashwood Lodge. There is a lot of disturbance but it is worth a quick stop, as rare grebes (e.g. Black-necked) have been seen here in winter among the common wildfowl. Little Ringed Plovers sometimes frequent the muddy edges.

This area is best visited early in the morning before the holidaymakers have stirred from their caravans. Be warned that lorries use this road at all times of the day and travel at a fair rate of knots.

A handful of Nightingales still cling on in the area of the Leisure Park lakes. Park in the car park at West Bilney Woods and listen for the distinctive song from late April to the end of May. Please do not disturb these birds.

There is a small car park at the entrance to West Bilney Wood (see Access section). Follow the wide track through the pine trees and you should see Goldcrest, Coal Tit, Great Spotted Woodpecker, Treecreeper and maybe even Tawny Owl and Crossbill.

155

Key points

- **Free car park (donations box) near Ranworth Staithe.**

- **Wheelchair-friendly toilets in The Maltsters pub car park. Do not use pub's car park – use designated NWT spaces.**

- **Boardwalk trail open at all times. Visitor centre open April to October (10am to 5pm).**

- **Groups should book in advance.**

- **Level terrain, fully wheelchair accessible.**

- **No cycling or dogs.**

- **Seasonal electric boat from Ranworth Staithe to visitor centre and around Ranworth Broad. Fee is charged. Book on 01603 270 479**

- **Sightings board, snacks at centre. Optics available for use upstairs.**

WHETHER you visit Norfolk Wildlife Trust's Ranworth Broad on foot or by the electric boat (or both), you are sure to see many species of common birds at any time of year. It is one of the most reliable sites in Norfolk at which to see an Osprey on passage and one often lingers through the summer.

Target birds *All year* – **Common wildfowl (100%), Cetti's Warbler (hear 70%, see 10%).** *Spring/summer* – **Common Tern (100%), Marsh Harrier (60%), Osprey (20%).** *Winter* – **Winter wildfowl (100%).**

Other possible bird species

All year		*Winter*
Egyptian Goose	Great Spotted Woodpecker	Wigeon
Shelduck	Common scrub birds	Gadwall
Common wildfowl	Marsh Tit	Teal
Cormorant (large roost)	Common woodland birds	Shoveler
Great Crested Grebe	Common finches	Pochard
Common waterbirds	Reed Bunting	
Sparrowhawk		*Occasional*
Regular gull species	*Spring/summer*	Lesser Spotted Woodpecker
Kingfisher	Cuckoo	
	Hirundines	Bearded Tit
	Summer warblers	

Background information and birding tips

RANWORTH BROAD is part of the Bure Marshes National Nature Reserve. Once you have found the reserve (sign-posting from the car park could be improved), a 500 yard boardwalk through carr woodland leads to the Norfolk Wildlife Trust's Ranworth visitor centre.

Alternatively, you can choose to arrive by the electric boat which departs from Malthouse Broad Staithe (near the NWT car park).

The carr holds many species of common birds including Cetti's Warblers and Marsh Tits, so take your time. Once at the centre, there is a sightings board, a shop, snacks, picnic tables and a viewing platform overlooking the Broad.

If you can manage the narrow spiral staircase to the upper floor, you'll be able to view the Broad through the telescopes and

binoculars set up to observe the tern breeding platforms and lake. An Osprey has been known to linger in the area all summer.

In winter, Ranworth Broad reserve attracts a large number of wildfowl but the centre itself is closed. Visiting birders can scan the Broad from a viewing platform (not wheelchair accessible) at the end of the boardwalk, adjacent to the centre.

Great Crested Grebes, Pochards, Goldeneyes, Teal, Shovelers and Tufted Ducks should all be in winter residence and there is a winter

Contacts

Ranworth Broad Centre, Ranworth – 01603 270 479
Norfolk Wildlife Trust – 01603 625 540
General Broads Authority – 01603 610 734

How to get there

(Eight miles NE of Norwich).

SAT NAV: NR13 6HY.

GPS: 52.677316; 1.489910.

By car: From B1140 (Acle to Wroxham road), follow signs into South Walsham village. In village centre take the road N to Ranworth. Follow road for 1.1 miles to a junction of roads at The Maltsters public house (pub on left, Granary Stores straight ahead).

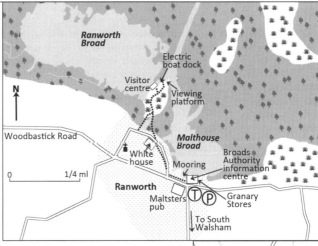

Turn right here, following signs to the Conservation Centre car park about 30 yards down on the right, indicated by a brown tourist sign.

Walk back to the pub and Ranworth Staithe. Look for a Norfolk Wildlife Trust sign indicating the start of the walk to the Conservation Centre (the electric boat to the visitor centre also leaves from this area).

Follow boardwalk (adjacent to the road, running west) towards church to its end. Turn immediately right (do not go straight on to the church) and follow for 0.2 miles to reserve entrance on the right (opposite a large white house). Follow the boardwalk through the alder carr to the visitor centre.

By boat: Head W from Wroxham along River Bure, through Horning and moor up at Ranworth Staithe. The

reserve notice board is on the right near the shop.

Follow the directions above to the visitor centre or catch the electric boat from the staithe (small fee payable).

roost of 400 or so Cormorants in the trees.

All in all, there is something here for everyone. The reserve is also good for butterflies and dragonflies in summer and a visit is usually an enjoyable one, though the trip might be made more enjoyable by using insect repellent.

An added attraction for visitors is the boat trip around Ranworth Broad (unfortunately this is not accessible for people in wheelchairs).

This visits areas not visible from the centre and the informative guide ensures an enjoyable trip. You may also get up close and personal

with a Marsh Harrier and the breeding terns along with Great Crested Grebes and maybe even a Kingfisher or an otter.

To make sure your day out goes well, I'd advise telephoning the centre to check sailing times and to book before you arrive.

Other nearby sites

Breydon Water, Buxton Heath, Cockshoot Broad, Great Yarmouth Beach, Hickling Broad, Hoveton Great Broad, How Hill NNR, Strumpshaw Fen, Upton Fen, Winterton Dunes.

157

Key points

- **NOA members only. Access by key dawn to dusk. (Permits from NOA Holme Observatory when a rarity is present).**
- **The key fits all NOA reserve hides. If membership lapses, please return your key!**
- **Boardwalked for wheelchair access.**
- **Free parking in field next to access gate when dry. One space by gate if parked CAREFULLY.**
- **Otherwise pay in beach car park or in lay-by on left after NWT payment hut.**
- **Telescope useful.**
- **Sightings book and fieldguide in hide.**

Contacts

Norfolk Ornithologists'
Association
01485 525 406;
e-mail: infonoa@
btinternet.com

THIS SMALL marshland site is fully wheelchair-accessible and worth visiting whenever you are in North Norfolk. It is a NOA members-only reserve but well worth the joining fee. Passage times see many species, such as Green and Wood Sandpipers and Yellow Wagtails, visiting the marsh and, in winter, one can sit for hours enjoying what turns up (expect raptors, wildfowl and waders).

Target birds *All year* – **Marsh Harrier (95%), Barn Owl (90%).** *Spring/autumn* – **Passage waders (75%).** *Winter* – **Winter raptors (25%).**

Other possible bird species

All year
Egyptian Goose
Common wildfowl
Common waterbirds
Little Egret
Kestrel
Lapwing
Redshank
Snipe
Regular gull species
Corvids
Skylark
Common scrub birds
Meadow Pipit

Pied Wagtail
Common finches

Winter
Brent Goose
Wigeon
Teal
Other common wildfowl
Winter thrushes

Summer
Hobby
Black-tailed Godwit
Avocet
Turtle Dove

Hirundines
Sedge Warbler
Lesser Whitethroat
Whitethroat
Blackcap

Spring/autumn
Little Ringed Plover
Little Stint
Ruff
Greenshank
Common Sandpiper
Yellow Wagtail

Background information and birding tips

REDWELL MARSH comprises 35 acres of marshland with an excellent wader scrape that attracts many bird species all year round.

The reserve's sole hide is only available to NOA members, though if a rarity is present day permits will be sold from the NOA Observatory at the end of the Holme access track.

To reach the hide, walk along a boardwalk from the Holme access track. This is fully wheelchair-accessible.

The scrape attracts numerous Green and Wood Sandpipers in spring and autumn, as well as Common and Curlew Sandpipers, Ruff, Little Stints, Whimbrels, Black-tailed Godwits and Greenshanks.

A few Yellow Wagtails regularly visit in spring and are usually to be found around the hooves of the resident cows. A Little Egret may drop in at any time of year.

In summer, small numbers of Avocets and Black-tailed Godwits may visit the marsh and, overhead, you may be lucky to see a Marsh Harrier or Hobby.

Black-headed Gulls breed on the marsh and you may wish to linger and observe the comings and goings at this lively colony. Keep an eye open for one of the wandering Holkham Spoonbills, which occasionally drop in during the summer.

Winter brings an array of common wildfowl to Redwell. Expect to see

Wigeon, Tufted Ducks, Gadwall, Teal and Mallards.

If these species become agitated, scan the marsh for a Hen Harrier, Merlin or Peregrine.

At any time of the year, Redwell Marsh is an excellent place to see a Barn Owl. A vigil in the hide for any reasonable length of time should result in superb views of this special bird.

Finally, don't neglect to scan the hedgerow alongside the boardwalk leading to the hide. This can hold several bird species, such as Goldfinch, Greenfinch, Bullfinch, Linnet, Dunnock and Blackbird which may all be encountered at any time of year. They will be joined by Sedge Warblers, Blackcaps and Whitethroats in summer.

The telegraph pole opposite the entrance gate seems to attract the local Great Spotted Woodpecker, especially when he's displaying in spring.

Redwell Marsh makes for an excellent diversion when combined with a visit to the NOA and NWT reserves. A full day's birding in the Holme area can be very rewarding whatever time of year you visit.

Other nearby sites

Brancaster Marsh, Gypsy Lane, Holme Dunes, Holme Observatory, Hunstanton, Ken Hill Wood, Sandringham, Snettisham, Titchwell Marsh.

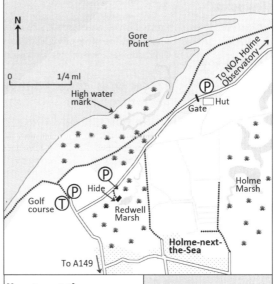

How to get there

(Two miles NE of Hunstanton).

SAT NAV: PE36 6LQ or Holme-next-the-Sea>Broadwater Road (postcode gets you onto rough access track).

GPS: 52.965715; 0.530461.

From Hunstanton head E on A149 to left turn (sign-posted NOA Watchpoint/NNT Reserve). Continue on this road for about half a mile, then turn right onto a rough track just before you reach the toilet block (note there are no facilities on site). Drive slowly as track is very bumpy.

0.2 miles after you have turned onto the track, look for a single car parking space by a

gate on the right. If dry, open the farm gate and park in the field. If soggy, either return to the beach car park where you turned off or continue for another 0.3 miles and park in the large sandy lay-by on the left (NWT charge may be asked for) and walk back.

Be careful not block the gate to the marsh as it will obstruct wheelchair users.

Key points

- **Free car parking.**
- **Free 24-hour mooring.**
- **Public footpath open at all times.**
- **800m of easy-access path.**
- **One hide.**
- **Two disabled spaces in the car park.**
- **No turning room in the hide for large wheelchairs. You may have to reverse 50m along the path to turn around.**
- **Facilities in the pub when open.**

ROCKLAND BROAD and its surrounds attract many common species of birds all year round, with Marsh Harrier, Barn Owl, Great Crested Grebe and Cetti's Warbler just some of the resident birds you might see. The site is particularly attractive to people with mobility difficulties, as the half mile long path to the hide is easy access all the way.

Target birds *All year* – **Cetti's Warbler (hear, 80%, see, 25%), Marsh Harrier (70%).**

Other possible bird species

All year		
Common wildfowl	Meadow Pipit	Chiffchaff
Common waterfowl	Pied Wagtail	Willow Warbler
Great Crested Grebe	Common finches	
Sparrowhawk	Reed Bunting	*Winter*
Kestrel		Winter wildfowl
Regular gull species	*Summer*	Winter thrushes
Barn Owl	Common Tern	
Kingfisher	Cuckoo	*Spring/autumn*
Green Woodpecker	Hirundines	Yellow Wagtail
Great Spotted Woodpecker	Sedge Warbler	
Corvids	Reed Warbler	*Occasional*
Skylark	Lesser Whitethroat	Osprey
Common scrub birds	Whitethroat	Hobby
	Blackcap	Arctic Tern
		Black Tern

Background information and birding tips

ROCKLAND BROAD is a somewhat overlooked site in The Norfolk Broads. An easy access path leads from the car park (opposite The New Inn) and from the adjacent boat moorings.

The route is part of the Wherryman's Way footpath, which links with the RSPB's Surlingham Church Marshes and The Ted Ellis Trust Reserve, though the easy access path only goes as far as the hide at Rockland St. Mary.

The birding starts in the car park where common species such as Chaffinch, Goldfinch, House Sparrow, Robin, etc can be encountered. In summer, Sedge and Reed Warblers sing from the vegetation around the staithe car park.

If the area is peaceful, listen out

for a Kingfisher along the mooring channel. First thing in the morning is best. Walk slowly along the path. You might hear a Cetti's Warbler in any of the bushes along the way.

Just past the mooring channel, you'll reach a wide kissing gate. The path now runs atop a raised bank with a marsh to your right and the broad to your left.

Scan the broad through the gaps in the bushes (you should see common wildfowl in the winter and Common Terns in the breeding season), while on the marsh you may see a Marsh Harrier or two drifting over or a Barn Owl hunting for voles. Snipe and Lapwing may be present in the winter.

The bushes and reeds along the path should also produce Sedge and Reed Warblers and Whitethroat

Contacts

General Broads Authority
01603 610 734

Strumpshaw Fen
01603 715 191

in the breeding season.

Green and Great Spotted Woodpeckers inhabit the trees at the back of the marsh to your right and they can sometimes be seen flying along the edges of the wood. Yellow Wagtails may be in the fields, especially in spring.

You'll eventually reach a hide, managed by the RSPB, which is the best place to view water birds such as Great Crested Grebe, Coot, Moorhen, Grey Heron, Mute Swan, Tufted Duck, Pochard and Gadwall. In spring and autumn, Black and Arctic Terns may pass through and Rockland is probably one of the best places to find a passage Osprey.

The windows at either end of the hide look into thick bushes – excellent places to catch a fleeting glimpse of Cetti's Warblers.

The easy access path continues for a short way after the hide. A bench that overlooks the inlet to Rockland Broad is another good place to sit quietly and wait for a Kingfisher to show. A narrow, muddy path then continues alongside the marsh and channel up to the River Yare. You may get closer views of Marsh Harrier here.

You can now retrace your steps to the car park or continue along the footpath, which rejoins the minor road at Claxton. You will then have to turn right along the road back to Rockland Staithe (approx 3.5 miles round walk).

You can also walk to the Ted Ellis Trust Reserve and the RSPB's Surlingham Church Marshes via the Wherryman's Way footpath accessed from near the car park in Rockland St. Mary (circular walk is seven miles long). Walk

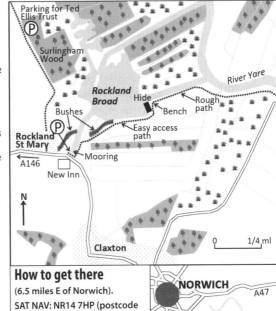

How to get there

(6.5 miles E of Norwich).

SAT NAV: NR14 7HP (postcode for New Inn).

GPS: 52.589727; 1.435063.

By boat: The reserve is situated along the River Yare about half an hour's journey SE from the Brundall boat yards. Moor in the channel at Rockland Staithe.

By car: From A47 Norwich bypass, turn onto A146 (sign-posted Lowestoft and Norwich). Head SE (away from Norwich) for about 100 yards until first set of traffic lights. Turn left to Bramerton. Stay on this minor road to Rockland then follow signs for Claxton (stay on minor road throughout). Beyond the

houses in Rockland, follow the small sign on left directing you to 'Rockland Staithe Car Park'. The reserve's car park is almost opposite the New Inn. Do not park in the pub car park.

From the designated car park follow the path over a small bridge towards the pub. The footpath to the reserve starts after you have crossed the mooring channel and continues to the River Yare.

onto the road and turn right. After 150 yards, turn right along a farm track (signed "playground") and follow

through to Surlingham Wood and the Ted Ellis Trust car park (approx. one mile distance).

161

Key points

- SSSI and Ramsar site managed by Wildlife Trust.
- No facilities.
- Free access and parking.
- Track to car park very rough.
- Poor access for wheelchair users, but raptors can be viewed from car park.
- Mainly level sandy tracks can be wet after rain.
- Take torch for return walk to car after Nightjar trips.
- A telescope useful for raptor watching.
- Use insect repellent in summer.
- All dogs on short leads at all times.

Contacts

Norfolk Wildlife Trust 01603 625 540. Downloadable leaflet: www. norfolkwildlifetrust. org.uk/Documents/ Reserves/Roydon_hires. pdf

ROYDON COMMON is rightly ranked among the top 50 National Nature Reserves in Britain thanks to a wide range of rare and scarce plants and animals supported by this rare heathland habitat. Birding interest includes a raptor roost in winter and breeding Nightjars and Woodlarks in spring and summer.

Target birds
Winter – **Marsh Harrier (95%), Hen Harrier (90%), Merlin (25%).** Summer – **Nightjar (90%), Woodlark (80%), Tree Pipit (60%), Nightingale (hear, 60%, see 20%).**

Other possible bird species

All year	Jay	Winter thrushes
Grey Partridge	Other corvids	*Spring/summer*
Sparrowhawk	Common scrub birds	Hobby
Kestrel	Marsh Tit	Hirundines
Lapwing	Skylark	Grasshopper Warbler
Snipe	Meadow Pipit	Lesser Whitethroat
Woodcock	Pied Wagtail	Other warblers
Curlew	Common finches	
Stock Dove	Yellowhammer	*Occasional*
Tawny Owl	Reed Bunting	Long-eared Owl
Barn Owl		Short-eared Owl
Green Woodpecker	*Winter*	
Great Spotted Woodpecker	Jack Snipe	

Background information and birding tips

ROYDON COMMON is a famous raptor roost site. A visit here in winter should result in sightings of Marsh Harrier, a couple of Hen Harriers and Barn Owls along with Kestrel, Sparrowhawk and, occasionally, Merlin.

It's best to turn up an hour before dusk between late October and early March (though I have found December through to February to be the optimum period) and scan the Common. The harriers can appear as if out of nowhere, so be alert.

Keep a close eye on Carrion Crows as any raptor in the area will be welcomed by a mass of mobbing corvids! Marsh Harriers and Barn Owls seem to be active about 90 minutes before dark, whereas Hen Harriers and Merlins appear much closer to nightfall. All species like to

circle the back of the heath before settling to roost.

Good numbers of Jack Snipe are present in winter, but seeing them involves a trek in freezing cold water up to your knees and is not advisable!

In summer, Roydon Common is a good place to see Nightjars, with up to 20 churring males to be heard on the reserve.

To see one, take the main track from the car park until you reach a junction with another sandy track (approx 200 yards on your left). The Nightjars can be anywhere along this second track, as well as Woodlarks and Tree Pipits. Nightjars can usually be seen as close as the junction of the two main tracks.

Visitors with mobility difficulties may park on the access track to the NWT car park and scan the

How to get there

(Four miles E of King's Lynn).

SAT NAV: PE32 1AP or Roydon>Lynn Road

GPS: 52.777904; 0.489715 (raptors & Nightjars) or 52.776567; 0.515558 (Nightingales).

For raptors: From King's Lynn bypass, take A148 towards Cromer. After 300 yards turn right (sign-posted to Grimston and Congham Hall Herb Garden). After 0.6 miles, take sandy track on right (with the wooden footpath sign). Park on the main track (in sight of the main road – break-ins common here!) and then walk along track away from m ain road. Flat, grassy viewing area is through large logs on the left, or take the first main sandy track off to the left to view heath where raptors roost and Nightjars breed.

For Nightjars: (Also general access to heath and bog) follow directions as above but after the new gate, take second track on left (by the NWT noticeboard). Nightjars can be seen anywhere from this track, which leads to Grimston Warren, a NWT reserve that is being restored to bog (currently no access but can be viewed from the fence).

For Nightingales: (TF 697 228) Follow instructions as for raptors (above) but instead of using car park, travel further along the Grimston road to just before the road junction. There is a small car park on the right that is not easy to see (if

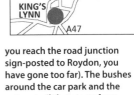

you reach the road junction sign-posted to Roydon, you have gone too far). The bushes around the car park and the nature trail that starts from this car park are very good for Nightingales.

---

heath for raptors from their car. Unfortunately, it is unlikely that you will see Woodlarks or Nightjars from here in summer.

Nightingales are present at Roydon in respectable numbers. Park in the eastern car park, taking care on this busy road. Nightingales are usually audible from this car park from mid April (approx 18th). Cross over a stile and follow the way-marked NWT trail through the wet wood.

The wood and pools along this trail are excellent for insects as well as birds. The wide, grass track accessed from the east of the car park (left as you turn in to the car park) is also excellent for butterflies and eventually leads to a sandy track.

Turn right along this sandy track (unbelievably, a 60mph road!) and you reach the gates to Roydon Common (on your right), follow the track to the raptor roost car park and Grimston Warren (on your left; no formal trails yet).

A lot of work goes into maintaining the habitat for all kinds of flora and fauna. The result is that Roydon Common, as well as being an excellent site for raptors and breeding birds, is also host to an amazing number of rare plants, dragonflies and moths and fully justifies its Ramsar designation.

Key points
- **Access at all times.**
- **Narrow roads, so please park with consideration.**
- **The only walking necessary is along level hard-surfaced roads. Good for wheelchair users.**

SALTHOUSE HEATH remains a reliable site for sought-after Nightjars and Nightingales and if you choose to visit on a still summer night you'll hear a thrilling dusk chorus. The Heath also hosts many species of common birds and is an attractive site for migrants.

Target birds *Summer* – **Nightjar (85%), Tree Pipit (May display flight 80%), Nightingale (hear 80%, see 20%).**

Other possible bird species

Summer		
Hobby	Tawny Owl	Common woodland birds
Woodcock	Great Spotted Woodpecker	Warblers
Cuckoo	Hirundines	Yellowhammer
	Common scrub birds	

Background information and birding tips

THE NAMES of the two most noteworthy species to be seen at Salthouse Heath give a clue to their habits. 'Night' suggests that both species, Nightingale and Nightjar, are only to be found during darkness. This is not strictly true of course but it is necessary to be on site at dawn or dusk for the best chance of locating either of these evocative species.

Nightingales arrive from about April 17 but I suggest you visit the Heath from a week later to be sure of connecting with one. I prefer to arrive around dawn on a mild day and listen for their beautiful, far-carrying song. It doesn't usually take long to locate a singing Nightingale, but seeing it is another matter!

The most promising place to look is in bushes lining the triangle of roads west of the crossroads where you park (see map). I have listened for an hour to a bird singing continually from thick cover three yards in front of me without catching a glimpse of the little devil.

Even more annoying was the fact that it kept moving from bush to bush and I still didn't see it! Eventually, I obtained good views,

demonstrating the benefits of patience.

There are stories of more than one Nightingale singing in full view on trees that haven't yet developed their leaves (in April) but I have never experienced this myself. Yet. The junction of the triangle of roads at TG 071 422 is supposed to be a good place for this.

Nightingales do sing through the day, especially on warm spring ones and in the evenings. If you turn up an hour before dark, you can listen to the Nightingales, then head back along the road for the chorus of Nightjars.

The Nightjars on Salthouse Heath are probably the most watched (and listened to) in Britain. On most nights there are several people standing around waiting for the first *'churrs'* of these birds. They arrive in mid to late May and entertain visiting birdwatchers until August.

Once parked, you need go no further. Male Nightjars should start 'churring' on the Heath north and south of the road just as it is getting dark. If you are really lucky, you may see one perched in a bare tree while it does its vocal

Contacts
None.

impression of a distant moped.

This is probably more likely on the north side of the road, the bird being silhouetted against the sunset. As the light dims, flying Nightjars can usually be seen over the road and a close encounter with one is certainly a life-enhancing experience!

Please remember that both Nightingales and Nightjars are sensitive to disturbance, so please do not chase after them or tape-lure them. If you see bad behaviour at this site, please remonstrate with the perpetrator.

Salthouse Heath is a traditional site for Tree Pipits, present from mid-April. There are only one or two pairs, so you may have to search a bit for them. They are much easier to find when they are performing their display flight from when they arrive until mid-May.

It is worth listening out for Woodlarks on the Heath from the end of February until early June. The habitat looks good for them but I don't think they are seen regularly.

Because of its position at the top of a hill (something of a rarity in Norfolk!), just inland from the sea, it is worth checking the Heath for migrants in early spring and autumn. It is under-watched at these times so who knows what you might discover.

Other nearby sites

Blakeney Point, Cley Marshes, Felbrigg Hall, Kelling Quags, Salthouse Beach, Swanton Novers, Walsey Hills, Weybourne.

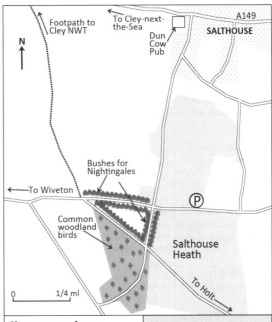

How to get there

(Six miles W of Sheringham).

SAT NAV: NR25 7XA. These coordinates are for The Dun Cow pub at Salthouse, on the A149 – from here follow directions below.

GPS: 52.939764; 1.083348. This reading is for a small, rough car park off Holt Road. Alternatively use tiny lay-bys on heath roads.

From A149 turn inland on a minor road (S) at the Dun Cow pub. After one mile, you reach a crossroads. Turn left and after about 150 yards there is a rough turn-off into a small car park.

Alternatively, park very

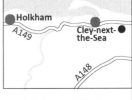

carefully in one of the few lay-bys along any of the very narrow lanes. Walk the lanes listening for singing birds. For either species, it should not be necessary to enter the heath.

You may also walk from Cley NWT/Walsey Hills to Salthouse Heath (or vice versa) along the public footpath.

Key points

- **Free access at all times.**
- **Marsh can be viewed from the road so suitable for wheelchair users.**
- **Terrain is level along shingle bank.**
- **Areas either side of beach car park owned by the National Trust.**
- **Snack van sometimes in car park.**

THE MAIN ATTRACTION at Salthouse is the regular overwintering flock of Snow Buntings. Attracted to seed put down by photographers, these delightful birds can be seen at close range. The surrounding fields and pools attract a host of winter geese and waders.

Target birds
All year – **Marsh Harrier (90%), Barn Owl (65%).** *Winter* – **Seabirds (40%), Snow Bunting (80%), winter raptors (20%).** *Spring/autumn* – **Passage waders, passage seabirds.**

Other possible bird species

All year	Great Crested Grebe	Whimbrel
Cormorant	Hen Harrier	Greenshank
Kestrel	Merlin	Green Sandpiper
Common waders	Peregrine	Wood Sandpiper
Regular gull species	Guillemot	Common Sandpiper
Skylark	Razorbill	Skuas
Meadow Pipit	Winter thrushes	Arctic Tern
Pied Wagtail	*Spring/autumn*	Yellow Wagtail
Reed Bunting	*(might include)*	Wheatear
Winter	Shearwaters	*Summer*
Brent Goose	Gannet	Sandwich Tern
Wigeon	Garganey	Common Tern
Long-tailed Duck	Little Ringed Plover	
Common Scoter	Little Stint	*Occasional*
Goldeneye	Temminck's Stint	Shore Lark (winter)
Red-breasted Merganser	Curlew Sandpiper	Lapland Bunting (winter)
Red-throated Diver	Ruff	

Background information and birding tips

SALTHOUSE MARSHES, to all intents and purposes, is an extension of NWT Cley Marsh reserve, thus the range of species to be seen is similar to its larger, more illustrious neighbour.

In winter, seed is laid out by bird photographers to attract Snow Buntings. These usually show superbly well close to the car park (which is therefore an ideal place for disabled birders to get to see this beautiful species).

If they are not there, wait for them to appear (they can sometimes be found around 'Little Eye', a small mound to the west of the car park or in roadside marshes). This flock is occasionally joined by one or two Shore Larks or Lapland Buntings.

You will also find Oystercatchers, Turnstones and Dunlins in the pools close to the car park, joined by Black-tailed Godwits and Avocets in the breeding season.

Further west, look out for Barn Owls and Marsh Harriers. Up on the shingle sea wall, seawatching can be productive at all times of year. The terns, divers, grebes, ducks, shearwaters and skuas listed for Cley can all be seen at sea from Salthouse, at the right time of year.

To the east, you may follow the Norfolk Coastal Path along the

Contacts

None.

shore to Sheringham, via Gramborough Hill and Weybourne, birdwatching all the way.

The road to the beach is an excellent area to watch birds at close range but it is important to stay in your car to avoid disturbance. Waders can be very close to the road here, particularly in autumn.

Little Stints are a speciality in September, while Green, Wood and Curlew Sandpipers can all give superb views. Redshanks are present all year round, possibly joined at migration times by a Greenshank or two. Whimbrels are regular visitors in spring.

Winter produces Brent Geese and Wigeon in the fields along the approach road. Yellow Wagtails can be seen here in spring and autumn and don't forget to watch out for one of the rarer races (Blue-headed, Syke's etc) among them.

Some birders prefer to park in the Iron Road car park and walk down to the Little Eye and seawall. This is generally a quieter route (fewer people, not fewer birds!) than from the beach car park but is essentially the same walk.

In between the Iron Road and Beach Road car parks, along the

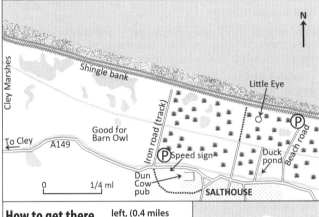

How to get there

(General area: five miles W of Sheringham).

SAT NAV: NR25 7XW (close to Beach Road – from here follow directions below).

GPS: 52.955412; 1.098161.

Beach Road: On A149, heading to Sheringham, you will pass the Dun Cow pub (on right) then the duck pond (on left) after leaving Salthouse village.

Take the next road left, (0.4 miles past the pub) sign-posted 'Beach Road' and follow this down to the shingle car park, scanning fields from your car to avoid disturbing the birds.

If available, use a small lay-by just after you have turned off the A149 for scanning.

Iron Road: Park in very small car park off A149, 1.2 miles E of Cley NWT visitor centre when

approaching from Cley TG 070 439; GPS: 52.953378; 1.080624).

If you reach the 40mph signs as you enter Salthouse, you have gone too far. Walk down the track to the shingle seawall.

A149, is a small duck pond. This usually holds a few loafing gulls, predominantly Black-headed and common ducks which love to be fed by children of all ages! Occasionally, a Mediterranean Gull joins the throng.

This is also a good place to stop as you can feed yourself in the pub or shop and no, you can't count all the feral geese on your list!

Other nearby sites

Blakeney Point, Cley Marshes, Felbrigg Hall, Kelling Heath, Kelling Quags, Salthouse Heath, Sheringham Sea Front, Sheringham Park, Swanton Novers, Walsey Hills, Weybourne.

167

Key points

- **House and some trails closed in winter.**

- **Country Park and visitor centre open all year.**

- **Free car parking.**

- **Level terrain along paved roads or rough tracks. Nightjar access along rough tracks.**

- **Take a torch (to light your walk back, NOT to shine on the Nightjars!).**

- **Bird hide (not accessible to wheelchair users).**

- **Restaurant and shop. Wheelchair access to toilets.**

- **Insect repellent may be needed in summer.**

Contacts

The Estate Office, Sandringham
01485 545 408;
e-mail: visits@
sandringhamestate.
co.uk

FAMOUS as the winter residence of the Royal Family, Sandringham is also the summer home to Nightjars and permanent quarters for many common species of birds. The woodland birds seem to show better here than at many other Norfolk sites, making it an ideal venue for photographers.

Target birds *All year* – **Crossbill (20%), Lesser Spotted Woodpecker (15%).** *Summer* – **Nightjar (90%).**

Other possible bird species

All year		*Summer*
Common wildfowl	Jay	Cuckoo
Common waterbirds	Coal Tit	Hirundines
Sparrowhawk	Marsh Tit	Warblers
Kestrel	Skylark	Spotted Flycatcher
Woodcock	Goldcrest	
Tawny Owl	Nuthatch	*Spring/autumn*
Green Woodpecker	Treecreeper	Winter thrushes
Great Spotted	Siskin	Redstart
Woodpecker	Redpoll	Passage migrants
	Other finches	

Background information and birding tips

SANDRINGHAM'S magnificent mixed woodland is home to many birds. A maze of footpaths through the woods connects the many parking places along the minor road to the main car park.

The pines around the main car park are excellent for Crossbills. Be prepared to stand for a while (or sit in your car), listening out for their loud 'chip chip' calls. Early mornings are best, when they may come down to drink from the puddles in the car park. I find the Jays are tamer here than anywhere else I know.

The colour-marked trails, (blue is one mile long, yellow two miles long), start from the children's play area to the left of the Sandringham shop. They weave in and out of the woods and are excellent walks to see common woodland species.

All three woodpecker species are present but Lesser Spotted Woodpeckers are becoming very hard to find. The best time to find them is in late March/early April when they are displaying.

The yellow trail splits from the blue one and leads to a hide overlooking a small pool. A few minutes here should produce good views of many common species and possibly a Crossbill flock coming down to drink.

The grounds of Sandringham hold six species of tit, Nuthatch, Treecreeper, Goldcrest and a whole range of woodland birds are easy to find here.

You can either find a quiet spot and wait for the birds to come to you or wander the trails looking for them. The estate makes for an excellent site for a dawn chorus vigil in spring.

The trails can be tricky to follow as the yellow and blue paint marks on tree trunks are sometimes hard to see. The arrows are sometimes ambiguous, too. If you go more

How to get there

(Six miles N of King's Lynn).

SAT NAV: PE35 6EH.

GPS: 52.829179; 0.504049.

The Sandringham Estate is well sign-posted from A149 (about six miles N of King's Lynn town centre).

Follow minor road down to the main car park (1 mile) or pull off wherever takes your fancy to walk into the woods. The 'Scenic Drive' is sign-posted off on the left of the access road.

For Nightjars: From King's Lynn take A147 past Castle Rising and a turn to West Newton (B1439). Take next right, marked by a blue cycle track sign to Sandringham. Park in 3rd muddy lay-by on left (approx. TF 676 269). Take narrow but obvious track on left into wood. Where it meets a wide 'ride', turn left and after 75 yards turn right to meet the line of telegraph poles and wires. Walk to open area and listen for the birds. Walk this in daylight to get your bearings before attempting it in the evening!

than 100 yards without seeing a coloured spot on a tree, I suggest you retrace your steps.

The trails may prove difficult for wheelchairs to negotiate but no matter, as there is a scenic drive (sign-posted from the main access road) that follows the general route of the trails and all species can be seen in this manner.

There are also several flat 'rides' that pass between the trees. A tractor carries tourists around the estate roads through the wood for an extra charge.

From the end of May to the end of August, visiting birders can see Nightjars in the clearings in Sandringham Woods. Because the forest is continually being felled, new clearings are formed and once-popular clearings for Nightjars gradually become overgrown. Currently, the best clearing can be found by following directions in the Access Section.

If you find my suggested clearing, you may also wish to adopt my method for seeing a Nightjar. Sit quietly by a telegraph pole or under the wires and one of these evocative birds will almost certainly come and sit on the wires and serenade you with its amazing 'churr'. There is no need to flap your handkerchief!

I recommend finding a suitable clearing during the day as a trial run to familiarise yourself with the route. If you cannot find my clearing, don't despair: Nightjars are easier to find at Dersingham Bog, just a few minutes' drive from Sandringham.

169

Key points

- **Free access dawn to dusk all year.**

- **Many paths accessible by wheelchair.**

- **Many trails to explore.**

- **Trail leaflet can be bought at Forest Enterprise offices in village (open 9am to 4.30pm).**

- **RADAR disabled toilets at St. Helen's picnic site, 1.5 miles and High Lodge, 3 miles by car (TL 807 864).**

- **Early visits best for most species, except Nightjar (dusk).**

- **Use insect repellent in summer.**

- **Dogs on leads please.**

Contacts

Forest Enterprise, 01842 810 271; e-mail: nicky.russell@forestry. gsi.gov.uk

High Lodge Forest Centre 01842 815 434

THERE ARE hundreds of miles of tracks and trails in the vast Thetford Forest, but the mixed habitats around Santon Downham gives the visiting birdwatcher the chance of seeing several sought-after species in a relatively small area. Some of these birds are elusive, so patience is a virtue!

Target birds *All year* – Firecrest (40%), Crossbill (40%), Lesser Spotted Woodpecker (25%), Goshawk (20%), Hawfinch (<15%), Golden Pheasant (5%), Long-eared Owl (1%). *Summer* – Nightjar (90%), Woodlark (75%). *Winter* – Brambling (70%).

Other possible bird species

All year	Marsh Tit	Hirundines
Sparrowhawk	Coal Tit	Redstart
Kestrel	Nuthatch	Whitethroat
Woodcock	Treecreeper	Garden Warbler
Stock Dove	Meadow Pipit	Blackcap
Tawny Owl	Siskin	Other warblers
Kingfisher	Redpoll	Spotted Flycatcher
Green Woodpecker	Yellowhammer	Tree Pipit
Great Spotted Woodpecker	*Spring/summer*	*Winter*
Jay	Hobby	Lapwing
Skyark	Turtle Dove	Snipe
Goldcrest	Cuckoo	Winter thrushes

Background information and birding tips

MANY OF THE scarcer species on offer here, for example Crossbill, Goshawk and Hawfinch, can be very elusive, due to the size of the area, but Nightjars and Woodlarks are easier to locate.

You can access the forest around Santon Downham from several car parks, but I recommend starting your visit at the Forest Enterprises car park where you can purchase a trail map and provisions.

You can then choose to walk whichever trails you like or cover the area by driving between car parks and exploring from each one: lazy birding and my own preferred method! The following is a glimpse at the best areas but you may wish to find your own.

Walk out of the car park and turn left along the narrow, winding lane

(good for common garden bird species). After about 100 yards, you'll reach a 'weak bridge' over the Little Ouse River, where it is worth scanning for the resident Kingfishers and summering Spotted Flycatchers and warblers.

Continue across the bridge and you will shortly reach a railway line: anywhere from the river to here is your best chance of seeing a Lesser Spotted Woodpecker, especially when they are displaying in late February through to early April. In between the river bridge and the railway, you will pass a road on your right, which leads to the St. Helen's picnic site (we'll come to this later).

Over the railway line is another large car park on your left. This gives access to an excellent, wide trail which opens out onto several

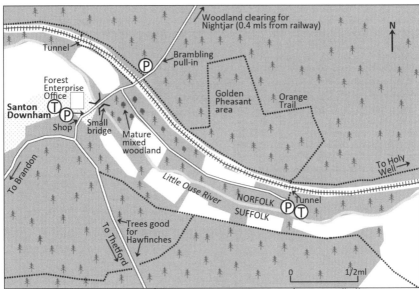

clearings along its length. This is my favourite spot for Nightjars in summer and Woodlarks from late February to July, though there are many clearings along the main road you may prefer to explore.

Woodcocks should be seen over any clearing in the area at dusk, Tree Pipits perform their parachuting display flight from early May and this track also provides a convenient look-out point to scan for soaring raptors (Sparrowhawk, Buzzard and Kestrel are all common and there is a chance of Goshawk, especially from late February to May).

In winter, this main lane, heading NE from the railway, is a very good site to watch Bramblings scuttling among the leaf litter below the beech trees: there is a pull-in on the right conveniently next to their favoured feeding area!

How to get there

(3.5 miles NW of Thetford).

SAT NAV: IP27 0TQ (close to Forestry Commission offices in the centre of Santon Downham).

GPS: 52.457941; 0.671451.

From Thetford, take theB1107, sign-posted Brandon. Take the first right turn (after approx. 3 miles) signed to Forest District Offices. As you drive down this road, keep an eye open for Hawfinch in the lime trees on either side. Follow this road to the Forest Office car park or continue to St. Helen's picnic site car park.

For St. Helen's (TL 825 873; GPS: 52.453641; 0.685807)

go past the offices and continue along the narrow road, cross the small bridge, then turn right immediately after this bridge (if you cross over the railway line you have gone too far). The car park is 0.75 miles down this road.

There is also a large car park past the turn off to St. Helen's, just after the railway line, on your left (TL 820 880; GPS: 52.460138; 0.678091).

Opposite the entrance to the car park by the railway line is a gate (on your right if coming from the FE offices) which leads you onto the Orange Trail, which you can follow all the way to St. Helen's picnic site. This wide path first passes through open grassland (listen for larks) and is an excellent place to sit/stand and watch the skies for raptors and Crossbills.

Further along, the way-marked Orange Trail diverts through pine woodland (or you can carry on along the main track to the railway tunnel junction – see below). Walk carefully and quietly and you may be lucky to pick out a Golden Pheasant in the dark leaf litter or a Firecrest singing from the pines. Crossbills can be anywhere around here.

After your diversion into the wood, if you follow the orange marker posts, you will reach

a junction with the wide track – right leads back to the main road at the railway, left takes you to the Holy Well and Oratory and straight on takes you through a tunnel under the railway to St. Helen's picnic site.

I usually go through the tunnel and turn right along the lane, which leads back to the junction between the railway and the river bridge).

In winter, scan around the edges of the St. Helen's car park, under the trees: it is a favoured spot for Bramblings and Chaffinches. Walk along the lane, not forgetting to look up for passing raptors now and again. The meadows on your left are good spots for thrushes, Lapwing and Snipe in winter and the resident Great Spotted and Green Woodpeckers. At the junction of roads, turn left back to the Forest Enterprise car park via the 'weak bridge' over the river.

If you venture along any of the trails south of the river, you will be in Suffolk, so I am not covering them here. You will have to go on an adventure, Forestry Enterprise map in-hand!

While the possibility of seeing Nightjars and Woodlarks makes the summer a favoured time to visit, Santon Downham has a good range of birds, including Yellowhammer, throughout the year.

THIS FANTASTIC Hawk & Owl Trust reserve attracts many species of birds while being extremely active in the promotion of conservation in the local community. The mile of boardwalk leads through dry and wet woodlands, fens, meadows, reedbeds and dykes and the reserve is carefully designed to allow visitors to see the maximum number of birds. One of my favourite reserves in Norfolk!

Target birds *All Year* – **Cetti's Warbler (hear 75%, see 15%), Barn Owl (50%), Lesser Spotted Woodpecker (15%).** *Summer* – **Marsh Harrier (85%), Grasshopper Warbler (hear, 75%, see, 10%).** *Winter* – **Water Rail (80%), Brambling (40%), Bittern (15%).**

Other possible bird species

All Year
Common wildfowl
Red-legged Partridge
Grey Partridge
Pheasant
Little Egret
Little Grebe
Buzzard
Sparrowhawk
Kestrel
Moorhen
Coot
Lapwing
Woodcock
Regular gull species
Stock Dove
Collared Dove
Tawny Owl
Kingfisher

Green Woodpecker
Great Spotted Woodpecker
Jay
Other corvids
Marsh Tit
Skylark
Goldcrest
Treecreeper
Nuthatch
Bullfinch
Other common finches
Reed Bunting
Yellowhammer

Spring/summer
Hobby
Cuckoo
Hirundines
Sedge Warbler

Reed Warbler
Blackcap
Willow Warbler
Chiffchaff
Spotted Flycatcher

Spring/autumn
Passage waders

Winter
Winter wildfowl
Lapwing
Winter thrushes
Siskin
Lesser Redpoll

Occasional
Hen Harrier (winter)
Honey Buzzard
Willow Tit

Background information and birding tips

SCULTHORPE MOOR Community Nature Reserve comprises 42 acres of reedbed, valley fen, alder carr and coppiced woodland leased from the parish council by the Hawk and Owl Trust.

Your first port of call should be the visitor centre where you will find a sightings board and a friendly receptionist or two to inform you what is around. There are some feeders at the rear of the centre which attract Marsh Tits and an array of common garden birds.

Follow the rough track to the start of the boardwalk. Keep scanning the fields to your left for the resident Barn Owl, winter thrushes, partridges, Lapwings, etc.

The boardwalk leads you through a dry wood to a hide (the boardwalk splits but you can go either way). This wood, and the feeders in front of the hide, is the place to look for Bramblings in winter, which mix with the resident Bullfinches, Chaffinches, Greenfinches and Goldfinches.

Key points
• **Reserve open April to Sept (Tues–Wed 8am–6pm, Thurs–Sun 8am–dusk); Oct to March (Tues–Sun 8am–4pm). Visitor centre open 9am – 4pm.**

• **Site closed Dec 25 and Mondays (except Bank Holidays).**

•**Toilets (inc wheelchair friendly) at visitor centre.**

•**Free parking, donation requested.**

• **4 wheelchair-accessible hides.**

•**1 mile boardwalk with seats; 400 yard soft, peaty path (wheelchair users may need a 'pusher').**

Contacts
Sculthorpe Moor Community Nature Reserve
01328 856 788;
e-mail: info@sculthorpemoor.org
www.hawkandowl.org

Cute voles and mice also visit the feeders!

As you leave the hide, look carefully under the holly bushes for the Golden Pheasants. Two Goldies turned up one winter and can usually be found skulking around the hide somewhere (though almost certainly 'untickable', they are always a treat to see).

There are a few benches in this wood where you can sit and watch more feeders to see what turns up. Marsh Tits are virtually guaranteed in this general area all year round and summer brings warblers such as Chiffchaffs, Willow Warblers and Blackcaps.

The boardwalk then winds through more woods, becoming wet woodland the further you venture along it. Listen for woodpeckers: Great Spotted is a common resident but Sculthorpe still holds a Lesser Spot or two (best in March and April when displaying).

The boardwalk opens onto a sedge bed. In summer, listen for Reed, Sedge and Grasshopper Warblers. Marsh Harriers may be seen hunting this open area (they return to breed during March) and if you go quietly, you might be lucky enough to see a Kingfisher or a water vole along the dykes.

You eventually reach the Whitley Hide. This is surrounded by wet woodland but affords an excellent view over the fen and reedbed. More feeders can be found in front of the hide where stunning views of Bullfinches can be had.

Perhaps the star species here is Water Rail, which feed around the base of the feeders in winter.

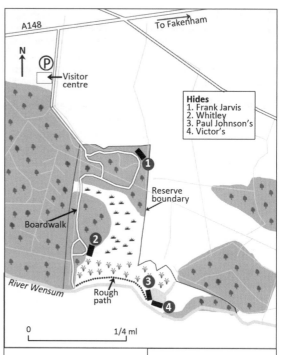

Hides
1. Frank Jarvis
2. Whitley
3. Paul Johnson's
4. Victor's

How to get there

(One mile west of Fakenham).
SAT NAV: NR21 9GN.
GPS: 52.838713; 0. 819404.

From King's Lynn, take the A148 road to Fakenham. Go through East Rudham and past the turn-offs for Dunton. Look out for a turning on your right to Sculthorpe Mill and you know you are close.

There is a road to Sculthorpe on your left but you need the next turning on your right (The Drift), almost directly opposite the second turning

left to Sculthorpe (there is a hand-made board for 'Sculthorpe Moor Community Nature Reserve'). The car park is down this track to your right, signed on a Hawk & Owl Trust board. Park your car and walk down the access track to the reserve entrance.

174

You may have to politely nudge one of the seemingly resident photographers out of the way in order to gain a vantage point!

On leaving the hide, follow the boardwalk out of the wood (a Tawny Owl may be roosting in its nest box near the hide. You will have to be sharp-eyed to spot it, though one of the regular birders may point it out to you) until you reach a sharp left bend. The seat here is a nice place to sit and relax and let the birds come to you.

The boardwalk ends here and the path continues along a soft, peaty surface to the final two hides (some wheelchair users may struggle if it is wet). This path may be closed in the breeding season to protect nesting birds from disturbance.

The path is bordered by a reedbed and the River Wensum, so walk slowly and quietly to the hides and you may get up close and personal with some of the bird species.

The hides overlook the reedbed, a pool and a few channels. In winter, carefully scan the reedy edges for a Bittern. Reed Buntings are resident, joined by Reed and Sedge Warblers in the breeding season.

Passage waders may be attracted to any muddy edges and common wildfowl may be present on the water. A Hobby or two may be hunting dragonflies in summer and early autumn.

Don't neglect scanning the woods in the distance at the rear of these hides or you might miss Buzzards, Kestrels and Sparrowhawks and, potentially, a Goshawk. Otters may be seen on the river if you are patient, quiet and lucky!

Retrace your steps back to the visitor centre, hopefully mopping up all of the species you missed on your walk out.

Sculthorpe Moor is a wonderful reserve, handily placed to nip in to on your way to the north coast or as part of a visit to the cluster of reserves around Fakenham. Alternatively, there is probably enough wildlife on site to keep you entertained for most of the day!

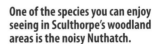

One of the species you can enjoy seeing in Sculthorpe's woodland areas is the noisy Nuthatch.

Key points

- **Pay-and-display parking.**
- **Park grounds open dawn to dusk daily.**
- **Mixture of undulating hard shingle and muddy paths, some steep – most not suitable for wheelchairs (?).**
- **Toilets, including wheelchair access.**
- **Cafe, shop and plant sales.**
- **National Trust visitor centre and Courtyard Café: open daily 10am to 5pm except Dec 27 to 31 (11am to 4pm).**

Contacts

Wood Farm,
Sheringham Park,
Upper Sheringham,
Norfolk NR26 8TL.
01263 820 550;
e-mail:
sheringhampark@
nationaltrust.org.uk

BOASTING SEVERAL areas of ancient woodland, heath, farmland, a wild garden, coastal cliff and collections of rhododendrons and azaleas, this huge National Trust estate is a wonderful place to see many species of common woodland birds. More dedicated birdwatchers also have a fighting chance of finding scarce or rare migrants in spring or autumn.

Target birds *All year* – Common woodland birds (100%), Firecrest (40%), Crossbill (20%). *Winter* – Brambling (40%). *October to March* – Pink-footed Goose (85%), Brent Goose (70%).

Other possible bird species

All year	Other corvids	Whitethroat
Grey Partridge	Starling	Blackcap
Red-legged Partridge	Marsh Tit	Garden Warbler
Pheasant	Skylark	Chiffchaff
Buzzard	Goldcrest	Willow Warbler
Sparrowhawk	Common scrub birds	Spotted Flycatcher
Kestrel	Nuthatch	Tree Pipit
Lapwing	Treecreeper	
Woodcock	Meadow Pipit	*Winter*
Stock Dove	Pied Wagtail	Winter thrushes
Woodpigeon	Siskin	
Barn Owl	Common finches	*Occasional*
Little Owl	Yellowhammer	Wildfowl (fly-overs)
Tawny Owl		Winter raptors
Green Woodpecker	*Summer*	Red Kite
Great Spotted Woodpecker	Cuckoo	Lesser Spotted Woodpecker
Jay	Hobby	Woodlark
	Hirundines	

Background information and birding tips

A NUMBER of colour-marked trails leading from the car park and visitor centre provide visitors with a wide choice of options depending on time and energy available. The red Ramblers' Route takes in all of the habitats should you wish to walk the full five miles of it!

After checking the sightings board at the centre, follow the wide, hard path for about 100 yards when it splits into the different trails. The red trail follows a muddy path through mature woodland: all three woodpeckers have been seen here, though Lesserpecker is very scarce now. Also watch and listen for Treecreeper, Nuthatch and other common species.

The path then drops down a relatively steep incline towards Weybourne Heath. At the bottom of the hill, there is a tiny drinking pool: approach carefully. To the side of this pool is a very small path to a hidden pool where I have found nesting Little Grebes. Sit quietly on the bench to see what birds come down to drink (Crossbill is a possibility because they are resident, thirsty birds on the estate!).

The red trail then opens out onto an area of mature pines. Listen and watch for Crossbills and this is the area I have been most successful with Sparrowhawks. Coal Tits and Goldcrests are common here and a Firecrest might also be seen (better in the rhododendron bushes near the visitor centre).

The trail now reaches a junction: left goes to Weybourne Station – handy if you fancy a ride on the North Norfolk Railway – and the main red route skirts Weybourne Heath.

There are several small paths onto the heath but please stay on them at all times. The heath is home to Nightjars, Tree Pipits and occasional Woodlarks in summer. Woodcocks perform their roding displays, but they and Nightjars are difficult to see here, mainly because the park is only open until dusk every evening! Check with the NT for any special birdwalks for these species.

Follow the red trail around a few bends and the view opens out to fields, a windmill, the A149 coast road and the North Sea. It is now time to start scanning for resident Barn Owls, soaring raptors, larks, corvids, partridges and, in spring and autumn, visible migration: the habitats in the park should be magnets to tired migrants.

In spring and autumn, check any seaward-facing woodland edge for passing migrants such as Redstarts, Wood Warblers and Pied Flycatchers, possibly joined by scarcer species such as Yellow-browed Warbler, Red-breasted Flycatcher and Pallas's Warbler later in the autumn. This is an under-watched site so you never know what you might find!

After a few hundred yards, the main trail bends inland. There are several bushes and brambles here which should be checked

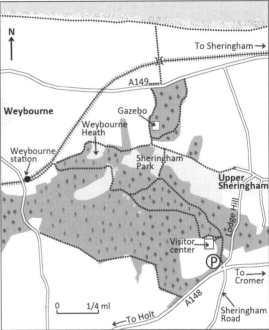

How to get there

(Approx. 2 miles SW of Sheringham)
SAT NAV: NR26 8TL.
GPS: 52.924406; 1.180778.
Take the A148 out of Holt (4 miles) or Cromer (5 miles). Turn down Lodge Hill (opposite Sheringham Road) signed to Upper Sheringham, following brown tourist signs for Sheringham Park and

Country House Hotel. As soon as you have turned off the A148, turn immediately left into the Park's large car park.

for migrants and breeding warblers such as Whitethroat. Follow the path into a delightful wet woodland where Marsh Tits love to hang out, joined by Siskins and Redpolls in winter.

The path then goes through more fields which look good for Quail, before reaching a gate. The Red Route takes a diversion here: you can

177

Key points

- **Two single-seater mobility vehicles/one multi-seater PMV for hire.**

- **Dogs on leads near grazing animals.**

- **Sightings board and accessible route map available in centre.**

- **Cycle racks at visitor centre.**

continue on to join the Blue Trail back to the visitor centre, or you can turn left down towards the coast.

If you turn left, there is a gazebo you can climb to view the woodland and the sea; an excellent place to watch for visible migration as well as the resident woodland birds. Tree-dwelling butterflies may also be seen in spring and summer from this tower.

If you continue down the hill, cross the road (through a gate) and the railway (over a bridge) to walk down to the sea, scanning for Barn Owls as you go. Turn right or left at the sea to search for birds in the cliff top fields (larks, pipits, buntings, etc.). At the right time of year, you may wish to undertake a seawatch for seabirds, geese and waders (see Sheringham Sea Front site, page 179, for possible species).

If returning to your car at Sheringham Park's car park, you now need to retrace your steps over the railway and road, up the hill to the gazebo and then turn left as you rejoin the Ramblers' Route.

Now the trail leads you through typical estate parkland with mature trees dotted around: a favourite area for Green Woodpeckers and Little Owls. Just past the house is a muddy-edged pool favoured by wagtails. Hirundines hunt over this area in summer.

The path then takes you past the temple, which is another place that

gives a superb view over the park. If you can get here in the early morning from October to March, you will see Pink-footed Geese flying over the park as they fly from their overnight roosting grounds to their feeding areas, often joined by Brent Geese (note: the % chance of seeing these presumes you will be at a viewpoint early or late in the day!).

Follow the path uphill and divert through the rhododendron bushes: this is the favoured habitat of Firecrest. Listen for a quite-like-a-Goldcrest-song-but-different and you might be lucky to see this gem of a bird.

Continue to the visitor centre and the car park (and if you are anything like me, by this time you will be needing the café!). You may just have time to seek out the bird feeding station in The Bower, near the visitor centre, where several species of common woodland birds can be seen at close range.

As I stated earlier, you do not need to walk the whole of the Ramblers' (Red) Route; you can walk along any of the other trails as the mood takes you. I have taken you on a long, pleasant walk through all of the park's habitats to give a flavour of what might be seen. I even found a roosting Tawny Owl in the ivy-clad tree above the pay-and-display machine in the car park a few years ago, so you never know what you might find at this productive site!

THE TOWN'S promenade is a well-established seawatching location and those hardy souls who spend hours staring out for birds in less than ideal conditions greatly appreciate the shelters here. From mid-July to the end of November, strong, prolonged northerly or north-westerly winds seem to provide the best results. Anything can fly past!

Target birds *Spring/autumn* – **Arctic Skua (60%), Great Skua (40%), Manx Shearwater (35%), Little Auk in November (10%), Balearic Shearwater (10%), other passage seabirds.**

Other possible bird species

All year	*Summer*	*Winter*
Common wildfowl	Gannet	Red-throated Diver
Fulmar	Kittiwake	Wigeon
Cormorant	Tern species	Common Scoter
Common waders	Hirundines	Red-breasted Merganser
Regular gull species		Auks

Background information and birding tips

SHERINGHAM'S Leas area is arguably the best seawatching spot in the county. In the right weather conditions (and sometimes even in seemingly unfavourable conditions), close views can be had of many of the passage seabird specialities.

From late July, Manx Shearwaters should be seen in small numbers with the chance of one or two Balearic Shearwaters passing, too. However, it is in autumn when this spot can really produce the goods.

Unfortunately, the best conditions for seawatching are strong onshore winds with rain or mist, which can make birding very uncomfortable at many coastal locations. At Sheringham, help is at hand in the form of shelters (with seats) on the promenade: luxury!

From these vantage points and in the conditions described above, the hardy birdwatcher can settle down to enjoy some excellent seawatching. Passing Common, Sandwich and Little Terns should be expected in the breeding season, along with common species of gulls and the odd Fulmar and Gannet.

Strong onshore winds may bring close views of Manx Shearwaters and a very occasional Balearic Shearwater. Storm-petrels are rare but not impossible.

As summer wears into autumn, skuas should be passing by (all four species are possible, though Arctic is the commonest followed by Great), a Grey Phalarope could be seen and the gulls and terns may be joined by a drop-dead-gorgeous Sabine's Gull. Guillemots, Razorbills and Gannets should be much in evidence.

By late October and into November, onshore winds should bring Little Auks close in. Frankly, anything can turn up, so the more you visit the more chance you have of connecting with something very special like a Fea's Petrel, etc.

When seabirds are passing in large numbers, the atmosphere in the shelter can be electric as every

Key points

• **A sheltered seawatching vantage point.**

• **Toilet block on the promenade, including disabled toilets.**

• **Early mornings or evenings seem best.**

• **Access via footpaths to flat terrace, perfect for wheelchairs.**

• **Free parking.**

• **Some shelter available on the prom for wheelchair users down a steep ramp.**

Contacts
None

few seconds someone picks out something new to test your ID skills.

A quick glance at the TV weather charts the previous night should help you decide if an early morning trip to the prom is going to be worthwhile. However, if things do look promising, arrive early as the shelter can get packed full of fellow nutters, erm, I mean seawatching fanatics.

Common wader species such as Turnstone, Ringed Plover and Sanderling, are seen daily and passage wildfowl may also be noted (Wigeon, Pink-footed Geese, Teal, etc).

Winter brings Red-throated Divers and Red-breasted Mergansers and the odd Pomarine Skua has been known to blast by in the right conditions.

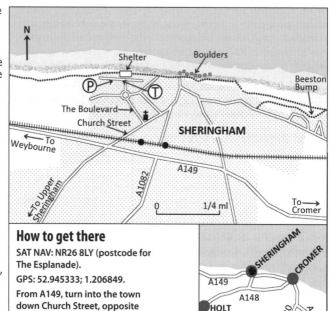

How to get there

SAT NAV: NR26 8LY (postcode for The Esplanade).

GPS: 52.945333; 1.206849.

From A149, turn into the town down Church Street, opposite B1157 to Upper Sheringham. Cross railway bridge and follow road to the church (about half a mile). Turn left into The Boulevard where you will find a small roundabout with a cenotaph on it. Take the second exit from the roundabout (dead end) and park by the concrete bridge straight ahead of you. This is the area known as The Leas.

Walk through the arch onto a terrace, which gives a superb view of the sea. If the weather is poor, go down the steps into a shelter with seats.

Winter is also the time to check for Purple Sandpipers on the boulders on the shore to the west of the seawatching shelters; if not present, you will almost certainly get superb views of Turnstones.

In addition to seawatching, the area to the east of the town, as far as Cromer, has become renowned as a raptor migration hotspot. In spring and autumn bird of prey species can include Marsh Harrier, Buzzard, Sparrowhawk and an occasional Goshawk.

Nearby, Beeston Bump (TG 168 433) has a track record of attracting migrants in spring and autumn and is a good place to view visible migration of species such as Tree and Meadow Pipits and winter thrushes.

Wheelchair users can park on the flat platform at the top of the prom or move down the steepish ramp to shelter under the bridge. The latter option restricts your field of view but it has kept me dry on many an occasion!

Other nearby sites

Blakeney Point, Cley Marshes, Holkham NNR, Salthouse Beach, Sheringham Park, Walsey Hills, Warham Greens, Wells Woods, Weybourne.

COMPOSED of marsh, scrub, reedbed and open water covering 143 acres, the Coastal Park also includes Heacham Harbour and is bordered by The Wash, so a respectable number of species is possible whenever you visit.

Target species *All Year* – **Waders (100%).** *Spring/summer* –**Grasshopper Warbler (hear 90%, see 50%).** *Winter* – **Pink-footed Goose (90%).** *Spring/autumn* – **Passage seabirds and migrants, Mandarin Duck (15%).**

Other possible bird species

All Year	*Summer*	*Spring/autumn (might include)*
Common Scoter	Hobby	Manx Shearwater
Eider	Avocet	Balearic Shearwater
Common wildfowl	Black-tailed Godwit	Sooty Shearwater
Red-legged Partridge	Cuckoo	Gannet
Fulmar	Sand Martin	Whimbrel
Little Egret	Other hirundines	Other passage waders
Little Grebe	Sedge Warbler	Kittiwake
Great Crested Grebe	Reed Warbler	Arctic Skua
Common water birds	Lesser Whitethroat	Great Skua
Marsh Harrier	Whitethroat	Pomarine Skua
Sparrowhawk	Blackcap	Long-tailed Skua
Kestrel	Chiffchaff	Garden Warbler
Water Rail	Willow Warbler	Spotted Flycatcher
Common waders		Pied Flycatcher
Regular gull species	*Winter*	Ring Ouzel
Barn Owl	Long-tailed Duck	Whinchat
Kingfisher	Red-breasted Merganser	Wheatear
Green Woodpecker	Red-throated Diver	Other passage migrants
Gt Spotted Woodpecker	Great Crested Grebe	
Corvids	Merlin	*Occasional*
Skylark	Peregrine	Montagu's Harrier
Common scrub birds	Purple Sandpiper	Shore Lark
Bullfinch	Short-eared Owl	Nightingale
Other common finches	Winter thrushes	Purple Sandpiper
Yellowhammer	Stonechat	Bearded Tit
Reed Bunting	Grey Wagtail	Snow Bunting

Background information and birding tips

SNETTISHAM COASTAL PARK, which was established in 1984, makes for a pleasant stroll after visiting the nearby RSPB reserve at any time of year. More than 120 species have been recorded in the park or on the adjacent beach and mudflats (The Wash).

When you enter the beach car park, park immediately on the right. The entrance to the park is across a little wooden bridge.

At migration times, it may be worth scanning the conifers bordering the car park to see if any birds have arrived. A good indicator species is Goldcrest: if they are in the pines, other species

Key points
• **Free access at all times.**

• **Car park charges apply.**

• **Car park locked 10.30pm – 8.30am.**

• **Mostly level terrain but some steep banks.**

• **Some paths muddy after rain.**

• **Seawatching shelter.**

• **Telescope useful.**

• **Nearest public toilets on W side of A149, Dersingham bypass.**

Contacts
Warden: M. Vowser, Village Farm, Hill Rd, Ingoldisthorpe, King's Lynn, Norfolk PE31 6NZ
01485 441 239

King's Lynn Borough Council,
015537 961 241

may have arrived too. There is an information board just inside the entrance to the park.

If you fancy starting from a different point, walk onto the seawall from the car park. Turn right to get to Heacham. (Note that you should not try to access the RSPB reserve this way, do so only from the Society's car park).

You can walk all the way along this seawall to Heacham south beach (approx. two miles), viewing The Wash on your left and the Coastal Park on your right. About a mile along the seawall, you reach a wooden hide, ideal for viewing The Wash in inclement weather.

Several species of waders such as Grey Plover, Knot, Oystercatcher, Turnstone, Dunlin, Golden Plover and Curlew will be joined on the mudflats by Whimbrel, Curlew Sandpiper and other waders on passage in spring and autumn.

Wader-watching is best in winter but birds begin to flock to the mudflats from July onwards. June is the quietest month but whatever time of year you visit, choose to view when the sea is reasonably close if you wish to see more than dots on the mud.

Also in winter, be in position on the seawall at dawn and dusk and you should be treated to thousands of Pink-footed Geese flying overhead. Views are probably better on the RSPB reserve but the Coastal Park may be an acceptable alternative, if you don't fancy the extra walking.

When the tide is fully in, look out for Great Crested Grebes and Red-throated Divers, occasionally joined by rare species such as Red-necked Grebe and Great Northern and Black-throated Divers in winter. Skuas and

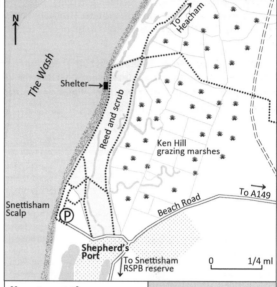

How to get there

Five miles south of Hunstanton).

SAT NAV. PE31 7PS (postcode for Snettisham beach road. Follow road to the very end).

GPS: 52.873888; 0.447032.

Follow the brown tourist signs to 'Snettisham Beach and RSPB reserve' from the A149 Dersingham bypass. Follow this narrow road for 1.9 miles to where it ends at the beach car park.

Walk along the main seawall or go into the park via the wooden walkway on the right near the car park entrance.

shearwaters could also be passing in autumn.

Seaducks such as Common Scoter and Eider could be present at any time of year, Long-tailed Duck and Red-breasted Merganser joining them in winter.

In spring and autumn, the Coastal Park is well worth exploring fully. Wheatear, Ring Ouzel and Whinchat are annual visitors and anything may turn up in favourable conditions.

The bushes attract passage warblers, which

join the breeders such as Lesser Whitethroat, Whitethroat and Blackcap. Nightingales can also be heard occasionally but are not present every year.

During the spring and summer, Snettisham is probably the best place in Norfolk to see Grasshopper Warblers. Seven or more birds can be heard reeling from isolated bushes from late April and into the summer months. They will usually show well if you are prepared be patient.

Walk into the park from the beach car park and head left along a wide stony path. After about 400 yards, there is a narrow, muddy path on your right leading into the heart of the park, which takes you past some bushes in the reeds. In my experience, this is the best place for 'Groppers', though they can be heard anywhere along the main track too.

This narrow path leads to the secondary seawall, accessed up some steps. Turn left along the uneven, grass track and head towards Heacham (right takes you back to the beach car park access road).

There is a channel on your right with a marsh behind. Kingfishers fly along this channel and Barn Owls hunt over the marsh. In winter, scan the marsh for grazing geese, wildfowl and Short-eared Owl.

This track affords excellent views over the park on your left. There is an extensive reedbed, home to Reed and Sedge Warblers in summer and Reed Buntings year round. It can

only be a matter of time before Bearded Tits take up residency and it also looks good for a wintering Bittern or two (though I have never seen one here).

There are several creeks and pools to your right, all should be checked for wildfowl on the water and waders on the muddy edges. Mandarin Ducks sometimes turn up in spring, though cannot be guaranteed and can be elusive.

After about a mile (opposite the hide on the main seawall) you have a choice. You can go down the steep seawall bank into the heart of the park, or you may wish to carry on along the track towards Heacham. Another footpath leading off to your right will take you all the way to Ken Hill Wood.

If you choose the Heacham route, the track bends inland. Once you reach the town you can return to the beach car park via the main seawall, making this a pleasant circular walk (approx 5 miles). The open areas of water on your left are excellent for hirundines in summer, usually pursued by a Hobby or two.

The varied habitats of the Coastal Park ensure an enjoyable and usually productive, hour or two's birdwatching at any time of year.

It is situated between Hunstanton to the north, Ken Hill Wood to the east, The Wash to the west and Snettisham RSPB to the south, making this stretch of Norfolk a perfect base for a birdwatching break.

Other nearby sites

Dersingham Bog, Gypsy Lane, Holme Dunes, Holme Observatory, Hunstanton, Ken Hill Wood, Redwell Marsh, Sandringham, RSPB Snettisham. Titchwell Marsh, Tottenhill Gravel Pits, Wolferton Triangle.

Key points

- Open at all times.
- Donation asked for in car park.
- Obey all 'Anglers Only' signs.
- Paths can be very muddy in winter.
- Three sets of steps to negotiate – otherwise flat terrain.
- Disabled drivers can park close to first hide by prior arrangement (at least 5 working days in advance).
- Wader roost best 3-4 days either side of a full moon. Arrive at hide 90 to 120 minutes before high tide.

Contacts

The Warden, Barn A, Home Farm Barns, Snettisham, King's Lynn, Norfolk PE31 7PD
01485 542 689;
e-mail: snettisham@rspb.org.uk

A WINTER VISIT to RSPB Snettisham at the highest tides will provide birdwatchers with an avian spectacle to rival any in the world. Thousands of waders move in spectacular shifting waves as the tide advances over The Wash, pushing them closer and closer to your viewing position on the reserve. Another treat is to watch the thousands of Pink-footed Geese leave or come into roost on The Wash at dawn or dusk in winter.

Target birds

All year – **Wader roost (100%), Barn Owl (60%), Short-eared Owl (10%).** *Winter* – **Pink-footed Goose (dawn & dusk, 90%), Peregrine (40%), Snow Bunting (30%), Scaup (20%).** *Summer* – **Avocet (99%), Marsh Harrier (75%).** *Spring/ autumn* – **Passage waders (100%).**

Other possible bird species

All year	Merlin	Whinchat
Cormorant	Golden Plover	Wheatear
Common wildfowl	Grey Plover	
Kestrel	Knot	*Summer*
Common waders	Sanderling	Hobby
Regular gull species	Bar-tailed Godwit	Black-tailed Godwit
Skylark	Winter thrushes	Common Tern
Meadow Pipit		Hirundines
Pied Wagtail	*Spring/autumn*	Sedge Warbler
Common finches	Little Stint	Reed Warbler
Reed Bunting	Curlew Sandpiper	Whitethroat
	Spotted Redshank	Other warblers
Winter	Greenshank	
Brent Goose	Green Sandpiper	*Occasional*
Goldeneye	Common Sandpiper	Bittern (winter)
Red-breasted Merganser	Black-tailed Godwit	Smew (winter)
Hen Harrier	Yellow Wagtail	Montagu's Harrier (spring)
		Shore Lark (winter)

Background information and birding tips

ENSURE YOU get the best out of Snettisham by checking the time of the highest tides before visiting. Tide tables for many key UK locations are published annually in *The Birdwatcher's Yearbook* (available from Buckingham Press). Alternatively, the RSPB Snettisham Office sells tide tables with the best wader tides marked on them, as does RSPB Titchwell Marsh's shop. If you catch the place at low tide you could be in for a very miserable visit!

The best time for watching the thousands of waders is over the highest tides from autumn to spring. This is because the Wash is a vast area of mud and the sea only pushes the waders within viewable distances when the tide is at its highest.

You should be in position 90 minutes before high tide and 120 minutes before the highest tides (marked on your tide tables) to get the best experience.

Another tradition for hardy winter birdwatchers at Snettisham is the

How to get there

(Five miles S of Hunstanton).

SAT NAV: PE31 7PS.

GPS: 52.868570; 0.452424.

Snettisham reserve is well sign-posted from A149's Dersingham bypass, 6.5 miles N of King's Lynn. Follow brown tourist signs for 'Snettisham Beach and RSPB reserve' down Beach Road. Continue for 1.5 miles to the RSPB car park on the left. If you arrive before 7.30am or after 9pm, you may have to park near the gate and walk through onto the access road. Follow the footpath from the reservevcar park for 1.5 miles to the hides.

dawn or dusk pilgrimage to witness thousands of Pink-footed Geese leaving or returning to their Wash roost (late November to the end of January). Avoid the three or four days either side of a full moon, as the Pinkies may stay in the fields to feed throughout the moonlit nights. **Please do not use torches once on the beach as this can scare the geese.**

Catch Snettisham at the right time and the spectacle of thousands of waders swirling through the air will leave you breathless.

A number of species roost throughout the year, except in June, with numbers highest between October and January. It cannot be overstated just what a stunning sight they make. I urge you to witness this magnificent avian spectacle and marvel at the number of birds present.

To reach the roost you have to walk nearly two miles through the reserve, though wheelchair users and people with mobility difficulties can take their car up to the first hide – Rotary Hide. **This must be arranged with the warden at least five working days before your visit.**

You will pass several pits on the way to The Wash, which are good for Tufted Ducks, Pochards, Goldeneyes, Gadwall, Mallards, etc and several fields good for Barn Owls, thrushes and finches.

The bushes and hedgerows hold common garden birds throughout the year, joined by Whitethroats in summer.

Once on the seawall, follow the wide track to the hides or the seats overlooking The Wash. Look out for Snow Bunting on the shingle in winter. There is also a circular route that cuts across two pits and through a field of rough grass (good for Skylarks, Meadow Pipits and owls).

The most numerous wader is Knot. In winter

185

Key points

- **Goose movements at dawn or dusk unpredictable around time of full moon.**

- **Essential to check tide times before visiting – see calculator in *The Birdwatcher's Yearbook*.**

- **Tide tables on sale at Snettisham Office or Titchwell Marsh.**

- **Wader ID charts in some hides, plus sightings sheet.**

- **Nearest toilets on west side of A149 Dersingham bypass.**

- **Café open in summer adjacent to car park entrance gate.**

- **Dogs on leads.**

they look plain grey, dumpy birds but if you visit in July/August many will be showing remnants of their red breeding plumage, whereas others will be grey. This gives the impression of someone having paved the mud with pretty bricks but a glance through your binoculars/telescope will reveal thousands of Knot constantly shifting position as the tide comes in.

Also in the mayhem, you should be able to pick out species such as Bar-tailed Godwit, Dunlin, Sanderling, Turnstone, Grey and Golden Plover, Curlew, Ringed Plover and Redshank.

And the fun really starts when a bird of prey comes in to reduce the throng by one. The waders take to the air in huge, swirling flocks to unsettle the raptor.

On very high tide days, many of the waders come in to roost on the southernmost pit, affording excellent views from the hides surrounding the lake. This also gives photographers ample opportunity to obtain close-up wader shots.

This pit is good for passage waders too and in summer, Black-headed Gulls, Common Terns and Avocets nest on the islands here. In winter, this pit is the favoured place for Smew and Scaup.

A winter walk at Snettisham can be a very cold experience so wrap up warmly. On the sea wall there is no respite from the bitter wind but the old saying 'no pain, no gain' is usually proven to be well-founded. And don't be lulled into thinking summer will be much warmer either: always be prepared for anything at Snettisham!

A final word about the beach car park area. This is reached by continuing past the RSPB car park turn off, following signs to the 'Beach'.

There is no access to the RSPB reserve from here but the Snettisham Coastal Park is adjacent to the car park (see page 183). The park is probably the best place in Norfolk to see Grasshopper Warbler, along with common finches and scrub birds. There is also a good chance of migrants in spring and autumn.

In winter, if you walk north from here, you can usually get views of Wigeon and other wildfowl on the marshy grasslands behind the second sea wall. You may also be treated to a good view of Pink-footed Geese flying over.

If you plan your trip carefully, Snettisham is *the* place in Norfolk, if not Britain, to witness one of the great marvels of the bird world; a mass wader roost. And that's not taking into account the 40,000 Pink-footed Geese flying overhead at dusk or dawn!

Other nearby sites

Dersingham Bog, Hunstanton, Ken Hill Wood, King's Lynn Docks, Sandringham, Snettisham Coastal Park. Titchwell Marsh, Wolferton Triangle,

THESE RECLAIMED gravel pits have become one of the most reliable sites in Norfolk to see Goosanders in winter. Grey Wagtails, another Norfolk scarcity, breed in the area and Common Terns, Sand Martins and Kingfishers breed on the reserve. Natural England's extension to this walk should produce sightings of some rapidly declining farmland bird species.

Target birds *All year* – **Grey Wagtail (65%).** *Summer* – **Common Tern (95%), Spotted Flycatcher (70%).** *Winter* – **Goosander (70%).**

Other possible bird species

All year	Common scrub birds	Whitethroat
Egyptian Goose	Marsh Tit	Blackcap
Common wildfowl	Common woodland birds	Chiffchaff
Cormorant	Meadow Pipit	Willow Warbler
Common waterbirds	Pied Wagtail	Reed Warbler
Buzzard	Bullfinch	
Sparrowhawk	Other common finches	*Winter*
Kestrel	Yellowhammer	Goldeneye
Little Grebe	Reed Bunting	Winter thrushes
Great Crested Grebe		Siskin
Regular gull species	*Summer*	Redpoll
Kingfisher	Oystercatcher	*Spring/autumn*
Little Owl	Cuckoo	Passage waders
Green Woodpecker	Turtle Dove	Yellow Wagtail
Great Spotted Woodpecker	Sand Martin	*Occasional*
	Other hirundines	Garganey
Skylark	Sedge Warbler	Little Ringed Plover
	Lesser Whitethroat	

Background information and birding tips

SPARHAM POOLS is a Norfolk Wildlife Trust reserve, reclaimed from former gravel workings. Lying north-west of Norwich, the pits and surrounding habitats are home to many common species all year round and offer a peaceful alternative to the nearby tourist traps of Dinosaur World and the Norfolk Wildlife Park.

Once you have found the NWT car park, (and it will take you a little while), there is a circular path round the pits. You can't get lost as the path does not veer off but leads you back to the car park whichever way you choose.

The track takes you through bushes and trees with occasional views over the pools themselves. Scan the islands in the pools for Egyptian Geese, Oystercatchers and Common Terns, which all nest in summer.

You should see plenty of common wildfowl whatever time of year you visit, though numbers increase in winter. Shovelers, Gadwalls, Mallards, Pochards and Tufted Ducks are joined by Goldeneyes and Teal in winter. Sparham has become a reliable site for Goosanders in recent winters, a welcome addition to any cold day's birding.

Key points

• **Free access at all times.**

• **No facilities other than a car park.**

• **Level terrain along narrow grass and mud paths.**

• **Not suitable for wheelchairs (though Grey Wagtail habitat is viewable from the road).**

• **Paths can be muddy after rain.**

• **No dogs on reserve except on leads on public footpath (northern edge of reserve).**

Contacts
Norfolk Wildlife Trust
1603 625 540

187

In the south-eastern corner of the pools, there is a private gravel pit which may be worth checking for waders such as Common, Green, Curlew and Wood Sandpipers, Greenshank, Ruff, Little Ringed Plover, etc during migration periods.

These pits can now be viewed from the new extension to the walk if you wish (see below for details).

The field adjacent to the road, near the car park, should be scanned for pipits, wagtails and larks especially when wet. The bushes and trees on the reserve should produce many species such as Bullfinch, Marsh Tit, Long-tailed Tit, Siskin, Redpoll, Great Spotted and Green Woodpeckers, etc.

Fifty yards from the entrance to the reserve is the best place to see Grey Wagtails in Norfolk. They are resident around the bridge over the River Wensum, though can go missing for long periods.

To view this area, walk out of the car park along the entrance track and turn left along the road. View from the bridge (no parking). In winter, this stretch of water doesn't freeze, so if the pits are frozen this will be the best place to see a Kingfisher. In summer, you may also see Spotted Flycatchers here.

The Farmland Bird Extension path can be accessed from the north-eastern part of the reserve. Look for a wooden sign-post with multiple direction signs and head east along the permissive footpath. There is a Natural England map and information board about this

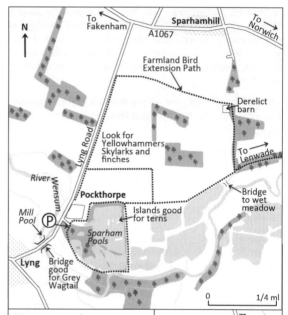

How to get there

(11.5 miles NW of Norwich).

SAT NAV: NR9 5QY (Postcode for houses close to reserve entrance).

GPS: 52.719514; 1.068580.

From Norwich outer ring road, take A1067 NW for approximately 11 miles (sign-posted Bawdeswell).

A mile beyond Lenwade, turn left down Lyng Road (sign-posted Lyng) and continue for 0.8 miles (if you reach the river bridge you have gone too far).

Turn down a narrow track on left to the car park (50 yards before the bridge). This is well hidden as the NWT sign is pointing towards Lyng village, so you may have to

turn around at the bridge and return to find the car park (look out for the wooden public footpath sign, also well hidden!).

From car park, take the path signed with yellow arrows (slightly uphill at 11 o'clock as you drive down the entrance track) or bear right from the access track along a narrow muddy path.

Ignore the path with the NWT sign as it doesn't lead anywhere.

188

new route. Basically, you are heading towards the large pits viewable from the reserve.

This walk takes you through habitat being farmed under the Higher Level Stewardship Scheme. The hedgerow on your left as you head towards the lakes can be bursting with resident finches and sparrows, joined by Whitethroats and other warblers in summer. Approach the pits carefully so as not to spook the wildfowl and gulls.

This first lake is deeper than the ones on the reserve and is the preferred base of many wintering birds such as Goldeneye. Gulls gather here to bathe in reasonable numbers. Scan any exposed edges in spring and autumn for passage waders.

After the lake, you reach another information board. There is an interesting diversion here: you may wish to cross the bridge over the stream (can be <u>very</u> muddy) and take a muddy path through a bit of wet grassland and wet woodland. This is a favoured area for woodpeckers and you may disturb a Snipe in winter.

Retrace your steps over the 'bridge' and walk uphill through a field, heading towards the right of a derelict barn. Scan the isolated trees for Little Owl, the bushes for summer warblers and the grass for winter thrushes, etc.

At the barn, turn left and follow the grassy farm track down towards the (Lyng) road. At the bottom of the hill turn left to walk adjacent to the road (on your right). Keep your eyes peeled all along the route for resident Yellowhammers, Skylarks, finches, etc. as well as Turtle Doves in summer.

At an obvious wide opening in the hedge, look right and you will see some houses: turn left here along a wide farm track (or you can keep straight on down to a small gap in the hedge at the bottom right of the field ahead of you, which takes you onto the road that leads to the car park entrance and the mill bridge).

At the junction of tracks, turn right down the hill towards the lakes you can see over the hedgerow. There is a gate at the bottom: turn right to go through the reserve and back to the car park.

This land is being managed to encourage scarce farmland birds to breed and is well worth the two mile extension from Sparham Pools. Together, these two trails make for a very pleasant birding visit at all times of year.

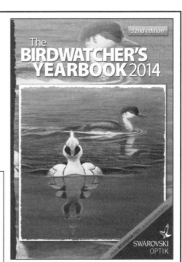

Key points

- **Free access at all times.**
- **Free parking.**
- **Obey all 'Private' signs – do not trespass.**
- **Terrain is level along muddy tracks (some stiles and steps may need to be negotiated).**
- **Not suitable for wheelchair users: view marsh from car parks at Morston or Stiffkey.**
- **Telescope very useful.**
- **Facilities available in village.**
- **Do not park on the road - use the small lay-by or the NT car park.**

STIFFKEY FEN and the surrounding area comprises a relatively large body of fresh water where common wildfowl gather, some enticing bushes for migrants, and a saltmarsh which you can park by at the end of the day to scan for winter raptors moving through to roost. What more could a visiting birdwatcher ask for?

Target birds *Winter* – **Wildfowl (100%), Marsh Harrier (85%), winter raptors (75%), Barn Owl (75%).** *Spring/autumn* – **Passage waders, passage migrants.**

Other possible bird species

All year	Pink-footed Goose	Redstart
Teal	Wigeon	Whinchat
Cormorant	Pintail	Wheatear
Shelduck	Goldeneye	Winter thrushes
Common wildfowl	Merlin	Barred Warbler
Grey Partridge	Peregrine	Goldcrest
Little Egret	Golden Plover	Spotted Flycatcher
Common waterbirds	Grey Plover	Pied Flycatcher
Kestrel	Winter thrushes	
Common waders	Rock Pipit	*Summer*
Great Spotted Woodpecker	*Spring/autumn (might include)*	Breeding waders
		Breeding gulls
Corvids	Scaup	Terns
Skylark	Little Stint	Hobby
Meadow Pipit	Ruff	Hirundines
Pied Wagtail	Whimbrel	Sedge Warbler
Common scrub birds	Greenshank	Reed Warbler
Common finches	Green Sandpiper	Other warblers
Reed Bunting	Wood Sandpiper	*Occasional species*
	Common Sandpiper	Scaup (winter)
Winter	Yellow Wagtail	
Brent Goose		

Background information and birding tips

THIS SITE can be approached from three directions: by walking along the North Norfolk Coastal Path from either Morston or Stiffkey, or by the public footpath from the A149. Any of these walks will produce many species of birds at any time of year.

From the lay-by on the A149, carefully cross the road, go through a gap in the hawthorn hedge and turn left. Follow the grass path (checking the hedge for scrub birds and migrants and the fields for gamebirds, buntings, finches, etc)

for approx. 300 yards. Cross the A149 again and head slightly right for a few yards before crossing a stile onto a muddy footpath (if you cross the stream by the A149 you have gone too far). You reach another stile, an excellent vantage point to scan the Fen!

Follow the footpath for 500 yards onto the seawall (up a few steps), with The Fen on your right. You can now turn left to Stiffkey (1.5 miles) or right to Morston (1.25 miles) along the Norfolk Coastal Path. This junction is a good place

Contacts

The National Trust, East Anglia Regional Office
01263 733 471

to scan for raptors in winter. They roost at Warham Greens, about 2.5 miles to the west but can be seen flying over the marsh in front of you up to two hours before dark.

With a telescope, you can also scan Blakeney Channel from here for terns in summer and wildfowl in winter. The muddy channels are excellent for waders at all times of year (a Lesser Yellowlegs overwintered here in 04/05).

Whether you choose to walk east or west, check the bushes along the path in spring and autumn as anything may turn up. Barred Warblers are regular vagrants in autumn and you should see commoner species such as Goldcrest, Garden Warbler, Whinchat, Redstart, etc.

Stiffkey Fen itself can be viewed from either the footpath from the A149 or the Coastal Path in winter but in summer, vegetation makes it difficult to view the Fen from the A149 footpath, so vertically-challenged individuals may have to climb the seawall to view the site.

The open water of the Fen

How to get there

(Four miles east of Wells-next-the-Sea).

SAT NAV: NR23 1AJ (Red Lion, Stiffkey) or NR23 1QF (Greenway – follow to the end for the car park).

GPS: 52.954731; 0.951189 or 52.956463; 0.923715.

From Wells, go through Stiffkey village (20mph), passing the Red Lion pub on your left.

After 1.2 miles (and several nasty bends), park in the muddy lay-by on your left (room for about 5 cars). Cross the road, go through a gap in the hedge and turn left for The Fen or right to the flooded field.

Stiffkey NT car park: (TF 965 439): From A149, turn down Greenway (unadopted road) at the western end of Stiffkey village (first left in Stiffkey if approaching from Wells). The car park is 500 yards down this track. Walk W to Warham Greens and Wells-next-the-Sea, or E to Stiffkey Fen and Morston Quay.

is home to common wildfowl such as Tufted Duck, Pochard, Shelduck, Egyptian Goose and Gadwall, joined by Goldeneye in winter. Scaup occasionally drop in on passage (unfortunately, they don't seem to stay for the winter), but Brent Geese frequently come in to bathe in winter.

The muddy islands attract

waders at all times of year. Avocets breed and you can also see Little Ringed Plovers and Black-tailed Godwits in summer. Passage periods bring Green, Wood and Common Sandpipers, Ruff, Whimbrel, Curlew Sandpiper, Little Stint, etc. In winter, the water level occasionally covers the islands, so wader-lovers should turn

191

their attention to the channels along the Coastal Path.

From the A149 lay-by, you also have access to a wonderful flooded field, alive with Wigeon and Lapwings in winter and common waders and wildfowl all year round.

Park in the small lay-by, as detailed for The Fen (always resist the urge to view the floods from your car on the winding A149!). Cross the road and go through the gap in the hedge. Turn right and follow the grass path for 0.2 miles when it meets the public footpath to Cockthorpe. View the flood/scrape from this junction but be careful not to flush the birds.

Stiffkey Fen can also be reached from a car park in Stiffkey village. Turn down Greenway and park in the National Trust car park at the end. The Norfolk Coastal Path runs east or west from here or you can walk onto the marsh to try to find winter flocks of Twite, Rock Pipits, Snow Buntings, etc (but keep to footpaths!).

Walk right from the car park to reach Stiffkey Fen. Campsite Wood, running east from the rear of the car park, should be explored thoroughly, before reaching the Fen.

The stunted trees here have an 'enchanted forest' feel and attract species such as Redstart, Pied and Spotted Flycatchers in spring and Yellow-browed Warbler and Firecrest in spring and autumn.

In winter, this car park is an ideal place for wheelchair users to sit and watch for raptors passing over the marsh, with Brent and Pink-footed Geese also likely.

If people fancy a bit of shelter, there is a small viewing hut ('hide' is too strong a word for it!) just to the left of the car park, accessed up a couple of steps.

Visiting birdwatchers could easily spend the whole day in the area. The Fen, flood pools, marsh, hedgerows and channels provide differing habitats for you to explore and you may also wish to combine your visit with a boat trip to Blakeney Point from Morston.

Fields surrounding the fen at Stiffkey, are always worth scanning for sightings of the increasingly rare Grey Partridge.

Other nearby sites
Blakeney Point, Cley Marsh, Felbrigg Hall, Holkham NNR , Holkham Park, Morston Quay, Salthouse Beach, Walsey Hills, Warham Greens.

STRUMPSHAW FEN is home to a number of sought-after bird species but is also an excellent site for the all-round naturalist. It is a large reserve of mixed habitats and some of the speciality birds can be elusive, so be prepared to spend several hours on site to maximise your chances of seeing as many species as possible.

Target birds *All year* – **Marsh Harrier (95%), Bearded Tit (70%), Bittern (20%), Lesser Spotted Woodpecker (10%).** *Winter* – **Hen Harrier (80%).** *Summer* – **Hobby (25%).**

Other possible bird species

All year
Common wildfowl
Cormorant
Little Egret
Great Crested Grebe
Sparrowhawk
Kestrel
Water Rail
Common waterbirds
Woodcock
Regular gull species
Barn Owl
Kingfisher
Green Woodpecker
Great Spotted Woodpecker
Jay
Skylark

Common scrub birds
Marsh Tit
Common woodland birds
Nuthatch
Treecreeper
Cetti's Warbler
Meadow Pipit
Pied Wagtail

Spring/autumn
Greenshank
Green Sandpiper
Common Sandpiper

Summer
Common Tern
Yellow Wagtail
Hirundines
Sedge Warbler

Reed Warbler
Garden Warbler
Grasshopper Warbler
Other warblers
Spotted Flycatcher

Winter
Common wildfowl
Water Rail
Winter thrushes
Redpoll
Brambling

Occasional
Garganey (passage)
Goosander
Spotted Crake
Merlin (winter)
Osprey (passage)

Background information and birding tips

VISITORS to Strumpshaw Fen should be prepared to walk quite a distance if they wish to see everything on offer, as it is a large reserve. It is a popular birding venue at all times of year with sought-after species being relatively easy to see – with patience.

Your walk starts at the reception centre just inside the reserve, but it is worth lingering around the car park as Lesser Spotted Woodpeckers occasionally visit the mature trees here.

On view from the reception centre should be common water birds and wildfowl, plus the chance of a Marsh Harrier. The dead branch protruding across the water to your right is a favoured perch of the resident Kingfisher.

This is also the place to be at dusk in winter when a few Hen and Marsh Harriers gather to roost, sometimes joined in December and January by a wonderful murmuration of Starlings.

My preferred route then proceeds through a small wood, home to several resident species of common woodland birds. Linger here as Nuthatches and Marsh Tits visit the feeders all year round, joined by one or two Bramblings in winter.

Key points

• **Free to RSPB members,** people arriving by train or bus (with valid ticket) and essential carers. Charge for all other visitors.

• **Open (sunrise to dusk) each day except Dec 25.**

• **Manned centre open 9 am to 5pm April to Sept; 10am to 4pm Oct to March.**

Toilets (inc. disabled).

• **One hide accessible to wheelchairs. Tower hide (1.2 miles from reception) involves steep steps.**

• **Only guide dogs allowed.**

Contacts:

RSPB Strumpshaw
01603 715 191;
e-mail: strumpshaw@rspb.org.uk

How to get there

(Seven miles E of Norwich).

SAT NAV: NR13 4HS (follow RSPB signs from this point).

GPS: 52.607209; 1.456465.

Leave A47 Norwich to Great Yarmouth road at the roundabout sign-posted to Brundall. Continue along this minor road for 0.4 miles. Bear left at the sharp bend onto The Street (sign-posted Brundall Station). Negotiate mini-roundabouts and the traffic-calmed area until, after 1.1 miles, you go under a railway bridge. Look for the sign for RSPB Strumpshaw Fen, turning right (Stone Road), then immediately right again (Low Road). Continue to RSPB car park by the railway line. Walk across the railway line at the crossing to the reception centre.

OR: From A47, turn S at signs to Cantley/ Beighton (just where the road becomes a dual carriageway) into Lingwood village. In Lingwood, take the left turn (sign-posted to Station/ Strumpshaw/Cantley & Freethorpe) along Station Road.

Continue past the station to a T-junction. Turn right to Strumpshaw/Norwich, along Norwich Road. Go into Strumpshaw village and turn left (at signs for Strumpshaw Fen and Household Waste Disposal Site) then immediately right down Low Road at the small brown RSPB sign (easily missed). Follow this road down to the RSPB car park.

Key

1. Boardwalk
2. Tower hide
3. Fen hide
4. Reception hide
5. Summer meadow
6. Pumphouse

The wood provides another chance to see or hear the scarce Lesser Spotted Woodpecker along with the commoner Great Spotted.

From the wood, walk along the wide, sandy track to Fen Hide. Listen for Grasshopper Warblers reeling from the isolated bushes in the reeds here. The hide gives a view over the large reedbed, so watch out for Bittern, Marsh Harrier and Bearded Tit at all times of year. Otters are seen regularly from this hide, so be prepared for a lengthy stay here!

If the fancy takes you, you can walk through the wood along the Woodland Trail. This takes you to the River Yare footpath, where you can turn right to join up with the Fen Hide footpath at the Pumphouse. This is a good spot to scan for the resident Barn Owls and a Hobby in the breeding season (the latter love to hunt the dragonflies on the reserve – up to 20 species have been recorded!)

The walk alongside the Yare should produce Great Crested Grebes, plus Sedge Warblers in the bushes on the water's edge (summer only). Listen out too for Cetti's Warbler in any clump of bushes.

Half a mile from Fen Hide is the Tower Hide, accessed up a steep flight of steps. The climb is worth the effort though, as Tower Hide affords superb views over the whole reserve. Sit here for as long as you can to increase your chance of seeing the more desirable species.

A long wait in Tower Hide may produce a flight view of one of the breeding Bitterns, or scan along the channels for one feeding at the edge of the reeds. In winter, the lagoons hold a good selection of common wildfowl, occasionally joined in spring by a Garganey or two.

Once you have had your fill from Tower Hide, continue along the footpath by the River Yare. Very soon, this path bears right to run alongside a small stream called the Lackford Run.

The hide that used to overlook a fine wader scrape has disappeared but you can still see the scrape from the path. Be careful not to flush the birds.

The bushes along the Lackford path hold common finches and scrub birds (Dunnock, Wren, etc) and also Cetti's and Grasshopper Warblers. If you are feeling adventurous, you can wait until dusk here and listen for the whip-like call of Spotted Crakes in spring.

Further along this path, you enter an area of what can only be described as a swamp, accessed along a boardwalk. This area, stretching a couple of hundred yards to the railway crossing, is the best place to *see* the Cetti's Warblers. They are easy to hear but do like to hide in the thick cover.

Once you have crossed the railway line, take the wide track to the right back to the car park (past a cottage). This completes a long, circular route, which produces many common and scarce species no matter what time of year you visit.

You should encounter at least a couple of the target species (but you may be unlucky and see nothing), the longer you stay, the more chance you have of seeing the birds.

Strumpshaw Fen is also an excellent place for other wildlife. In summer, many species of dragonfly and butterfly can be seen along with a number of scarce plants.

Key points

• **Access from car park is across a railway line. Wheelchair users should use phone by the gate to check for trains.**

• **Hearing loop in manned reception hide.**

• **Level terrain. Some hard-standing paths but mostly grass, which can be muddy at any time of year.**

• **Well-marked trails (benches at regular intervals).**

• **Picnic tables and bike racks by reception.**

• **Binoculars available for hire.**

• **Snacks and hot and cold drinks available from reception.**

Other nearby sites

Breydon Water, Buckenham Marshes, Buxton Heath, Great Yarmouth Beach and Cemetery, Hardley Flood, Rockland Broad, Surlingham Church Marshes, Ted Ellis Reserve.

Key points

• Place entrance fee (for non-NWT members) in donations box at visitor centre.

• Park in NWT Hickling Broad car park and walk to mill.

• Blue Badge holders may park at the mill (TG 437 220), but do not block farm access

• Access road can be muddy or flooded.

• Wheelchair users can now access the viewpoint bank. The viewpoint is on a level gravel bank (with 2 benches).

• NWT visitor centre closed in winter, though toilets usually open.

•Sightings book at watchpoint.

Contacts

The Warden, Hickling Broad National Nature Reserve 01692 598 276

Norfolk Wildlife Trust 01603 625 540

THERE CAN BE no better end to a winter day's birding in The Broads than to watch the raptors and Cranes come in to roost from the Stubb Mill watchpoint. Marsh Harrier numbers can run into three figures and more than 30 Cranes are sometimes seen. It is well worth braving the cold wind to witness this spectacle!

Target birds *Winter* – Marsh Harrier (99%), Crane (85%), Hen Harrier (85%), Barn Owl (70%), Merlin (60%).

Other possible bird species

Winter	Lapwing	Winter thrushes
Pink-footed Goose (in flight)	Woodcock	Meadow Pipit
	Regular gull species	Pied Wagtail
Wigeon (in flight)	Skylark	Common finches
Sparrowhawk	Jay	
Kestrel	Common scrub birds	

Background information and birding tips

HARDY birdwatchers are virtually guaranteed to see Cranes in winter at this famous site. A large number of Marsh Harriers also roost on the marsh at Stubb Mill, joined by one or two Hen Harriers and Merlins.

A Barn Owl will almost certainly put in an appearance, usually approaching closer than the roosting raptors and Cranes.

In recent winters the watchpoint has become very busy with birders, so it is best to arrive at least an hour and a half before dusk to stake your claim on a good viewing position. Regularly scan the fields, as raptors seemingly appear from nowhere.

If it is raining it is probably worth postponing your visit. The birds still fly in to roost but I have found that they tend to hunker down quickly in wet weather. Apart from that, there is no shelter here so you'll get wet too! If it is foggy, there is absolutely no point in visiting the site.

In fine weather, the raptors quarter the fields in search of a last meal before roosting. I have noted that Hen Harriers tend to come in later than the other birds, so do not despair if it is getting late and you still haven't seen one.

The Merlins will quite often be seen mobbing the harriers and, if you are lucky, you may see one land on a fence post in reasonable light.

Once on the ground, the Cranes can be surprisingly difficult to see. This sounds impossible for a four foot tall, three foot long shaggy mop but it is remarkable how they melt away into the tall grass when feeding.

This is a fantastic way to end a day's birding in this corner of Norfolk. What could be better than listening to the evocative '*cronk, cronk*' of the Cranes as they fly over two species of harrier being mobbed by a lightning-fast Merlin?

Other species seen from the watchpoint include a thousand or so Pink-footed Geese flying over to roost, as well as Woodcock, Jay, Fieldfare, Redwing, Kestrel and Sparrowhawk.

Be alert and you may be lucky to see a Short-eared Owl that occasionally drifts by. I was once lucky enough to watch a Great White Egret fly over just as the light faded into blackness. Also look out for the Chinese water deer, a small introduced species.

One cautionary note: it is highly likely that the road to the mill watchpoint will be flooded, or at best very muddy, so wear Wellingtons.

Many birdwatchers tend to spend the day in the Horsey/Martham area, searching for the Cranes and raptors, or on the NWT's Hickling Broad reserve, then end up at the Stubb Mill roost in the late afternoon – a perfect winter day out.

Stubb Mill is at its best from November to March, but does provide a handy raised viewpoint to scan the marshes at other times of year. Cranes are resident but do not roost when breeding. Marsh Harriers and a Barn Owl or two can be seen at all times and a Hobby may be hunting hirundines and dragonflies in summer. At this time of year, the hedgerows down to the watchpoint from the visitor centre will hold species such as Whitethroat but otherwise things will be quiet.

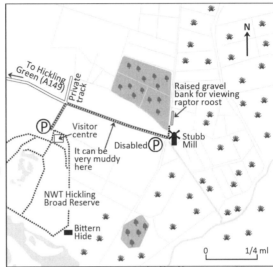

Other nearby sites

Breydon Water, Buckenham Marshes, Burgh Castle, Great Yarmouth Beach, Haddiscoe Marshes, Hickling Broad, Horsey, Martham Broad, Strumpshaw Fen.

How to get there

(14 miles NE of Norwich).

SAT NAV: NR12 0BW (from here follow brown tourist signs to Hickling Broad visitor centre).

GPS: 52.742155; 1.594859.

From A149, about one mile south of Potter Heigham, turn NE at the sign-post to Hickling. Follow all the way to Hickling Green, then turn right at the Greyhound pub.

Follow the brown duck signs to Norfolk Wildlife Trust's car park. DO NOT DRIVE DOWN TO THE MILL. Blue Badge holders may park by the mill in the designated area. There is only room for a couple of cars here, so please do not block farm access.

From the car park, retrace your steps down the road. After about 100 yards you will reach an obvious cross roads

(straight on is a private farm track).

Turn right down the muddy road and walk for about half a mile down to the disused Stubb Mill. Do not enter the mill and cottage grounds but watch the marsh and fields from the obvious raised gravel bank where the track ends (TG 437 220). There is free entry to NWT members but non-members should pay a fee. This is difficult as the visitor centre is closed in winter and I have never seen a warden on site to issue permits. The raised bank can get crowded at times so get there early.

Key points

- **Open all year.**
- **Circular route on rough paths. Some shallow steps en- route.**
- **Not suitable for wheelchairs.**
- **Limited free parking by Surlingham Church and near Woods End Tavern, Bramerton.**
- **One hide, one viewing screen.**
- **Waterproof footwear advisable.**
- **Keep dogs under control.**
- **Stick to paths at all times.**
- **RSPB notice board and map at Surlingham Church.**
- **Sightings board and ID posters in hide.**

Contact

RSPB Mid-Yare Reserves
01603 715 191;
e-mail: strumpshaw
@rspb.org.uk
www.rspb.org.uk/
reserves/guide/s/
surlingham/index.aspx
RSPB East Anglia Office
01603 661 662

ONE OF THE RSPB's five Mid-Yare Nature Reserves, Surlingham's 1.5km circular walk may produce several species of bird at any time of year, but in view of its small size it is probably best combined with a visit to nearby sites to ensure you see as many Broadland birds as possible.

Target birds *All year* – **Marsh Harrier (70%), Cetti's Warbler (hear 70%, see 20%), Kingfisher (50%).** *Winter* – **Hen Harrier (50%).** *Spring/autumn* – **Passage waders.** *Summer* – **Hobby (60%), Grasshopper Warbler (hear 50%, see 10%).**

Other possible bird species

All year		*Summer*
Gadwall	Green Woodpecker	Cuckoo
Shoveler	Great Spotted	Hirundines
Other common wildfowl	Woodpecker	Yellow Wagtail
Cormorant	Jay	Sedge Warbler
Great Crested Grebe	Other corvids	Reed Warbler
Little Grebe	Long-tailed Tit	Grasshopper Warbler
Common waterfowl	Skylark	Whitethroat
Sparrowhawk	Meadow Pipit	Blackcap
Kestrel	Pied Wagtail	*Occasional*
Water Rail	Common finches	Bittern (winter)
Lapwing	Reed Bunting	Jack Snipe (winter)
Snipe	*Winter*	Bearded Tit
Regular gull species	Winter wildfowl	
Barn Owl	Winter thrushes	

Background information and birding tips

SURLINGHAM Church Marshes is one of the lesser known RSPB reserves. It is quite difficult to find but is worth the effort. Though quite a small area (68ha), it holds some desirable species for the visiting birdwatcher.

My suggested route starts from Surlingham Church. Follow the reserve sign-post straight down the grassy track past the cottage. This runs downhill along a bush-lined path to a dyke.

The hedgerow is good for common scrub birds (Robin, Blackbird, Dunnock, etc) and common finches. When you reach the River Yare turn right and follow the grass path.

Listen for the resident Cetti's

Warblers along the path, as well as other warblers in summer (Blackcap, Willow warbler, Whitethroat, etc). Scan the fields across the river for hunting Hobbies in the breeding season and Marsh Harriers and Barn Owls all year round.

Common species on the river itself include Coot, Moorhen, Grey Heron and Great Crested Grebe, with a good chance of Kingfisher.

The hide is reached by a short grass path to your right and there is also a viewing screen a few hundred yards further along the main path. Both overlook a large pool that holds breeding Gadwall and Shovelers. In front of the hide you should see Reed and Sedge

How to get there

(Five miles E of Norwich).

SAT NAV: NR14 7DF (Surlingham Church). Other parking in Bramerton at NR14 7ED. Walk E on Wherryman's Way to reserve.

GPS: 52.606994; 1.403693.

By car: From A47 Norwich bypass, turn onto A146 (sign-posted to Lowestoft & Norwich). After 100 yards, turn left to Bramerton and Kirby Bedon at first set of traffic lights.

After 2.5 miles you will reach a green with the Bramerton village name-post on it. Turn left here (no destination sign-posted) and continue all the way into Surlingham.

Take a left turn in Surlingham village down Church Lane (a dead end), sign-posted to the Church and park there. The reserve is sign-posted either straight on or to the right by the cottage (circular route).

By boat: Moor up at the Ferry House pub, which is about half way between Norwich and Rockland Broad on the River Yare.

There is a permissive footpath

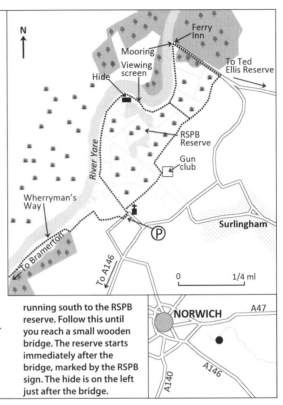

running south to the RSPB reserve. Follow this until you reach a small wooden bridge. The reserve starts immediately after the bridge, marked by the RSPB sign. The hide is on the left just after the bridge.

Warblers in summer and Reed Buntings all year.

Cetti's Warblers may also show in the bushes around the hide all year round. If the water level in the pool is low, watch the muddy edges for the resident Water Rails and passage waders such as Green and Common Sandpipers.

In winter, Hen and Marsh Harriers fly in to roost and give good views from the hide and screen. The pools become flooded and attract decent numbers of common wildfowl such as Tufted Duck, Pochard and Shelduck.

The marshy edges of the pool should be scrutinised for Water Rails in winter, occasionally joined by Jack Snipe.

After the hide, you can either retrace your steps to the car or boat, or complete the circuit of the reserve, via the viewing screen. As the river bends to the left, the footpath bears right and skirts a marshy field that is good for Snipe, Lapwing and Pied Wagtail, with Yellow Wagtails regularly recorded in spring.

You will then reach a T-junction of public footpaths. Cross a stile and turn right to walk along a narrow boardwalk towards the gun club. The marshes are regularly shot over on Sundays and Thursdays after 10am.

After the gun club, the path becomes a rough farm track. Follow this for another quarter of a mile back to the church car park, scanning the bushes and small wood for common woodland birds and finches.

199

Key points

- **No access to woods.**
- **No walking involved.**
- **Donation requested.**
- **Telescope recommended.**
- **Information leaflets in box by entrance gate.**
- **No facilities.**
- **Dogs on leads.**

THOUGH THIS raptor watchpoint used to be one of the few sites where you could see Honey Buzzards in Britain, their appearances are now infrequent. However HBs are renowned for deserting and then re-colonising breeding sites, so keep your eyes on the bird news services for up-to-date information. In the meantime, you can still expect to see several other species of raptor from the viewpoint.

Target birds Honey Buzzard - in years when present (70%).

Other possible bird species

Spring/summer	Corvids	Common finches
Common Buzzard	Hirundines	Yellowhammer
Marsh Harrier	Common scrub birds	*Occasional*
Sparrowhawk	Whitethroat	Red Kite (increasing)
Kestrel	Lesser Whitethroat	Goshawk
Lapwing	Blackcap	Tree Sparrow
Turtle Dove	Skylark	

Background information and birding tips

HONEY BUZZARDS nested in the Great Wood, visible from the car park at Swanton Novers, from 1989 until 2011.

Birds are still seen over the site, especially early in the season, though nesting is sporadic. Bird news services will be the best source of information for each season. For instance, HBs deserted the site in 2011/12 but were present in 2013.

Note that the watchpoint at Great Ryburgh was closed in 2012 but may reopen should HBs return to nest: again, keep an eye on bird news services.

Swanton Great Wood is owned and managed by the Astley Estate. More than 50 species breed within the woodland but access is by permit only (no, you won't get one so don't even bother asking!).

It is perhaps the lack of general access to the wood, that makes the site such a good place for breeding birds.

There is a donation box at the entrance to the grass car park and a Natural England warden is often present.

Even if Honey Buzzards are not nesting, Swanton Novers is still a good place to watch for raptors and visible migration. Buzzards are common, while Hobbies are regular along with Kestrels and Sparrowhawks.

Red Kite sightings are increasing and I have also seen Goshawk here, so who knows what else may fly over?

Honey Buzzards are often seen from the viewpoint when they return to Britain, from mid to late May, even if they don't settle down to breed here.

Scan the sky at regular intervals, as raptors appear as if out of nowhere. A telescope is useful, as birds can be some way off over the wood.

While waiting, scan the surrounding fields and hedgerows. Whitethroats are common and an array of other summer warblers

Contacts

Natural England
01603 620 558
Site Manager
01485 543 044

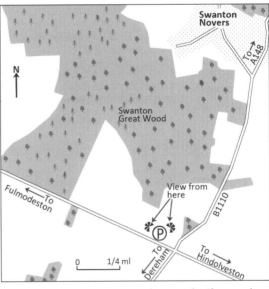

How to get there

(Five miles E of Fakenham).

SAT NAV: NR21 0NG (postcode for Fulmodeston Road and then follow written directions to car park. Alternatively, try Hindolveston>Fulmodeston Road).

GPS: 52.832101; 0.982420.

At the roundabout in Holt, on A148 King's Lynn to Cromer road, turn off onto B1110 to East Dereham. After about five miles, cross B1354 (you need to turn right then immediately left, sign-posted Guist). After a further two miles, turn right at the crossroads to Fulmodeston.

The raptorwatch car park is 0.4 miles on the right: turn into the field at the wooden sign-posts and view the woods from here.

If approaching from Fakenham on A148, take the turning off right after the Fakenham bypass, sign-posted "Fulmodeston 2 miles" (opposite the Kettlestone Road crossroads – if you reach The Green Man pub you have gone too far).

Follow to Fulmodeston where you go straight over at the crossroads down Hindolveston Road.

Follow the road down to the raptorwatch car park on the left after 3.3 miles (turn into the field at the brown sign – if you reach the B1110 crossroads you have gone too far).

breed in the area including Blackcap, Chiffchaff, Willow Warbler and Lesser Whitethroat. Yellowhammers breed in the grassland and Turtle Doves may still be heard cooing away.

If the two buzzard species are in the air together, be sure to note the raised wings of the Common and the flat wings of the Honey.

Honey Buzzard also has a more protruding head with longer wings and tail than Common. If you are really lucky, you may see an HB perform its wing-clapping display.

Also, keep an eye on the bird table in the bottom right hand corner of the car park field as this is kept topped up with seed for the Greenfinches, Goldfinches, etc to feed on, joined by an occasional Tree Sparrow.

Other nearby sites

Hempton Marsh, Salthouse Heath, Salthouse Marshes, Pensthorpe, Thursford Wood.

Key points

- **Free parking and access every day but please give generously at donations box.**
- **Small study centre with toilets (see warden for key).**
- **Wheelchair access OK for hide/study centre.**
- **Reserve maps/ leaflets in car park dispenser.**
- **Hide has info boards plus drawing paper for children.**
- **Level terrain on muddy tracks, boardwalks and uneven grass paths.**
- **Keep to paths at all times.**
- **Cycle racks in car park.**
- **Use insect repellent in summer.**
- **No dogs.**

Contacts

Warden: David Nobbs - 01508 538 036; e-mail: wheatfen@aol.com www.wheatfen.org.uk

A SUPERB, secluded reserve in the south Broads. Visitors will enjoy a quiet stroll around varied habitats which support a wide range of bird species, including the increasingly scarce Lesser Spotted Woodpecker.

Target birds *All year* – **Marsh Harrier (85%), Cetti's Warbler (hear 75%, see 20%), Lesser Spotted Woodpecker (March/April 60%, rest 10%), Bearded Tit (30%).**

Other possible bird species

All year	Green Woodpecker	Winter thrushes
Common wildfowl	Great Spotted Woodpecker	*Summer*
Common waterbirds	Common scrub birds	Hobby
Red-legged Partridge	Marsh Tit	Cuckoo
Grey Partridge	Common woodland birds	Sedge Warbler
Great Crested Grebe	Nuthatch	Reed Warbler
Little Grebe	Jay	Other warblers
Sparrowhawk	Pied Wagtail	Hirundines
Kestrel	Bullfinch	
Woodcock	Common finches	*Occasional*
Regular gull species	Reed Bunting	Bittern
Little Owl		Osprey
Barn Owl	*Winter*	
Kingfisher	Hen Harrier	

Background information and birding tips

THIS RESERVE, sometimes known as Wheatfen Broad, is owned by the Ted Ellis Trust and is a wonderful memorial to a respected naturalist, writer and broadcaster who died in 1986.

The Trust's Patron, David Bellamy, once said: "Wheatfen Broad is, in its way, as important as Mount Everest or North America's redwood forests. It is probably the best bit of fenland we have because we know so much about it. That is purely because one man gave his life trying to understand it – Ted Ellis".

It is a well hidden reserve near Surlingham but once discovered I predict you will return again and again to stroll along the three miles of paths.

Your first port of call should be the leaflet dispenser in the car park. This is an excellent publication that tells you what you can see and where you can see it (don't forget to put a donation in the box).

The trails pass through many different habitats, all of which can hold several desirable species. Cetti's Warblers are resident in the thick bushes around the reserve and Marsh Harriers and Bearded Tits inhabit the reedbeds. Lesser Spots are best seen when displaying and drumming on fine days in March and early April either in Surlingham Wood or in the wood near the reedbed (see map). Kingfishers may be seen along the ditches or along the banks of the River Yare.

Nuthatches and Treecreepers are in the woodland all year round, with Siskins, Redpolls, Redwings and Fieldfares in winter. In summer, a host of warblers join the residents, including Blackcap, Whitethroats and Grasshopper, Willow, Reed and Sedge Warblers. The Summer Path may be closed due to flooding in wet years.

In summer, after strolling along the path through the reeds hoping for a glimpse of the Marsh Harriers, you can walk to the River Yare.

From here you can see Great Crested Grebe, Coot, Moorhen and quite probably Kingfisher as you wave to the passing boats. However, be warned that this path may also be closed, even in summer, as the reserve can be very wet underfoot.

This is a superb site for the all-round naturalist. There are some excellent birds to be seen (including an occasional Bittern) but the place is also alive with scarce and rare plants, butterflies (17 species) and dragonflies (14 species).

You are guaranteed a very friendly welcome from the staff who are only too pleased to tell you what can be seen and the current warden, David Nobbs, is one of the friendliest chaps you could wish to meet.

It is possible to walk from the reserve to Rockland Broad. Leave the car park and turn left along the access track (away from the way you drove in). This track passes alongside Surlingham Wood and eventually (approx one mile) comes out onto the main road at Rockland St Mary.

Once on the road, turn left to the New Inn and the path to Rockland Broad (approx 150 yards).

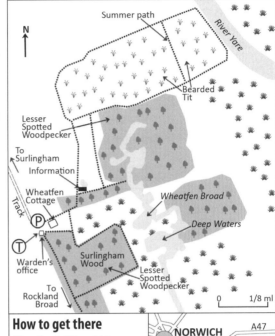

How to get there

(Six miles E of Norwich).

SAT NAV: NR14 7AL (postcode gets you onto the correct lane. Follow to where tarmac turns to rough track and follow signs for reserve).

GPS: 52.598940; 1.431531.

From A47 Norwich bypass, turn onto A146 (sign-posted Lowestoft). Head SE for about 100 yards until first traffic lights, where you turn left to Bramerton.

After 2.5 miles , by the Bramerton village name-post on a patch of grass, turn left (not sign-posted anywhere!) and continue all the way into Surlingham.

In Surlingham, go through the village to a small pond. Take the next left turn (The Green). Follow for half a mile and turn right into The Covey (sign-posted to the Ted Ellis reserve).

This becomes a rough track but reserve is well sign-posted at the end.

The trail to the hide is straight on as you enter the car park, access to the wood is behind the warden's small wooden office. Pick up a leaflet before you enter the reserve for more detailed trail directions.

Key points

- Free on-road parking.

- Open dawn to dusk every day; free entry.

- Terrain is flat on muddy paths.

- Access over a railway bridge: steep steps!

- Free 24hr Broadland boat mooring on site (Commissioner's Cut).

- No facilities other than one viewing screen.

- Cafe, shops and pub on nearby Yarmouth Road.

- Dogs on leads please.

- Download map here: www. honeyguide. co.uk/ documents/ NWTThorpe Marshes.pdf

Contacts

Norfolk Wildlife Trust, 01603 625 540.

A FORMER gravel site by the River Yare now restored to a nature reserve, Thorpe Marshes attracts several species of common wildfowl in winter and common breeding warblers and scrub birds in summer. There is a certain amount of interchange of waterbirds between this site and Whitlingham Country Park across the river.

Target birds *All year* – Cetti's Warbler (hear 70%, see 20%). *Winter* – Winter wildfowl (75%). *Spring/summer* – Little Ringed Plover (60%), Marsh Harrier (40%), Grasshopper Warbler (hear 60%, see 20%). *Spring/autumn* – Passage waders (20%).

Other possible bird species

All year		*Winter*	*Occasional*
Mute Swan	Common woodland birds	Shelduck	Hobby
Egyptian Goose	Pied Wagtail	Common wildfowl	Oystercatcher
Great Crested Grebe	Meadow Pipit	Goldeneye	Common Tern
Sparrowhawk	Common finches	Water Rail	Cuckoo
Kestrel	Reed Bunting	Coot	Hirundines
Peregrine		Snipe	Warblers
Lapwing	*Winter*	Regular gull species	
Stock Dove	Shelduck	Winter thrushes	*Occasional*
Tawny Owl	Common wildfowl		Goosander (winter)
Kingfisher	Goldeneye	*Spring/summer*	Rarer ducks and grebes (winter)
Green Woodpecker	Water Rail	Grey Heron	Little Egret
Great Spotted Woodpecker	Coot		Buzzard
Jay	Snipe		Barn Owl
Other corvids	Regular gull species		Yellow Wagtail (passage)
Goldcrest	Winter thrushes		Grey Wagtail (winter)

Background information and birding tips

THORPE MARSHES, the newest Norfolk Wildlife Trust reserve and its only urban one, consists of 25ha of grazing marsh, river, broad and reedbed. A circular route around the reserve is a mixture of permissive and public paths.

In spring and summer, listen for a Grasshopper Warbler reeling as soon as you cross the railway bridge and then home in on the song if you can. The bush-lined track straight ahead leads to the River Yare and is full of visiting warblers, breeding finches, etc. In winter, look for Fieldfares and Redwings.

There are two ways around the reserve: option one is a path that turns left off the main track and

crosses the grazing marshes before bearing right to join the river path. Turn right to walk to Commissioner's Cut, past the viewing screen overlooking St. Andrew's Broad and back to the railway bridge.

Alternatively, continue straight down the track from the bridge which ends at the river. Turn left past the screen to a gate on your left. Go through here across the marsh and turn left again to return to the bridge. It's all very simple!

I usually take the first turn left after crossing the railway bridge. Again, the bushes hold common scrub birds. You soon reach a gate: approach carefully as there may be pipits, wagtails or Lapwings on the

How to get there

SAT NAV: NR7 0QA (or Thorpe-St. Andrew>Whitlingham Lane).

Park on Whitlingham Lane at Thorpe. Only room for two cars, so if full return to lights at main road. Go straight across onto Thunder Lane (sign-posted to Sprowston) and park considerately.

GPS: 52.626003; 1.346435.

Turn off the A47 Norwich bypass onto A1042 sign-posted to Norwich N&E and Thorpe St. Andrew. Follow signs to Thorpe St. Andrew (across two roundabouts) and on to Yarmouth Road. After 0.4 miles, bear left at a mini-roundabout, sign-posted to Norwich A1242 (still Yarmouth Road).

After 0.7 miles, you reach a set of traffic lights: turn right (signed to Sprowston) to park on Thunder Lane and then walk back across the lights onto Whitlingham Lane (i.e. left as you look at the lights as you came in). Walk to the end of the lane and cross the railway bridge to the reserve.

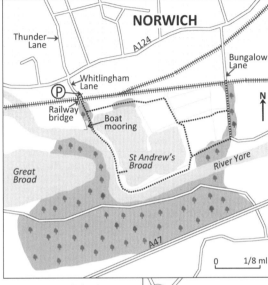

muddy fields, joined by Snipe in winter.

Cross the marsh, scanning as you go. Bear right and you soon reach the river footpath through a kissing gate. Listen here for the resident Cetti's Warblers, joined by Chiffchaffs, Whitethroats, Blackcaps, etc in spring and summer. Common Terns regularly patrol the area in summer.

After about 200 yards, the viewing screen on your right affords an excellent view over the broad, where you may see grebes and wildfowl in winter and find Reed and Sedge warblers in spring and summer. If scarce or rare grebes or ducks are at Whitlingham Country Park, they occasionally cross the river to visit this broad.

If there are any muddy edges, look for passage waders in spring and autumn; Green, Common and Wood Sandpipers are possible. Little Ringed Plovers attempt to breed on the pebbles each year.

Continue along the riverside path, scanning

for birds. As you round the bend at the mooring channel (Commissioner's Cut) and head back towards the railway bridge, there is a gravel path to your right. Walk slowly here to the rocky shore as LRPs, Oystercatchers and Shelduck may be roosting on this spit.

Continue towards the bridge where you will complete your circuit. In winter, any of the ditches might hold a secretive Water Rail. And don't forget to glance up once in a while – raptors include resident Kestrels and Sparrowhawks, while Marsh Harriers are possible in summer along with Hobby.

As Thorpe Marshes is an excellent site for dragonflies and damsels, Hobbies can be active (right up until late September). Though on the edge of Norwich, you really do feel like you are away from it all when you are on this reserve.

Key points
- **Open every day dawn to dusk.**
- **Free parking.**
- **Information board and map in car park.**
- **Facilities in nearby Fakenham.**
- **No dogs.**
- **Can be muddy at all times of year.**
- **Uneven paths. Slight inclines. Not suitable for wheelchairs.**
- **Paths can become overgrown with bracken.**

Contacts
Norfolk Wildlife Trust, 01603 625 540.

THIS TEN HECTARE stand of ancient woodland, managed by the Norfolk Wildlife Trust, is normally packed full of common woodland birds. There is nothing rare here but the waymarked trail leads you through wonderful mixed woodland where it is unlikely you will meet another soul. Bluebells in spring and fungi in autumn are the icing on the cake.

Target birds *All year* – **Common woodland birds (100%).**

Other possible bird species

All year		*Summer*
Red-legged Partridge	Long-tailed Tit	Cuckoo
Grey Partridge	Blue Tit	Hirundines
Pheasant	Great Tit	Blackcap
Sparrowhawk	Marsh Tit	Willow Warbler
Kestrel	Skylark	Chiffchaff
Stock Dove	Wren	Spotted Flycatcher
Woodpigeon	Dunnock	
Barn Owl	Robin	*Winter*
Tawny Owl	Blackbird	Grey Wagtail
Green Woodpecker	Song Thrush	Winter thrushes
Great Spotted Woodpecker	Mistle Thrush	Siskin
Jay	Goldcrest	Lesser Redpoll
Magpie	Nuthatch	
Jackdaw	Treecreeper	*Occasional*
Rook	Pied Wagtail	Mallard
Carrion Crow	Chaffinch	Barn Owl
Starling	Greenfinch	Kingfisher
	Goldfinch	Brambling

Background information and birding tips

THIS COMPACT NWT woodland reserve is worth popping in whenever you are visiting the larger sites around Fakenham such as Sculthorpe Moor, Pensthorpe, etc or on your way to the coastal hotspots.

The habitat is known as woodland pasture, one of the rarest in Norfolk. The oak trees were once pollarded here and the NWT plans to restore the wood to its former glory with help from The Heritage Lottery Fund.

From the car park, follow the main waymarked trail (on the left as you enter the car park) through the wood. Some of the trees you will encounter may be over 500 years old, making them among the oldest in the county! Resident birds are typical woodland species such as Great Spotted Woodpecker, Nuthatch, Treecreeper, tits, finches and corvids. Tawny Owls breed here but you will be lucky to find one (listen for the excited alarm calls of small birds mobbing the owl, if they find a roosting bird).

The main trail, marked on posts with green NWT arrows, leads downhill through the trees. At the bottom of the hill, turn right at a T-junction to a secluded oxbow of the River Stiffkey. Approach this area very quietly: occasional

Kingfishers and Grey Wagtails visit but are very easily disturbed if you go crashing through the trees. This is an excellent drinking/bathing pool, so stay quiet and hidden for as long as possible for best results. You now need to retrace your steps back to the main path and the T-junction.

From the junction, carry straight on (as if you turned left coming down the hill along the main track). This is the return path to the car park (or you can retrace your steps uphill). This part of the loop may become overgrown with bracken but it all adds to the adventure!

This narrow path runs uphill and allows you further chances of finding some of the birds you missed on the walk down. Check any coniferous trees for Coal Tits and Goldcrests and also listen out for the distinctive high-pitched sneeze 'pitchoo' of the Marsh Tit. This path rejoins the main path where you turn right back to the car park.

Another short trail leads from the right of the car park (as you enter) and takes you to a small pool through a less dense stand of trees. It is worth waiting here to see what species come in to drink. This area of the reserve probably provides your best chance of seeing a Brambling or two in winter.

The path ends at a field boundary where you can scan for partridges, thrushes and Skylarks, etc and here is your best chance of seeing a hunting Barn Owl.

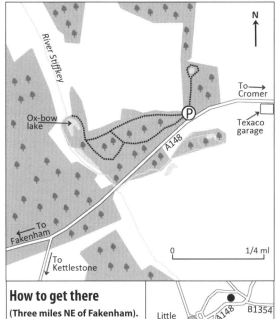

How to get there

(Three miles NE of Fakenham).
SAT NAV: NR21 0BD.
(postcode for general area on A148 – then follow detailed directions below).

GPS: 52.860773; 0.939383.

It's tricky to find the car park! Leave Fakenham on A148 towards Cromer and go through Little Snoring. As you leave the village, the road becomes wooded on either side. After passing a sign to 'Kettlestone 1 mile', watch out 0.3 miles after this sign for a 'Police Enforcement Cameras' sign. 0.2 miles after the camera sign (and just before **the bend warning sign) is the small, muddy pull-off into the small car park (unsigned!). If you reach a grass field on your left and crop fields on your right, you've gone too far.**

Coming from the Cromer direction, go past the Texaco petrol station: the reserve turn off is 0.4 miles after this on the right.

Thursford Wood will provide you with an hour or so's diversion among some scarce Norfolk habitat. It isn't the quietest place given the proximity of the busy A148 (take extra care when leaving the car park!) but the birds don't seem to mind. It is much quieter if you visit very early in the morning. Even if there isn't much birding activity, it is still a delightful walk.

207

Key points

- **Pay-and-display car park – free to RSPB members (display card on dashboard).**
- **Reserve open at all times.**
- **Visitor centre open: 9.30am-5pm (4pm from Nov to Feb).**
- **Cafe open 9.30am-4.30pm (4pm from Nov to Feb). Visitor centre and cafe closed Dec 25 and 26.**
- **Toilet block in car park, including disabled access.**
- **Regular guided walks.**
- **Books, clothes, optics etc for sale in visitor centre.**
- **Binoculars for hire.**

Contacts

RSPB Titchwell Marsh
01485 210 779;
e-mail: titchwell
@rspb.org.uk

THIS MUCH-MODIFIED RSPB site remains my favourite bird reserve in the whole of Britain. Not only is there always something to see, whether it be on the marshes, in the trees around the visitor centre or on the sea, but it is usually easy to see it. And the pasties are the best in the country!

Target birds
All year – **Marsh Harrier (98%), Cetti's Warbler (hear 80%, see 45%), Bearded Tit (60%), Bittern (20%).** *Winter* – **Red-throated Diver (75%), Spotted Redshank (70%), seaduck and grebes (65%), winter raptors (40%).** *Spring/summer* – **Avocet (99%), Little Gull (60%).** *Autumn* – **Passage seabirds, passage waders.**

Other possible bird species

All year
Shelduck
Eider
Common Scoter
Velvet Scoter
Common wildfowl
Cormorant
Little Egret
Little Grebe
Sparrowhawk
Kestrel
Water Rail
Black-tailed Godwit
Common waders
Barn Owl
Great Spotted Woodpecker
Skylark
Long-tailed Tit
Corvids
Meadow Pipit
Pied Wagtail
Bullfinch
Linnet
Reed Bunting

Winter
Brent Goose
Pintail
Goldeneye
Red-breasted Merganser
Hen Harrier

Merlin
Peregrine
Water Rail
Golden Plover
Grey Plover
Knot
Woodcock
Guillemot
Razorbill
Stonechat
Common (Mealy) Redpoll
Lesser Redpoll
Brambling

Spring
Garganey
Little Ringed Plover
Black-tailed Godwit
Whimbrel
Greenshank
Little Gull
Sand Martin
Yellow Wagtail

Summer
Sandwich Tern
Common Tern
Little Tern
Turtle Dove
Hirundines
Sedge Warbler
Reed Warbler
Whitethroat

Blackcap
Chiffchaff
Lesser Whitethroat
Willow Warbler

Autumn
Shearwaters
Gannet
Garganey
Hobby
Avocet
Little Ringed Plover
Little Stint
Curlew Sandpiper
Ruff
Whimbrel
Greenshank
Green Sandpiper
Wood Sandpiper
Common Sandpiper
Skuas

Occasional
Black Brant (winter)
Spoonbill
Hobby (summer)
Yellow-legged Gull
Mediterranean Gull
Short-eared Owl (winter)
Shore Lark (winter)
Twite (winter)
Arctic Redpoll (winter)

Key

1. Viewpoint
2. Bare ground (good for buntings/finches)
3. Parrinder hides
4. Island hide
5. Fen hide
6. Dead trees (good for Marsh Harriers)

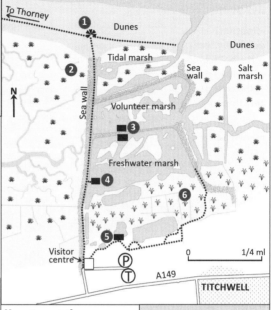

Background information and birding tips

THE BEAUTY of Titchwell is that there is always something to see, no matter what the weather conditions, no matter what time of year you visit. You are guaranteed half a day's birding at least and at certain times of the year a whole day can be spent tootling around.

In 2010, the RSPB decided to build a new sea wall half way across the reserve. At high water, this would mean the northern half of the reserve would be allowed to flood, but would preserve the freshwater marsh and reedbed for another 50 years.

New Parrinder hides were installed – some consider these to be rather grandiose constructions, but others find them a welcome addition to the reserve's facilities – I'll let you decide!

This really is a five star reserve that deservedly draws big crowds, so if you like your privacy see the Gypsy Lane site (page 90).

Birdwatching starts in the car park. The surrounding bushes are full of common birds eager to share your food and Chaffinches and Robins often come to take crumbs off your wing mirror.

Before leaving the car park you should have 'ticked off' the common tits, finches and thrushes and, if lucky, a Bullfinch or two, and a wintering Chiffchaff or Blackcap. In summer

How to get there

(Five miles E of Hunstanton).
SAT NAV: PE31 8ED.
GPS: 52.962609; 0.605527.
The reserve is sign-posted off A149, between the villages of Thornham and Titchwell. There is a large car park on site. The reserve is accessed via a public footpath, which is open at all times.

Turtle Doves, Willow Warblers and Blackcaps join the throng.

The marked path from the car park to the visitor centre takes you through some dense scrub and alder trees. In winter, a Woodcock can occasionally be seen roosting just off the path, usually in full view.

Check the alders for redpoll species and Siskins. In summer, the bushes are full of common scrub birds and warblers. Feeders by the visitor centre are popular and Bramblings can join common species in winter.

Key points

- **Footpath generally level but wheelchair users may need assistance at certain points.**

- **All hides wheelchair accessible.**

- **Wheelchair available for loan. Contact visitor centre for details.**

- **Well-behaved dogs allowed on main (west bank) public footpath but not in the hides or along the named trails.**

- **Picnic site adjacent to car park.**

The main reserve lies either side of a 1km track down to the sea. The only deviations allowed are down the short paths to the hides, though unless it is raining heavily it is hardly necessary to enter them as birds seem unperturbed by our constant comings and goings on the main track.

The closest hide to the visitor centre is the Fen Hide, which is reached along a 250 metre long boardwalk – the best place to listen and look for the resident Cetti's Warblers.

Fen Hide affords excellent views of breeding Marsh Harriers in summer and roosting Hen Harriers in winter. Bearded Tits should be encountered here and a patient wait should result in a glimpse of a Bittern. Sightings are usually of a bird in flight and can be quite brief, so be alert!

In 2012, the RSPB opened the East Trail, which is an extension of Fen Trail. This path heads east (obviously!) into newly developed and previously inaccessible areas that give great views over new areas of reedbed and the inland side has been specially planted with shrubs to attract migrant and nesting birds.

From the eastern end of East Trail, Autumn Trail also opened in 2012. It provides excellent views of the freshwater marsh, particularly in the early morning when the position of the sun can make for difficult viewing from the main reserve footpath.

In order to protect nesting and roosting birds, Autumn Trail will only be open in the August to October period each year. Both trails are 'easy access'.

Retrace your steps to rejoin the main track via the boardwalk and scan the fields to your left. These are good for Barn Owls (mornings and evenings best) all year round, and Golden Plover and Lapwing flocks in winter. Look to your right in the ditches for Water Rail (best in winter) or a fly-over Woodcock at dusk.

Follow the track and you will soon see Thornham Pool on your left. This is good for winter wildfowl. Pause a while as this is an excellent point from which to see a flying Bittern, quartering Marsh Harriers and to witness the dusk winter harrier roost.

Further along, check the reeds on your right for Bearded Tits (windless days are best). I have found autumn the best time to get close views, as the adults feed their noisy young right next to the path. In summer, the reedbed is alive with Reed Warblers and Reed Buntings, while Wrens and Sedge Warblers sing from the small bushes and trees.

Look over the bank to your left at regular intervals for raptors and geese in winter. Redshanks take flight at the slightest thing and are often your indicator that a raptor is in the vicinity. Also on the marsh in winter you should see Snipe, Curlews and Wigeon feeding in the grass.

Brent Geese are guaranteed in winter and spring (sometimes up until May) occasionally joined by their American cousin: the Black Brant. This is also a good place to look for a Little Egret at any time of the year. They occasionally fly over the path giving excellent views, especially at dusk.

Two paths lead off to your right, the first to Island Hide and the second to Parrinder Hides North & South. The former is ideal for spotting Bearded Tits, Marsh Harriers, Bitterns, Water Rails and Reed Buntings all year round and Reed Warblers in the breeding season.

A good selection of wildfowl can also be seen from this hide, along with many species of waders and gulls. In spring and summer, pay particular attention to the gull flock, as Little and Mediterranean Gulls may join the throng and Yellow-legged Gull sightings are increasing.

The new Parrinder Hides (love 'em or hate 'em!) - opened in 2010. The South Hide gives great views over the Freshwater Marsh and its breeding Avocets in summer, close views of passage waders in spring and autumn (e.g. Curlew Sandpiper and Little Stint) and a plethora of wildfowl in winter.

A winter speciality is Spotted Redshank: one or two over-winter every year, so keep your eyes peeled for this dainty beauty.

The North Hide holds smaller numbers of similar birds and looks over the tidal Volunteer Marsh. When winter water levels are low, a flock of finches (including occasional Twite) may be seen feeding on the vegetated islands. In winter, scrutinise any muddy island for Rock and Water Pipits.

The main path continues down to the beach. Due to the shifting nature of the dunes, access cannot always be guaranteed for wheelchair users along the final 50 metres of boardwalk.

The bare ground to the left of the boardwalk has been an excellent area for feeding flocks of Linnets and Skylarks in winter but Shore Larks and Twite are now scarce. If the birds are not here, try walking east (right) along the beach.

The area of pebbles around here is another good place for all the above species and Snow Buntings, though none can be guaranteed as they tend to roam along the beach as far as Hunstanton and Holkham.

Each winter is different, so check recent records to ensure you are not disappointed. To avoid disturbing birds, only take this route in winter and don't walk onto the salt marsh, which can be dangerous.

To view the sea/beach you can either sit on the wooden viewing platform (good for wheelchair users but too bouncy for easy telescope use) or settle down out of the wind on the beach (note that the platform and adjoining boardwalk may be covered with sand!).

Winter should produce large numbers of waders on the beach and an unpredictable number of sea duck/grebes/divers out to sea. High tide is best as all birds are closer to the viewer at this time.

In winter, you can expect the beach to be alive with Turnstones, Sanderlings and Oystercatchers, some of which remain on site all summer. Grey Plovers and Knot join the party in the autumn and remain into late spring.

Common Scoters can be present all year round, though they range as far as Hunstanton so cannot be guaranteed. Some years up to 3,000 can be seen and in other years hardly any. Also watch out for the white wing-flashes of Velvet Scoter among the Commons.

Winter sea enthusiasts can have their days enlivened by regular Red-throated Divers and, if lucky, the not so regular Black-throateds or Great Northern Divers. Long-tailed Ducks are unpredictable in their numbers, as are Slavonian and Red-necked Grebes.

One or two Guillemots and Razorbills are regularly seen in winter. The onset of spring is heralded in late March by the return of Sandwich Terns, joined by Little and Common Terns in May.

Autumn seawatching, preferably in a strong onshore wind, can be very good from the beach at Titchwell. Skuas are regularly seen, with Great and Arctic being the commonest but Pomarine and Long-tailed are occasionally spotted.

Manx Shearwaters can virtually be guaranteed from August to October and look out for the rarer shearwaters (Sooty, Balearic, Great and Cory's). Little Auks pass by in November storms.

Titchwell has an excellent record for turning up rarities. On one notable day in 2011, Cattle Egret, Buff-breasted Sandpiper and Little Bittern were all present on the same day! Arctic Redpolls are regular winter visitors and passage scarcities such as Red-necked Phalarope, Temminck's Stint and Pectoral Sandpiper are almost expected

Key points

- **The pits can be viewed at all times from the road.**

- **Do not enter the fenced-off areas.**

- **No walking necessary.**

- **Wheelchair users may find pits obscured by bushes.**

THIS FLOODED gravel pit, which is a traditional wintering site for Smew in varying numbers, can be viewed from the road. Rumours of Nightingales present in the thick bushes along the roadside are unsubstantiated by me. The pits are private and you must not enter the site.

Target birds Winter – Smew (30%).

Other possible bird species

Winter	Sparrowhawk	Long-tailed Tit
Wigeon	Coot	Marsh Tit
Gadwall	Moorhen	Common woodland birds
Teal	Regular gull species	Pied Wagtail
Shoveler	Kingfisher	Common finches
Goldeneye	Great Spotted	Reed Bunting
Pintail	Woodpecker	
Egyptian Goose	Goldcrest	*Early spring*
Other common wildfowl	Nuthatch	Sand Martin
Cormorant	Treecreeper	Swallow
Great Crested Grebe	Common scrub birds	House Martin

Background information and birding tips

TOTTENHILL continues to attract wintering Smew in varying numbers but Willow Tits, its other speciality, have disappeared from the site. Winter wildfowl are drawn here because the pool is sheltered by trees and so rarely freezes over.

Impressive gatherings of 700-plus Pintails, 300-plus Pochards and 200-plus Teal have been counted on the lake.

While scanning the lake for Smew, you should also see more common ducks such as Gadwall, Wigeon, Tufted Ducks, Pochards and Goldeneye.

Smew can remain on site until

The delicate beauty of Smew is always appreciated by birders and the gravel pits at Tottenhill have a good track record for attracting this species in winter

Contact

None

April, by which time you will be able to watch the comical head-tossing courtship displays of the drake Goldeneyes as they try to impress the females who are usually more occupied with feeding.

Great Crested Grebes should also be present and coming into their resplendent breeding plumage by February. Look out for their elaborate courtship rituals, including the famous 'weed dance' and synchronised head bobbing and shaking.

Several species of common woodland birds frequent the trees. By the end of March, you should also encounter the first Chiffchaffs, Blackcaps and Sand Martins of the year as they pour in from their African wintering grounds.

In the summer months the bushes along the road completely obscure the view of the pits. Besides, bird activity is confined to very common species which are readily seen elsewhere, so a visit is probably only advised while the Smew are in residence, unless you wish to investigate reports of Nightingales in the area.

The large pit on the left of the A10, just past the junction with the A134, attracts several species of common wildfowl in winter, including an occasional Smew, but viewing is uncomfortable thanks to very heavy traffic on the A roads.

There is a lay-by on the A134 about 100 yards from the roundabout where you can park. You then have to cross the busy road and stand on the grass verge to view the pit. I advise against it, though!

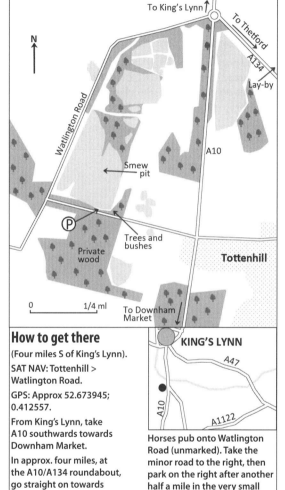

How to get there

(Four miles S of King's Lynn).

SAT NAV: Tottenhill > Watlington Road.

GPS: Approx 52.673945; 0.412557.

From King's Lynn, take A10 southwards towards Downham Market.

In approx. four miles, at the A10/A134 roundabout, go straight on towards Downham. After 1 mile, turn right opposite the Dray &

Horses pub onto Watlington Road (unmarked). Take the minor road to the right, then park on the right after another half a mile in the very small pull-off. The gravel pits can be viewed from the road here.

Other nearby sites

Blackborough End Tip, Denver Sluice, Flitcham Abbey Farm, Hunstanton, Ken Hill Wood, Roydon Common, Sandringham, Snettisham, Welney, Wolferton Triangle.

213

Key points

- Site is a designated SSSI.

- £1 donation requested (collection point at reserve gate).

- Small car park, otherwise no facilities.

- Trail not suitable for wheelchairs.

- Terrain is level along muddy, grass paths and a short boardwalk.

- Walking boots (at least) recommended.

- Use insect repellent in spring/summer.

- No dogs on reserve. Keep under close control on public footpaths.

Contacts

Norfolk Wildlife Trust, 01603 625 540

General Broads Authority 01603 610 734

THE RESERVE at Upton can be tricky to locate but once there you will find a mosaic of way-marked paths through varied habitats packed full of wildlife. You might see many species of birds but this large reserve is also home to many scarce plants, animals and creepy crawlies!

Target birds All year – **Marsh Harrier (90%), Lesser Spotted Woodpecker (March 20%, rest 5%).** Summer – **Hobby (65%).** Winter – **Winter raptors (30%).**

Other possible bird species

All year	Common scrub birds	Chiffchaff
Mallard	Cetti's Warbler	Willow Warbler
Grey Heron	Goldcrest	Yellow Wagtail
Lapwing	Marsh Tit	Common finches
Sparrowhawk	Common woodland birds	Reed Bunting
Kestrel	Meadow Pipit	
Buzzard		*Winter*
Coot	*Spring/summer*	Curlew
Moorhen	Turtle Dove	Snipe
Water Rail	Cuckoo	Hen Harrier
Woodcock	Hirundines	Peregrine
Green Woodpecker	Sedge Warbler	Merlin
Great Spotted Woodpecker	Reed Warbler	Winter thrushes
Jay	Grasshopper Warbler	
Other corvids	Lesser Whitethroat	*Occasional*
Starling	Whitethroat	Common Tern
Skylark	Garden Warbler	(summer along river)
	Blackcap	

Background information and birding tips

THIS Norfolk Wildlife Trust reserve is best known for its dragonfly populations but it has much to offer birdwatchers as well.

A way-marked trail around the reserve consists of muddy grass paths and boardwalks (long loop is 3km, the short trail is 1.6km). You should see Skylark, Linnet, Yellowhammer, Goldfinch, etc along the hedges and in the fields as you approach the car park.

The walk starts at the Turf Ponds, small pools just inside the reserve entrance. This is an excellent area for dragonflies, while birds can include Garden Warbler, Blackcap, Chiffchaff, Kestrel, Sparrowhawk,

Swallow, Swift and House Martin. Listen out for the explosive song of Cetti's Warbler.

Follow the marked trail straight ahead into a wet woodland. Migrant warblers, Goldcrest and Marsh Tit are seen regularly along with common woodland birds.

The wood opens onto a cleared area – an excellent place to see Whitethroats and Sedge Warblers. There is usually a Grasshopper Warbler reeling at the back of the clearing and a Marsh Harrier may drift over. Green and Great Spotted Woodpeckers sometimes fly along the edge of the woodland. Lesser Spotted Woodpeckers are seldom seen now but still listen out for them in late March / early April when they may be displaying. This is the best area for swallowtail butterflies in season.

The trail splits into two at a blue marker. The right fork takes you along a dyke to the viewpoint. The left hand path is a short cut back to the car park. On the way to the viewpoint, you should see Reed Warblers and Reed Buntings.

The path reaches a marsh, an excellent place to wait for Hobbies pursuing hirundines and dragonflies, as well as to enjoy views of Marsh Harriers. In winter, there may be a Hen Harrier, Merlin or Peregrine hunting here. A Barn Owl or two should be encountered in the evenings or early mornings at any time of year.

The path rejoins the main track after about a quarter of a mile. You should turn right towards the Turf Ponds and car park, watching for warblers and scrub birds along the way.

Walking boots or preferably wellingtons are recommended at all times of year and the summer mosquitoes are some of the most vicious I have encountered on my travels around the world!

However, the combination of birds, dragonflies, butterflies and unusual plants guarantee a successful visit to this first-rate site. As well as the excellent birds, this is a superb place for rare butterflies (swallowtail), dragonflies (Norfolk hawker) and plants (marsh fern).

There is also a car park at Upton, along Boat Dyke Road (TG 402 127, GPS: 52.659444;

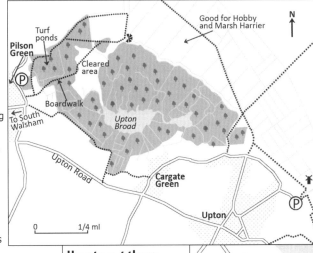

How to get there

(Ten miles NE of Norwich).

SAT NAV: South Walsham>Low Road (or Marsh Road).

GPS: 52.668531; 1.518414.

Upton Fen can be a devil to find! Basically, you need to head for Pilson Green, NE of South Walsham.

From the B1140 (Wroxham to Acle road), follow signs for South Walsham/Ranworth.

In the village, keep heading E, past the church, then take the left turn sign-posted to Pilson Green/Fairhaven Water Gardens.

Take second left turn

(ignoring the one signed to 'Broad') sign-posted 'Upton 1 mile'. Once past the houses, take the first left down Low Road, which is a dead end.

The small reserve car park is approx. 200 yards on the right, just before the house. If you have made it this far, you deserve to see everything on the reserve!

1.551053). Park by Palmer's Drainage Mill and follow footpath signs along the River Bure to view the extensive marshes (several paths cut into the reserve from this main path) or head west (left) to access the reserve and its waymarked trails.

Key points

- **NOA members dawn to dusk access, non-members 9am - 5pm.**

- **When warden is present you may be asked for a donation. Report to visitor centre at top of steps.**

- **Small visitor centre closed when warden is absent.**

- **£5 deposit for key which fits all NOA hides. Return key if membership lapses!**

- **ID & sightings book in hide**

- **Public footpath is level, but path to visitor centre involves steep steps.**

- **Warden usually present.**

- **Telescope very useful.**

- **No dogs allowed.**

Contacts

Norfolk Ornithologists'
Association
01485 525 406;
e-mail:info@noa.org.uk
www.noa.org.uk

THIS TINY RESERVE is a wonderful place for a bit of relaxed birdwatching. The hide allows panoramic views over Cley Marshes and the surrounding thick bushes attract an array of common birds throughout the year.

Target birds *All year* – **Marsh Harrier (90%), Barn Owl (60%), Cetti's Warbler (hear 75%, see 15%).** *Spring/autumn* – **Passage migrants.** *Winter* – **Water Pipit (30%), raptors (15%).** *Summer* – **Lesser Whitethroat (65%), Grasshopper Warbler (hear 50%, see 5%).**

Other possible bird species

All year	*Summer*	
Egyptian Goose	Hobby	Wheatear
Other common wildfowl	Cuckoo	Barred Warbler
Little Grebe	Hirundines	Yellow-browed Warbler
Sparrowhawk	Sedge Warbler	Firecrest
Kestrel	Reed Warbler	Pied Flycatcher
Common waders (distant)	Other warblers	Red-backed Shrike
Regular gull species	*Spring/autumn (might include)*	*Winter*
Common scrub birds		Brent Goose
Common finches	Passage migrants	Winter thrushes
Reed Bunting	Redstart	*Occasional species*
	Whinchat	Bittern
		Turtle Dove

Background information and birding tips

DESPITE ITS SMALL size, there is always something to see on or from this three acre reserve owned by the Norfolk Ornithologists' Association. It is covered by thick bushes and gorse, ideal for attracting migrants in spring and autumn and an array of breeding summer visitors.

Start your visit with a scan of Snipe's Marsh, the small reed-fringed pool on your right as you enter the reserve along the public footpath from the car park.

The bushes offer your best chance of seeing the resident Cetti's Warblers. Much more in evidence will be the resident Reed Buntings, summering Reed Warblers, common winter wildfowl and maybe an occasional Bittern if you are quiet.

Enter the reserve through a small gate on the left, a few yards along the main footpath. You'll have to climb steep steps wooden steps to reach the visitor centre at the top of the hill but there are a couple of benches along the way to stop and catch your breath.

If a warden is present, you may be asked for a donation (usually £3). If you are visiting on a warm day, it may be worth asking the warden to show you the resident slow worms and adders!

You can scan Cley Marshes (telescope essential) from benches at the centre or wait to see which birds come to visit the feeders. I find this to be a perfect picnic spot.

NOA members can access the hide adjacent to the centre (£5 deposit

How to get there

(Six miles W of Sheringham)

SAT NAV: NR25 7SA (This postcode is for Cley reserve – drive E for 0.5 miles).

GPS: 52.954633; 1.066850.

Head E from Cley on A149 towards Sheringham. About half a mile after passing the NWT Cley Marsh visitor car park on right, turn onto the rough lay-by on the right signed 'NOA Watchpoint' (virtually opposite Cley East Bank).

All visitors should enter the reserve via the path leading from the car park and report to the small visitor centre up the steep steps on the left.

for key) for an even better overview of Cley Marshes.

You should soon tick off Marsh Harrier and Barn Owl at any time of year, Wigeon, Brent Geese, raptors in winter, and distant waders on Arnold's Marsh. Water Pipits are sometimes seen in winter on the marsh just across the road, often viewable from Walsey.

After a rest, take the only other footpath down the hill, slowly checking the bushes and feeders for birds. Common residents may be joined by scarcer species at migration times.

These have included Yellow-browed, Hume's Leaf, Barred and Icterine Warblers, Red-backed, Woodchat and Great Grey Shrikes, Firecrest, Wryneck etc.

In summer, an array of warblers breed on the reserve. These include the locally scarce Lesser Whitethroat, along with the more common Blackcaps, Whitethroats, Willow Warblers, Chiffchaffs and Garden Warblers. Grasshopper Warblers are often heard from the car park but seldom seen.

Take as long as possible to cover this small reserve. Cover is thick but the potential to find something very unusual is really quite high at this site!

Retrace your route back to the visitor centre as there is no access to the public footpath from this second track. This gives you another chance to scrutinise the bushes along the way.

Leave Walsey the way you entered: down the steps to the public footpath. Turn left and follow the narrow path through yet more thick cover looking and listening for birds all the way. The path opens out at a field (worth scanning for partridges all year round and Curlews in winter).

If you turn left at this junction, you reach Salthouse at the Dun Cow public house and if you go straight on, you reach Salthouse Heath after about a mile. Both routes can produce some good birds.

217

Key points
- **Part of the Holkham National Nature Reserve.**
- **Narrow, very rough access road.**
- **Small car park.**
- **Terrain is level along grass paths. Narrow, muddy paths to marsh.**
- **Wheelchair users may view raptors from car parks but the paths are definitely not accessible.**
- **Avoid walking onto the marsh to prevent disturbance to birds.**

Contacts
Natural England
01603 620 558

THE BUSHES along the coastal path at Warham have a proven track record of attracting migrants in spring and autumn. In winter, the marsh is home to roosting Hen & Marsh Harriers and in summer, several species of waders, etc. settle down to breed.

Target birds *All year* – **Marsh Harrier (90%).** *Winter* – **Winter raptors (40%).** *Summer* – **Breeding waders (60%).** *Spring/autumn* – **Passage migrants (70%).**

Other likely bird species

All year	Dunlin	*Summer*
Shelduck	Whimbrel	Hirundines
Little Egret	Greenshank	Sedge Warbler
Kestrel	Green Sandpiper	Whitethroat
Red-legged Partridge	Wood Sandpiper	Blackcap
Grey Partridge	Common Sandpiper	Chiffchaff
Lapwing	Wryneck	Willow Warbler
Snipe	Yellow Wagtail	
Curlew	Bluethroat	*Winter*
Redshank	Black Redstart	Brent Goose
Regular gull species	Redstart	Wigeon
Barn Owl	Whinchat	Seaduck
Skylark	Wheatear	Short-eared Owl
Meadow Pipit	Ring Ouzel	Stonechat
Pied Wagtail	Barred Warbler	Winter thrushes
Starling	Lesser Whitethroat	Rock Pipit
Reed Bunting	Blackcap	
Spring/autumn (might include	Goldcrest	*Occasional*
	Firecrest	Hobby
Little Stint	Pied Flycatcher	Twite
		Snow Bunting

Background information and birding tips

WARHAM GREENS is part of Holkham National Nature Reserve. It first came to my notice when I heard of a strange harrier in the fields here, rumoured to be a Pallid Harrier. After spending an hour trying to find the place, the bird turned out to be a Montagu's but was still thrilling to see. Since then, Warham has produced Rufus-tailed Robin and a Blyth's Reed Warbler to mention but a few goodies, including Pallid Harrier!

Summer is the quietest period, though Shelduck, Snipe, Curlews, Redshanks and Black-headed Gulls all nest on the marsh. The hedgerows around the car parks hold Whitethroats, Blackcaps and Chiffchaffs and common scrub species and the bushes along the edge of the marsh attract breeding Sedge Warblers.

Marsh Harriers frequently hunt over the marsh and it would be unusual for you not to see a Little Egret or two in the channels. One hot July afternoon, I drove down the deserted track and was treated to a delightful family party of two adult and six young Grey Partridges dust-bathing in the car park.

The main attraction in winter is the raptor roost. Hen Harriers are seen daily between December and February, appearing from about an hour before dark. Merlins are also regularly seen here but are never guaranteed.

Sharing the marsh in winter are varying numbers of Brent Geese and Wigeon. A Short-eared Owl is occasionally seen but Barn Owls are noted more regularly. A few Twite may be among the flocks of Goldfinches, Linnets, Greenfinches etc and if you are really lucky maybe even a Snow Bunting or two. Rock Pipits also winter in small numbers but can be hard to locate.

Warham's reputation as a migrant trap, particularly in autumn, is well founded. The bushes running east and west from the car park can hold species such as Redstart, Chiffchaff, Willow Warbler, Blackcap, Pied Flycatcher, Garden Warbler, etc. Be alert, too for something a little special, such as Firecrest or Barred Warbler.

If you walk west from the car park, check the small, bush-lined, sheltered hollow on the left after about 800 yards, rather grandly known as 'the quarry'. Walk east for about 500 yards from the car park and you will come across 'The Gibbet': a curious structure surrounded by migrant-filled bushes particularly favoured by Wrynecks.

The marsh and bushes around the edges of the marsh should also be checked for migrant Wheatears and Whinchats etc but don't ignore the sky for a passing Honey Buzzard or, more likely, migrating thrushes, hirundines, etc.

The pools and creeks on the marsh may attract passage waders such as Greenshank, Whimbrel, Little Stint, etc along with Yellow Wagtails in spring.

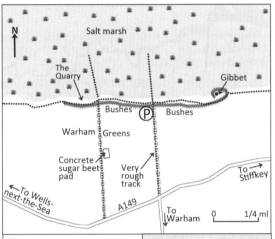

How to get there

(1.5 miles E of Wells-Next-The-Sea).

SAT NAV: NR23 1QD. Postcode should get you onto main A149 east of Wells-next-the-Sea, then look out for the rough track opposite the turn off to Warham village (Stiffkey Road). Far easier to follow written directions below!

GPS: 52.956116; 0.899703.

Head E from Wells along A149 towards Sheringham. To find the most convenient Warham car park turn N onto a very rough track opposite the turn-off to Warham (look for a small, partly hidden sign-post).

The track is sign-posted 'not suitable for vehicles'. If you worry about the suspension

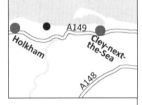

on your car, park here and walk the rest of the way. If not, drive slowly to a small car park at the end (about half a mile).

From here walk straight ahead onto the marsh, or to the left or right to view the bushes during passage periods.

Raptors can be seen from the car park but particularly recommended is the area surrounding The Gibbet, a strange metal structure on a concrete base, 500 yards to the right.

Key points

- **Free access from dawn to dusk all year.**

- **Paths level but can be muddy.**

- **Telescope very useful if viewing the marshes.**

- **Wheelchair access difficult: powertrikes may handle some of the forest tracks when dry.**

- **Part of area can be viewed from pavement on road bridge (see Haddiscoe Marshes).**

- **Facilities: pub nearby; toilets sign-posted off A143 in St. Olaves (approx. TM 460 993).**

THIS EXTENSIVE area of mixed woodland leads down to a view of Haddiscoe Marshes. Common woodland species should be in evidence all year round and the marshes are at their best in winter when one or two Rough-legged Buzzards have become regular visitors.

Target birds *All year* – **Common woodland birds (100%), Marsh Harrier (85%), Bearded Tit (30%).** *Winter* – **Winter raptors, inc. Short-eared Owl and Rough-legged Buzzard (30%).**

Other possible bird species

All year
Mute Swan
Greylag Goose
Mallard
Red-legged Partridge
Grey Partridge
Pheasant
Cormorant
Little Egret
Grey Heron
Buzzard
Sparrowhawk
Kestrel
Peregrine
Coot
Moorhen
Lapwing
Woodcock
Regular gull species
Stock Dove
Woodpigeon
Barn Owl
Tawny Owl
Little Owl
Green Woodpecker

Great Spotted Woodpecker
Jay
Magpie
Other corvids
Starling
Long-tailed Tit
Blue Tit
Great Tit
Coal Tit
Skylark
Blackbird
Song Thrush
Mistle Thrush
Wren
Dunnock
Robin
Goldcrest
Nuthatch
Treecreeper
Pied Wagtail
Meadow Pipit
Chaffinch
Greenfinch
Goldfinch

Siskin
Lesser Redpoll
Reed Bunting

Summer:
Cuckoo
Hirundines
Blackcap
Willow Warbler
Chiffchaff
Spotted Flycatcher

Winter
Pink-footed Goose
Wigeon
Teal
Golden Plover
Winter thrushes

Occasional
Whooper Swan (winter)
Bewick's Swan (winter)
Hobby (summer)
Yellow Wagtail (passage)
Brambling (winter)

Background information and birding tips

THE MOST popular spot in Waveney Forest is called 'The Mound' where birders gather in winter to scan the marshes. A Rough-legged Buzzard or two have become regulars here in winter, joining the resident Marsh Harriers and occasional Short-eared Owls. The reeds in front of you are home to Bearded Tits.

The longer you stay, the more birds you will see and if you are there at dusk you should also catch a glimpse of a Woodcock or two.

To reach 'The Mound', park considerately on the verge at the end of New Road (room for about four cars) and take the obvious rough track through a metal gate on the left. Walk past a cottage on the right and keep going until you see the river in front of you. There is a path on your left: follow this to a clearing and this is the area

Contacts
None

known as 'The Mound'. Scan the marshes from here.

Alternatively, park in the large car park (I usually park on the verge opposite the car park so my vehicle is in full view!) and take the wide track through the forest, through a metal gate (you can see this gate on the left just before you enter the car park). Follow this muddy track all the way down to the marsh where you will find a pile of rubble. Stand here to scan the marshes.

In addition to the above mentioned raptors, Kestrels and Sparrowhawks can be seen as well as Peregrines and Barn Owls. Hen Harriers and Merlins occasionally hunt the marsh in winter. Pink-footed and White-fronted Geese are sometimes seen along with wild swans and common wildfowl such as Wigeon and Teal.

But Waveney is much more than the marshes. Most birders neglect the woods themselves, but this can be a mistake. The extensive woodland is home to many common species of birds, so you will be hard pushed to miss Great Spotted Woodpeckers and locally scarce Treecreepers and Nuthatches.

Jays and Coal Tits are among the resident species, joined by Redwings and Fieldfares in winter with the chance of Brambling.

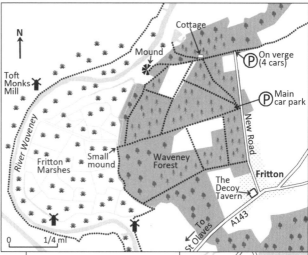

How to get there

(Seven miles SW of Great Yarmouth)

SAT NAV: NR31 9HR.

GPS: 52.549119; 1.635733.

Take A12 to Lowestoft out of Great Yarmouth, passing over the bridge across Breydon Water. Turn off the dual carriageway to follow signs to Diss on the A143 and Beccles on the A146 (also Burgh Castle and Gorleston).

At the bottom of the slip road, turn right at the lights (to pass under the A12). After 5 miles, you reach Fritton: look for the Decoy Tavern on your right. Turn onto New Road (immediately before the pub) and follow for 0.4 miles to the car park on the left, or continue right to the end of the road and park on the verge.

The woods are easily explored along the maze of paths. If you get lost, just head uphill and you will soon hit the road or the car park. The woods are popular with dog walkers and most seem approachable should you need to ask for directions! If you want to view the marsh from the viewpoint, don't forget to leave enough time to get the best out of it; it is easy to be distracted by woodland birds!

Finally, it might be worth taking a torch with you if staying on 'The Mound' until dusk in winter: the track back to your car can be very dark.

221

Key points

- Open daily (April to Sept) 7am to dusk (check NWT website for current times).
- Charge for non-NWT members. Tickets from visitor centre (open April to July 10am – 5pm) or use honesty box in car park.
- Terrain is level along mulched paths. Woodland walk (4.5km) is on unmade paths and tracks – not suitable for wheelchairs.
- Visitor centre and hides are wheelchair accessible.
- Visitor centre sells hot and cold drinks, snacks, books, etc. Toilets (inc. Blue badge) in centre.
- Guide dogs only on reserve but Forest Walk OK for all dogs.

Contacts

Norfolk Wildlife Trust
01603 625 540

WEETING is a superb Breckland reserve famous for its breeding Stone-curlews. The hides are accessed along short paths through a pleasant conifer wood, packed with common woodland species. The new Forest Walk gives you the chance to stretch your legs and find some Crossbills and Tree Pipits. All in all, a superb reserve!

Target birds Spring/summer – Woodlark (90%), Stone-curlew (90%), Tree Pipit (70%), Hobby (60%), Crossbill (20%).

Other possible bird species

Spring/summer		Common woodland birds
Buzzard	Corvids	Marsh Tit
Sparrowhawk	Skylark	Meadow Pipit
Kestrel	Hirundines	Siskin
Lapwing	Common scrub birds	Linnet
Regular gull species	Summer warblers	Other common finches
Little Owl	Goldcrest	Yellowhammer
Green Woodpecker	Spotted Flycatcher	
Great Spotted Woodpecker	Wheatear	Occasional
	Mistle Thrush	Marsh Harrier

Background information and birding tips

WANT TO SEE Stone-curlew? Then head for Weeting Heath. There are other sites, of course but please avoid these to prevent them being targeted by egg collectors.

The return of heathland species to Weeting each spring depends entirely on the rabbit population busily nibbling away, keeping the plants low enough for Stone-curlews and Woodlarks to nest. You may see both species from either the east or west hides, though the latter seems more productive.

The Stone-curlews prefer to nest over the ridge from the west hide, so patience may be required to see these ground-nesting birds. They are nocturnal, so an early morning or evening visit is best, though they can be seen at all times of day.

Be aware, a wicked heat haze during the day can severely hamper viewing. If you are lucky, you may even hear the eerie call of the Stone-curlew, a loud, haunting 'tudlooweeet tudlooweet' (when

you hear it, you will know what I mean).

While you are waiting for the SCs to show, keep an eye on the skies above the heath. Sparrowhawk and Kestrels are common, one or two Hobbies may dash through and Buzzards and Marsh Harriers are seen occasionally.

Green Woodpeckers and Mistle Thrushes love the heath and you may be lucky and find a Little Owl perched on fence posts to the right of west hide. Wheatears may be seen on passage and stoats regularly hunt the rabbits.

In the pine trees surrounding the hide, you should see Spotted Flycatcher, Marsh Tit, Long-tailed Tit, Blackcap, Goldcrest, etc. Crossbills and Tree Pipits are seen occasionally.

Please note that the visitor centre may close whenever the warden needs to be out and about on the reserve itself. If you fancy a walk, head towards the west hide through the wood. At the end of this path is a tiny hide overlooking some well-stocked feeders where you can get excellent views of common woodland species.

Continue to the road and cross carefully (traffic moves very fast along here). Follow the narrow grass path through some mixed woodland and onto a wide track. Turn right and walk slowly uphill looking for Linnets feeding along the open edges of this track.

At the top of the hill, take a sharp left down a gravelled drive. Check the paddocks around the house for thrushes and other feeding birds. The way-marked trail now takes you around the edges of several fairly new plantations, home to Yellowhammers, Linnets and a smattering of Tree Pipits. Chiffchaffs, Willow Warblers and common scrub birds are seen frequently. Woodlarks love these clearings too.

Some of the way-marking posts can be difficult to find in late summer when obscured by overgrown vegetation but I managed to follow my nose successfully. The trail eventually leads downhill towards the main road, and then bears left to run adjacent to the road.

You then reach the main track (where you originally turned right to go uphill), so you need to go straight across and back along the narrow grass path to the car park. You eventually return to the car park where you may wish to have another look for the Stone-curlews, Woodlarks, etc. from the hides, especially if you missed them earlier.

Along the whole of this circuit, constantly be alert for the loud *'chip' chip'* calls of Crossbills flying over.

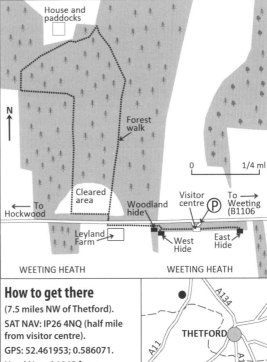

WEETING HEATH   WEETING HEATH

How to get there

(7.5 miles NW of Thetford).

SAT NAV: IP26 4NQ (half mile from visitor centre).

GPS: 52.461953; 0.586071.

Head N on A1065 from Brandon towards Swaffham. Immediately after crossing the railway turn left onto B1106, sign-posted to Weeting.

After 1.5 miles turn left at the green to Hockwold. After a further 1.5 miles the reserve is sign-posted off to the left. Obtain your permit from visitor centre (NWT members free). The centre is open from April to Sept.

All in all, this is a first-class reserve and you are guaranteed a friendly welcome from the wardens, who are only too happy to spend time with you to show you what is around.

Visiting birdwatchers who spend a leisurely hour or two here should see many sought-after Breckland species, though be sure to remain quiet throughout your visit to avoid disturbing these sensitive, vulnerable species.

223

Key points

- **Large pay and display car park, open dawn until dusk.**
- **Blue Badge holders also charged.**
- **Two toilet blocks on site.**
- **Café on site.**
- **Some tracks are wheelchair accessible (after negotiating a tight kissing gate).**
- **Terrain is level along a wide track but several narrower paths are steep.**
- **Managed by English Nature as part of its Holkham NNR.**
- **Dogs on leads allowed.**
- **Bike racks in car park.**
- **For birding in the area at other times of year, please see Holkham Pines NNR page.**

Contacts

Natural England
01603 620 558

ONE OF THE BEST sites in Norfolk to find migrants in spring and especially autumn, Wells Wood covers a large area but has a proven track record of attracting common, scarce and rare migrants. The maze of paths provide an ideal opportunity for rarity hunters to find their own birds.

Target birds *Spring/autumn* – **Common, scarce and rare migrants, potentially including: Wryneck, Redstart, Whinchat, Wheatear, Ring Ouzel, winter thrushes, Barred Warbler, Firecrest, Red-breasted Flycatcher, Pied Flycatcher, etc.**

Other likely bird species

Spring/autumn		
Woodcock	Skylark	Goldcrest
Regular gull species	Hirundines	Common woodland birds
Green Woodpecker	Common scrub birds	Treecreeper
Great Spotted Woodpecker	Lesser Whitethroat	Meadow Pipit
Jay	Garden Warbler	Crossbill
Other corvids	Blackcap	Other common finches
	Chiffchaff	Siskin
	Willow Warbler	Lesser Redpoll

Background information and birding tips

THOUGH birds such as Spotted Flycatcher breed in Wells Woods, and common woodland birds plus Crossbill and Jay can be found all year round, the most productive periods are during spring and autumn migration times, with autumn being the best.

Wells Woods is part of Holkham National Nature Reserve but I have split this site from Holkham Gap/Pines for ease of coverage. The whole area can provide a superb day searching for grounded migrants, though be warned that it is a huge area to cover thoroughly.

From the beach car park, take the path at the right hand edge of the boating lake. After a few yards the path splits left or straight on; the choice of route is yours and either is good for migrants.

The path straight ahead leads to a toilet block. The berry bushes opposite the block are excellent for warblers and it is well worth pausing here for quite some time to see what flits out of the thick cover. If it starts raining there is the added attraction of good shelter offered by the block's roof.

This path continues up a boardwalk into The Dell, a patch of woodland criss-crossed by undulating paths and a favoured area for migrants, so search the area thoroughly. Another narrow path skirts the wood on its seaward side and runs the length of the forest to Holkham Gap.

Alternatively, take one of several paths behind the toilet block. These all lead to the wide path which you would have reached if you had taken the left fork just past the boating lake.

It sounds complicated but you cannot get lost as you either hit the beach on the northern side or the wide track to Holkham on the southern side. All areas can be good for migrants.

Rare and scarce migrants also favour the Drinking Pool. This is difficult to find but is best reached by going onto the main track from the car park and then taking the first track left following the Norfolk Coastal Path signs (the boating lake should be on your left).

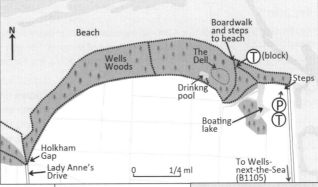

Keep on the main Coastal Path as it bends sharp right. Ignore any side tracks until you reach a bench dedicated to Raymond Kenneth Sparkes. About 200 yards past this bench is a single pine tree and a gorse bush isolated in quite a large grassy area. Turn right into the wood just after this pine tree and you soon reach the pool, complete with a homemade shack in which you can shelter! Approach carefully so as not to scare any bathing/drinking birds.

Once you have found the pool wait quietly around the edge to see what pops out of the bushes. The pool may be empty in dry years but the area is still excellent for migrants

How to get there

(15 miles E of Hunstanton).

SAT NAV: NR23 1DR (or Wells-next-the-Sea>Beach Road).

GPS: 52.972351; 0.847865.

About half way between Sheringham and Hunstanton, turn off A149 at the signposts for Wells Quay/Wells Beach.

In town, follow signs for Beach Car Park and Pinewoods Caravan Site. This road runs adjacent to Wells harbour and ends in a large pay and display car park. The path into the wood starts at the western end of the car

park, behind the boating lake.

Alternatively, park in Lady Anne's Drive, opposite the main entrance to Holkham Park and walk east (right) at the bottom. This takes you through Wells Woods and to the car park/toilets after about 1.5 miles.

I always try to find a sheltered area of berry bushes, ideally with a bit of sun on them. This usually produces Garden Warbler, Blackcap, Dunnock, Wren and Blackbird and hopefully a Barred Warbler in autumn. Another tip is to find a flock of tits because Firecrests and Yellow-browed Warblers tend to join with them.

Wells harbour can be very good for wintering wildfowl and grebes, especially in harsh weather. The harbour wall can be reached from the beach car park via some steps adjacent to the car park exit or from Wells town centre.

Also scan the football pitch to the west of the harbour wall for geese and winter thrushes.

Other nearby sites

Blakeney Point, Cley Marshes, Holkham Hall, Holkham NNR, Kelling Quags, Kelling Heath, Salthouse Beach, Salthouse Heath, Swanton Novers, Walsey Hills.

225

Key points
- **Open every day except Dec 25.**
- **Entrance fee for non-members. Collect permit at reception.**
- **Nov to Feb opening times: Mon to Wed (10am to 5pm – last admissions 4.30pm); Thurs to Sun (10am to 8pm – last admissions 6.30pm). March to Oct: 9.30am to 5pm (last admissions 4.30pm).**
- **Cafe open in winter: Mon to Fri 10am to 4.30pm; Sat & Sun 10am to 6.15pm. Summer: open 10am to 4.30pm daily (changes to 10am - 4pm daily from April 1).**
- **Toilets, incl. disabled.**

Contacts
The Wildfowl & Wetlands Trust, 01353 860 711; e-mail: info.welney@ wwt.org.uk www.wwt.org.uk/visit/ welney/plan-your-visit/

THE HEATED observatory overlooking the main lake ensures this is my wife's favourite winter reserve! Thousands of winter wildfowl visit this 1,000-acre wetland and there are several scarce breeding species present in spring and summer. The wild swan feeding sessions are extremely popular with the public but Welney offers far more than this to active birdwatchers.

Target birds
All year – **Whooper Swan (99%), Bewick's Swans (95%: a few injured birds of both species remain on site), Marsh Harrier (80%), Corn Bunting (60%), Tree Sparrow (20%).** *Winter* – **Winter wildfowl (100%), winter raptors (25%), Brambling (10%).** *Spring/summer* – **Avocet (95%), Little Ringed Plover (80%), Black-tailed Godwit (80%), Garganey (40%).** *Autumn* – **Passage waders (40%).**

Other likely bird species

All year	Pied Wagtail	Black Tern
Common wildfowl	Common finches	Ringed Plover
Red-legged Partridge	Yellowhammer	Little Stint
Grey Partridge	Reed Bunting	Temminck's Stint
Cormorant		Curlew Sandpiper
Little Egret	*Winter*	Dunlin
Great Crested Grebe	Pintail	Ruff
Sparrowhawk	Peregrine	Whimbrel
Kestrel	Winter thrushes	Greenshank
Lapwing		Green Sandpiper
Black-tailed Godwit	*Summer*	Wood Sandpiper
Snipe	Hobby	Common Sandpiper
Redshank	Common Tern	Grey Wagtail
Regular gull species	Oystercatcher	Winter thrushes
Barn Owl	Turtle Dove	
Little Owl	Hirundines	*Occasional (winter)*
Kingfisher	Yellow Wagtail	(Tundra) Bean Goose
Green Woodpecker	Sedge Warbler	Pink-footed Goose
Great Spotted Woodpecker	Reed Warbler	Smew
	Whitethroat	Hen Harrier
Corvids	Blackcap	Merlin
Skylark		Short-eared Owl
Meadow Pipit	*Passage*	Crane
	Little Gull	
	Arctic Tern	

Background information and birding tips

WELNEY is owned by the Wildfowl and Wetlands Trust and is worth a visit at any time of year. It is particularly famous for its winter birds when the feeding of swans and ducks is a feature of many a family visit. Every afternoon and most evenings, a staff member scatters a wheelbarrow load of grain for the wildfowl.

Birding should start before you arrive at the main centre. Drive slowly along the access road, scanning fields and hedgerows as you go. Species such as Tree Sparrow, Corn Bunting and Yellowhammer may well be your first sightings and raptors such as Hen Harrier, Peregrine, Short-eared Owl and Merlin occasionally quarter the fields in winter.

Once parked, enter the main building and obtain your permit from the reception desk (on the first floor, accessed by stairs or lift). Be aware that the advertised fee is the Gift Aid price; you may pay less if you want to.

The cafe overlooks the Lady Fen area, where you may watch wildfowl and waders while you eat and drink.

The bridge leads to the main (heated) observatory, which overlooks the main lake. From here, you should see thousands of wildfowl in winter including Bewick's and Whooper Swans, Wigeon, Teal, Pintail, Goldeneye, Mallard, etc., along with occasional Scaup and Smew.

Garganeys will be one of the first spring migrants, usually arriving in March. Waders should include many Lapwings, Curlews, Golden Plovers, etc with a few Dunlins and Ruff thrown in for good measure. Black-tailed Godwits and Avocets usually overwinter here and occasional Tundra Bean Geese and Cranes drop in.

In spring and the breeding season, Little Ringed Plovers and Oystercatchers join the semi-resident waders such as Black-tailed Godwits to breed on the reserve if water levels drop sufficiently. Garganeys also breed but become more elusive as the season wears on. Marsh Harriers regularly hunt over the area.

The Little Ringed Plovers usually breed on the island in front of the main hide, giving superb

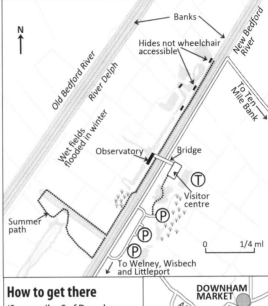

How to get there

(Seven miles S of Downham Market).

SAT NAV: PE14 9TN.

GPS: 52.525920; 0.277855.

From the north: The reserve is off A10, seven miles S of Downham Market (look for Ten Mile Bank/Welney on a brown tourist sign). Follow road for 0.8 miles to a bridge. Turn left, then immediately right down Station Road (there is a brown tourist sign but it is difficult to see). Follow Station Road for about 4.5 miles to the reserve car park on the left. Be warned: this road is straight but keep your speed down as there are severe undulations and potholes along the route.

From the south: From Ely, head N on A10 to Littleport. Turn left onto A1101 towards Wisbech. After about four miles the road turns sharply right to run alongside a high bank. At the next sharp left bend, take the minor road straight on. The reserve centre is approximately 1.3.miles further on.

views as they raise their chicks. A useful comparison with the similar Ringed Plover can usually be made as they argue over the best feeding areas.

227

Key points

• **Wild Swan Feeds: 12 noon daily (Boxing Day to mid March); 3.30pm daily (end Oct to mid March); 6.30pm floodlit feeds (Thurs to Sun only, Nov to Feb).**

• **Book ahead for free hire of wheelchairs (one with motor).**

• **Binoculars for hire.**

• **Hearing loop in main hide to amplify bird sounds.**

• **Shop stocked with books, bird food, etc.**

• **Access to reserve may be affected by flooding. CHECK BEFORE YOU VISIT!**

• **Only guide dogs allowed.**

• **Telescope useful. Usually one or two set up in main observatory.**

• **Photo hide for hire (pre-book).**

In summer, the WWT opens up a two and a quarter mile long trail allowing visitors the chance to explore the marsh, home to Black-tailed Godwits and other breeding waders. This trail is along rough paths that may be flooded if water levels are high in the area. The short reedbed boardwalk is also worth a look-see.

Avocet chicks can be seen from mid-June, along with odd-looking Shelduck youngsters. Several injured Bewick's and Whooper Swans also summer at the reserve. Turtle Doves often sit on the phone wires along the access road in summer.

The main hide is the most popular viewpoint but there are several more hides that overlook the marshes. Most are wheelchair accessible but paths may become muddy (or completely flooded) after prolonged rain, making access difficult.

For those who like to count their Mallard flocks in peace, there are one or two glass-fibre mini-shelters along the track which hold one person; they look like Portaloos but some hardy birders prefer them to the luxurious heated hide.

This is a very good reserve at all times of year. There is usually a warden in the main hide to show the visitor what is around.

Most birdwatchers turn up in winter when the wildfowl are in attendance but this reserve should not be overlooked in spring and autumn – one or two species of wader usually drop in on passage – or summer.

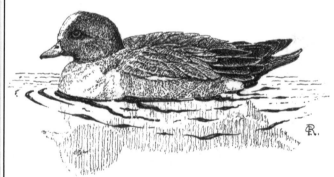

Welney's watery expanses offer a refuge to a wide variety of wildfowl species and you are sure to see good numbers of Wigeon in winter.

WEYBOURNE is a place for those who like to find their own birds, whether it be a secluded seawatch or a trek along the coastal path to scour the grassland and ploughed fields for migrants. One may wander for miles in each direction along the grassy clifftop in search of birds.

Target birds *Spring/autumn* – **Passage migrant passerines, passage seabirds.** *Summer* – **Sandwich Tern, Common Tern, Arctic Tern, Little Tern (all 100%).** *Winter* – **Seaduck and seabirds.**

Other likely bird species

All year
Cormorant
Common waders
Regular gull species
Skylark
Meadow Pipit
Pied Wagtail
Common finches
Reed Bunting

Winter
Red-throated Diver
Great Crested Grebe
Red-necked Grebe
Slavonian Grebe
Pink-footed Goose
Brent Goose
Eider

Common Scoter
Velvet Scoter
Goldeneye
Red-breasted Merganser
Hen Harrier
Merlin
Peregrine

Spring
Hirundines
Yellow Wagtail
Black Redstart
Whinchat
Wheatear
Ring Ouzel

Summer
Hirundines

Sedge Warbler
Reed Warbler
Whitethroat
Blackcap

Autumn (might include)
Sooty Shearwater
Manx Shearwater
Balearic Shearwater
Gannet
Skuas
Kittiwake
Little Auk
Black Redstart
Winter thrushes

Occasional
Lapland Bunting (winter)

Background information and birding tips

WEYBOURNE is a site with an excellent track record of attracting migrants in spring and autumn. It is also a good seawatching site at all times of year, though Sheringham offers a bit more shelter in bad weather conditions.

Your birding starts in the car park, where to your left, a small area of reeds holds Reed Buntings all year round, plus Reed and Sedge Warblers in summer.

The small pond sometimes attracts common wildfowl and waterbirds, mainly Mallard and Coot. The bushes behind you are on private land but you can see into them from the car park to check for migrants.

From the car park, there is a choice: if you choose to walk right (east), go up the slight incline onto the cliff top and follow the grass track. After about half a mile there is a hedgerow near a cottage, which is worth searching for migrants in spring and autumn.

The extensive grassy area attracts Skylarks and Meadow Pipits all year and migrants such as Yellow Wagtails and Ring Ouzels in spring and autumn. Rarer species such as Short-toed Lark are a distinct

Key points
• **Pay and display car park, including spaces for blue badge holders.**

• **Steepish incline onto the cliff, then flat track.**

• **Free access at all times.**

• **A public house and shop close by.**

Contacts
None

229

possibility. In winter, raptors sometimes hunt over this area and Lapland Buntings occasionally make the ploughed fields their winter home.

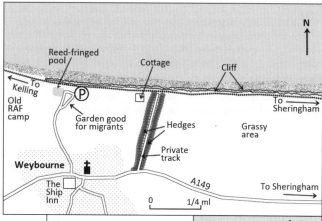

The cliff is a superb place from which to seawatch. In winter, look out for Great Crested, Red-necked and Slavonian Grebes, all three diver species, Red-breasted Mergansers, Goldeneye, Long-tailed Ducks, Velvet and Common Scoters.

In spring, you may be able to see incoming migrants make landfall, or winter visitors such as Fieldfares and Redwings departing for warmer climes. In autumn, the reverse happens.

Nothing is guaranteed, of course but watch the weather forecasts to assist you in deciding whether to visit Weybourne at migration times.

In spring, if there is a low pressure system over East Anglia coupled with high pressure over the rest of Europe and easterly winds, then sit and watch the birds stream in! In autumn, high pressure over Scandinavia with a low pressure system over Britain and onshore winds is likely to produce the best results.

In summer, terns will be fishing offshore and, from late July onwards, watch out for species such as Manx Shearwater, all four species of skua, Sabine's Gull etc.

If you walk west (left) from the car park, the going is slightly rougher but there are some good fields and bushes that attract migrants, especially around the disused RAF camp. Ring Ouzel and Black Redstart are specialities around this area.

How to get there

(Three miles W of Sheringham).

SAT NAV: NR25 7SR or Weybourne>Beach Lane. Follow access road to car park. GPS: 52.948583; 1.140075.

Turn off A149 in Weybourne village opposite The Ship Inn (from Hunstanton this is just before the church, from Sheringham just after the church).

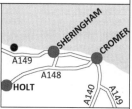

Follow this rough road down to a pay-and-display car park at the end. Walk E (right) onto the cliff or W (left) to the disused RAF camp.

It is possible to walk all the way to Kelling Quags and beyond, to Cley and Blakeney Point if you so desire. On foggy or drizzly spring and autumn mornings the whole area can be dripping with newly arrived migrants.

My personal Weybourne triumph came on July 21, 2001 when I decided to do some seawatching before heading up to Kelling Heath for Nightjar. The first bird I saw out to sea, as I stood on the shingle by the car park, was a Caspian Tern!

Other nearby sites

Blakeney Point, Cley, Kelling Heath, Kelling Quags, Salthouse Heath, Sheringham Park, Sheringham Sea Front, Walsey Hills.

BECAUSE IT IS only a couple of miles from the centre of Norwich, the park is extremely popular with non-birding visitors, but its varied habitats are home to a wide range of bird species. There is something to see at all times and it is establishing a reputation as a magnet for rare and scarce waterbirds in winter.

Target species *All year* – **Common water and woodland birds (100%).**

Other likely bird species

All year

Common waterfowl
Egyptian Goose
Cormorant
Grey Heron Little Grebe
Great Crested Grebe
Sparrowhawk
Kestrel
Regular gull species
Stock Dove
Tawny Owl
Kingfisher
Great Spotted Woodpecker
Green Woodpecker
Jay
Other corvids
Skylark
Common scrub birds

Blackcap
Goldcrest
Tree Sparrow
Pied Wagtail
Common finches
Reed Bunting

Winter

Common wildfowl
Lapwing
Winter thrushes
Grey Wagtail
Meadow Pipit

Spring to autumn

Common Tern
Cuckoo
Sand Martin
Other hirundines
Reed Warbler

Sedge Warbler
Summer warblers

Occasional

Rarer grebes and wildfowl (winter)

Marsh Harrier
Hobby
Oystercatcher
Little Ringed Plover
Mediterranean Gull
Little Gull
Arctic Tern
Black Tern (passage)
Passage waders (spring/autumn)

Nightingale
Wheatear (passage)
Brambling (winter)

Background information and birding tips

WHITLINGHAM Country Park has been developed from former gravel workings and is managed by the Whitlingham Charitable Trust with assistance from The Broads Authority. It lies just two miles from Norwich city centre and comprises several developing habitats that attract many common species of birds. It was opened in 2004, so these habitats have still to mature but the potential is there for this to be a very good birdwatching site.

You can start your walk from a number of points in the park. The beauty of Whitlingham is that you can cover the whole site in one go or visit one of the distinctly different areas as the mood takes you. These include the two broads, a mature wood and a small marsh. Each bit has its own car park so lazy birders, such as me, or people with just a few minutes to spare at lunchtime can drive between/to areas to maximise birding time!

The downside of this easy access and proximity to a large city is that the park can become very busy, especially at weekends and holiday times. There are usually some areas that remain quiet and there are always birds to see.

The main car park is situated adjacent to Whitlingham Great Broad, probably the principal

Key points

• **Cafe and toilets (plus map/visitor info) at visitor centre (01603 617 332).**

• **Pay-and-display car park (inc. Blue Badge holders).**

• **Great Broad path (2.3 miles) is wheelchair friendly. Benches at regular intervals.**

• **Dogs on leads in conservation area. No dogs allowed in Little Broad area July 1 to Aug 31.**

• **River Bus from Station Quay and Griffin Lane, Norwich (01603 701 701).**

• **Solar-powered boat trips around Great Broad, April to Sept. (wheelchair friendly; sound amplification system on board). Book on 01603 756 094 or 617 332**

• **Part of the Wherryman's Way long distance footpath.**

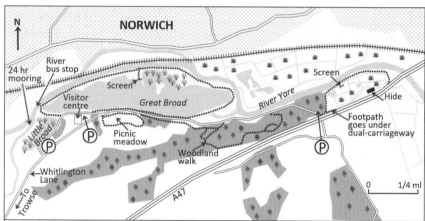

How to get there

SAT NAV: NR 14 8TR (or Trowse>Whitlingham Lane).

GPS: 52.620756; 1.327740.

Leave the A47 Norwich bypass on the A146 (dual carriageway) signed to Norwich, Lowestoft, Trowse & football traffic. After 0.6 miles, turn right on the ring road (A1054 to City Centre & Trowse).

After 0.3 miles, turn right at the roundabout to Trowse. Go over a bridge and turn left onto Whitlingham Lane, (0.3 miles after the roundabout).

Follow this road to your desired car park (Little Broad, Great Broad, Picnic Meadow, Woodland or Whitlingham Marsh – up to two miles from the start of Whitlingham Lane).

feature for visiting birdwatchers. A level path runs around the whole broad.

Obtain a map of trails from the visitor centre and also book for the boat (in season) if you want a leisurely cruise.

The main path splits the two broads. Little Broad hosts Reed and Sedge Warblers in summer but as it is the main boating lake the birdlife tends to be disturbed on a regular basis.

Continue walking clockwise round the lake, keeping Great Broad on your right and the River Yare on your left. The path is lined with trees and bushes where you should see resident common finches and scrub birds joined by warblers in summer (Blackcap, Willow Warbler, Chiffchaff, Whitethroat, etc).

You may wish to walk up the bank on your left at regular intervals to see what is on the river (Great Crested Grebe and other common waterbirds should be expected and Kingfisher is a possibility). There are one or two narrow, grass paths off to your right that lead to the broad's edge, though these are principally for fishermen to use.

After approx a quarter of a mile, you reach a gravel path signed to the 'Bird Screen'. Follow this track for about 75 yards to the screen, which overlooks the Great Broad (there is also an information board here).

The posts in the water will be occupied by gulls or Cormorants but check for Kingfishers too. The broad itself holds common ducks all year round, joined by Goldeneye, Pochard and Teal in winter.

Check the water carefully, as there are several records of rare and scarce grebes and ducks dropping in at Whitlingham in winter.

Cetti's Warblers are resident in the bushes and Nightingales have bred here.

The path continues to the far end of the broad. Check the rocky edges here first thing in the morning (before disturbance by dog-walkers, etc) for waders such as Common Sandpiper during spring and autumn passage times and Grey Wagtail in winter. You may also see birds coming down to this shallow edge to drink.

Follow the path to the opposite bank of the broad. You may choose to then divert left along the access road to the wood or marsh, or continue along the side of Great Broad to the car park and visitor centre (for refreshments?).

There is a picnic meadow along the access road, a pleasant place for an outdoor gathering. The woodland walk has its own car park, approx one mile from the park entrance gate, on your right. This is surrounded by trees and you may see species such as Great Spotted Woodpecker, Long-tailed Tit and Goldcrest, from your car.

The woodland walk starts along the access road (away from the park entrance), then across the grass/lawn to the grotty-looking toilet block (there are some cycle rails here also). Follow blue signs through the trees (be aware the start of path is not obvious behind the 'toilets').

Some of the way is quite steep but there are one or two viewpoints into some shaded dells, ideal for feeding warblers and common scrub birds in inclement weather. The path loops around the wood, onto the access road and back to the car park.

Whitlingham Marsh (owned by Norwich County Council) car park is a further 0.3 miles from the woodland car park, just before you go under the A47. There is an information board in the car park. Follow the hard path that starts by the access gate and this leads you to the River Yare.

Turn right along a rough grass track and after 20 yards there is a bird screen overlooking the marsh. To be honest, better views can be obtained from the footpath! The marsh may hold Snipe, with Reed and Sedge Warblers in summer. There is a large reedbed here but I haven't seen many birds in it.

The path continues through a patch of scrubby wood, which looks good for Cetti's Warbler, though I haven't heard of any in this area. You then have to walk under the A47 (very eerie as lorries thunder overhead) where the path continues to the right of the bridge stanchion.

After 100 yards, go through a wooden gate on your right. The muddy path leads to a boardwalk and hide. This overlooks a tiny pond, optimistically called a scrape. I believe the council are working towards making this a better area for wildlife, so the marsh will improve for birdwatchers too.

Retrace your steps back to the footpath and turn right to the car park (this is the old Norwich to Yarmouth road!) 400 yards along.

If you are feeling energetic, you can walk the whole country park from the main car park, following the course of the River Yare.

There are a number of activities in the park to engage non-birdwatching family members, and surely everyone would enjoy a cruise on Great Broad on the solar-powered boat. Close views of common wildfowl can be had from this quiet vessel and it is even suitable for wheelchair users. The boat leaves from a ramp near the visitor centre.

Whitlingham Country Park would make a superb local patch for a Norwich birder as it is the sort of place where some good birds will definitely be seen if the site is watched regularly.

Contacts

Whitlingham CP Ranger. 01603 610 734.

www.nccoutdooreducation.co.uk (01493 368129).

Whitlingham Charitable Trust, c/o Broads Authority, Yare House, 62-64 Thorpe Road, Norwich, Norfolk, NR1 1RY. 01603 610 734 (e-mail link on website).

Beccles Broads Information Centre on 01502 713 196.

Key points

- **National Nature Reserve and SSSI, managed by Natural England.**

- **Access on foot only.**

- **RSPB visitor hut open when Little Terns are nesting.**

- **Keep dogs under control.**

- **Keep to paths at all times as there are many rare plants and animals.**

- **Beach car park closes at 8pm in summer, 4pm in winter. Double yellow lines strictly enforced at all times of year but street parking OK after 8pm (May – Sept).**

- **Toilet block in car park.**

Contacts

Natural England
Norfolk Office
01603 620 558

WINTERTON is a dream site for those who love to find their own birds or like to mix birding with a sprinkling of rare plants, amphibians and insects. The whole area has a strong track record of attracting common, scarce and rare migrants in spring and autumn, while in summer there is a delightful Little Tern colony on the beach.

Target birds *Summer* – **Little Tern (95%), Nightjar (85%), Grasshopper Warbler (hear 55%, see 10%).** *Spring/autumn* – **Passage migrants.** *Winter* – **Winter raptors (25%), Short-eared Owl (10%).**

Other likely bird species

All year
Seaduck
Sparrowhawk
Kestrel
Marsh Harrier
Oystercatcher
Turnstone
Ringed Plover
Regular gull species
Barn Owl
Tawny Owl
Green Woodpecker
Corvids
Skylark
Common scrub birds
Stonechat
Meadow Pipit
Pied Wagtail

Yellowhammer
Reed Bunting

Summer
Sandwich Tern
Common Tern
Cuckoo
Hirundines
Summer warblers

Spring/autumn (might include)
Passage seabirds
Gannet
Skuas
Long-eared Owl
Wryneck
Red-backed Shrike
Bluethroat

Redstart
Whinchat
Wheatear
Ring Ouzel
Winter thrushes
Barred Warbler
Pallas's Warbler
Yellow-browed Warbler
Firecrest
Pied Flycatcher
Richard's Pipit
Tawny Pipit
Yellow Wagtail
Ortolan Bunting

Occasional overhead
Crane
Pink-footed Goose

Background information and birding tips

THIS NATIONAL NATURE RESERVE is part of an extensive nine-mile-long dune system. In recent years, it has become one of the 'in-places' for birdwatchers to find rare and scarce migrants in Norfolk.

In truth, Winterton is much more than a migrant hotspot, with Nightjars and Little Terns on offer in summer, several raptor species to savour in winter and the possibility of some excellent seawatching in autumn.

After parking in the beach car park (or in one of the small pull-ins along the beach road) you have a choice of walking north or south through the dune system. In spring and autumn the bushes at the bottom of the hill can hold many common (Redstart, Pied Flycatcher, Goldcrest, etc), scarce (Firecrest, Barred and Icterine Warblers, etc) or rare (Pallas's Warbler, Dusky Warbler, etc) migrants.

Spring and summer see breeding warblers such as Whitethroat and Blackcap joining the resident species.

The whole dune system, north and south, should be searched thoroughly at migration times for anything that moves! Wheatears,

How to get there

(Eight miles N of Great Yarmouth).

SAT NAV: NR29 4DD (postcode for Beach Road, Winterton. Follow to end for car park).

GPS: 52.717970; 1.698268.

From Yarmouth: Follow signs for Caister-on-Sea along A1064. At a roundabout after a stretch of dual carriageway near Caister, take B1159 to Winterton (second exit) and continue for approximately 4.5 miles. As you enter village, take Hermanus Road on right, sign-posted 'Beach'. Turn right at T-junction (down The Craft), then park in the small lay-bys by the dunes, or in car park at the end of the road. Walk left (N) or right (S) into the dunes, or straight ahead to the beach.

From north and west: Enter Winterton village on B1159. At a sharp bend, turn down Black Street (signed 'Beach'). Continue past the chapel and post office (Black Street now becomes Beach Road) to the car park. This closes at 8pm, so for Nightjar parking, turn down Black Street off the main B1159 at the church. Continue to just before the Post Office and turn left onto Market Place and then onto North Market Road (dead end). Park considerately and walk through onto the dunes at the end of NM Road. Follow the wide path, keeping the fenceline on your left as far as you like: this path leads to the concrete blocks.

(Postcode for N. Market Rd is NR29 4BH).

Map labels: Concrete blocks; To Horsey Gap; N; Pools for natterjack toads; Area best for Nightjars; Usual area of Little Tern colony; Fence; Dunes; Beach; Totem pole; North Market Road; P P; East Somerton; B1159; Winterton-on-Sea; Dunes; Bushes; 0 1/2 ml; To A1064; A149; A47; GREAT YARMOUTH

Whinchats, Ring Ouzels, pipits, wagtails, etc, should all be encountered and Wryneck and Red-backed Shrike are regularly reported from here.

When I say search the dunes thoroughly, I mean stay on the paths criss-crossing the site, scanning regularly with your binoculars. This method usually pays dividends, with the added bonus of not disturbing other rare animals and plants in the process (though dog owners allow their animals to roam uncontrolled with impunity and they may flush a hidden bird or two).

If you choose to head north you may wander for many miles, passing Horsey Gap, Waxham and Sea Palling. All hold the promise of migrants popping up at any time. On the way, about 500 yards from the car park, you will find an object protruding from the sand. This is fancifully called 'The Totem Pole' and is often referred to in bird reports/bird newslines, etc.

In addition to the migrants, you should encounter many resident species such as Kestrel, Yellowhammer, Meadow Pipit, Reed Bunting, Skylark, Green Woodpecker and the delightful Stonechat. Marsh Harriers and Barn

235

Key points

- **Cafe in car park open every day (mid Feb – Oct, 9am-5pm plus winter weekends and NY Day and Boxing Day).**

- **Terrain generally level along wide, rough, sandy tracks. Difficult wheelchair access.**

- **Take a torch to light your way back (NOT to point at the Nightjars!!)**

- **No horses**

- **No motorbikes.**

- **If you see any disturbance at the Little Tern colony phone 07899 901 566 immediately.**

- **Do not touch any strange objects on the beach – unexploded missiles turn up occasionally!**

Owls regularly hunt over fields to the west of Winterton Dunes (look towards Horsey Mill), with sightings almost guaranteed all year round for the former species.

In winter, this can seem a barren place. However, hardy walkers may be rewarded with sightings of Hen Harrier, Merlin, Peregrine and Short-eared Owl, though none are guaranteed. Skeins of Pink-footed Geese regularly fly overhead, especially in the early mornings and evenings.

Crane is another species to watch out for around the Winterton area, though they are usually seen more frequently around Horsey and at Stubb Mill. However, I had two adults and two juveniles fly overhead at Winterton in November 2001 (accompanied by a Sacred Ibis!), so keep your eyes peeled at all times.

The sea should not be ignored at Winterton either, as winter can produce reasonable numbers of Red-throated Divers, Red-breasted Mergansers, Common Scoters, Long-tailed Ducks and other scarce grebes and divers. In autumn expect Manx Shearwaters, Gannets and Arctic and Great Skuas.

In summer, the main attractions are Nightjars and Little Terns. The Little Tern colony is usually north of the beach car park (from there, head onto the beach and walk left to find the RSPB warden's hut by the colony).

The area is fenced off and a warden is on site to answer questions and to keep dogs out of the nesting area.

Little Tern colonies are notorious for shifting venue from one year to the next (the Great Yarmouth colony has now moved to Caistor,

with some birds boosting the numbers at Winterton). Check on the RSPB website to see if the colony is still present at Winterton before you visit.

Also, usually hanging around this area are Oystercatchers, Turnstones and Ringed Plovers. Out to sea, you should see Common and Sandwich Terns busily fishing for food to raise their young at colonies nearby.

For Nightjars, take the main track north following the fence on your left, with trees at the back. Nightjars can be anywhere in this fenced-off area, though I have found the best spot to be about half a mile from the beach road, by the concrete blocks at the northern entrance to the reserve.

Green Woodpeckers continually 'laugh' at waiting birders, while a Tawny Owl occasionally shows itself. If you wait quietly, Nightjars will come and perch on fence posts at the edge of the main track.

Winterton Dunes is home to one or two pairs of Grasshopper Warblers in summer, though they are extremely difficult to see. You will more likely hear them 'reeling' from the bushes dotted around the dunes.

They may also join natterjack toad, Nightjar, Green Woodpecker, Woodcock and Tawny Owl in the dusk chorus for an uplifting end to the birdwatching day!

Other nearby sites

Alderfen Broad, Barton Broad, Breydon Water, Burgh Marshes, Great Yarmouth Beach, Great Yarmouth Cemetery, Hickling Broad, How Hill Trust Reserve, Martham Broad, Ranworth Broad, Ted Ellis Reserve.

THE MAIN species of interest at Wolferton is the extravagant Golden Pheasant. There are one or two common woodland species to be seen but it is the pheasants that draw in the visitors. As suggested by its name, the site is a triangle of roads, bordered by thick bushes. The pheasants occasionally emerge from these bushes to feed along the grass verges.

Target birds *All year* – **Woodcock (60%), Golden Pheasant (40%).** *Summer* – **Nightjar (40%), Woodlark (30%).**

Other likely bird species

All year	Long-tailed Tit	*Summer*
Pheasant	Goldcrest	Summer warblers
Tawny Owl	Common finches	*Occasional*
Great Spotted Woodpecker	*Winter*	Lesser Spotted Woodpecker
Common scrub birds	Pink-footed Goose (overhead)	Crossbill
Common woodland birds		

Background information and birding tips

WOLFERTON TRIANGLE is a site of limited interest as regards species numbers but is the best site in the country for Golden Pheasants. Patient birdwatchers should be rewarded with good views of these gaudy introductions as long as certain rules are followed.

Though the target birds are present all year round, I have found early mornings and late afternoons in winter and spring provide the best chances of seeing a Goldie. The most important thing to remember is to never get out of your car or the pheasants will scuttle into the undergrowth.

Simply cruise very slowly around the triangle of roads keeping an eye on the grass verges for the birds, or park up considerably at a likely looking spot and sit quietly to wait for the Goldies to emerge.

In my experience, the most productive stop-off is the small, muddy lay-by on the south-eastern edge of the triangle at TF 673 277.

From here, it is possible to see into the wood where Goldies may be seen scratching for food in the leaf litter. If you see anyone in this wood, please ask them to leave!

While waiting for the Golden Pheasants to show, you can amuse yourself by watching some commoner bird species (Robin, Wren, Blackbird) or grey squirrels which sometimes approach the car.

If you visit Wolferton at dawn and dusk, you may be lucky to see one or two Woodcocks on the roadside verges. They freeze as you drive by, allowing superb views of this usually skulking species.

Great Spotted Woodpeckers are seen regularly, Lesser Spotted Woodpeckers have been recorded in recent years and Crossbills occasionally visit the conifers in the triangle.

Coal Tits and Chaffinches are probably the commonest species to be seen or heard and Goldcrests should also be seen here.

Key points

• **Woods are private – do not enter.**

• **No need to even get out of your car.**

• **Access at all times.**

• **Do not impede the progress of local traffic – keep checking the rear view mirror as you crawl along.**

• **Do not run over any pheasants!**

How to get there

(Approx. five miles N of King's Lynn).

SAT NAV: Wolferton.

GPS: 52.821713; 0.481058.

Between Hunstanton and King's Lynn off A149. Wolferton is sign-posted opposite the turn-off for Sandringham. Once off the A road, drive round the triangle of minor roads (about one mile in total) skirting the dense bushes.

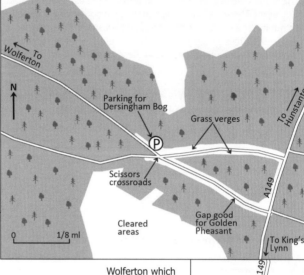

The chance of connecting with Golden Pheasants is quite good, though several of my friends refuse to believe these birds actually exist! They are becoming more elusive, probably due to disturbance from people entering the private wood.

There is another problem: the Goldies are interbreeding with other pheasants, so it is essential you make sure there are no signs of 'foreign genes' in the birds you see. An untainted Goldie should have a pure reddish breast with no sign of any black and the tail should be all brown with no hint of white feathers.

Maintenance work has created a clearing at Wolferton which is now home to a handful of Nightjars, Woodlarks and Tree Pipits.

A tiny part of this clearing can be viewed from a barrier almost opposite the layby mentioned earlier. THIS IS A PRIVATE AREA AND YOU SHOULD NOT CROSS THE BARRIER! If you want better views of these species, you should visit Dersingham Bog nearby.

Other nearby sites

Dersingham Bog, Flitcham Abbey Farm, Gypsy Lane, Holme Dunes, Holme Observatory, Hunstanton, Redwell Marsh, Ken Hill Wood, Roydon Common, Sandringham, Snettisham, Titchwell Marshes.

THE NORFOLK BIRD LIST

THIS IS a run-down of all species of birds which have been seen in Norfolk, detailing when and where to see them. This is mainly aimed at beginners who may not be aware of when and how often some species are present in the county. The list can be used as a checklist as there are boxes to record your Norfolk life list and an individual year.

I have to stress that these notes are from my personal experiences of the birds in Norfolk and many folk will disagree with my verdicts! For instance, I see Marsh Harrier every time I visit Norfolk, no matter what time of year, hence my assessment that they are common. Obviously, they aren't common in the true sense but you can't argue with a 100% strike rate! Also included are several races of species which are sometimes mentioned in bird magazines, and which may be given full species status in future (indicated by italics).

I have assigned all species to one of the following categories.

COMMON
Very abundant, or very easy to see ev there aren't many of them around.

SCARCE
Not very common, or hard to see in the field even if fairly abundant in numbers. Not likely to be seen by a casual visitor unless they are specifically looking for a particular species (eg. Hawfinch). See specific site pages for more details of when to visit and how likely you are to see the target species.

MODERATELY RARE
Hardly any seen during the year, and certainly almost never by the casual visitor.

RARE
Probably only a handful of records, or several records many years ago. You will not see this species unless alerted to a new sighting by a pager or birdline service.

EXTREMELY RARE
Probably only one mention in the history of record-keeping! Probably more chance of winning the National Lottery than seeing one of the species in this category on a casual visit. Only intrepid birders looking for rare birds will find one of these in a lifetime, or twitchers travelling to see these rarities are likely to see them.

The jangling song of Corn Bunting is an increasingly rare sound in Norfolk – Choseley Barns is probably the best place to connect with this species.

		Common Name	Scientific Name	Status and Key Locations
		Mute Swan	*Cygnus olor*	Common resident on all wetlands.
		Bewick's Swan	*C. columbianus*	Localised winter resident. Best at Welney.
		Whooper Swan	*C. cygnus*	Localised winter resident. Best at Welney.
		(Tundra) Bean Goose	*Anser fabalis rossicus*	Moderately rare winter visitor, mainly at Welney.
		(Taiga) Bean Goose	*A.f. fabalis*	Up to 300 winter at Buckenham Marshes (Nov to Feb).
		Pink-footed Goose	*A. brachyrhynchus*	Thousands in winter. Snettisham, Horsey and Holkham favoured sites or on fields anywhere near coast.
		White-fronted Goose	*A. albifrons*	Winter resident, best at Holkham and Buckenham.
		Lesser White-fronted Goose	*A. erythropus*	Extremely rare winter visitor.
		Greylag Goose	*A. Anser*	Common resident, feral population on all wetlands.
		Snow Goose	*A. caerulescens*	Rare winter visitor. Beware escapes!
		Canada Goose	*Branta canadensis*	Common resident on all waters.
		Barnacle Goose	*B. leucopsis*	Moderately rare winter visitor. Try Holkham.
		(Pale-bellied) Brent Goose	*B. bernicula*	Moderately rare winter visitor among dark-bellied flocks.
		(Dark-bellied) Brent Goose	*B.b. hrota*	Very common winter visitor to all north coast marshes.
		Black Brant	*B.b. nigricans*	Moderately rare winter visitor among dark-bellied Brent flocks. Titchwell and Cley are best bets.
		Red-breasted Goose	*B. ruficollis*	Rare winter visitor. Scan Brent goose flocks.
		Egyptian Goose	*Alopochen aegyptiacus*	Increasingly common feral resident on many Broadland rivers and coastal marshes.
		Ruddy Shelduck	*Tadorna ferruginea*	Extremely rare. Recent records due to escapes?
		Shelduck	*T. tadorna*	Common resident mostly on coastal marshes.
		Mandarin	*Aix galericulata*	Rare.
		Eurasian Wigeon	*Anas penelope*	Common winter resident, all marshes. One or two stay for winter?
		American Wigeon	*A. americana*	Rare.
		Gadwall	*A. strepera*	Common resident all waters.

			Common Name	Scientific Name	Status and Key Locations
			Teal	A. crecca	Common winter resident. A few over-summer.
			Green-winged Teal	A. carolinensis	Rare.
			Mallard	A. platyrhynchos	Very common resident.
			Pintail	A. acuta	Fairly common winter resident. Try Welney, with smaller numbers at Titchwell.
			Garganey	A. querquedula	Scarce on passage, plus a few pairs breed: Cley, Hickling or Welney.
			Blue-winged Teal	A. discors	Extremely rare.
			Shoveler	A. clypeata	Common resident.
			Red-crested Pochard	Netta rufina	Rare.
			Pochard	Aythya ferina	Common winter resident all waters, some breed.
			Canvasback	A. valisineria	Extremely rare.
			Ring-necked Duck	A. collaris	Rare.
			Ferruginous Duck	A. nyroca	Rare.
			Tufted Duck	A. fuligula	Common winter resident all waters, some breed.
			Scaup	A. marila	Scarce winter visitor. Try Snettisham RSPB pits.
			Common Eider	Somateria mollisima	Scarce sea duck. Try Titchwell all year round.
			King Eider	S. spectabilis	Extremely rare.
			Steller's Eider	Polysticta stelleri	Extremely rare.
			Long-tailed Duck	Clangula hyemalis	Scarce winter sea duck. Coast between Hunstanton and Horsey.
			Common Scoter	Melanitta nigra	Up to 3,000 off the north coast. Hunstanton, Holme and Titchwell.
			Surf Scoter	M. perspicillata	Extremely rare.
			Velvet Scoter	M. fusca	Scarce sea duck in with Common Scoters – scan flocks for tell-tale white wing patches.
			Bufflehead	Bucephala albeola	Extremely rare.
			Goldeneye	B. clangula	Fairly common winter visitor. At sea or on inland pits.
			Smew	Mergellus albellus	Scarce winter visitor. Best at Tottenhill Pits, also Hickling and Snettisham.
			Red-breasted Merganser	M. serrator	Fairly common at sea in winter. North coast sites.

THE NORFOLK BIRD LIST

			Common Name	Scientific Name	Status and Key Locations
			Goosander	*M. merganser*	Scarce in winter. Try Denver Sluice, Nunnery Lakes, Sparham Pools.
			Ruddy Duck	*Oxyura jamaicensis*	Rare.
			Red-legged Partridge	*Alectoris rufa*	Common resident. Scan any field.
			Grey Partridge	*Perdix perdix*	Declining resident in fields. Roydon Common best.
			Quail	*Coturnix coturnix*	Present most summers in wheat fields. Check bird newslines for locations.
			Pheasant	*Phasianus colchicus*	Common resident everywhere.
			Golden Pheasant	*Chrysolophus pictus*	Scarce resident. Wolferton Triangle and Santon Downham.
			Red-throated Diver	*Gavia stellata*	Relatively common at sea in winter. Rare inland.
			Black-throated Diver	*G. arctica*	Fairly rare at sea in winter. Rare inland.
			Great Northern Diver	*G. immer*	Fairly rare at sea in winter. Rare inland.
			White-billed Diver	*G. adamsii*	Extremely rare.
			Black-browed Albatross	*Thalassarche melanophins*	Extremely rare.
			Fulmar	*Fulmarus glacialis*	Relatively common resident. Hunstanton is the best place, or any seawatching site.
			Zino's/Fea's Petrel	*Pterodroma madeira/ fea*	Extremely rare.
			Black-capped Petrel	*P. hasitata*	Extremely rare.
			Cory's Shearwater	*Calonectris diomedia*	Rare passage sea bird. Late summer to October.
			Great Shearwater	*Puffinus gravis*	Extremely rare passage seabird. Late summer to October.
			Sooty Shearwater	*P. griseus*	Moderately rare passage seabird. Early autumn off seawatching sites.
			Manx Shearwater	*P. Puffinus*	Scarce (but most common shearwater) passage seabird. Late summer to October at seawatching sites.
			Balearic Shearwater	*P. mauretanicus*	Moderately rare passage seabird. Late summer at seawatching sites.
			Little Shearwater	*P. assimilis*	Extremely rare.
			Storm Petrel	*Hydrobates pelagicus*	Moderately rare seabird, from late July – late September.
			Leach's Petrel	*Oceanodroma leucorhoa*	Rare seabird in autumn.
			Gannet	*Morus Bassanus*	Relatively common passage seabird. Autumn best.

			Common Name	Scientific Name	Status and Key Locations
			Cormorant	*Phalacrocorax carbo*	Common resident at coastal sites plus inland waters.
			Shag	*P. aristotelis*	Moderately rare passage seabird at seawatching points.
			Bittern	*Botaurus stellaris*	Extremely secretive, scarce resident. Look over reedbeds at Hickling, Cley, etc. Best seen in icy conditions which force them to feed in open areas.
			Little Bittern	*Ixobrychus minutus*	Extremely rare.
			Night Heron	*Nycticorax nycticorax*	Rare.
			Squacco Heron	*Ardeola ralloides*	Extremely rare.
			Cattle Egret	*Bubulcus ibis*	Rare.
			Little Egret	*Egretta garzetta*	Scarce breeder. Relatively common on all marshes throughout year.
			Great White Egret	*E. alba*	Rare.
			Grey Heron	*Ardea cinerea*	Common resident at all wetlands.
			Purple Heron	*A. purpurea*	Rare.
			Black Stork	*Ciconia nigra*	Extremely rare.
			White Stork	*C. ciconia*	Rare.
			Glossy Ibis	*Plegadis falcinellus*	Extremely rare.
			Spoonbill	*Platalea leucorodia*	Scarce breeder at Holkham NNR. Families wander to Cley and Titchwell.
			Pied-billed Grebe	*Podilymbus podiceps*	Extremely rare.
			Little Grebe	*Tachyaptus ruficollis*	Fairly common on inland waters.
			Great Crested Grebe	*Podiceps cristatus*	Common at sea in winter. Breeds on inland waters, stronghold in The Broads.
			Red-necked Grebe	*P. grisegena*	Scarce at sea in winter.
			Slavonian Grebe	*P. auritus*	Scarce at sea in winter.
			Black-necked Grebe	*P. nigricollis*	Mainly seen on passage on inland waters.
			Honey Buzzard	*Pernis apivorus*	Rare breeder (possibly 2 pairs). Swanton Novers mid-May to mid-Sept.
			Black Kite	*Milvus migrans*	Extremely rare.
			Red Kite	*M. milvus*	Scarce but increasing visitor.
			White-tailed Eagle	*Haliaeetus albicilla*	Rare winter visitor.
			Marsh Harrier	*Circus aeruginosus*	Common on most marshes throughout the year.
			Hen Harrier	*C. cyaneus*	Scarce winter visitor. Roosts at Stubb Mill and Roydon

		Common Name	Scientific Name	Status and Key Locations
		Pallid Harrier	C. macrourus	Extremely rare.
		Montagu's Harrier	C. pygargus	Rare breeder. Details not given at request of RSPB. Sometimes seen on migration at Snettisham or Cley.
		Goshawk	Accipiter gentilis	Scarce breeder. Try any vantage point in Thetford Forest from late Feb to early May for displaying birds.
		Sparrowhawk	A. nisus	Common resident in virtually all woodland.
		Buzzard	Buteo buteo	Relatively common resident.
		Rough-legged Buzzard	B. lagopus	Usually one in winter. Check telephone newslines for current site.
		Golden Eagle	Aquila chrysaetos	Extremely rare.
		Osprey	Pandion haliaetus	Scarce on passage. May and September best months.
		Kestrel	Falco tinnunculus	Common resident everywhere.
		Red-footed Falcon	F. vespertinus	Moderately rare spring vagrant.
		Merlin	F. columbarius	Scarce winter visitor. Most marshes but best at Stubb Mill roost.
		Hobby	F. subbuteo	Scarce but increasing summer visitor. Hickling and Lakenheath Fen best.
		Eleonora's Falcon	F. eleonorae	Extremely rare.
		Gyrfalcon	F. rusticolus	Extremely rare.
		Peregrine Falcon	F. peregrinus	Scarce winter visitor, most marshes. Holkham NNR and Buckenham Marshes seem favoured spots.
		Water Rail	Rallus aquaticus	Secretive resident. More commonly seen in winter. Try Cley and Titchwell.
		Spotted Crake	Porzana porzana	Moderately rare autumn visitor. Titchwell is a favoured haunt.
		Little Crake	P. parva	Extremely rare.
		Baillon's Crake	P. pusilla	Extremely rare.
		Corncrake	Crex crex	Moderately rare passage migrant. Usually seen when flushed from Blakeney Point.
		Moorhen	Gallinula chloropus	Common resident, all waters.
		Allen's Gallinule	Porphyrula alleni	Extremely rare.
		Coot	Fulica atra	Common resident, all waters.
		Common Crane	Grus grus	Small population resident in Horsey/Hickling area.
		Sandhill Crane	Grus canadensis	Extremely rare.

		Common Name	Scientific Name	Status and Key Locations
		Little Bustard	*Tetrax tetrax*	Extremely rare.
		Great Bustard	*Otis tarda*	Extremely rare.
		Oystercatcher	*Haematopus ostralegus*	Common coastal resident.
		Black-winged Stilt	*Himantopus himantopus*	Rare.
		Avocet	*Recurvirostra avosetta*	Fairly common breeder. Cley, Titchwell, Welney. Winter at Breydon Water.
		Stone Curlew	*Burhinus oedicnemus*	Moderately rare but increasing breeder. Weeting Heath (April to Sept).
		Cream-coloured Courser	*Cursorius cursor*	Extremely rare.
		Collared Pratincole	*Glareola pratincola*	Rare.
		Oriental Pratincole	*G. maldivarum*	Extremely rare.
		Black-winged Pratincole	*G. nordmanni*	Extremely rare.
		Little Ringed Plover	*Charadrius dubius*	Moderately rare breeder. Welney best (April to late August).
		Ringed Plover	*Charadrius hiaticula*	Common coastal resident, plus inland scrapes.
		Killdeer	*C. vociferus*	Extremely rare.
		Kentish Plover	*C. alexandrinus*	Moderately rare spring vagrant. Favours Breydon Water.
		Greater Sandplover	*C. leschenaultii*	Extremely rare.
		Caspian Plover	*C. asiaticus*	Extremely rare.
		Dotterel	*C. morinellus*	Moderately rare passage migrant.
		American Golden Plover	*Pluvialis dominica*	Extremely rare.
		Pacific Golden Plover	*P. fulva*	Extremely rare.
		Golden Plover	*P. apricaria*	Common winter visitor. Snettisham or Titchwell best.
		Grey Plover	*P. squatarola*	Fairly common winter visitor. Any coastal wader site.
		Sociable Plover	*Vanellus gregarius*	Extremely rare.
		Lapwing	*V. vanellus*	Common resident all marshes.
		Knot	*Calidris canutus*	Common winter visitor. Snettisham at high tide.
		Sanderling	*C. alba*	Common on beaches in winter.
		Semipalmated Sandpiper	*C. pusilla*	Rare.

		Common Name	Scientific Name	Status and Key Locations
		Western Sandpiper	Calidris mauri	Extremely rare.
		Red-necked Stint	C. ruficollis	Extremely rare.
		Little Stint	C. minuta	Scarce passage wader – autumn at Titchwell and Cley.
		Temminck's Stint	C. temminckii	Passage wader. Cley in May is best.
		White-rumped Sandpiper	C. fuscicollis	Rare.
		Baird's Sandpiper	C. bairdii	Rare.
		Pectoral Sandpiper	C. melanotos	Moderately rare vagrant, usually September.
		Sharp-tailed Sandpiper	C. acuminata	Extremely rare.
		Purple Sandpiper	C. maritima	Scarce winter visitor. Rocks at Sheringham seem the best bet.
		Dunlin	C. alpina	Common resident wader. All pits and coast.
		Broad-billed Sandpiper	Limicola falcinellus	Rare. Favours Breydon Water.
		Stilt Sandpiper	Micropalama himantopus	Extremely rare.
		Buff-breasted Sandpiper	Tryngites subruficollis	Rare. Usually in September.
		Ruff	Philomachus pugnax	Fairly common resident, scarcer in winter. Cley, Holme, Titchwell, Snettisham, etc.
		Jack Snipe	Lymnocryptes minimus	Moderately rare winter visitor. Very secretive. Surlingham, Holme, Cley, Roydon Common.
		Snipe	Gallinago gallinago	Common resident on all marshes and pits.
		Great Snipe	G. media	Extremely rare.
		Long-billed Dowitcher	Limnodromus scolopaceus	Rare.
		Woodcock	Scalopax rusticola	Common but secretive resident. Dusk at Buxton Heath
		Black-tailed Godwit	Limosa limosa	Relatively scarce at all times of year. Try Breydon Water and Cley in winter, Welney and Cley in summer.
		Bar-tailed Godwit	L. lapponica	Relatively common all year. Any wader hotspot in winter and Titchwell in summer.
		Little Whimbrel	Numenius minutus	Extremely rare.
		Whimbrel	N. phaeopus	Scarce on passage. Try Blakeney Point, Cley, Breydon Water and Salthouse Beach.

			Common Name	Scientific Name	Status and Key Locations
			Curlew	N. arquata	Common in winter, all marshes, scarcer in summer. Breeds at Roydon Common, Warham Greens.
			Spotted Redshank	Tringa erythropus	A few winter at Titchwell. Passage best at Snettisham.
			Redshank	T. totanus	Common on all pits and marshes all year.
			Marsh Sandpiper	T. stagnatilis	Extremely rare.
			Greenshank	T. nebularia	Scarce on passage. Cley, Breydon Water, Snettisham, Holme etc.
			Greater Yellowlegs	T. melanoleuca	Extremely rare.
			Lesser Yellowlegs	T. flavipes	Rare.
			Solitary Sandpiper	T. solitaria	Extremely rare.
			Green Sandpiper	T. ochropus	Common passage wader. Holme is good but any scrape can attract them.
			Wood Sandpiper	T. glareola	Scarce passage wader. Cley, Holme, Salthouse Beach are all favoured areas.
			Terek Sandpiper	Xenus cinereus	Rare.
			Common Sandpiper	Actitis hypoleucos	Relatively common on passage. Favour sites used by Green and Wood Sandpipers.
			Spotted Sandpiper	A. macularia	Rare.
			Turnstone	Arenaria interpres	Common resident on coast.
			Wilson's Phalarope	Phalaropus tricolor	Extremely rare.
			Red-necked Phalarope	P. lobatus	Cley in May is a traditional stop-over. Moderately rare.
			Grey Phalarope	P. fulicarius	Moderately rare from seawatching points in autumn.
			Pomarine Skua	Stercorarius pomarinus	Moderately rare seabird. Autumn best but sometimes seen in winter.
			Arctic Skua	S. parasiticus	Scarce on autumn passage. From late July harassing terns at sea.
			Long-tailed Skua	S. longicaudus	Moderately rare seabird. Autumn best.
			Great Skua	S. skua	Scarce seabird. Best from Aug to Oct harassing birds at sea.
			Mediterranean Gull	Larus melanocephalus	Moderately rare breeder. Best seen on Great Yarmouth beach.
			Laughing Gull	L. atricilla	Rare.
			Franklin's Gull	L. pipixcan	Rare.
			Little Gull	L. minutus	Scarce on passage at Titchwell, Breydon Water, Kelling Quags. May is best month.

		Common Name	Scientific Name	Status and Key Locations
		Sabine's Gull	*L. sabini*	Moderately rare autumn seabird at seawatching points.
		Bonaparte's Gull	*L. philadelphia*	Extremely rare.
		Black-headed Gull	*L. ridibundus*	Very common breeder and resident. All waters and marshes.
		Slender-billed Gull	*L. genei*	Extremely rare. Favours Cley.
		Ring-billed Gull	*L. delawarensis*	Rare.
		Common Gull	*L. canus*	Relatively common resident.
		Lesser Black-backed Gull	*L. fuscus*	Relatively common resident. All waters and marshes.
		Herring Gull	*L. argentatus*	Common resident on coast.
		Yellow-legged Gull	*L. michahellis*	Scarce summer visitor. Cley is best.
		Caspian Gull	*L. cachinnans*	Rare vagrant, usually summer.
		American Herring gull	*L.smithsonianus*	Extremely rare.
		Iceland Gull	*L. glaucoides*	Moderately rare winter visitor. Phone bird newslines for details.
		Glaucous Gull	*L. hyperboreus*	Moderately rare, usually winter, visitor. Favours King's Lynn Docks.
		Great Black-backed Gull	*L. marinus*	Common resident on all waters and coast.
		Ross's Gull	*Rhodostethia rosea*	Extremely rare.
		Kittiwake	*Rissa tridactyla*	Relatively common seabird at all watchpoints. From late July to October best.
		Ivory Gull	*Pagophila eburnea*	Extremely rare.
		Sooty Tern	*Onychopion fuscata*	Extremely rare.
		Little Tern	*Sternula albifrons*	Common summer visitor. From May to September at all seawatching points. Colonies at Blakeney Point and Winterton.
		Gull-billed Tern	*Gelochelidon nilotica*	Rare.
		Caspian Tern	*Hydroprogne caspia*	Moderately rare summer vagrant. Any tern colony/ roost.
		Whiskered Tern	*Chlidonias hybrida*	Rare.
		Black Tern	*C. niger*	Scarce on spring and autumn passage. Lakenheath is a favoured site, but watch all Broads.
		White-winged Tern	*C. leucopterus*	Rare passage vagrant.
		Sandwich Tern	*Sterna sandvicensis*	Common summer visitor. All seawatching points (April to Sept). Colony at Blakeney Point.

			Common Name	Scientific Name	Status and Key Locations
			Lesser Crested Tern	S. bengalensis	Extremely rare.
			Common Tern	S. hirundo	Common summer visitor. From April to September at
			Roseate Tern	S. dougallii	Moderately rare summer visitor. Cley scrapes are a favoured site but also at Blakeney Point.
			Arctic Tern	S. paradisaea	Moderately rare summer visitor. Breeds on Blakeney Point. Also on passage on any water – The Broads in April/May are best.
			Guillemot	Uria aalge	Scarce at seawatching points.
			Razorbill	Alca torda	Scarce at seawatching points.
			Black Guillemot	Cepphus grylle	Moderately rare, winter.
			Little Auk	Alle alle	Scarce during strong onshore winds in November. All seawatching points.
			Puffin	Fratercula arctica	Moderately rare. Pot luck at any seawatching point spring/autumn.
			Pallas's Sandgrouse	Syrrhaptes paradoxus	Extremely rare.
			Rock Dove/Feral Pigeon	Columba livia	Descendant of Feral Pigeon. Pure birds now only found on Scottish islands.
			Stock Dove	C. oenas	Relatively common resident.
			Woodpigeon	C. palumbus	Very common everywhere.
			Collared Dove	Streptopelia decaocto	Common in all villages.
			Turtle Dove	S. turtur	Declining summer visitor. Still seen in The Broads, the Brecks and Flitcham Abbey Farm.
			Rufous Turtle Dove	S. orientalis	Extremely rare.
			Ring-necked Parakeet	Psittacula krameri	Rare. Probably all escapes!
			Great Spotted Cuckoo	Clamator glandarius	Rare.
			Cuckoo	Cuculus canorus	Common summer visitor. Best seen in May when displaying.
			Barn Owl	Tyto alba	Common resident. Any marsh or field at any time of day, but dawn and dusk preferred.
			Scops Owl	Otus scops	Extremely rare.
			Snowy Owl	Nyctea scandiaca	Extremely rare.
			Little Owl	Athene noctua	Scarce resident. Best seen at Flitcham Abbey Farm.
			Tawny Owl	Strix aluco	Common resident. More often heard than seen.

		Common Name	Scientific Name	Status and Key Locations
		Long-eared Owl	*Asio otus*	Scarce resident. Breeds in extensive woodlands but rarely seen. Listen out for squeaks of the young at Dersingham Bog, Thetford Forest etc. Possible on passage at Holme or Winterton Dunes.
		Short-eared Owl	*A. flammeus*	Scarce resident. Best seen in winter on any marsh but Waveney Forest most reliable site.
		Tengmalm's Owl	*Aegolius funereus*	Extremely rare.
		Nightjar	*Caprimulgus europaeus*	Common summer breeder. Mid May to the end of August at Salthouse Heath, Roydon Common, Dersingham Bog, Winterton etc.
		Common Swift	*Apus apus*	Common in summer. From May to August everywhere, but best at Titchwell.
		Pallid Swift	*A. pallidus*	Rare.
		Pacific Swift	*A. pacificus*	Extremely rare.
		Alpine Swift	*A. melba*	Rare.
		Little Swift	*A. affinis*	Extremely rare.
		Kingfisher	*Alcedo atthis*	Scarce resident. Try Strumpshaw, Flitcham Abbey Farm, Nunnery Lakes.
		Bee-eater	*Merops apiaster*	Moderately rare spring vagrant. Usually in flight.
		Roller	*Coracias garrulus*	Rare.
		Hoopoe	*Upupa epops*	Moderately rare. Can turn up at any time of year.
		Wryneck	*Jynx torquilla*	Scarce passage vagrant. Winterton, Holkham and Holme Dunes best bets, usually in autumn.
		Green Woodpecker	*Picus viridis*	Common resident in most woods, parks etc. Listen for its loud laughing call.
		Great Spotted Woodpecker	*Dendrocopos major*	Common resident in all woodland.
		Lesser Spotted Woodpecker	*D. minor*	Hard-to-see but declining resident. Best at Holkham Park or Ted Ellis Trust Reserve when displaying.
		Golden Oriole	*Oriolus oriolus*	Rare breeder., now only at Lakenheath. Passage migrant.
		Isabelline Shrike	*Lanius isabellinus*	Rare.
		Red-backed Shrike	*L. collurio*	Moderately rare autumn vagrant. Usual migrant hotspots.
		Lesser Grey Shrike	*L. minor*	Rare.

			Common Name	Scientific Name	Status and Key Locations
			Great Grey Shrike	L. excubitor	Scarce to rare winter visitor.
			Woodchat Shrike	L. senator	Rare.
			Jay	Garrulus glandarius	Increasingly common resident. Holkham Park, Hickling, Sandringham Estate.
			Magpie	Pica pica	Increasingly common resident. Moving into all areas.
			Nutcracker	Nucifraga caryocatactes	Extremely rare.
			Jackdaw	Corvus monedula	Common resident everywhere.
			Rook	C. frugilegus	Common resident everywhere.
			Carrion Crow	C. corone	Common resident everywhere.
			Hooded Crow	C.c cornix	Rare winter visitor to Horsey/Roydon Common.
			Raven	C. corax	Rare winter visitor to the Horsey area.
			Goldcrest	Regulus regulus	Common resident. Any woodland but especially coniferous.
			Firecrest	R. ignicapillus	Scarce passage migrant, some now breed. Try Felbrigg Hall and Sandringham Park.
			Penduline Tit	Remiz pendulinus	Rare vagrant but Titchwell has produced regular January records, so stay alert by the reedbed!
			Long-tailed Tit	Aegithalos caudatus	Common and increasing resident everywhere.
			Blue Tit	Parus caeruleus	Common resident everywhere.
			Great Tit	P. major	Common resident everywhere.
			Coal Tit	P. ater	Common resident. Coniferous forests best.
			Willow Tit	P. montanus	Very scarce resident. Occasional sightings at Barnhamcross Common, Hempton Marsh and Strumpshaw Fen.
			Marsh Tit	P. palustris	Common resident around The Broads.
			Bearded Tit	Panurus biarmicus	Common resident. Most reedbeds, but pick a windless day for best results. Hickling, Cley, Titchwell, Gypsy Lane all good.
			White-winged Lark	M. leucoptera	Extremely rare.
			Black Lark	Melanocorypha yeltoniensis	Extremely rare.
			Short-toed Lark	Calandrella brachydactyla	Moderately rare passage vagrant.

			Common Name	Scientific Name	Status and Key Locations
			Woodlark	Lullula arborea	Increasingly common in suitable areas. Weeting Heath best but any clearing in Thetford Forest.
			Skylark	Alauda arvensis	Common resident all marshes and fields.
			Shore Lark	Eremophila alpestris	Scarce winter visitor. Check bird newslines for favoured areas but usually Titchwell, Salthouse Beach or Holkham Gap.
			Sand Martin	Riparia riparia	Common summer visitor. On passage at all coastal sites plus all summer at Pentney Gravel Pits, Cley etc.
			Swallow	Hirundo rustica	Common summer visitor, everywhere.
			Red-rumped Swallow	H. daurica	Rare.
			House Martin	Delichon urbica	Common summer visitor everywhere.
			Cetti's Warbler	Cettia cetti	Scarce resident. Very skulking. Ted Ellis Reserve, Rockland Broad seem best for actual sightings, but widespread around other Broads.
			Pallas's Grasshopper Warbler	Locustella certhiola	Extremely rare.
			Lanceolated warbler	L. lanceolata	Extremely rare.
			Grasshopper Warbler	L. naevia	Heard more often than seen. Try Winterton, Horsey Gap, Upton Fen, Hickling. Relatively scarce.
			River Warbler	L. fluviatilis	Extremely rare.
			Savi's Warbler	L. lusciniodes	Rare breeder, with one or two pairs usually in The Broads. Details not given at request of RSPB.
			Aquatic Warbler	Acrocephalus paludicola	Extremely rare.
			Sedge Warbler	A. schoenbaenus	Common summer breeder. Any marsh or riverside vegetation.
			Paddyfield Warbler	A. agricola	Extremely rare.
			Blyth's Reed Warbler	A. dumetorum	Extremely rare.
			Marsh Warbler	A. palustris	Moderately rare passage migrant. Sings from vegetation anywhere around water. Early June only.
			Reed Warbler	A. scirpaceus	Common summer breeder. Any reedbed.
			Great Reed Warbler	Acrocephalus arundinaceus	Rare.
			Booted Warbler	Iduna caligata	Extremely rare.

		Common Name	Scientific Name	Status and Key Locations
		Sykes's Warbler	*I. rama*	Extremely rare.
		Icterine Warbler	*H. icterina*	Moderately rare passage migrant, any migration hotspot (Warham Greens, Winterton, Holkham Pines, Holme, Wells Wood).
		Melodious Warbler	*H. polyglotta*	Rare.
		Blackcap	*Sylvia atricapilla*	Common summer breeder, increasingly seen in winter (try Titchwell). Breeds in all woods.
		Garden Warbler	*S. borin*	Common summer visitor. Lynford Arboretum, The Broads, etc.
		Barred Warbler	*S. nisoria*	Moderately rare autumn migrant. Warham Greens, Blakeney Point, Winterton Dunes, Wells Woods, etc.
		Lesser Whitethroat	*S. curruca*	Relatively scarce summer visitor. Seeks thick cover but not as skulking as Cetti's Warbler. Try Holme.
		Desert Warbler	*S. nana*	Extremely rare.
		Whitethroat	*S. communis*	Common summer visitor in hedgerows.
		Spectacled Warbler	*S. conspicillata*	Extremely rare.
		Dartford Warbler	*S. undata*	Rare.
		Mamora Warbler	*S.sarda*	Exteremly rare.
		Ruppell's Warbler	*S. rueppelli*	Extremely rare.
		Subalpine Warbler	*S. cantillans*	Rare.
		Sardinian Warbler	*S. melanocephala*	Rare.
		Greenish Warbler	*Phylloscopus trochiloides*	Rare.
		Arctic Warbler	*P. borealis*	Rare.
		Pallas's Warbler	*P. proregulus*	Moderately rare autumn vagrant (lat Oct/ early Nov). Wells Woods, Winterton, Yarmouth Cemetery and Holkham Pines seem best.
		Yellow-browed Warbler	*P. inornatus*	Annual but rare autumn vagrant. See Pallas's Warbler sites.
		Hume's Yellow-browed Warbler	*P. humei*	Rare.
		Radde's Warbler	*P. schwarzi*	Rare.
		Dusky Warbler	*P. fuscatus*	Rare.
		Western Bonelli's Warbler	*P. bonelli*	Extremely rare.

			Common Name	Scientific Name	Status and Key Locations
			Wood Warbler	*P. sibilatrix*	Rare breeder. Has bred at Kelling Triangle and Felbrigg Hall.
			Chiffchaff	*P. collybita*	Common summer breeder, increasingly seen in winter (try Titchwell). Breeds in all woods.
			Iberian Chiffchaff	*P. ibericus*	Extremely rare.
			Willow Warbler	*P. trochilus*	Common summer visitor, most woods.
			Bohemian Waxwing	*Bombycilla garrulus*	Scarce winter visitor, not every year. Watch any berry bushes and check bird newslines.
			Red-breasted Nuthatch	*Sitta canadensis*	Only one. Sorry, there won't be another one!
			Nuthatch	*S. europaea*	Localised resident. Holkham Park best place, but also Ashwellthorpe Wood and Ken Hill Wood.
			Wallcreeper	*Tichodroma muraria*	Extremely rare.
			Treecreeper	*Certhia familiaris*	Localised resident. Secretive. See Nuthatch for sites.
			Wren	*Troglodytes troglodytes*	Common resident everywhere.
			Starling	*Sturnus vulgaris*	Common resident everywhere.
			Rose-coloured Starling	*S. roseus*	Rare.
			Dipper	*Cinclus cinclus*	Member of black-bellied race occasionally winters in the county.
			White's Thrush	*Zoothera dauma*	Extremely rare.
			Siberian Thrush	*Z. sibirica*	Extremely rare.
			Ring Ouzel	*Turdus torquatus*	Scarce passage migrant. Coastal watchpoints plus Choseley Barns.
			Blackbird	*T. merula*	Common resident everywhere.
			Black-throated Thrush	*T. fuficollis*	Extremely rare.
			Fieldfare	*T. pilaris*	Relatively common winter resident everywhere.
			Song Thrush	*T. philomelos*	Relatively common resident everywhere.
			Redwing	*T. iliacus*	Relatively common winter resident everywhere.
			Mistle Thrush	*T. viscivorus*	Common resident, especially in coniferous woods.
			Spotted Flycatcher	*Muscicapa striata*	Localised breeder. Weeting Heath and East Wretham etc.
			Robin	*Erithacus rebecula*	Common resident everywhere.

		Common Name	Scientific Name	Status and Key Locations
		Rufous-tailed Robin	*Larvivora sibilans*	Extremely rare.
		Thrush Nightingale	*Luscinia luscinia*	Extremely rare.
		Nightingale	*L. megarhynchos*	Scarce and declining. End of April to early June best at Salthouse Heath and Pentney.
		Bluethroat	*L.a svecica*	Scarce on passage, usually spring. Blakeney Point, etc.
		Red-breasted Flycatcher	*Ficedula parva*	Moderately rare autumn vagrant. Try Wells Woods, Holme, etc.
		Collared Flycatcher	*F. albicollis*	Extremely rare.
		Pied Flycatcher	*F. hypoleuca*	Passage migrant. Holme, Holkham, Winterton, Yarmouth Cemetery, etc.
		Alder Flycatcher	*Empidonax alnorum*	Extremely rare – the bird on Blakeney not accepted by BOURC at time of going to press.
		Black Redstart	*Phoenicurus ochruros*	Scarce on passage, usually spring. Usual migrant hotspots. Rare breeder.
		Redstart	*P. Phoenicurus*	Relatively common on passage: try Holme, Holkham Pines, Wells Woods, Yarmouth Cemetery. Scarce breeder.
		Rock Thrush	*Monticola saxatilis*	Extremely rare.
		Whinchat	*Saxicola rubetra*	Scarce passage migrant. Holme, Winterton, Holkham Pines, Wells Woods etc.
		Stonechat	*S. torquata*	Scarce Resident at Horsey Gap. Winter at Cley, Titchwell etc.
		Siberian Stonechat	*S. maurus*	Rare passage migrant.
		Isabelline Wheatear	*Oenanthe isabellina*	Extremely rare.
		Wheatear	*O. Oenanthe*	Common on passage at coastal sites.
		Pied Wheatear	*O. pleschanka*	Rare.
		Black-eared Wheatear	*O. hispanica*	Extremely rare.
		Desert Wheatear	*O. deserti*	Rare.
		Dunnock	*Prunella modularis*	Common resident everywhere.
		Alpine Accentor	*Prunella collaris*	Extremely rare.
		House Sparrow	*Passer domesticus*	Common resident everywhere, especially towns and villages.
		Tree Sparrow	*P. montanus*	Moderately rare resident. Try Flitcham Abbey Farm or Welney.
		Rock Sparrow	*Petronia petronia*	Extremely rare.

			Common Name	Scientific Name	Status and Key Locations
			Yellow Wagtail	Motacilla flava flavissima	Scarce migrant plus summer breeder. Cley (east bank), Buckenham Marshes, Kelling Quags etc.
			(Blue-headed Wagtail)	M.f. flava	Moderately rare spring migrant. Try Cley east bank.
			(Black-headed Wagtail)	M.f. feldegg	Rare.
			(Grey-headed Wagtail)	M.F thunbergi	Rare.
			(Syke's Wagtail)	M.f. beema	Rare.
			Citrine Wagtail	Motacilla citreola	Rare.
			Grey Wagtail	M. cinerea	Scarce resident. Best in harsh weather on ice free waters. Try Sparham Pools.
			Pied Wagtail	M. yarellii	Common resident everywhere. A large roost in Norwich city centre is a spectacular sight!
			White Wagtail	M. alba	Scarce spring migrant on coast.
			Richard's Pipit	Anthus novaeseelandiae	Moderately rare autumn passage migrant. Try Blakeney Point, Winterton or Holme.
			Blyth's Pipit	A. godlewskii	Extremely rare.
			Tawny Pipit	A. campestris	Moderately rare passage migrant. Declining records, try sites for Richard's Pipit.
			Olive-backed Pipit	A. hodgsoni	Rare, autumn.
			Tree Pipit	A. trivialis	Scarce summer breeder. Dersingham Bog, Roydon Common, Thetford Forest. Also on passage on coast.
			Meadow Pipit	A. pratensis	Common resident, all marshes.
			Red-throated Pipit	A. cervinus	Rare passage migrant.
			Rock Pipit	A. petrosus	Localised winter resident. Breydon Water, Blakeney.
			Water Pipit	A. spinoletta	Scarce winter resident. Titchwell and Serpentine at Cley often host a few winter birds.
			Chaffinch	Fringilla coelebs	Common resident everywhere.
			Brambling	F. montifringilla	Scarce winter visitor. Try Holkham Park or Welney.
			Serin	Serinus serinus	Moderately rare vagrant, any time of year.
			Greenfinch	Carduelis chloris	Common resident everywhere.
			Goldfinch	C. C.	Common resident everywhere.

			Common Name	Scientific Name	Status and Key Locations
			Siskin	C. spinus	Localised resident. Usually coniferous forests.
			Linnet	C. cannabina	Common resident everywhere.
			Twite	C. flavirostris	Scarce winter resident. Best places include Holkham Gap and Titchwell.
			Common Redpoll	C. flammea	Moderately rare winter visitor.
			Lesser Redpoll	C. cabaret	Scarce resident. Numbers vary year to year. Try East Wretham Heath.
			Arctic Redpoll	C. hornemanni	Moderately rare winter visitor.
			Two-barred Crossbill	Loxia leucoptera	Rare, only in irruption years.
			Common Crossbill	L. curvirostra	Scarce resident. Numbers vary year to year. Try Lynford Arboretum, Dersingham Bog, Holkham Pines, Wells woods etc.
			Parrot Crossbill	L. pytyopsittacus	Extremely rare.
			Trumpeter Finch	Bucanetes githagineus	Extremely rare.
			Common Rosefinch	Carpodacus erythrinus	Passage vagrant. Winterton, Holme, Holkham Pines, Wells Woods, etc. Occasionally breeds.
			Bullfinch	Pyrrhula pyrrhula	Scarce resident. Try Titchwell car park, Holme (Redwell Marsh hedges) Pentney Gravel Pits.
			Hawfinch	Coccothraustes	Scarce and decreasing resident, best seen in winter. Lynford Arboretum.
			Black and White Warbler	Mniotilta varia	Extremely rare.
			Lark Sparrow	Chondestes grammacus	Extremely rare.
			White-crowned Sparrow	Zonotrichia leucophrys	Extremely rare.
			White-throated Sparrow	Z. albicollis	Extremely rare.
			Dark-eyed Junco	Junco hyemalis	Extremely rare.
			Lapland Bunting	Calcarius lapponicus	Moderately rare winter resident. No reliable sites any more though Salthouse Beach and Cley eye field are regularly visited.
			Snow Bunting	Pletrophenax nivalis	Localised winter visitor. Small flocks around Yarmouth Beach, Holkham Gap and along coast from Hunstanton to Brancaster. Very mobile!
			Pine Bunting	Emberiza leucocephalos	Extremely rare.

			Common Name	Scientific Name	Status and Key Locations
			Yellowhammer	E. citrinella	Relatively common resident. Flitcham Abbey Farm, Salthouse Heath, Kelling Heath, Choseley Barns, etc.
			Cirl Bunting	E. cirlus	Extremely rare. Unlikely to be another one.
			Ortolan Bunting	E. hortulana	Moderately rare autumn vagrant. Try Blakeney Point.
			Yellow-browed Bunting	E. chrysophrys	Extremely rare.
			Rustic Bunting	E. rustica	Rare.
			Little Bunting	E. pusilla	Rare.
			Yellow-breasted Bunting	E. aureola	Extremely rare.
			Reed Bunting	E. schoeniclus	Common resident, all marshes and waterways.
			Black-headed Bunting	E. melanocephala	Extremely rare.
			Corn Bunting	Miliaria calandra	Scarce resident. Try Flitcham Abbey Farm, Welney or Choseley Barns all year round.
			Rose-breasted Grosbeak	Pheucticus ludovicianus	Extremely rare.

DEFINITIONS OF BIRD GROUPS USED IN THIS BOOK

SOME GENERAL TERMS have been used in the 'Target Birds' and 'Other Likely Species' sections, to save space. Here are the birds typically included in each group.

COMMON WILDFOWL
Mute Swan, Greylag Goose, Canada Goose, Egyptian Goose, Mallard, Gadwall, Tufted Duck, Pochard, Teal.

WINTER WILDFOWL
Includes **Common Wildfowl** in greater numbers than in summer, plus Goldeneye, Wigeon, Pintail. May include Pink-footed

and Brent Geese though these are usually mentioned specifically.

SEADUCKS AND SEABIRDS
Most likely are Red-throated Diver (winter), Great Crested Grebe, Eider, Long-tailed Duck (winter), Common Scoter, Velvet Scoter, Goldeneye (winter) and Red-breasted Merganser, but also look out for scarcer species such as Black-throated and Great Northern Divers (winter), Red-necked Grebe (winter), Black-necked Grebe and Slavonian Grebe (winter) and Pomarine Skua.

PASSAGE SEABIRDS
Includes **Seaducks, Winter Seabirds, Skuas** and **Terns** plus Gannet, Sooty Shearwater, Manx Shearwater, Kittiwake, Guillemot and Razorbill. Less likely but not impossible are Balearic Shearwater, Storm Petrel, Grey Phalarope, Sabine's Gull and Little Auk (the latter in November storms). Rarities include Leach's Petrel, Cory's and Great Shearwaters.

COMMON WATERBIRDS
Includes **Common Wildfowl**, but more specifically Little Grebe, Great Crested Grebe, Cormorant, Grey Heron, common wildfowl, Moorhen, Coot.

WINTER RAPTORS
Hen Harrier, Merlin, Peregrine. Also can include Rough-legged Buzzard, Short-eared Owl and Barn Owl. Marsh Harrier should also now be included and take it as read that Kestrel and Sparrowhawk are included too.

COMMON WADERS
Oystercatcher, Ringed Plover, Golden Plover, Grey Plover, Lapwing, Knot, Sanderling, Dunlin, Snipe, Black-tailed and Bar-tailed Godwits, Curlew, Redshank, Turnstone.

PASSAGE WADERS
Little Ringed Plover, Ringed Plover, Little Stint, Curlew Sandpiper, Dunlin, Ruff, Whimbrel, Spotted Redshank, Greenshank, Green Sandpiper, Wood Sandpiper, Common Sandpiper. Scarcer passage waders may include Temminck's Stint and Red-necked Phalarope.

REGULAR GULL SPECIES
Black-headed Gull, Common Gull, Lesser Black-backed Gull, Herring Gull, Great Black-backed Gull.

TERNS
Common Tern the most likely species seen inland. On the coast, Common and Sandwich are the most likely followed by Little, Arctic and Roseate in that order.

SKUAS
Most likely are Arctic and Great but Long-tailed and Pomarine are seen regularly in autumn.

CORVIDS
Jay, Jackdaw, Carrion Crow, Rook, Magpie.

HIRUNDINES
Sand Martin, Swallow, House Martin, Swift (not a hirundine but included here to save space).

WINTER THRUSHES
Blackbird, Fieldfare, Song Thrush, Redwing, Mistle Thrush.

SUMMER WARBLERS
Lesser Whitethroat, Whitethroat, Garden Warbler, Blackcap, Chiffchaff, Willow Warbler. Grasshopper, Sedge and Reed Warblers are also summer visitors, but these are specifically mentioned in Other Likely Species where they occur.

PASSAGE MIGRANTS/MIGRANTS
Most likely will include **Hirundines, Winter Thrushes, Summer Warblers,** plus Meadow and Tree Pipits, Yellow and White Wagtails, Redstart, Black Redstart, Whinchat, Wheatear, Ring Ouzel, Goldcrest, Spotted and Pied Flycatchers and Brambling. Over water, look out for Arctic and Black Terns and Little Gull and on the marshes try to find a Garganey.

Scarcer migrants that are regularly seen include Short-toed Lark, Richard's Pipit, Hoopoe, Wryneck, Bluethroat, Barred Warbler (autumn), Yellow-browed Warbler (autumn), Firecrest, Red-breasted Flycatcher and Red-backed & Great Grey Shrikes.

DEFINITIONS OF BIRD GROUPS USED IN THIS BOOK

Rare migrants: You can let your imagination run wild, as Norfolk has an incredible track record of turning up rare birds at any time of year. It is impossible to mention them all but just have a look at the Norfolk Bird & Mammal Reports to whet your appetite!

COMMON WOODLAND BIRDS
Includes **Common Scrub Birds, Corvids, Common Finches** and some **Summer Warblers**, but also Great Spotted Woodpecker, Woodpigeon, Stock Dove, Goldcrest, Coal Tit, Nuthatch and Treecreeper.

COMMON FINCHES
Chaffinch, Greenfinch, Goldfinch, Siskin, Linnet, Lesser Redpoll.

COMMON SCRUB BIRDS
Can include **Common Woodland Birds, Summer Warblers** and **Common Finches**, plus Wren, Dunnock, Robin, Blackbird, Song Thrush, Mistle Thrush, Long-tailed Tit, Blue Tit, Great Tit and House Sparrow. Marsh and Willow Tits may fall into this category but are mentioned specifically at any site where they are present. Willow Tit will be a Target Species being as they are now so rare!

BIBLIOGRAPHY

The Birds of Norfolk
By Moss Taylor, Michael Seago, Peter Allard and Don Dorling (Pica Press 1999).

Norfolk Bird Atlas: Summer and Winter Distributions 1999-2007
By Moss Taylor and John H Marchant (BTO, 2011).

Birds New To Norfolk
By Keith Dye, Mick Fiszer and Peter Allard (Wren Publishing, 2009).

The Birds of Cley
By Steve Gantlett. Available from Books For Birders, Stonerunner, Coast Road, Cley-next-the-Sea, Norfolk NR25 7RZ.

The Birds of Blakeney Point
By Andy Stoddart and Steve Joyner (Wren Publishing, 2005). Available from North Norfolk Birds, 7 Elsden Close, Holt, Norfolk NR25 6JW.

Shifting Sands (History of Blakeney Point)
By Andy Stoddart. Available from North Norfolk Birds (see above).

Where To Watch Birds in East Anglia
By Peter and Margaret Clarke (Helm, 2002).

Norfolk Bird & Mammal Report
Published annually by the Norfolk and Norwich Naturalists' Association.

Norfolk: A Birdwatcher's Site Guide
By Phil Benstead, Steve Rowland and Richard Thomas (Shoebill Press, 2001).

Guardian Spirit of the East Bank (Biography of Richard Richardson)
By Moss Taylor (Wren Publishing, 2002).

Cley Bird Club 10km Square Bird Report
Available from Peter Gooden, 45 Charles Road, Holt, Norfolk NR25 6DA.

Nar Valley OS Annual Report
Available from Ian Black, Three Chimneys, Tumbler Hill, Swaffham, Norfolk PE37 7JG.

Norfolk Ornithologists' Association Annual Report
Available from Holme Bird Observatory, Broadwater Road, Holme-next-the-Sea, Norfolk PE36 6LQ.

BIRD NEWS, RECORDS AND INFORMATION

County Recorders
Dave and Jacquie Bridges;
e-mail: dnjnorfolkrec@btinternet.com

Birdline East Anglia
09068 700 245 premium rate number.
Phone news to 0800 0830 803.

BROADS AUTHORITY VISITOR CENTRES

Beccles
The Quay, Fen Lane. 01502 713 196;
e-mail: becclesinfo@broads-authority.gov.uk

Hoveton/Wroxham
Station Road. 01603 782 281;
e-mail: hovetoninfo@broads-authority.gov.uk

How Hill
Ludham. Toad Hole Cottage Museum and
'Electric Eel' Wildlife Water Trail. 01692 678 763;
e-mail: toadholeinfo@broads-authority.gov.uk

Potter Heigham
The Staithe. 01692 670 779;
e-mail: potterinfo@broads-authority.gov.uk

Ranworth
The Staithe. 01603 270 453;
e-mail: ranworthinfo@broads-authority.gov.uk

For winter enquiries:
Broads Authority, Yare House, 62-64 Thorpe
Road, Norwich, Norfolk, NR1 1RY. 01603 610
734; e-mail:broads@broads-authority.gov.uk
www.broads-authority.gov.uk/index.html

TOURIST INFORMATION CENTRES

Aylsham
Bure Valley Railway Station, Norwich Road,
Aylsham, Norfolk NR11 6BW.
01263 733 903/01263 733 858;
e-mail: aylsham.tic@broadland.gov.uk

Burnham Deepdale
Deepdale Farm, Burnham Deepdale, Norfolk,
PE31 8DD. 01485 210 256;
e-mail: info@deepdalefarm.co.uk

Cromer
Prince of Wales Road, Cromer, Norfolk
NR27 9HS. 01263 512 497;
e-mail: cromertic@north-norfolk.gov.uk

Downham Market
The Priory Centre, 78 Priory Road, Downham
Market PE38 9JS. 01366 383 287; e-mail:
downham-market.tic@west-norfolk.gov.uk

Great Yarmouth
Maritime House, 25 Marine Parade, Great
Yarmouth, Norfolk NR30 2EN. 01493 846 345;
e-mail: tourism@great-yarmouth.gov.uk

Holt
3 Pound House Market Place, Holt, Norfolk
NR25 6BW. 01263 713 100;
e-mail: holttic@north-norfolk.gov.uk

Hoveton
Station Road, Hoveton, Norfolk NR12 8UR.
01603 782 281;
e-mail: hovetoninfo@broads-authority.gov.uk

Hunstanton
Town Hall, The Green, Hunstanton, Norfolk
PE36 6BQ. 01485 532 610;
e-mail: hunstanton.tic@west-norfolk.gov.uk

King's Lynn
The Custom House, Purfleet Quay, King's Lynn,
Norfolk PE30 1HP. 01553 763 044;
e-mail: kings-lynn.tic@west-norfolk.gov.uk

Loddon
Tourist Information Point, The Old Town Hall, 1
Bridge Street, Loddon Norfolk NR14 6ET. 01508
521 028.

Norwich
The Forum, Millennium Plain, Norwich, Norfolk
NR2 1TF. 01603 727 927;
e-mail: tourism@norwich.gov.uk

Sheringham
Station Approach, Sheringham, Norfolk NR26
8RA. 01263 824 329;
e-mail: sheringhamtic@north-norfolk.gov.uk

Swaffham
The Shambles, Market Place, Swaffham, Norfolk
PE37 7AB. 01760 722 255;
e-mail: swaffham@eetb.info

Thetford
4 White Hart Street, Thetford, Norfolk IP24
2HA. 01842 820 689;
e-mail: info@thetfordtourism.co.uk

Wells-next-the-Sea
Staithe Street, Wells-next-the-Sea, Norfolk
NR23 1AN. 01328 710 885;
e-mail: wellstic@north-norfolk.gov.uk

Wymondham
The Market Cross, Market Place, Wymondham,
NR18 0AX. 01953 604 721;
e-mail: WymondhamTIC@btconnect.com
www.wymondham-norfolk.co.uk

WILDLIFE GROUPS AND ORGANISATIONS

Birding For All (formerly Disabled
Birders Association), Bo Beolens, 18 St
Mildreds Rd, Margate, Kent CT9 2LT. www.
disabledbirdersassociation.org.uk

British Trust for Ornithology
The Nunnery, Thetford, Norfolk IP24 2PU.
01842 750 050. www.bto.org

Cley Bird Club
The Membership Secretary, Cley Bird Club,
Turnstone Cottage, The Street, Sharrington,
Melton Constable, Norfolk, NR24 2AB.
www.cleybirdclub.org.uk/cbc/default.asp

Disabled toilets leaflet
RADAR, 12 City Forum, 250 City Road, London
EC1V 8AF. 0207 125 03222. Textphone: 020
7250 4119;
e-mail: enquiries@disabilityrightsuk.org
www.radar-shop.org.uk/Detail.aspx?id=0

Forest Enterprise
Santon Downham, Brandon, Suffolk IP27 0TJ.
01842 810 271;
e-mail: eandem@forestry.gsi.gov.uk

General Broads Authority
18 Colgate, Norwich, NR3 1BQ. 01603 610 734.
High Lodge Forest Centre. 01842 815 434.

How Hill Trust
How Hill, Ludham, Great Yarmouth NR29 5PG.
01692 6788 555; www.how-hill.org.uk

The National Trust
East of England Regional Office, Westley
Bottom, Bury St Edmunds, Suffolk IP33 3WD.
01284 747 500;
www.nationaltrust.org.uk/visit/east-of-england/

Natural England
(Norwich Office): Dragonfly House, 2 Gilders
Way, Norwich, Norfolk, NR3 1UB. 0845 600
3078; www.naturalengland.org.uk

Norfolk and Norwich Naturalists' Society
Hon treasurer: David Richmond, N&NNS, 42
Richmond Rise, Reepham, Norfolk, NR10 4LS.
www.nnns.org.uk

Norfolk Ornithologists' Association
Holme Observatory, Broadwater Road, Holme-next-
the-Sea, Norfolk PE36 6LQ. 01485 525 406;
www.noa.org.uk

Norfolk Wildlife Trust
Bewick House, 22 Thorpe Road, Norwich NR1 1RY.
01603 625 540; www.norfolkwildlifetrust.org.uk

RSPB Eastern England Regional Office
Stalham House, 65 Thorpe Road, Norwich NR1
1UD. 01603 661 662;
www.rspb.org.uk/nearyou/index.aspx?c=norfolk

RSPB Mid-Yare Reserves
Staithes Cottage, Low Road, Strumpshaw, Norwich
NR13 4HF. 01603 715 191.

RSPB Snettisham Reserve Office
Snettisham Business Centre, 43a Lynn Road,
Snettisham PE31 7LR. 01485 542 689.

Ted Ellis Trust
Ted Ellis Trust at Wheatfen Nature Reserve,
Surlingham, Norfolk NR13 5PT;
www.tedellistrust.org.uk

BEST SITES WITH DISABLED ACCESS

THIS IS a quick-reference chapter to show the various ways you can reach your chosen destination. For instance, if you are relying on public transport, turn to the relevant page to see which reserves are easily accessible to you. You can then turn to the Site Guide page for more details sites listed in alphabetical order. Simple!

Take it as read that all reserves are accessible by car, with the exceptions of Berney Arms Marsh, which can only be reached by train and Hoveton Great Broad, which can only be reached by boat.

SITES FULLY ACCESSIBLE TO WHEELCHAIR USERS

The sites listed here are ones I consider to be accessible by wheelchair users, and several have been field-tested by a disabled friend. However, I strongly advise that you check with the contact number listed on the Site Guide page for specific guidance before you visit. I apologise profusely now if you turn up at a site and it is not accessible to you. Please let me know if this happens and I will amend the details for future editions.

Barton Broad

Cockshoot Broad

Flitcham Abbey Farm

Haddiscoe Marsh

Hempton Marsh – need key to hide from NOA.

Herbert Barnes Riverside Park

Hickling Broad – most of the reserve is accessible.

Hunstanton

King's Lynn Docks

Norwich City Centre

Ranworth Broad

Redwell Marsh – need key to hide from NOA.

Rockland Broad

Sheringham

Stubb Mill – park by the mill but do not obstruct the lane.

Swanton Novers

Titchwell Marsh – might need a push over the steep hump on the public footpath near the brackish marsh. Boardwalk to beach viewing platform may be covered with sand!

Tottenhill Gravel Pits – view from car.

Wolferton Triangle

SITES PARTLY ACCESSIBLE TO WHEELCHAIR USERS

Listed here are sites where I consider some sections can be reached by wheelchair users, together with a short description of the accessible area. Please check with the contact number listed on the Site Guide page before you visit.

Ashwellthorpe Wood
Gravel path onto reserve from car park, Flat, grass paths ('rides') should be pushable but can become muddy.

Bayfield Estate
Some farm tracks may be accessible.

Blickling Hall
Some estate roads and paths are accessible.

Brancaster Marsh
Marsh viewable from the road and beach car park.

Buckenham Marsh
Park by hide at bottom of rough access track. Hide fully accessible.

Burgh Castle
Marsh and Breydon Water viewable from the Angles Way footpath.

Choseley Barns
Barns viewable from road, bunting fields not accessible.

Cley Marshes
Easy access track from visitor centre to Cley village and East Bank car park, giving wheelchair access to four hides. East Bank not accessible. Fields along Beach Road viewable from car and beach car park.

Dersingham Bog
Muddy access ramp from Scissors Crossroads car park may be accessible for Powertrikes and people with strong pushers. Nightjar area about half a mile away on muddy and stony paths.

East Wretham Heath
Wide track alongside reserve.

Fairhaven Woodland & Water Garden
Some paths accessible. Boat is accessible to 'people with some level of mobility'.

Felbrigg Hall
Some of the woodland trail.

Great Yarmouth
Med Gulls from piers and Promenade. Main paths in cemetery accessible.

Hickling Broad
Most of the reserve is accessible.

Holkham Hall
Trees viewable from estate roads.

Holkham NNR
Washington Hide, Lady Anne's Drive, viewing platform behind Washington Hide, some of woods along sandy track.

Holme Bird Observatory
Blue Badge parking near reserve entrance. Ramp and accessible paths to several hides and observation platform.

Holme Dunes
One large hide overlooking wader scrape, access track from car.

Horsey
Mere viewable from 'Easy Access' track. Fields visible from the road. Boat tour on Broad is possible (phone to check – see site page for details).

How Hill Trust
A few paths may be accessible. Check before you go.

Kelling Heath
Nightjars may be possible from large, flat car park on Holgate Hill accessed from Weybourne (see site page for directions).

Kelling Quags
Access down a very rough track. Ask the NOA's opinion.

Lakenheath Fen
Sandy tracks from visitor centre to New Fen Viewpoint. Wardens report that one or two wheelchair users have managed to reach Joist Fen along the extremely pitted and sometimes muddy riverside public footpath: sometimes I can hardly walk it!!

Lynford Arboretum
Many paths wheelchair accessible.

Morston Quay
Limited view of saltmarsh from the car park.

Nunnery Lakes & Barnhamcross Common
Spring Walk from Nuns' Bridges car park is easy access (chance of otter!). Some areas of Barnhamcross Common are flat and grassy.

Pensthorpe
Blue and yellow trails only.

Pentney Gravel Pits
Leisure Lake viewable from the road, but of limited interest.

Roydon Common
Access down rough tracks, which can be wet. Ask the NWT first.

Salthouse Beach
Fields visible from the road, including Snow Bunting area.

Salthouse Heath
Limited view from road; difficult access onto heath.

Sandringham
Several tracks and roads, plus part of the trails.

Santon Downham
Several wide sandy tracks and tarmac roads.

Sculthorpe Moor
Most of the reserve is accessible along boardwalks. Final 300 yards to the furthest two hides is along a soft, peaty track which some wheelchair users will manage.

SITES PARTLY ACCESSIBLE TO WHEELCHAIR USERS

Sheringham Park
Some trails accessible

Snettisham
Rotary hide. Phone at least five working days before you visit.

Stiffkey
Saltmarsh viewable from the NT car park.

Strumpshaw Fen
Main hide, plus track to railway crossing, good for Cetti's Warbler.

Walsey Hills
Lower path only. Narrow and muddy, but level.

Warham Greens
Very limited view of saltmarsh from car park.

Weeting Heath
Two hides accessible along path (watch out for tree roots!). Woodland walk not accessible.

Welney
Most of the reserve is accessible.

Wells Woods
Some wide, slightly rough tracks.

Whitlingham Country Park
Easy access path around Great Broad. Broad boat tour accessible.

ACCESS BY PUBLIC TRANSPORT

GETTING AROUND Norfolk by public transport is not easy! In the previous edition of this book, I tried to give a brief rundown of how to get to each site by public transport but situations changed so quickly I felt this was a hopeless case for this edition. However, the following contact details should provide visiting birdwatchers with everything they need to plan their own journeys.

Another useful tool is the GPS co-ordinates listed on each site page. Type these into Google Earth and you can then zoom down to find the reserve and its environs. Look for a small blue and white bus icon near each site and click on it to give the number of the bus and a contact web address (though this will only be as up-to-date as the last update of Google Earth in that area!). Good luck!

It goes without saying that it is important to check for up-to-date information on all trains and buses BEFORE you travel.

PUBLIC TRANSPORT CONTACTS

AIR

Norwich International Airport
Amsterdam Way, Norwich NR6 6JA, with more than 300 worldwide connections via Manchester, Paris and Amsterdam. 01603 411 923; e-mail: infodesk@norwichinternational.com www.norwichairport.co.uk

Stansted Airport
Within easy reach of all the key Norfolk birding sites by road. 01279 680 500; www.stanstedairport.com

BICYCLE

National Cycle Network
Contact Sustrans 0845 113 0065; www.sustrans.co.uk

BUS

Traveline national transport planner
0871 200 22 33; http://traveline.info/

Traveline East Anglia
www.travelineeastanglia.co.uk/ea/XSLT_TRIP_REQUEST2?language=en&timeOffset=15

PUBLIC TRANSPORT CONTACTS

I have found by far the best website for planning a journey in Norfolk is: www.travelineeastanglia.co.uk/ea/XSLT_TRIP_REQUEST2?language=en&timeOffset=15 where you can type in your set-off point and destination, choose your mode of transport and time of travel and the website does the rest!

COACH

There are daily services from all major cities to Norwich operated by National Express, which also operates regular connections from Stansted, Heathrow and Gatwick airports.

National Express
08705 808 080; www.nationalexpress.com

Coasthopper (Green) Bus Service
Norfolk Green, Hamlin Way, King's Lynn, Norfolk PE30 4NG. 01553 776 980;
e-mail: enquiries@norfolkgreen.co.uk
www.norfolkgreen.co.uk/services/service.aspx?serviceid=1029

FERRY

Stena Line
08447 707 070; www.stenaline.co.uk

DFDS Seaways
0870 533 3000; www.dfdseaways.co.uk

TRAIN

InterCity half-hourly services operate between Norwich and London Liverpool Street with local connecting services within East Anglia.

Average journey time from London 1 hour 50 minutes. There are connecting services from the Midlands, the North of England and Scotland via Peterborough.

Local Broads stations are located at: Acle, Beccles, Berney Arms, Brundall, Brundall Gardens, Buckenham, Cantley, Great Yarmouth, Haddiscoe, Hoveton and Wroxham, Lingwood, Lowestoft, Norwich, Oulton Broad, Reedham, Salhouse, Somerleyton and Worstead.

National Rail Enquiries
08457 484 950; www.nationalrail.co.uk
www.thetrainline.com

Greater Anglia Railway
0845 600 7245 www.greater anglia.co.uk

Central Trains
0870 6096 060 www.centraltrains.co.uk
www.bitternline.com – for northern Broads and north Norfolk.

www.wherrylines.org.uk – for central and southern Broads, Great Yarmouth and Lowestoft.

OTHER USEFUL INFORMATION

The Broads Authority
These produce a series of leaflets titled *Birds by Boat, Birds by Train* and *Birds by Bus* see contacts section, page 261.

Norfolk Wildlife Trust
The NWT offers a 50% discount off the reserve entry fee for anyone who can produce a valid ticket from public transport.

SITES WITHIN WALKING DISTANCE OF BUS OR RAIL STOPS

Alderfen Broad	Blackborough End Tip
Ashwellthorpe Wood	Blakeney Point
Barton Broad	Blickling Hall
Berney Arms Marshes	Brancaster Marsh
Bayfield Estate	Breydon Water North Shore

Buckenham Marshes
Burgh Castle
Buxton Heath
Choseley Barns
Cley Marshes
Cockshoot Broad
Denver Sluice
Dersingham Bog
East Wretham Heath
Fairhaven Water Gardens
Felbrigg Hall
Flitcham Abbey Farm
Foxley Wood
Great Yarmouth
Gypsy Lane
Haddiscoe Marshes
Hardley Flood
Hempton Marsh
Herbert Barnes Riverside Park
Hickling Broad
Holkham Hall
Holkham Pines
Holme Bird Observatory
Holme Dunes
Horsey
Hoveton Great Broad
How Hill Trust
Hunstanton
Kelling Heath
Kelling Quags
Ken Hill Wood
King's Lynn Docks
Lakenheath Fen
Lynford Arboretum
Martham Broad
Morston Quay
Norwich City Centre

Nunnery Lakes/Barnhamcross Common
Pentney Gravel Pits
Pensthorpe
Ranworth Broad
Redwell Marsh
Roydon Common
Salthouse Marshes
Salthouse Heath
Sandringham
Santon Downham
Sheringham
Sculthorpe Moor
Sheringham Park
Snettisham Coastal Park
Snettisham RSPB Reserve
Sparham Pools
Stiffkey Fen
Strumpshaw Fen
Stubb Mill
Swanton Novers
Surlingham Church Marsh
Ted Ellis Nature Reserve
Thorpe Marshes
Thursford Wood
Titchwell
Tottenhill Gravel Pits
Upton Fen
Walsey Hills
Warham Greens
Weeting Heath
Wells Woods
Welney
Weybourne
Winterton Dunes
Whitlingham Country Park
Wolferton Triangle

Authors note:
One thing to bear in mind is that some of the more rural bus routes operate on 'Norfolk Time' i.e. half an hour either way of advertised time. I once stood in Halvergate for a bus that was 40 minutes late! GOOD LUCK!

BROADLAND BOAT MOORINGS

THESE SITES have mooring facilities at or close to the reserve, and these make for ideal stop-offs during your Norfolk Broads holiday. A river map is an essential aid to planning your holiday, and I can recommend the one produced by GEOprojects UK Ltd, 9-10 Southern Court, South Street, Reading RG1 4QS (0118 939 3567).

Barton Broad
Moor at Gay's Staithe and walk to reserve, about half a mile.

Breydon Water
Moor on River Bure and walk past train station to view Breydon Water.

Berney Arms Marshes
Free mooring at Berney Arms along the Berney Arms Reach of the River Yare at the west end of Breydon Water. A short walk to the reserve.

Buckenham Marshes
Free mooring at Cantley along the River Yare; walk back along the river footpath to Buckenham RSPB about 2 miles.

Burgh Castle
Moor at Burgh Castle Marina and walk north for half a mile.

Cockshoot Broad
Moor in channel at reserve entrance.

Fairhaven Water Garden
Turn off the River Bure onto Fleet Dyke (just north-west of St. Benet's Abbey) and moor on South Walsham Outer Broad. Follow footpath signs to village. No mooring allowed on South Walsham Inner Broad!

Great Yarmouth Beach
Moor on River Bure. 15 minute walk to beach.

Great Yarmouth Cemetery
Moor on River Bure. 15 minute walk.

Haddiscoe Marshes
Moor at St. Olaves on the River Waveney and then walk south-west along the A143 to stand on the road bridge over the railway (approx. 0.75 miles).

Halvergate Marshes
Moor in Yarmouth, then train to Berney Arms, then walk.

Hardley Flood
Moor on River Chet near the Flood.

Herbert Barnes Riverside Park
Moor at Yarmouth and walk to park

Hickling Broad
Nearest mooring is at Hickling Sailing Club, over a mile away.

Horsey
Moor at Horsey Mill.

Hoveton Great Broad
Moor on River Bure at reserve entrance.

How Hill Trust
Moor on River Ant at reserve entrance.

Martham Broad
Moor at West Somerton on the River Thurne.

Norwich
24hr mooring (fee charged) at Norwich Yacht Station on the River Wensum (01603 612980). You are advised to moor up against the tide unless the wind is stronger. Indicate your intentions to the quay rangers so they can guide you in. Ten minute walk to cathedral.

Ranworth Broad
Moor at Ranworth village and walk 500 yards.

Rockland Broad
Moor at Rockland staithe on the River Yare.

Surlingham Church Marshes
Moor at Ferry House and walk half a mile.

Ted Ellis Trust Reserve
Moor at Rockland Staithe on the River Yare and walk about a mile along a public footpath to the reserve OR moor at Ferry House, Surlingham, on the River Yare and walk along the river path or through village approx 3 miles.

Thorpe Marsh
24hr free mooring at Commissioner's Cut just north of Whitlingham Bends on the River Yare. Straight onto reserve. Editorial note: Need to add this mooring cut on site page map.

Upton Fen
Moor at Upton Dyke on the River Bure and walk 2 miles to the reserve.

Waveney Forest
Moor at St. Olaves on the River Waveney and then walk approximately 1.25 miles north-east along the A143. Turn left onto New Road (at the Decoy Tavern) to the forest.

Whitlingham Country Park
24 hour mooring on the River Yare adjacent to the Country Park.

INDEX OF NORFOLK'S TOP TARGET SPECIES

To assist readers in finding the most interesting birds that occur regularly in Norfolk, we have selected a batch of 'target species' for each site and these are included in the index below. Common species that occur broadly across the region are not included.

INDEX OF SITES

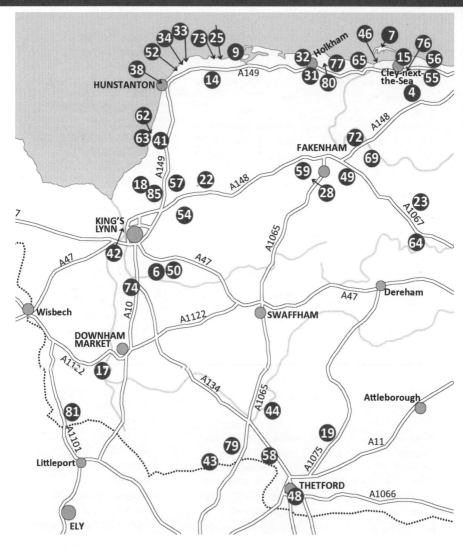

KEY TO SITES